JOHN KENNEI

Scottish Religious Cultures *Historical Perspectives*

Series Editors: Scott R. Spurlock and Crawford Gribben

Religion has played a key formational role in the development of Scottish society shaping cultural norms, defining individual and corporate identities, and underpinning legal and political institutions. This series presents the very best scholarship on the role of religion as a formative and yet divisive force in Scottish society and highlights its positive and negative functions in the development of the nation's culture. The impact of the Scots diaspora on the wider world means that the subject has major significance far outwith Scotland.

Available titles

George Mackay Brown and the Scottish Catholic Imagination
Linden Bicket

Poor Relief and the Church in Scotland, 1560–1650
John McCallum

Jewish Orthodoxy in Scotland: Rabbi Dr Salis Daiches and Religious Leadership
Hannah Holtschneider

John Kennedy of Dingwall, 1819–1884: Evangelicalism in the Scottish Highlands
Alasdair J. Macleod

Miracles of Healing: Psychotherapy and Religion in Twentieth-Century Scotland
Gavin Miller

George Strachan of the Mearns: Seventeenth-Century Orientalist
Tom McInally

Scottish Liturgical Traditions and Religious Politics: From Reformers to Jacobites, 1560–1764
Edited by Allan I. Macinnes, Patricia Barton and Kieran German

Dissent After Disruption: Church and State in Scotland, 1843–63
Ryan Mallon

Scottish Presbyterianism: The Case of Dunblane and Stirling, 1690–1710
Andrew Muirhead

The Scots Afrikaners: Identity Politics and Intertwined Religious Cultures in Southern and Central Africa
Retief Müller

The Revival of Evangelicalism: Mission and Piety in the Victorian Church of Scotland
Andrew Michael Jones

The Bantu Presbyterian Church of South Africa: A History of the Free Church of Scotland Mission
Graham A. Duncan

Forthcoming titles

The Dynamics of Dissent: Politics, Religion and the Law in Restoration Scotland
Neil McIntyre

William Guild and Moderate Divinity in Early Modern Scotland
Russell Newton

Protestantism, Revolution and Scottish Political Thought: The European Context, 1637–1651
Karie Schultz

edinburghuniversitypress.com/series/src

JOHN KENNEDY OF DINGWALL, 1819–1884

Evangelicalism in the Scottish Highlands

ALASDAIR J. MACLEOD

EDINBURGH
University Press

Edinburgh University Press is one of the leading university presses in the UK. We publish academic books and journals in our selected subject areas across the humanities and social sciences, combining cutting-edge scholarship with high editorial and production values to produce academic works of lasting importance. For more information visit our website: edinburghuniversitypress.com

© Alasdair J. Macleod, 2023, 2024

Edinburgh University Press Ltd
13 Infirmary Street
Edinburgh EH1 1LT

First published in hardback by Edinburgh University Press 2023

Typeset in 10/12 ITC New Baskerville by
Cheshire Typesetting Ltd, Cuddington, Cheshire

A CIP record for this book is available from the British Library

ISBN 978 1 3995 0389 1 (hardback)
ISBN 978 1 3995 0390 7 (paperback)
ISBN 978 1 3995 0391 4 (webready PDF)
ISBN 978 1 3995 0392 1 (epub)

The right of Alasdair J. Macleod to be identified as author of this work has been asserted in accordance with the Copyright, Designs and Patents Act 1988 and the Copyright and Related Rights Regulations 2003 (SI No. 2498).

Contents

Acknowledgements and Note regarding Referencing	vi
Introduction	1
1 Ministry	15
Kennedy the Highland Evangelical	15
Kennedy the Preacher	25
Kennedy the Pastor	48
Conclusion	60
2 Writing	71
Kennedy the Historian	71
Kennedy the Biographer	89
Kennedy the Mystic	100
Conclusion	109
3 Constitutionalism	117
Kennedy and the Atonement	118
Kennedy and the Union Controversy	132
Kennedy and the Establishment Controversy	147
Conclusion	160
4 Controversy	171
Kennedy and Worship	171
Kennedy and Mass Evangelism	184
Kennedy and Biblical Criticism	201
Conclusion	216
Conclusion	227
Bibliography	229
Index	243

Acknowledgements

I would like to express my gratitude to my supervisors, Professor Ewen A. Cameron and Professor Stewart J. Brown, for their consistent encouragement and support during the course of this project. I have appreciated the support of my doctoral examiners, Professor Robert Dunbar and Professor John R. McIntosh, in the publication of this work. For assistance with primary sources, particular appreciation is due to Mr Maurice Grant, the late Rev. John MacLeod, Rev. Angus MacRae and Dingwall Free Church, and Mr Roy Middleton. I am especially grateful to my late grandmother, Mrs Christina Johnston, for the translation of primary source material in Scottish Gaelic. For general discussion and advice, I extend my thanks to Dr Donald Boyd, Mr Norman Campbell, Rev. John Keddie, Rev. William Macleod and Rev. Dr Douglas Somerset.

Finally, I am deeply appreciative for the support of my wife, Esther, and children, James, Marcus and Emily, throughout the preparation of this book.

Note regarding Referencing

In citations, honorifics have been used to distinguish individuals with the same name: for example, 'Rev. Donald Munro'. Note also that 'John Macleod' should not be confused with 'John MacLeod'.

For the primary sources by John Kennedy, I have cited the fullest nineteenth-century edition. The only exceptions are two instances where exceedingly rare publications have been reprinted in modern editions, which are widely available and which I have therefore cited in preference. These are:

1. John Kennedy, *Hyper-evangelism, 'Another Gospel', though a Mighty Power* (Edinburgh, 1874); Horatius Bonar, *The Old Gospel: Not 'Another Gospel' but the Power of God unto Salvation* (Edinburgh, 1874); and John Kennedy, *A Reply to Dr Bonar's Defence of Hyper-evangelism* (Edinburgh, 1874); republished and cited hereafter as *Evangelism: A Reformed Debate* (Gwynedd, 1997).
2. Articles in the *Perthshire Courier*, 4 February to 1 April 1879; later published as John Kennedy, *The Present Cast and Tendency of Religious Thought* (Edinburgh, 1902); republished and cited hereafter as *Signs of the Times* (Aberdeen, 2003).

Introduction

On 3 October 1843, the Chanonry Presbytery of the newly separate Free Church of Scotland licensed a young divinity student as a minister. John Kennedy had not yet finished his divinity course, having completed three of the four years, but the need for ministers was pressing, especially for those who were fluent in Gaelic. There were newly established Free Church congregations throughout the Highlands, and many were vacant charges seeking a minister, such as Dingwall, where Kennedy would shortly be called to his life's work as the first Free Church minister. In the Disruption of May 1843, the great majority of the members and adherents of the Established Church of Scotland in the Highlands had responded to the call of Thomas Chalmers to abandon the temporal properties of the Establishment in defence of the crown rights of Jesus Christ over His church. Thus the Highlands had participated enthusiastically in a truly national religious movement in 1843. But in the later years of the nineteenth century, a divergence became increasingly evident. The Highlands became known as the 'chief bastion' of Calvinism, in the face of the theological, critical and confessional revolutions that profoundly changed the face of Lowland evangelicalism. If John Kennedy began his ministry in 1843 as a mainstream Free Churchman, he ended it at his death in 1884 as a perceived hardliner and conservative, a leader of the so-called 'Constitutionalist' party that included the majority of the Highland Free Church. Yet it was others who had changed in their opinions, not him. The resulting divergence between the two regions was a formidable one, identified by one author as 'a divide between two different cultures, two languages, two value-systems, two economic realities, and, more than anything else, two different forms of Christianity'.[1]

This divergence in religious outlook requires explanation, as its scale can scarcely be exaggerated. Highland evangelicals like John Kennedy largely rejected any modification of Calvinistic theology, opposed Biblical higher criticism, maintained a commitment to the Establishment Principle, and objected to any proposal for loosening the strict confessional subscription required of office bearers in the Presbyterian churches. Many thousands of people eventually separated themselves from the national churches to form distinct and overwhelmingly Highland denominations committed to these principles: namely, the Free Presbyterian Church and the continuing Free Church after 1900. Even within the churches of national scale, the United Free Church and the Established Church, the Highland congregations retained their own distinctive character, culturally, certainly, but also in theological terms.[2] Yet, as Allan MacColl has demonstrated, the later nineteenth century was actually a period of growing integration between Highlands and Lowlands in broader social, cultural and economic terms.[3] The divergence was in theology, religious outlook and religious practice, and this largely rooted in Lowland change and Highland continuity. Furthermore, the divergence was progressive: the opposition to union between the Free Church and the United Presbyterian Church during their first period of negotiations, 1863–73, by the so-called constitutionalist party, was broadly national in character, albeit drawing substantial support from the North; but by the time of the second round of negotiations, 1896–1900, the opposition came overwhelmingly from the Highlands. Nor was the divergence subtle: on the contrary, by 1887, the Free Church Moderator criticised the Calvinistic theology of the Highland congregations from the chair of the General Assembly.[4] Above all, the divergence was self-perpetuating as one controversy followed another. Increasingly, mutual suspicion tarnished relations between the Highlanders and even Lowlanders generally in sympathy with Calvinistic theology, as they clashed over the correct application of these principles, in, for example, the choice of materials of praise for public worship, and the proper response to American evangelistic campaigns.

Yet despite general acknowledgment of the dramatic Highland–Lowland divide in nineteenth- and twentieth-century Scottish evangelicalism, no one historical explanation can be said to command general agreement. To sum up the question: *Why did the evangelicalism of the Scottish Highlands diverge so dramatically and enduringly, in theology, worship, piety and practice, from that of Lowland Scotland, between the years 1843 and 1900?* This crucial question continues to await an adequate resolution, and the aim of the present study is to contribute towards such an answer.

For the purposes of this study, 'evangelicalism' will be defined as that form of orthodox Protestantism stressing the transformative power of the gospel of salvation by faith in Jesus Christ, and the need for personal experience of such a change. Undeniably, the evangelicalism typical of the Highlands had certain distinctive characteristics. In his important survey, still the standard work on the Highland Church in the eighteenth century, John Macinnes lists seven core doctrines characteristic of the indigenous Highland Calvinism that endured from the seventeenth century: namely, the distinction between law and grace; the difficulty of obtaining assurance; the centrality of the gospel call; the necessity of conversion; the necessity of sanctification; the reality of sacramental grace; and the concept of 'the secret of the Lord', a special insight regarding the reality of Christian profession, granted by the Spirit through the Word.[5] Kenneth Ross identifies the different view of evangelism, the different view of the Church arising from the predominant respect and religious observance in Highland communities, the different view of the sacraments, and the loyalty to charismatic individuals and consequent high place given to certain laymen.[6] Donald Meek, rather, lists the Highland distinctives as serious worship, the centrality of the Scriptures, emphasis on preaching, Sabbath observance and especially the theological stress on the sovereignty of God.[7] Allan Macinnes addresses especially the role of the Men – the traditionally outspoken laymen who were the key local leaders of Highland evangelicalism – in going beyond the 'arid institutional approach' of the Established Church, and bringing a distinctive vigour and character to the Highland Church.[8] Finally, David Paton identifies the 'pillars' of Highland evangelicalism as: Gaelic, lay participation, individual self-abnegation and revivalism.[9] Yet despite all these observations, when allowance is made for the exigencies of continuing the Church's witness in the distinct cultural, linguistic and geographic region of the Highlands, the key point to be emphasised is that the Highland Church stood in continuity with Scotland's Reformation, Calvinistic and Covenanting heritage, and, in the first half of the nineteenth century, in fellowship with evangelical Presbyterianism in Lowland Scotland.

The Highlands may be defined as the upland north of the Highland Boundary Fault, a line drawn from Helensburgh to Stonehaven, but excluding the North-East.[10] The north-eastern counties, together with Orkney and Shetland, have no share in the discussion, not exhibiting the religious divergence under consideration. The Highland counties were not, of course, monolithic in their religiosity: the distinctive Highland evangelicalism identified obtained especially strongly in the core Highland counties of Sutherland, Inverness, the Hebrides and especially Kennedy's native Ross-shire, and only to a lesser degree in the more peripheral regions such as Caithness, Argyllshire and Highland Perthshire.[11] But even when both variety and fluidity are acknowledged in the religiosity of the Highlands, the general loyalty of the nineteenth-century Highland population to evangelical Presbyterianism is clear.

The chronological boundaries of the study refer to the crises of Scottish church history: 1843, the year of the Disruption, and 1900, the year of the union of the Free Church with the more liberal United Presbyterian Church, which a minority, chiefly in the Highlands, declined to enter. From 1843 to 1893, the vast majority of people in the Highlands associated themselves with the Free Church of Scotland. The Established Church retained a presence throughout the Highlands, as State funding of stipends continued, but in rural areas the actual attendances were sometimes so small as to render the national church effectively defunct.[12] For these reasons, the terms 'Highland evangelicalism' and even 'the Highland Church' may be regarded as virtually synonymous with the Free Church for the period from 1843 to 1893, and additionally to refer thereafter to the Free Presbyterian Church, and from 1900 also to the Highland congregations of the United Free Church. By contrast, Lowland evangelicalism was always more heterogenous, due to the variety of secession and independent churches present, particularly in the cities, but especially was represented in the Free and United Presbyterian Churches. It should be noted that the United Presbyterian Church had little presence in the Highlands, and so the union of 1900 was largely a division in terms of the experience of the Highland Church, between the majority who entered the union, and the minority who continued as the Free Church.

Undoubtedly, the divergence that developed between Highland and Lowland evangelicalism in the later nineteenth century largely reflected change in the latter. William Enright examined the changing face of the evangelical sermon during the nineteenth century, demonstrating how radical change was evident even at the most basic level of the communication of popular religious instruction from the pulpit. An older, formally structured, doctrinal message, wholly focused on salvation in an eternal sense, proclaiming God as Judge and Sovereign, exemplified in the preaching of older Lowland preachers such as Andrew Thomson (1779–1831) and William Cunningham (1805–61), gave way to a liberal–evangelical address, unstructured, practical, dealing with character rather than status, stressing the Fatherhood and advancing Kingdom of God, exemplified in the sermons of William Robertson Smith (1846–94) and George Adam Smith (1856–1942).[13] Alec Cheyne is helpful on the sheer scale of transformation involved, arguing that the Victorian Church went through not one but several revolutions, over issues such as the authority of Scripture, worship and confessional subscription.[14] As these revolutions by-passed the Highlands, the gulf widened, but even more so as Highland leaders, pre-eminently John Kennedy, assailed these changes as evidence of declension in the Lowland Church. The fundamental question therefore remains: Why were the Highlands not impacted by these huge intellectual and cultural changes?

This study suggests that more attention should be given to the significance of the writings and leadership of the Highland minister John Kennedy (1819–84) as one major factor in the divergent character of Highland evangelicalism. Kennedy was an able and prominent Highland minister, who pastored Dingwall Free Church for forty years from 1844 until his death, being recognised in the later years of his ministry, from about 1860 onwards, as the effective leader of Highland evangelicalism. Even after his death he remained a pervasive influence, holding an almost totemic significance for the sundered factions of Highland evangelicalism. His writings were repeatedly republished, and mostly remain in print today, and his theological and historical views continue to influence opinion within the conservative churches. The principal focus of this study will be consideration of the significance of these works in addressing the question, especially in comparison to earlier writings on Highland evangelicalism devoid of the positive stress on Highland distinctives characteristic of Kennedy, and to subsequent writings that help to demonstrate the ubiquity of Kennedy's influence.

The key sources used are Kennedy's own published works and his private letters, diary entries and sermon notes. Use has also been made of a large manuscript volume of Kennedy's handwritten notes, which was discovered during the recent renovations of Dingwall Free Church, including first-draft texts of some of his publications. Comparative use has been made of other writings on the Highland Church, both prior to and subsequent to Kennedy's publications, from which his influence on the later writers is clear. Other primary sources include newspaper articles, General Assembly reports, and the posthumous biography of Kennedy by his friend Alexander Auld, published in 1887.[15] Secondary sources used include the discussion of Kennedy by Alan Sell, the works on the church history of the Highlands by John Macinnes and Douglas Ansdell, and the key monograph on the factors behind the separation of 1893 by James Lachlan MacLeod.[16]

In the academic literature, there has been widespread acknowledgment of Kennedy's significance as the leader of late nineteenth-century Highland evangelicalism, but little real analysis of how that influence was exercised or what it entailed. Many sketches of his life have been produced, often promoting him as an ideal of the Reformed minister, as a Christian believer worthy of emulation and as a writer worthy of being read.[17] He has been promoted by means of such profiles within the three main strands of Highland Presbyterianism: the Free Presbyterian Church,[18] continuing Free Church[19] and United Free Church of Scotland.[20] Equally, we may note the many works of popular church history emulating the concerns and approach of Kennedy's writing: for example, in stressing the distinctive character of Highland religion, and in demonstrating openness to accepting instances of apparently supernatural insights.[21]

Among modern historians, Alan Sell has discussed Kennedy in terms of the dramatic shift in mainstream theological outlook accomplished in the years 1860 to 1920, considering him as an example of unchanging doctrinal orthodoxy in contrast to many of his contemporaries, especially in his writing on the atonement.[22] Sandy Finlayson considered him as a participant in the Disruption, stressing the variety of different traditions encompassed within the Free Church of Scotland in 1843, and including Kennedy's Highland evangelicalism as one aspect of that mix.[23] John Smith considered Kennedy's politics in a useful journal article, showing how his Conservative sympathies differed from the strongly Liberal inclination of much of the rest of the Free Church, especially over the issue of disestablishment, which he vigorously opposed in later life, despite annual resolutions of the Free Church General Assembly urging Parliament to enact this measure.[24]

Most significantly for this book, the journalist and popular historian John MacLeod argued that John Kennedy reinvented Highland evangelicalism in his writings, and positively created divergences from the South not previously extant.[25] This argument probably attributes too much influence to Kennedy, but underlines Kennedy's recognised importance within the Highland Church. In comparable terms, Murdoch Campbell has commented of 'the Highland evangelical movement, [that] Dr Kennedy gave it solidity and depth', and described him as 'the Calvin of the north'.[26] A similar, if perhaps more balanced perspective, was given by Donald Meek, who analysed the literature of Highland evangelicalism as an example of successful image creation, with 'the archetype of such image making' being Kennedy's most famous book, *The Days of the Fathers in Ross-shire*.[27]

What other answers have historians offered to explain the divergence in Scottish evangelicalism? These fall into the broad categories of racialist, geographical, linguistic and sociological.

The whole concept of race was central to Victorian thought, and the perception of a racial division in Scotland between the Highland Celts and the Lowland Anglo-Saxons informed much of the contemporary explanation of the divergences within Scottish Christianity. The characteristics of Highland evangelicalism were regarded as reflecting supposed racial propensities of the Gaels, chief among them a servile willingness to follow charismatic leaders, an impulsive haste towards radical action, and a widespread incapacity for logical thought, all of which were felt to be exemplified in the Highland support for the Jacobite rebellion of 1745–6.[28] Contemporary writers suggested that the Highlanders had a native tendency to loyalty that led them to transfer to their religious leaders, such as Kennedy, the fealty they had once accorded their clan chiefs.[29] Taylor Innes, a prominent Free Church layman, offered this crude analysis within a thoughtful contemporary appraisal of Highland religion, taking account of the writings of defenders, such as John Kennedy and Alexander Auld, alongside hostile Lowland critiques. Innes accepted Highland religion as both objective and subjective in emphasis, strong on both doctrinal and experimental teaching, but weak in its lack of practical emphasis on the activity of the Christian life. He marred his insightful account with unflattering reflections on the 'Highland character', the supposed source of the divergence, and thus can only be said to describe rather than to explain the Highland–Lowland division in evangelicalism.[30]

The racialist tendency was evident even in sources written by Highlanders, such as Kenneth Macdonald's chapter 'Highlanders Are Simply Human', which conceded racial differences despite its title.[31] While most of the ecclesiastical sources exhibiting this tendency displayed condescension rather than hostile racism, Krisztina Fenyő demonstrated its darker side, in the angry and vitriolic response to the Highland Famine that she found in her exhaustive study of the columns and letter pages of the contemporary press.[32]

The whole notion of a meaningful racial divide in Scottish society now seems fanciful, and certainly inadequate as an explanation for the substantial intellectual divergence between Highland and Lowland evangelicalism in question. Douglas Ansdell has decisively debunked the notion of ministers as clan chiefs, showing how the Highland response to the union of 1900 demonstrated independent judgment rather than acquiescence, and often involved rejection of the guidance of local ministers, the great majority of whom did enter the union.[33] James Lachlan Macleod, however, has argued that contemporary racism directed against Highlanders was a substantive cause of the divergence leading to the first division of 1893, one of four he identified, on the grounds that it served to alienate Highland evangelicals from their Lowland counterparts.[34] In my view, this argument, while useful, is overstated: racism was scarcely a true ground of divergence in religion, and was probably no more than an exacerbating factor in undermining communication between North and South. MacColl described well 'the incomprehension with which Lowlanders – frequently buttressed in their opinions by theories of economic, social, and even racial superiority – looked upon Highland society and religion'.[35] This factor may thus have aided religious divergence but was not its cause.

The assertion that geographical isolation was a principal cause for the Highland–Lowland divergence is found in both contemporary and modern authors. Writing in 1922, Norman Maclean commented that, during the nineteenth century, 'The Grampians lay as an impassable barrier between two worlds, alien in thought, in spirit and in language.'[36] As early as 1851, enough of a divergence could be distinguished to lead an anonymous author to suggest that the differing climate could be responsible, that the 'want of sun' contributed to the 'want of animal spirits' apparently evidenced in Highland evangelicalism![37] The pejorative implication of the geographical argument was rendered more explicit, however, in one historian's narrative:

> Industrialisation and trade favoured the Lowland merchants and workers and the Lowland towns, where there was a quickening and broadening of social life and thought, while the Highlands remained economically poor and relatively unchanged. Indeed, the Highlanders reacted hostilely to most attempts at change, which they interpreted as further threats to their stability and integrity.[38]

As one ecclesiastical historian notes: 'These regions have always stood outside the main evolution of Scottish religion, and have been slow to catch up with the movements that have powerfully affected the rest of the country'.[39] John Boyd Orr, later famed as a nutritionist, but as a young man a partisan of the 1900 anti-unionists, neatly turned this argument about in his published defence of the continuing Free Church, suggesting that the unvarying landscape of the Highlands permitted rather a profounder spirituality and view of God. He wrote in florid prose:

> The Highland shepherd has ever before his eyes the vast mountain peaks stretching up towards heaven and lonely moors alternately clad in purple velvet and scourged by the storms [. . .] These see God's hand in the radiance of the sunrise and hear his voice in the desert silence or in the howl of the tempest. They communicate direct with the Eternal. Every one is an incipient poet and philosopher, and the

truths of religion are awful realities. Hence, theology is common property and common study.[40]

It must be said that the one explanation was probably as dubious as the other!

Andrew Drummond and James Bulloch acknowledged the Highland–Lowland distinction, 'the existence of two nations in Scotland', but tended to resort to the geographical explanation. The Highlands, they wrote, contributed 'little to the national life beyond romance and rebellion'. This broadly dismissive attitude was reflected in consistently antagonistic descriptions of Highland piety, always unfavourably contrasted to religion in the Lowlands, a divergence firmly rooted by the authors in 'the isolation, both cultural and geographical, of this Gaelic community'.[41] Callum Brown appeared to concur, proposing 'topography' as an answer to the divergence.[42] It is difficult not to regard such explanations as essentially reductive, taking an unwarranted step from geographical distance to intellectual, as though the Highlands' very landscape inhibited the intellectual progression of its inhabitants at the pace of the Lowlands. An obvious answer to the argument was the vigorous loyalty to Highland evangelicalism of many Highlanders who moved to the Scottish cities, or to Canada, and formed large and enthusiastic congregations of the separate Highland denominations after 1893 and 1900, and passed on this legacy to the next generation, long after the impact of geographical distance had been vitiated. The geographical argument also fails to account for the growing rather than weakening confidence of Highland evangelicalism during the period in question, despite the reduction in isolation achieved by educational Anglicisation, the telegraph and the railway.

Recently, and more positively, a whole Ph.D. thesis has been constructed on this very subject, considering the impact of the geography of the Highlands – in the broader sense of both landscape and language – on the religious development of the area. John Stephen advanced some striking thoughts in a work of considerable originality, suggesting that the remote and isolated communities of the Highlands tend to foster distinctive local patterns of religious development, with divergent strongholds of Roman Catholicism, Episcopalianism and Presbyterianism. He considered the high places in the topography of the Highlands to promote an enduring faith and obedience to Scriptural injunctions, suggested that the nearness of death in small rural settlements promoted an emphasis on resurrection and eternity, and pointed out that the over-large parishes that have always characterised Highland Church provision lead naturally to a strong emphasis on lay leadership. Crucially for the question in hand, he considered the linguistic barrier and the isolating geography to pose a serious obstacle to influence from without, and rooted the comparative lack of challenge to the Established Church in the North prior to 1843 principally in these factors.[43] However, as regards the specific divergence of the late nineteenth century, Stephen's insights must be weighed against the reality that Free Church ministers were all trained in the same colleges, read the same authors and periodicals, attended the same General Assemblies, and yet in the Highlands largely opposed the intellectual revolutions that the mainstream Church embraced. Furthermore, the outcomes of the revolutions tend to defy simplistic explanations: Shetland and Orkney, geographically separated far from the Lowlands, though culturally never part of the Highlands, followed a more conventional religious development, and had no significant involvement in the 1893 and 1900 movements. While geographical isolation cannot be disregarded, it cannot be the principal explanation.

Another argument concerns the linguistic isolation of the Highlands, due to the prevalence of Gaelic throughout the period in question. This was stressed as a factor by contemporary observers, such as Allan MacKillop, who supplied pulpits as a probationer of the incipient United Free Church, prior to emigrating to Australia. He noted that from Kennedy's old congregation in Dingwall, a substantial body of the English section had followed their minister into the union, but that a 'mere shadow' of the Gaelic-speaking section had done so. Equally, in Kingussie, he observed the division to reflect largely the extant linguistic division of the charge.[44] Yet this factor must not be over-emphasised: inevitably, a language section of a congregation in a society where many were monolingual in one direction or the other would tend to form a fairly cohesive community, particularly in the event of division. For example, Alexander Beith observed that the English congregation in Inverness in 1843 had largely remained in the Established Church.[45] The question is rather why the Highlanders, local to these areas, who would form the bulk of the Gaelic congregations, tended to support denominations characterised by a more traditional evangelicalism.

Many historians have concurred in the significance of the language: Charles Withers stressed the connection between the Gaelic language and evangelicalism, which was spread through Gaelic services and with the Gaelic Bible.[46] Victor Durkacz argued that the evangelicals made Gaelic 'a language fully developed as a Gospel medium', in contrast to the Anglicising policies of the moderates, by stressing engagement with the written word in the people's own language, through translation and education. The result was to bind the Highlands to the Free Church 'by grace and Gaelic'.[47] John Macinnes, in a thoughtful article, argued similarly that evangelical religion added a new dimension to the Gaelic language, and concludes that the evangelical Revival was 'a cultural revolution, which went some way at least toward forging a new Gaelic identity'.[48] Allan MacColl placed language at the centre of his analysis:

> Above all else, the Gaelic language was the principal cause of Highland religious distinctiveness. [. . .] The notion of Gaelic being a theological and spiritual barrier to the inculcation of innovatory beliefs is

given extra credence when the preponderance of translations of Puritan divinity in Gaelic is considered. For example, the Westminster Assembly's *Shorter Catechism* went through almost one hundred Gaelic editions between 1659 and 1951. [...] Thus, the religious tradition that was followed by most Highlanders in the nineteenth century, evangelical Presbyterianism, had also become intrinsically identified with the cultural identity of the region.[49]

Highland evangelicalism established itself through the use of Gaelic and, through its continued use, limited the ability of preachers and writers from beyond the Highlands to reach the people with new ideas. Yet even if this is granted, there were limits to the significance of Gaelic to Highland evangelicalism. In particular, Caithness, despite having a more limited prevalence of Gaelic than other parts of the Highlands, was significantly influenced by Highland evangelicalism in the nineteenth and early twentieth centuries. The hostile commentator 'Investigator', a partisan of the Established Church in the aftermath of the Disruption, insisted that Gaelic was no barrier to the evangelical religion of the Highlands, with the influence of the Gaelic-speaking 'Men' extending into Caithness, and English-speaking Christians aspiring to emulate their conduct and profession.[50] But above all, for the leadership of the Highland Church, English was no barrier. All the ministers and Gaelic schoolmasters, together with those of the elders who worked in professions involving trade of any significant nature, were fluent in speaking and reading English, and were just as familiar as their Lowland counterparts with the new developments in Biblical criticism emanating from Germany, the new scientific challenges to the interpretation of Genesis, and the arguments for changes in worship. The difference was an intellectual one: the general rejection of these ideas in the Highlands, by ministers, elders and people alike. Thus, language was an important part of the context of Highland evangelicalism, and may have helped to sustain its distinctness as a community within the Free Church, and its comparative uniformity of doctrine and practice, but is inadequate as a fundamental explanation for the Highland–Lowland divergence.

The sociological argument, popularised by James Hunter in particular, contends that Highland evangelicalism emerged as a psychological response to a period of social and economic trauma, exacerbated by an ecclesiastical Disruption that was really the sublimation of social protest against the abuse of the prerogatives of land ownership, and thus retained a wholly distinct character from the more conventional religious development of the Lowlands. The movement towards militancy and confrontation in the Land War of the 1880s mirrored the increased confidence and boldness of the 'Highland Host' as a conservative voting bloc in the Free Church General Assembly, just as the institutional independence and popular appeal of the Highland Land Law Reform Association (HLLRA) reflected the newly separate and primarily Highland denominations of

1893 and 1900.⁵¹ The parallels are interesting, of course, and would seem to reflect a greater social confidence and assertion in the Highlands by the end of the nineteenth century, which John Kennedy's writings in the 1860s certainly helped to promote, but as an explanation for theological divergence this is unconvincing on many levels. MacColl has demonstrated that some constitutionalist leaders were actively opposed to land reform, while others such as Kennedy's successor, Murdoch MacAskill, took a leading part, yet alongside leaders of the Free Church progressive party such as Robert Rainy, not to mention Church of Scotland ministers and even Roman Catholic priests.⁵² Therefore framing the land debate on religious lines is unsustainable. Furthermore, the sociological narrative is open to objections of condescension, crude psychoanalysis, and the refusal to accept the primary testimony of Highland people to account for their own actions. Indeed, the sociological narrative breaks down particularly in the 1890s, given that the crofters had proven, through their effective agitation for land reform, that they were able to effect social reform through journalistic and political channels. What need was there, then, to sublimate their social protest in religious movements such as those of 1893 and 1900? This book suggests rather that the divergence was intellectual and theological, and driven at least in part by the writings and influence of John Kennedy.

In structure, this study takes a thematic approach, while following the broad contours of Kennedy's life. The chapters consider consecutively his work as a preacher and pastor; his writings; his role as a leader of the constitutionalist party in the Free Church of Scotland; and his involvement in controversies in the public sphere.

Notes

1. James Lachlan MacLeod, *The Second Disruption* (East Linton, 2000), 125.
2. Even after the divisions of 1893 and 1900, there were still enough Highland conservatives to lead the attempted prosecution of the higher critical scholar George Adam Smith in 1902; cf. Iain D. Campbell, *Fixing the Indemnity: The Life and Work of Sir George Adam Smith, 1856–1942* (Carlisle, 2004), 136ff.
3. Allan W. MacColl, *Land, Faith and the Crofting Community* (Edinburgh, 2006), 88.
4. Andrew L. Drummond and James Bulloch, *The Church in Late Victorian Scotland, 1874–1900* (Edinburgh, 1978), 262–3.
5. Rev. John Macinnes, *The Evangelical Movement in the Highlands of Scotland, 1688–1800* (Aberdeen, 1951), 167–93.
6. Kenneth R. Ross, *Church and Creed in Scotland: The Free Church Case 1900–1904 and its Origins* (Edinburgh, 1988), 239–43.
7. Donald E. Meek, *The Scottish Highlands, the Churches and Gaelic Culture* (Geneva, 1996), 35.
8. Allan I. Macinnes, 'Evangelical Protestantism in the Nineteenth-century Highlands' (43–65), in G. Walker and T. Gallagher, eds, *Sermons and Battlehymns: Protestant Popular Culture in Modern Scotland* (Edinburgh, 1990), 44ff.
9. David Paton, *The Clergy and the Clearances* (Edinburgh, 2006), 108ff.

10. Given, e.g., in Donald Macleod, 'The Highland Churches Today' (146–76), in James Kirk, ed., *The Church in the Highlands* (Edinburgh, 1998), 146.
11. This distinction between core and periphery would appear to be more meaningful in terms of religiosity than imposing a north/south or east/west distinction within the Highlands.
12. Cf. Colin Macnaughton, *Church Life in Ross and Sutherland* (Inverness, 1915), 384ff., esp. 392.
13. W. G. Enright, 'Preaching and Theology in Scotland in the Nineteenth Century: A Study of the Context and the Content of the Evangelical Sermon' (Unpublished Ph.D. thesis, University of Edinburgh, 1968), *passim*.
14. A. C. Cheyne, *The Transforming of the Kirk* (Edinburgh, 1983), *passim*.
15. Alexander Auld, *Life of John Kennedy, D.D.* (London, 1887).
16. Alan P. F. Sell, *Defending and Declaring the Faith: Some Scottish Examples, 1860–1920* (Exeter, 1987), Ch. 1; Macinnes, *Evangelical Movement in the Highlands*; Douglas Ansdell, *The People of the Great Faith: The Highland Church, 1690–1900* (Stornoway, 1998); MacLeod, *Second Disruption*.
17. E.g., Maurice J. Roberts, 'John Kennedy of Dingwall' (4–31), *Banner of Truth* (August–September 1984).
18. Neil M. Ross [then Free Presbyterian minister of Dingwall], 'Introduction – A Prince Among Preachers' (vii–xxv), in John Kennedy, *Sermon Notes 1859–1865* (Lochmaddy, 2007).
19. Hugh M. Cartwright [then Free Church minister of Urquhart], 'Dr John Kennedy' (210–12), *Monthly Record of the Free Church of Scotland* (October 1983).
20. Norman C. Macfarlane [then Church of Scotland, and formerly United Free Church minister of Juniper Green, Edinburgh], *Apostles of the North* [first pub. 1931] (Stornoway, n.d.), 100–5.
21. E.g., Murdoch Campbell, *Gleanings of Highland Harvest* (Stornoway, 1958). Campbell discusses Kennedy himself (73–87) as one of the 'Fathers' he is now commemorating in turn.
22. Sell, *Defending and Declaring the Faith*, Ch. 1.
23. Sandy Finlayson, *Unity and Diversity: The Founders of the Free Church of Scotland* (Fearn, 2010), Ch. 11.
24. John A. Smith, 'Free Church Constitutionalists and the Establishment Principle' (99–119), *Northern Scotland*, xxii (2002).
25. John MacLeod, *Banner in the West: A Spiritual History of Lewis and Harris* (Edinburgh, 2008), 187, 363.
26. Campbell, *Gleanings of Highland Harvest*, 73.
27. Meek, *Scottish Highlands*, 61.
28. Examples of this argument in contemporary sources include Patrick Carnegie Simpson, *The Life of Principal Rainy*, 2 vols (London, 1909), i, 429–69 (esp. 448–50); and Norman Maclean, *Life of James Cameron Lees* (Glasgow, 1922), 48, 58ff.
29. E.g., William Garden Blaikie, *After Fifty Years* (London, 1893), 88; David Mackeggie, *Social Progress in the Highlands Since the Forty Five* (Glasgow, 1906), 26–7.
30. A. Taylor Innes, 'The Religion of the Highlands' (413–46), *British and Foreign Evangelical Review*, xxi (July 1872).
31. Kenneth Macdonald, *Social and Religious Life in the Highlands* (Edinburgh, 1902), 9–14.

32. Krisztina Fenyő, *Contempt, Sympathy and Romance: Lowland Perceptions of the Highlands and the Clearances During the Famine Years, 1845–1855* (East Linton, 2000), esp. Ch. 2.
33. Douglas Ansdell, 'The Disruptive Union, 1890–1900 in a Hebridean Presbytery' (55–103), *Records of the Scottish Church History Society*, xxvi (1996), 57–8.
34. MacLeod, *Second Disruption*, 235. The other factors he identifies are the context of social and economic change, the challenge from science and criticism, and the move to revise confessional orthodoxy. The first of these points will be addressed more fully below under sociological factors, while the other two are really descriptive rather than explanatory: the point at issue is surely why the Highland answer to these challenges differed from the Lowland answer.
35. MacColl, *Crofting Community*, 88.
36. Maclean, *Cameron Lees*, 83.
37. [Anon.], 'Puritanism in the Highlands' (307–32), *Quarterly Review*, lxxxix 178 (September 1851), 307.
38. T. O. Beidelman, *W. Robertson Smith and the Sociological Study of Religion* (Chicago, 1974), 15.
39. J. R. Fleming, *A History of the Church in Scotland, 1843–1874* (Edinburgh, 1927), 13.
40. John B. Orr, *The Scotch Church Crisis: The Full Story of the Modern Phase of the Presbyterian Struggle* (Glasgow, 1905), 28–9.
41. Andrew L. Drummond and James Bulloch, *The Church in Victorian Scotland 1843–74* (Edinburgh, 1975), esp. 274–5, 321–8; Drummond and Bulloch, *Church in Late Victorian Scotland*, esp. 84–8, 150–3, 195, 262–70, 321–2.
42. Callum G. Brown, *The Social History of Religion in Scotland Since 1730* (London, 1987), 116.
43. John Rothney Stephen, 'Challenges posed by the Geography of the Scottish Highlands to ecclesiastical endeavour over the centuries' (Unpublished Ph.D. thesis, University of Glasgow, 2004), esp. 22–3, 33, 145–50.
44. Allan Macdonald MacKillop, *A Goodly Heritage*, Sine Martin, ed. (Inverness, 1988), 102, 109.
45. Alexander Beith, *A Highland Tour* (Edinburgh, 1874), 244.
46. C. W. J. Withers, *Gaelic Scotland: The Transformation of a Culture Region* (London, 1988), 338.
47. Victor Edward Durkacz, *The Decline of the Celtic Languages* [first pub. 1983] (Edinburgh, 1996), 6ff., 96–133.
48. Dr John Macinnes, 'Religion in Gaelic Society' (222–42), *Transactions of the Gaelic Society of Inverness*, lii (1980–2), 239–42.
49. MacColl, *Crofting Community*, 73–4.
50. 'Investigator', *The Church and her Accuser in the Far North* (Glasgow, 1850), 49–51. 'Investigator' was Kenneth Phin, minister of Galashiels; Hew Scott, *Fasti Ecclesiae Scoticanae*, 6 vols [New Edition] (Edinburgh, 1917), ii, 178–9.
51. I have not found this position stated so decisively in the secondary literature, but it is the natural implication of James Hunter, *The Making of the Crofting Community* [New Edition] (Edinburgh, 2000), esp. 155–7, 217. The parallels between land reform and ecclesiastical controversy are usefully discussed in Ewen A. Cameron, 'Embracing the Past: The Highlands in Nineteenth-century Scotland' (195–219) in Dauvit Broun, R. J. Finlay and Michael Lynch,

eds, *Image and Identity: The Making and Re-making of Scotland Through the Ages* (Edinburgh, 1998), esp. 195–8, and MacColl, *Crofting Community*, 88–95.
52. MacColl, *Crofting Community*, 96ff. Note that despite their opposing positions on ecclesiastical questions, MacAskill and Rainy served together in the Edinburgh HLLRA.

CHAPTER ONE

Ministry

Kennedy the Highland Evangelical

John Kennedy was born on 15 August 1819, the fourth son of John Kennedy (1772–1841), himself a highly respected Gaelic preacher, and minister of the parish of Killearnan in the Black Isle. He therefore lived through a major period of transition within the Scottish Highlands. At his birth in 1819, the last Jacobite rebellion lay within living memory, when fear and suspicion of Highlanders had been general. The Highlands as he knew them in his youth were, as they always had been, comparatively primitive, and while very much a part of Scotland and Britain for the purposes of military recruitment, and considerably modernised in agricultural practices from previous generations,[1] they remained geographically remote from the major urban centres. Many Highlanders were monolingual in a language marginalised even within Scotland, many were illiterate, and few had capacity for engagement in national governance and public affairs. Travel was uncomfortable and sometimes hazardous,[2] and the fastest way to journey across land was still on horseback, as it had been for centuries. Roads were few and poor, and there was still not even a daily coach running between Inverness and Thurso.[3] Yet by the time of Kennedy's death in 1884, much had changed. The railway brought swift, comfortable and dependable travel to the furthest points of the mainland Highlands, while the telegraph permitted rapid communication with the wider world. Highlanders had access to elementary education, and were reading newspapers and voting in elections (albeit with property restrictions), while Parliament was coming to recognise the need for Highland land reform. Indeed, legislation was already at an advanced stage of planning that would grant security of tenure to the Highland crofters. In wider society, fear of the Highlander had given way to romanticism; a professorial chair of Celtic at Edinburgh University, the adorning of even Lowland Scottish regiments with the sartorial paraphernalia of the Highlands, and Queen Victoria's public embrace of Highland life all indicated a growing appreciation for Gaelic Scotland.

Not all the changes were positive. Kennedy's lifetime was also marked by high emigration from the Highlands, with a population in steady decline, and the modest developments did little to address the heavy economic and cultural dependence on the Lowlands. The popularisation of Darwinian evolution from 1859 appeared to offer scientific credibility to assertions of racial difference. The cultural difference always recognised between

Lowlander and Highlander could now be expressed in pseudo-scientific terminology, and the age-old disregard, even disdain, for 'the other' north of the Highland line was justified as legitimate scientific observation. The young John Kennedy, who grew up speaking Gaelic and was educated alongside the local children at the parish school, could not but be shaped by a public discourse that often treated the Highlander in racial terms as a 'noble savage', a 'warrior', the 'contemporary ancestor'; or, alternatively, as a 'fool' and a 'rogue'.[4] The Established Church journalist known as 'Investigator' probably expressed the attitude of many when he wrote disparagingly of the 'semi-savage peasantry' on whose support the popular evangelicalism of the Highland Church relied.[5] As Kennedy's life progressed, the language would change in sophistication but not in import, and as a result Kennedy was deeply conscious of his identity, not just as a Scot, but as a Highlander.

His contemporary and sometime colleague, John Watson, writing as 'Ian Maclaren', only expressed the view of educated Scots when he wrote in one of his novels:

> Scotland contains within it two races; and partly because their blood is different, and partly because the one race has lived in the open and fertile Lowlands, and the other in the wild and shadowy Highlands, the Celt of the north and the Scot of the south, are well-nigh as distant from each other as the east from the west.[6]

The language asserted difference but with broad hints of Lowland superiority. Patrick Carnegie Simpson, the biographer of Kennedy's ecclesiastical opponent Robert Rainy, concurred: 'Between the Celtic, or, rather, Gaelic and the more strictly Scottish sections of the Church is a difference of race,' which he saw as a leading cause of the ecclesiastical divisions of the Free Church from the late 1860s. He added of the Highlanders that 'they were constitutionally prejudiced against all change, for their lives, physically and intellectually, knew little variety'.[7]

It is against the background of such attitudes that Kennedy must be assessed. Facing an instinctive prejudice that regarded him and his people as both racially inferior and intellectually backward and inflexible, it was not surprising that his writing was often robust and combative, countering the prejudices of the Lowlands with his bold assertion of the superiority of the religious piety and practice of the Highlanders. He argued that, conscious of the difference in religious tone, 'the Southrons have been anxious to make out that the difference is owing to some defect or excess that may be charged against the north'. His disparaging term reflected his instinctive reaction against those too ready to criticise the Highland Church. The threatened feeling, as a member of a community under critical assault, became evident in his mention of the Lowland detractors of a 'Ross-shire Father' with a military metaphor, as 'the hosts across the Spey marshalled against him'.[8]

Furthermore, Kennedy's loyalty was always to the Highland *Church*. He was born into a manse of the Established Church of Scotland, and was committed to the Protestant and Presbyterian allegiance of his father from his earliest days. As a Protestant, he considered medieval Romanism to have been a system of superstition which was sustained by popular ignorance, and from which the Reformation had delivered Scotland. This outlook informs the historical narrative in the first chapter of *The Days of the Fathers in Ross-shire*:

> Fearing no competing religion, the priesthood had been content to rule the people, without attempting to teach them. His ignorance and superstition made the rude Highlander all the more manageable in the hands of the clergy, and they, therefore, carefully kept him a heathen ... [He] was found by the Reformation as Popery had left him, an utter heathen in ignorance, a very fanatic in superstition, and, in his habits, a lawless savage.[9]

Kennedy's narrative thus rooted the spiritual life of the Highlands in the Reformation itself, as a deliverance from an oppressive religious structure; in particular, he celebrated the actions of the Church of Scotland, as an institution, in appointing a commissioner, and thereafter a supply of ministers and readers, to establish the Protestant faith in Ross-shire.[10] This new spiritual life was rooted in the Calvinistic theology of the Scottish Reformation, which recent research has demonstrated was notably influential in the Highlands, even in the early years following the Reformation.[11]

But Kennedy's narrative was also explicitly Presbyterian, which was the form of ecclesiastical governance developed in Scotland, and in parallel forms on the Continent, as the institutional vehicle of Calvinism. For Kennedy, Presbyterianism was the form of government mandated by the New Testament, and those Church of Scotland ministers who had resisted the Stewart imposition of Episcopalian governance at the Restoration of the monarchy in 1660 'were found faithful in the day of trial', while the Episcopalian curates were disparaged as 'such rubbish as had filled' the parishes during the Episcopalian hegemony. Presbyterianism was faithfulness to God, while the Episcopalians acted 'in opposition to the cause of the Gospel'.[12] It would be a mistake, however, to regard this account as the record of a long-forgotten battle: on the contrary, there were still substantial remnants of indigenous Episcopalian worship in the eighteenth- and even into the nineteenth-century Highlands. Even in Killearnan, 300 Episcopalians were recorded living in the parish in 1813,[13] the year that Kennedy's father became minister. This number only reduced thereafter, as his popular and effective ministry wore down opposition to Presbyterianism.[14] The point of Kennedy's narrative was clear: the Presbyterian Church of Scotland was, under God, the means of spiritual life and blessing to the Highlands. The pride in the ministers who spearheaded the successful extension of Presbyterianism throughout the Highlands in the eighteenth century was evident, as was Kennedy's sense that he was, and sought to be, loyal to their legacy.

There may be something purposeful in this self-presentation, as there can be an uncomfortably dislocating element to the identity of a 'son of the manse'. Socially, in a community like Killearnan, the manse family did not fit naturally into one social class. The parish manse, still extant today, though in private ownership, is a large stone house of considerable grandeur, which by appearances would tend to put the Kennedys on a par with the wealthier landowners of the district, yet the parish minister's dealings were as much with the lower classes of society, and his income would not permit a lifestyle comparable to that of the wealthy. Kennedy grew up living in the manse but attended the parish school alongside the local children. In a cohesive Highland community, he would be uncomfortably conscious that his parents had moved to the Black Isle only in 1813, and that all their family roots were in far-away Wester Ross. The fact that Kennedy felt a need to work to improve his spoken Gaelic during his student years[15] suggests that it was not the principal language of the home, and that there may have been limits to the extent that he and his brothers were permitted to socialise with the local boys as they grew up. In his description of the long and distinguished tradition of Highland ministry he describes in *Days of the Fathers*, reaching a pinnacle in the glowing elegy to his own father, he firmly located and embraced his own identity as a Highland Presbyterian minister.

Thus we may infer that Kennedy recognised and accepted his identity as a Presbyterian from early youth; that he considered the Presbyterian Church to be the historical, confessional and legitimate Church of Scotland, the means of spiritual blessing to Lowlands and Highlands alike; and that he therefore possessed a clear and decisive institutional commitment. In this, he shared the general loyalty of the Highlands of his day, well expressed in the standard history:

> The Presbyterian Church, in 1688 an alien intrusion offensive to the majority of the Gaelic people, became in a relatively short time the beloved and venerated spiritual Mother from which it was not only grievous loss but also sin to be separated.[16]

It was in this loyalty and commitment that Kennedy presented himself in 1840, in his twenty-first year, as a candidate for the ministry of the Church of Scotland. Having graduated M.A. from King's College that year, he proceeded immediately to enter the Aberdeen Divinity Hall in preparation for the ministry. During his divinity studies, he supported himself by work as a tutor in the household of the well-known author Dr Henderson at Caskieben.[17]

Curiously, it was only after he began his divinity studies that Kennedy experienced an evangelical conversion. Stewart Brown makes the interesting comment that, in 1811, Thomas Chalmers's 'conversion became a symbol of the Evangelical revival in Scotland'.[18] John Kennedy's personal experience in the year 1841 was more private, but equally intense and permanent in effect, and in the change effected from outward conformity to evident spiritual vigour and passion, could equally stand as symbolic of the evangelical transformation in the Highlands occurring at that time. As a young student, Kennedy was upright in life, and is described at King's College, Aberdeen, as a 'universal favourite'.[19] He gave evidence of academic ability and application, with a fellow-student recalling his 'plain and easy' progress through the arts course,[20] and Kennedy himself later recalling winning a money bursary at the close of one session, which he used to take a sightseeing trip to Glasgow.[21] He also worked as a private tutor to support himself financially during this time. He gave every appearance of training for the Presbyterian ministry, holidaying on the west coast to improve his Gaelic, presumably with the intention of having a preaching capacity in that language. He even travelled on summer missionary cruises with the well-known philanthropist Isaac Lillingston, an Englishman and nephew of William Wilberforce, who resided at Balmacara and used his wealth and energies to promote the spread of the evangelical religion.[22] Yet his personal Christian commitment seemed less than heartfelt, as his fellow-student John Mackay wrote of his student days:

> There was not much in his conversation to give any special promise of that high-toned personal piety and power as a preacher by which he afterwards became distinguished. Indeed, the stage was then believed to possess nearly as great attractions for him as the pulpit, while the fictions of Walter Scott occupied fully more of his time than the facts of Calvin's 'Institutes'. [. . .] Apart from this, there was nothing in his character or conduct outwardly inconsistent with his profession. But to his intimate acquaintances there appeared a want of that high sense of the sacredness and solemnity of the ministerial office which might be expected . . . Mr Kennedy's religion – if such it can be called – seemed to consist in little more than a strong dislike to a cold and heartless moderatism, a high admiration and peculiarly warm affection for his venerated father, and great confidence in the efficacy of that father's prayers.[23]

The key emphases to draw from this testimony are the young Kennedy's evident respect for distinctively evangelical religion, and yet his lack of personal experience of its truth as the way of salvation. Undoubtedly, the young Kennedy as described by Mackay must have seemed to most acquaintances a committed Christian already in principles and conduct. Yet Mackay's testimony cannot be lightly dismissed when it is so consistent in terms of the nature and timing of his spiritual change with Kennedy's own testimony. After this period of change, Mackay saw Kennedy marked by 'high-toned personal piety', a sincere concern for consistent Christian conduct not previously evident and by 'power as a preacher', an evident passion for Christian teaching only now witnessed. Both Mackay and Kennedy himself thus testify to a dramatic change to his inward attitudes during this period, even if it may not have been largely evident in his outward conduct.

In one respect, the change may have been very definite, in terms of convictions regarding Christian doctrine. Many years later, Kennedy made the striking statement that he 'was deceived and almost ruined' by Amyraldianism,[24] the doctrine that, contrary to strict Calvinism, Christ died for everyone. Presumably he was referring to his unconverted student days, as his whole later ministry was marked by clear and decisive Calvinist theology; it may be that he was putting his trust at this period in some vague sense that Christ had died in a general sense for all, and that he simply needed to acknowledge that in faith for salvation. This teaching, though not orthodox by the Westminster Confession, was not unknown among Church of Scotland evangelicals, most famously being promulgated by John McLeod Campbell, albeit latterly from outside the bounds of the Established Church.

Kennedy himself testified that the circumstance that, at least in the human sense, led to his conversion was the unexpected death of his father on 10 January 1841. This minister, John Kennedy of Killearnan, 'Kennedy of Redcastle', had been one of the principal leaders of Highland evangelicalism, well known throughout the Highlands as a frequent assistant at communion seasons. For his father, as indicated in the quotation above, the younger Kennedy cherished the highest regard, as he further proved subsequently by appending a short biography of John Kennedy, senior, to his first book.[25] Crucially, he testified regarding this bereavement: 'The memory of that loss I can bear to recall, as I cherish the hope that his death was the means of uniting us in bonds that shall never be broken.'[26] One biographer describes how, on receiving this news, 'he threw himself on top of his bed and lay there for a whole night drenched and drowned in sorrow'.[27] He left early in the morning for Killearnan, but felt unable even to enter the house when he arrived, and instead 'retired to the garden, and there poured out his soul to God'.[28] Alexander Auld describes three states of mind that Kennedy passed through during his fortnight's stay in Killearnan, as his subject had personally described them to him. These are worth giving in full:

(1.) Indescribable agony of mind under a sense of sin against God, especially in the neglect of his admonitions, instructions, and example of his father, now lost to him for ever.
(2.) Striving to keep himself from sinking into utter despair of God's mercy by betaking himself to prayer and to meditation on passages of Scripture.
(3.) An apprehension that the way of salvation by Jesus Christ was opened in the Gospel to the very chief of sinners.[29]

This testimony indicates that Kennedy experienced a sense of the reality of his sin; an awareness of the judgment of God upon this sin; a recourse to Scripture in search of hope; and thus, eventually, access to Jesus Christ in the gospel, as offering hope, love and a personal relationship with God, even for a sinner such as him. This is a classical evangelical description of personal salvation. Kennedy's spiritual diary from 1841, *Annotationes Quotidianae* [Daily Jottings], expressed the intensity of the experiences that he went through at this time: 'The Atheism of my heart again raging. IT IS MY SIN, I now see "the fool is in my heart, the guilt at my door".'[30]

The end result of these experiences was an evidently changed life, for Mackay calls him 'another, and to all appearance a new, man', and adds:

> No change could be more complete than that which was visible in his whole nature. His former indifference to Divine things had given place in his mind to a deep seriousness, his self-sufficiency to self-abasement, the things of time to the things of eternity . . . The new song [i.e. assurance of saving faith] alone seemed to be wanting.[31]

The experience was plainly a real and meaningful turning point in his life, from which arose his passionate and lifelong dedication to evangelical Christianity. That it was recognised as such at the time, by his professors and fellow-students alike, is evident in a contemporary account of him 'as one of the most active students on the Evangelical side, and as one that incurred the strong dislike of a certain cold Aberdeen Professor of Divinity for his warm Evangelical views'.[32] It may have been the same Professor who, commenting on a popular discourse of Kennedy's, described it as 'containing much that was excellent, and which gave promise of future eminence, but at the same time too Methodistical in its tone and emphasis'. This reference to the evangelical nonconformist movement generally known by this name was plainly an attempt to deprecate Kennedy's preaching by comparison with preachers regarded as firebrand enthusiasts. Hence one can understand Kennedy's recorded remark on the occasion: 'I have no ambition for any higher praise . . . if that be the spirit of Methodism, I trust it shall never cease to be one of the characteristics of my pulpit ministrations.'[33] In such a comment, whatever the theological nuances, he identified himself with the bold gospel spirit of men like Whitefield and the Wesleys.

However, Kennedy would soon have to take a bolder step to follow his evangelical convictions with consistency. On 18 May 1843, the bulk of the evangelical party within the Church of Scotland separated themselves from the Establishment, choosing to form the Free Church of Scotland rather than allow the spiritual independence of the Church to be compromised by allowing the State to enforce the law of patronage in the appointment of ministers to vacant charges and to interfere in matters of internal ecclesiastical discipline. The sacrifices required of many individual ministers were immense, requiring them to leave manses, glebes and stipends for an uncertain future, dependent on the freewill offerings of congregations for support, rather than on the teinds and endowments of the Establishment. But students also took a bold step into the unknown, leaving the wealthy vacancies and comfortable prospects of the Church of Scotland for the vulnerable situation and uncertain future of the Free Church. Kennedy never seems for a moment to have considered any other course than enthusiastic embrace of the stance of the Free Church, which was wholly consistent with his evangelical convictions. He later conceded that it was 'a time of sifting trial'[34]: that is, a time when the truth of professed convictions became evident in conduct. Much the same conclusion was reached across the Highlands, and the great body of the Highland people flocked into the new Free Church, which could soon command adherence levels of more than 90 per cent in the three core Highland synods of Caithness and Sutherland, Ross and Glenelg.[35] As one commentator remarked, in the Highlands, 'the Church came out'.[36]

This comment is crucial: Stewart Brown has stressed that historians entirely misunderstand the purpose of the Disruption if they consider it merely as the formation of another denomination. Chalmers's vision was nothing less than that the Scottish national Church would, as a body, withdraw from its connection to the British State, rather than submit to the infringement of Christ's Headship it saw in the imposition of unwanted ministers by patronage, backed by the full force of the law. In the Highlands, this is what happened: a concerted movement of the popular community away from the Established Church. It was, rather, the Lowlands that were divided, with large numbers of ministers and congregations choosing to remain within the Established Church. Chalmers had hoped to force the Tory Government of Sir Robert Peel to back down from its commitment to enforce the law of patronage in the Scottish Established Church by united, concerted action, or, failing that, to build in Scotland a godly commonwealth with a national Church free of State connection; yet, judged by either objective, the Disruption had really failed to achieve its objectives.

Later in life, when he opposed the Free Church campaign for the disestablishment of the Church of Scotland, Kennedy was accused of lacking loyalty to Free Church principles, and it was insinuated that his lack of personal experience of Disruption sacrifice as a minister was at least one reason for this. His response was a frank personal testimony, in a published lecture:

> But I did know something of trial in that sifting time. I was then, on the eve of license, living in a manse, which was my brother's, on whose kindness I was quite dependent, and which, along with my mother and my sisters, I had to abandon. I had to lock the door of the old manse, which had been the place of my birth and the home of my boyhood, with my weeping mother leaning on my arm, and to accompany her to a house, which had for years been untenanted except by birds, with all its windows broken, and its floors covered with a thick coating of

clotted dust, with no prospect before us but pinching poverty during the remainder of our days on earth. I had that much of an experience of Disruption trial.[37]

Kennedy knew what it was for a family to suffer privation in the cause of the Free Church, and the Disruption testimony, and his family had made the sacrifices willingly to safeguard what they viewed as the principle of the Headship of Christ.

The Disruption raised immense practical problems for the young Free Church throughout the Highlands. The near-unanimous support of the Highland people did not equate to unanimity amongst the ministry; indeed, dozens of Highland ministers were Moderates, who had no intention of entering the Free Church. Many congregations now wished to call their first evangelical minister, but the supply of preachers with a command of Gaelic was limited. The 1843 General Assembly noted no fewer than 151 vacant congregations and preaching stations throughout the Highlands.[38] Consequently, students at advanced stages of their courses were asked to present themselves for licence, and Kennedy, having completed three of the usual four sessions of divinity studies, was formally licensed by the Free Presbytery of Chanonry on 3 October 1843.[39] Despite challenges, this was an exciting time in the Scottish Church; William Walker pointed out that the Disruption opened up about 1,000 new positions of ministry, as every parish that lost a minister to the Free Church sought a replacement, and the Free Church tried as quickly and as far as possible to duplicate that nationwide structure.[40] The days were gone when able probationers lingered in dissatisfied service as teachers and tutors, sometimes all their lives, for want of a well-disposed patron to grant them a living.

Fittingly, Kennedy's first sermon was preached in Killearnan, in a scene ably described by his colleague John Fraser, also a native of that parish:

> [He] preached his first sermon in a sweet spot, sloping to the shore, and within a hundred yards of the old manse and church where he was born and baptised, and where the Free Church congregation worshipped till such time as the first Free church was erected. In few, if in any parish in the Highlands, did the parishioners, as in Killearnan, almost in a body cast in their lot with the Free Church.[41]

One can imagine the scene: the beauty of the natural surroundings; the delight of the congregation in hearing one of their own, after so many years of study and some hard experiences, preach for the first time the gospel message; and yet the poignancy that it must be in the open air because, as a Free Church congregation, for all their unanimity, their parish church was barred to them for worship.

The difficulties of Killearnan were duplicated across Scotland, as congregations entering the Free Church lost the use of their church building, but it was in the Highlands that the problem was most keenly felt, due to the lack of public buildings that could serve as alternatives, the inclemency of the weather and, above all, the extreme uniformity of land ownership. In some cases, whole parishes, such as Kilmallie, formed part of larger estates, and these landowners had the right, which many of them exercised, to deny a congregation a piece of land on which to erect a church building. In some cases, landowners went further and refused permission to Free Church congregations even to gather for worship in the open air on their lands. The *Annals of the Disruption* document congregations reduced to worshipping on the public road, as the only land in the parish not owned by the landowner, or, in the most extreme cases, in gravel-pits or stretches of shoreline below the high tidemark, which lay outside the landlord's jurisdiction.[42] While Dingwall, as a town congregation, did not endure these hardships, Kennedy himself certainly experienced what it was to be denied a place of worship in the Highlands, both in Killearnan and in many other congregations, as he supplied pulpits and assisted at communions. The cruel situation of a congregation having to worship outdoors in all weathers due to the obstinacy of their landlord continued, in the case of Shieldaig Free Church in Wester Ross, where Kennedy was a regular assistant at communions, until 1877, five years after they at last obtained their own minister, Donald Macdonald, who later found fame as one of the founding fathers of the Free Presbyterian Church of Scotland.[43] Schoolteachers who sided with the Free Church were dismissed, and there were also reports of individual tenants being evicted and employees being dismissed for their affiliation with the Disruption movement.[44] In this context, one can understand the observation of John Macleod, that 'The Disruption is the great epoch in the Church life of the Highlands. Its memories furnish them with the heroic materials that Scotland as a whole finds in the Covenanting struggle.'[45]

Stewart Brown has indicated how the Free Church took consolation from the imagery of martyrdom, even though the relevant instances were largely restricted to the Highlands.[46] The Disruption generation of Highlanders were considered, as Ansdell noted, to have demonstrated qualities of 'commitment, faithfulness and sacrifice', and albeit that the more extreme sufferings were restricted to the few, even in the North, this 'minority experience was adopted as the prevailing ethos of the Highland Free Church'.[47] The Highlanders considered themselves, and were considered by the wider Free Church, to have shown a particularly zealous commitment to the Free Church cause, and to have underlined this commitment by the privations they had experienced. On the one hand, this gave the Free Church a heightened status in the Highlands, so that, as Allan MacKillop has remarked, 'The Free Church practically took possession of the Highlands after 1843.'[48] But crucially, this also led the Free Church to consider itself to have a special obligation to the Highlands.[49] As one particularly practical example, Donald Macleod notes that the Free Church was 'conscious of a special responsibility' for the Highlands when the Potato Famine of 1846 brought first shortages, and eventually a very real threat of starvation, and so was the first body to organise relief efforts.[50] As an evangelical and a Free Church minister, Kennedy felt himself bound by ties of loyalty to the Highland congregations who had taken their stance with the Disruption movement, and this undoubtedly coloured his attitude thereafter, of loyalty to evangelical truth and to the Highland congregations that professed it.

Thus while Kennedy's evangelical identity was rooted in his family background, and especially in his profound respect for his father, his individual evangelicalism was also forged in a powerful personal experience of spiritual conversion, whereby he acknowledged his personal sin and embraced the Biblical offer of salvation by means of the atoning work of Christ. He accepted the implications of his conversion when he left the Established Church at the Disruption. His identity, like that of the Highland Church, was therefore one of decisive commitment to evangelical Christianity on the basis of personal spirituality, and of sacrifice and even suffering in the fulfilment of that commitment. This was the commitment that Kennedy maintained in the many conflicts of his later years. The young minister did not have to wait long to receive a call, and on 13 February 1844, John Kennedy was ordained and inducted as the first minister of the Free Church of Scotland in Dingwall.

Kennedy the Preacher

Dingwall was a royal burgh, the administrative centre of Ross and Cromarty, in the heart of the Scottish Highlands. In the mid-nineteenth century, it was a busy market town with a settled population of around 2,000 people.[51] Like much of the Highlands, Dingwall was firmly Episcopalian during the seventeenth century. An attempt to hold a Presbyterian service there in 1704 was thwarted by a mob, and an attempted settlement of a Presbyterian minister four years later was similarly prevented.[52] However, over the course of the eighteenth century, a peaceful and stable Presbyterian ministry had been established. The parish church had experience of evangelical ministry, notably from the famed Alexander Stewart, whose conversion from Moderatism in 1796, when minister of his previous charge of Moulin, was emblematic of the impact of evangelicalism across the Highlands and led to a significant revival in that part of Perthshire. Stewart served as minister of Dingwall from 1805 to 1820, and his *Memoirs* offer valuable insight into the spiritual state of the town in that period.[53] Stewart testified to having two distinct congregations in the town: the Gaelic, which was largely solemn and receptive to his evangelical teaching; and the English, whom he found to be, in a spiritual sense, 'careless'. Overall, however, he considered his ministry there to have met with 'little success'.[54]

The Dingwall population by 1843 was largely Presbyterian, with only 40–50 Episcopalians and around 12 Methodists. The parish minister, Hector Bethune, was evangelical in doctrine, but when the Disruption came he remained within the Church of Scotland. A majority of the congregation 'came out', but not an overwhelming one, and a later description of the English section of the Free Church congregation as numbering 'probably not more than 120' following the Disruption suggests that the division Stewart discerned in his congregation thirty years before was reflected to some extent in the parting of ways in 1843.[55] The Established Church congregation in Dingwall was larger than any other in Ross-shire, and reportedly included 'the greater part of the upper strata of society'.[56] The first Free Church building was erected on Castle Street in 1844, designed to seat 800, which was adequate given the separate services held for the Gaelic and English sections of the congregation. The manse was built in 1848, the year of Kennedy's marriage, with the debts on both buildings paid off by 1858.[57]

The Free Church communicant membership in the Dingwall congregation was initially around 140,[58] although the actual size of the congregation is difficult to estimate. The conventional rule of thumb that one in eight in nineteenth-century Highland congregations were communicants[59] would suggest an initial congregation with a little over 1,000 people at least loosely connected, which would be consistent with a majority of Dingwall's Presbyterian population adhering to the Free Church. However, Kennedy's call as placed before the Dingwall Presbytery in 1843 is recorded as having just 249 signatures appended.[60] This must have included a clear majority of the communicant membership, as the call was sustained without question, and indeed was stated in one biographical sketch to have been unanimous,[61] but could only have been actively subscribed by a small minority of adherents. The probability is therefore that the adherent base was nominally large but somewhat disengaged from the activity of the congregation. By contrast, after thirteen years of Kennedy's ministry, he was reportedly presented with an address signed by 1,400 members and adherents of the Dingwall congregation – which, given the town population, must have included the overwhelming majority connected with the charge – appealing to him not to accept the calls to Greenock or Tain, which were then being presented.[62] This suggests a church that had both grown in size, and become more concerted and cohesive in its activity. By 1863, when Kennedy received a call to Glasgow, the number of members and adherents signing a similar address had risen to 1830, which would seem to indicate substantial further growth and cohesion since 1857, remarkable over so brief a period.[63] The communicant membership increased, though not dramatically, and mostly varied between 150 and 190 through the years of Kennedy's ministry, with a small dip to 133 on the roll at the time of his death in 1884.[64]

The charge was demanding, with five regular services conducted every week, each requiring a full-length sermon: two Sabbath morning services, Gaelic and English, a Sabbath evening service alternating between the two languages, and separate weekly prayer meetings in Gaelic and English.[65] Preaching was central to ministry in the Highland evangelical tradition,[66] and it was through his proficiency in the pulpit that Kennedy earned his place as a leading minister, and later *the* leading minister, in the Highland Free Church. 'The pulpit was Dr Kennedy's throne,' declared one contemporary tribute,[67] and in his own congregation his resultant popularity was immense. Even visiting fully twenty years after Kennedy's death, Allan MacKillop found many in Dingwall keen to reminisce about his sermons.[68] Norman Macfarlane noted how one aspect of his preaching was reserved solely for Dingwall:

> [He had] a genius for preaching (or lecturing) engagingly to boys and girls. Whether in sermon or lecture – on a text from the Scripture or on the wonders of Science or his descriptions of his travels – he could captivate and charm as few could, young and old revelling in the delights of his wonderful brilliance on such occasions. [. . .] He gave quarterly sermons to the young to which young and old flocked. The thickest-witted grown-ups were there, for he preached or lectured on their level.[69]

The only criticism in Dingwall was the rigorous extent of his preaching, with some former hearers complaining to MacKillop that Kennedy's full-length discourses at midweek meetings had been too demanding on their attention, particularly an exhaustive series of consecutive sermons working through the entire book of Psalms, which he preached at these meetings over the course of almost forty years of ministry.[70]

The fruit of his painstaking ministry in the town was a growing and attentive congregation, such that by the 1860s the original church building was considered inadequate. A large new church was erected on a prominent site in the heart of Dingwall with seating for more than 1,000 people, and opened for worship in 1870. This building was well filled for both the Gaelic and the English services,[71] with the latter in particular developing over the course of his ministry, so that a newspaper reported at the time of his death: 'The handsome new Gothic edifice in which he preached would contain an audience of a thousand persons, listening with eagerness to his chaste elegance in the English tongue.'[72] One unusual feature of the church was the pulpit, designed to Kennedy's own requirements, as a platform just below the level of the gallery, across the whole width of the church. Apparently, Kennedy liked to stride from end to end as he preached, holding an ever-present white handkerchief.[73] This platform pulpit, the focal point of the whole church, was and is an architectural statement of the centrality of Kennedy's preaching to his ministry in Dingwall.

Beyond his own congregation, Kennedy rapidly built a reputation as a notably talented preacher. As early as 1849, he was invited to preach before the General Assembly of the Free Church on the Sabbath of their meeting, a signal honour for a minister not yet thirty.[74] That same year, the renowned 'Apostle of the North', John Macdonald of Ferintosh, whom Kennedy would later commemorate in an appreciative biography, died aged sixty-nine. The young pastor of Dingwall thereafter became known as the minister who had 'seized the mantle' of Macdonald as the leading preacher of the Free Church in the Highlands.[75] The tradition of yearly or twice-yearly communion seasons, with well-known preachers invited to help to attract visitors from other congregations, obtained throughout the Highland Free Church, and facilitated Kennedy's growing popularity as a preacher beyond his own congregation.

In 1848, Kennedy married Mary Mackenzie, who was a year his senior and of high social standing. She was born in Stornoway Castle in 1818, to Forbes Mackenzie, the 'Chamberlain of the Lewis', and his wife, Catherine Nicolson, and resided from 1822 at Fodderty Lodge.[76] The Kennedys seem to have had a very happy marriage, and to have been likeminded in religious matters. They went on to have several children, of whom twin girls survived to adulthood. An affectionate memoir of Mrs Kennedy by a cousin of her husband, Rev. John Kennedy of Caticol, was included as an appendix to the posthumous fifth edition of Kennedy's book *The Days of the Fathers in Ross-shire*. It praises Mary Kennedy for her intelligence and hospitality, and notes in particular that she served as her husband's amanuensis in his composition of his published sermons.[77]

His new family life did not inhibit John Kennedy's preaching. By the height of his ministry, Kennedy was reportedly spending half the year travelling around communion seasons[78]: for example, being 'an unfailing helper at the August communion' of Olrig Free Church in Caithness, and in that capacity 'a great attraction',[79] and one of two principal assistants each year at the Creich communions.[80] *The Glasgow Herald* reported that 'his popularity as a preacher was such that none of the great sacramental gatherings in Ross-shire would be regarded as quite complete unless he partook in them'.[81] One biographer recorded that, latterly, a railway car was reserved for his use in this extensive programme of travel, such was the respect accorded to his ministry by the company directors.[82] Through this wider ministry, Kennedy helped to mould the thought and the spirituality of the Church across the Highlands.

Kennedy's popularity as a preacher was also reflected in the numerous calls[83] he received to other charges, all of which he declined. As early as 1853, he was called to the large town of Dunoon, to succeed Mackintosh Mackay, a former Moderator of the Free Church, who had accepted a call to Australia.[84] The following year, Kennedy was himself called to an overseas city charge in Sydney, Australia, and ten years later to a major city-centre congregation, Renfield Free Church in Glasgow.[85] At one meeting in 1857 his Presbytery had to consider concurrent calls addressed to him from two separate congregations, Tain and Greenock Gaelic, to succeed two of the most celebrated Highland ministers of the Free Church,[86] indicating that he was already being reckoned in a similar category himself. The latter congregation went on to call him again in 1872.[87] These calls were generally to minister primarily to Highlanders, even the Sydney and Glasgow calls probably having regard to the large populations of Highlanders in both cities, who might be expected to flock to join a church under Kennedy's ministry.

The readiness of Highlanders everywhere to gather for his preaching underlines the respect which they held for Kennedy: for example, he reported that on visits to London, he could always gather a congregation of more than 300 for a Gaelic service, even at just two or three days' notice.[88] Indeed, his final sermon was at a Gaelic service he conducted in his hotel in London in April 1884, while on his final journey back to Scotland, and was so appreciated that some of those in attendance thereafter formed the London Gaelic Services Committee to ensure that Gaelic services would continue in the metropolis. The resulting quarterly Gaelic services, conducted by ministers from a variety of denominations, have continued right to the present, now usually held at Crown Court Church of Scotland.[89] He was also well known in Edinburgh as a communion assistant, preaching annually in the Highland congregation, Free St Columba's, from the early 1850s onwards, and equally in the congregation of Newington on a yearly basis after he forged a close friendship with the minister, James Begg, during the First Union Controversy (1867–73).[90] His sermon in Edinburgh after the death of Begg drew so immense a crowd that the press reported that Newington Free Church 'was crowded to excess, every available inch of space being occupied, including the pulpit steps, lobbies and staircases'.[91] He also preached regularly in the Aberdeen Highland congregation, again called St Columba's,[92] in Dundee, Glasgow, Greenock, and more occasionally at communions in other Lowland congregations, such as Roxburgh Free Church, Edinburgh, in 1882.[93]

Greatest of all, however, were the communion gatherings of the Highlands. One newspaper report described Kennedy assisting at the open-air summer communion in Creich, Sutherland, in 1873:

> It has long been affirmed that the assemblage of worshippers on such occasions was the largest in Scotland, and, if our experience can be taken, we should fully endorse the statement. On a careful calculation, the members present were not less than seven thousand. There were people present from the outskirts of the Reay Country, about 130 miles off, from Grantown and Strathspey, a like distance, from Inverness, from Dingwall, and, in short, from all the district round. [... Following the administration of the sacrament,] the assemblage was afterwards addressed outside, the minister standing on top of a sloping piece of ground, while his audience stood or reclined on the slope below. The scene was certainly an impressive one.[94]

As stated, Creich may have been the largest regular sacramental gathering but there were many other vast assemblies throughout the year, and the materials gathered in Kennedy's biography bear witness to his busy exertions in preaching at various gatherings across northern Scotland. Letters tell of his preaching to the fishermen in Wick, in Burghead, Gairloch,

Strathpeffer and Thurso. Further letters speak of a preaching tour in Lewis and Lochbroom, and of 'having been weeks successively at Communions throughout the Highlands', and in another place of 'having been, since coming home from Aberdeen, at communions in Rosskeen, Inverness and Urray'.[95] These letters testify to a great deal of travel and an extraordinary capacity for rapid pulpit preparation, as sermons could not be readily reused when hearers sometimes travelled from communion season to communion season. Yet for all the labour involved, these vast gatherings, which Kennedy addressed with such frequency all over the Highlands and Islands, gave to him an opportunity to exert and demonstrate leadership over the vast numbers of the Highland Church. This leadership was always rooted in the quality of his preaching, and it was his power in the pulpit that enabled him to win and retain to the last the loyalty of the Highland evangelical people: they respected him as an expounder of Scripture in pastoral and evangelistic matters, and so were inclined also to respect his judgment on ecclesiastical questions, the more so as he did not hesitate to use the pulpit to address controverted ecclesiastical questions.

The respect he received for his homiletical gifts extended beyond the ordinary members of the Free Church, to Kennedy's brother-ministers and elders in the North, as was evidenced in his nomination by a number of the Highland church courts for vacant professorial chairs.[96] With a much lower profile in the Lowlands, however, he never received nominations from a sufficient number of courts to be a serious candidate for any vacancy, even had he desired to move to an academic position. Interestingly, despite his eminence as a leader of the Highland Church, Kennedy was never appointed to the highest position of the Free Church, to serve as Moderator of the General Assembly. Kennedy had been one of six ministers proposed to be Moderator of the 1876 General Assembly, but being presumably unlikely to secure the nomination at this stage in his ministry, had withdrawn his name from consideration at an early juncture.[97] As a minister ordained after the Disruption of 1843, Kennedy lacked the stature of one who had abandoned his stipend and benefits in the Established Church to serve the Free Church, and this seems to have been an operative factor in the selection of Moderators. Crucially, the Free Church would not appoint a Moderator from the generation of ministers ordained after the Disruption until 1887, well after Kennedy's death, with the first such chosen being his frequent ecclesiastical opponent, Robert Rainy.[98] Had he lived until the Inverness General Assembly of 1888, Kennedy would, as the leading Highland minister, presumably have been chosen as Moderator rather than his less prominent friend, Gustavus Aird.[99] Nevertheless, it is telling that throughout the whole of Kennedy's long ministry, only twice did the Assembly's choice as Moderator fall on the minister of a Highland congregation[100]: an indication of the peripheral standing of the Highland ministers within the national Free Church.

However, Kennedy's brother-ministers across the Highlands showed their appreciation in the frequency of the invitations he received to assist at communion seasons. Individual fellow-ministers, such as John Fraser, William Robertson Nicoll and his principal biographer, Alexander Auld, have left appreciative tributes to his ministry.[101] Nicoll's testimony is especially significant as that of a minister entirely unsympathetic to Kennedy's stance in the nineteenth-century Free Church controversies, praising him as 'beyond comparison the ablest Highland preacher of his generation'.[102] A minister of a later generation, John Macleod, the leading theologian of the twentieth-century Free Church, stated emphatically the view of many: 'He was the great preacher of his generation in Scotland.'[103]

But how did skills in preaching make Kennedy a significant popular leader in the Highlands? It is a question that reveals the massive gulf between Kennedy's society and that of the present day. The importance of sermons in pre-twentieth-century British society has only gradually come to be recognised in academic circles, but the incipient discipline of Sermon Studies has gone some way to redress this balance. One recent text in this field identified the period 1689–1901 as 'a "golden age" of sermons', noting the popularity and ubiquity of the experience of listening to preaching. The authors explained:

> It was a period in which the religious culture and polity of Britain was largely defined by the sermon: Britain was a sermonic society in which preaching was one, if not the principal, shared experience of all classes and conditions of people.[104]

Keith Francis pointed out the consequent need for sound academic study of sermons:

> Sermons, as opposed to preaching, have 'escaped' scholarly scrutiny until the last decade. As the preceding chapters have shown, the varieties of sermons and the ways in which they were used mean that there is, putting it metaphorically, a rich seam of material that scholars ought to mine.[105]

Given the importance of Kennedy's ministry in the nineteenth-century Highlands, his sermons are well worthy of such scrutiny. Francis proposed two simple categories for sermons: those teaching the Christian life and those given in response to specific occasions. Kennedy's body of sermons fall overwhelmingly into the former category, as he very rarely gave any attention to contemporary news or developments. They can therefore be analysed directly as his vision of the Christian life, based on his exegesis of Scripture. In considering and evaluating Kennedy as a preacher, the present study will draw both from contemporary accounts of the effects of his pulpit ministry, and from fresh analysis of the literary remains of his sermons.

As a preacher, Kennedy was noted for his fluency and command of language, in both Gaelic and English, remarkably so given that he never used notes in the pulpit, and even tended to close the Bible after reading his text at the commencement of his sermon, such was his ability to quote relevant passages from memory.[106] One assessment comments that he spoke 'in English as if he did not know a word of Gaelic, and in Gaelic as if he did not know a word of English', although many hearers considered that 'it was in Gaelic he got nearest the hearts of his hearers'.[107] His proficiency in the latter language was clearly the product of practice and effort, but his English skills were, according to his college friend William Walker, at least partly rooted in his love of reading Shakespeare.[108] Robertson Nicoll, himself a noted Victorian literary critic, observed a special quality in his English preaching: 'He at once fascinated us by the arresting solemnity of his manner and the spring-like newness of his English.'[109] Norman Macfarlane, who, like Nicoll, opposed Kennedy on the establishment question and was later a minister of the United Free Church, gave a rather florid testimony to the effectiveness of Kennedy's language:

> His eloquence was unrivalled in the Highlands [...] Kennedy's lips poured forth an even stream of liquid silver of the choicest thoughts and choicest words [...] One could sit listening to Dr Kennedy by the hour. The effortlessness of his beautiful speech amazed one as it ran out of a face, which in itself was a picture.[110]

His eloquence was highlighted in comparison with the greatest of Victorian preachers, being termed the 'Spurgeon of the Highlands'.[111]

However, it is plain that the popularity of Kennedy's preaching rested on more than just the quality of his language. Contemporary accounts concur that there was an intellectual depth and profundity to his sermons that commanded the attention of discerning hearers. Following his death, the *Northern Chronicle* commented: 'It says much for John Kennedy, a young man, [...] that he should have at once taken a foremost rank among the foremost preachers of the Disruption Church.' The *Nairnshire Telegraph* added: 'Dr Kennedy's death deprives the Highlands of its greatest orator and preacher [...] He could keep vast crowds under the spell of his genius as no other preacher living could.' The *Daily Review* added a particularly striking account of the effect of Kennedy's preaching:

> The sermon was built up, block upon block, of granite reasoning. Each of those fundamental propositions was presented with intense and over-powering earnestness. The blocks were laid upon each other *red hot* [...] As the discourse went on and the reasoning became molten into fiery flood [...] the labouring breath struggled into voice and rang over the hillside like a clarion [...] and the whole responding multitude bent forward.[112]

This description is particularly useful, as it stresses that logical force rather than rhetorical flourish was the basis for the power of Kennedy's sermons:

the construction of an exegetical and theological argument with unanswerable force and direct and pointed application.

Journalist James Barron adds a further salient testimony to Kennedy's effect in the pulpit:

> John Kennedy was an orator capable of moving any assembly in the world. He deserves to be named among the finest speakers of his day. It has been the privilege of the present writer to hear most of the great speakers of the time; and he has no hesitation in saying that for sheer power over an audience – power refined as well as impressive – he has heard none to surpass Dr Kennedy at his best. His sermons and addresses consisted of close, compact reasoning, fused with passion and lighted up with imagination. Circumstances placed Dr Kennedy in a corner of Scotland, but in natural gifts, especially as preacher and debater, he was the peer of any man in English speaking lands.[113]

Again, he stresses the importance of Kennedy's flow of reasoned argument to the force of his preaching, with the effect only heightened by his additional qualities of passion and imagination. Another former hearer, who placed Kennedy on a par with the legendary London Baptist preacher C. H. Spurgeon himself, observed that his 'preaching went forth with the greatest authority to compel, as it were, submission, while the heavenly sweetness of the Gospel message, as delivered by him, was very winning'.[114] He thus concurred that Kennedy's solid content was complemented by effective presentation: the argument compelled his hearers but the sweetness won them over.

Unfortunately, Kennedy's depth of thought could make him challenging to appreciate. A Highland church historian recorded of one of 'the Men', George Grant of Brora: 'He was a great admirer of Dr Kennedy, Dingwall, and his fine mind and rich Christian experience helped him to understand the flights of that eminent preacher,'[115] which suggested that many may have struggled to follow the more intellectually demanding and experimentally mature passages of his sermons. This is further borne out by the record that, on an announcement that he was coming to assist at the Kilmallie communion, one commented: 'What is the use of his coming, for they say his preaching is so profound, that we in Lochaber cannot understand him?'[116] Norman Macfarlane recorded the comment of at least one sermon that 'no-one could understand' it.[117] This tends to suggest a self-indulgent use of the pulpit for a display of theological acumen, rather than an exercise in profitable communication. If this had been generally typical of Kennedy's public preaching, then he would have been shooting far over the heads of most of his hearers, many of whom had little or no formal education, though they were steeped in Scriptural knowledge.[118] However, given the many testimonies of the usefulness of Kennedy's preaching to individuals, even those without much theological understanding, it is likely that this was an occasional rather than habitual failing. Equally, for those who could follow his thought on the occasion of these more demanding flights, this depth must have added richness to his presentation of Christian doctrine.

Overall, Kennedy's regular teaching ministry seems to have been generally very effective in communicating theological instruction. It is recorded of one hearer, for example, that

> His youthful mind seems to have been absorbed with Dr Kennedy's entrancing presentation of the Saviour King executing the plan of salvation, and also captivated by the intellectual vitality that gave freshness, vigour, and a new significance to the great doctrines of grace, reiterated by others in a phraseology worn threadbare by generations of usage, and then falling on sensitive ears with deadly monotony.[119]

Equally, another contemporary tribute praised his 'vivacity' in preaching,[120] while a recent writer remarked, on the basis of such testimony, that Kennedy's sermons 'came across to his contemporaries as stylish and thrilling', and thus he 'succeeded in being a modern preacher'.[121]

The result was that Kennedy excelled as an evangelistic preacher. The journalist and Free Church elder Archibald MacNeilage commented in a published letter: 'The greatest preacher, the fullest and freest exponent of the glorious Gospel of free grace some of us have ever known, was Dr Kennedy of Dingwall.'[122] One account suggests that this was not a feature of the early stages of his ministry, but was the result of an experience he had during the course of his ministry. John Macleod, a Free Church minister of the early twentieth century, describes it as follows, in his sketch of the life of Archibald Crawford, a noted elder from Cowal:

> Dr Kennedy was laid aside with a somewhat serious illness at the time. Crawford was shown in to his bedroom, and sympathised with him in his trouble. 'Yes', said the Doctor, 'I am laid aside for the time, and I have learned the reason for it.' 'If that be the case,' said Crawford, 'there is no need for me to tell you.' From the time he recovered from this illness there was a change in Dr Kennedy's preaching. It had always been full and richly doctrinal [. . .] The new note that was to be detected in his subsequent teaching was the emphasis that he laid on the hearer's responsibility for receiving the Gospel.[123]

Whatever the substance of the change suggested in this passage, Kennedy was certainly not lacking in clear emphasis on the urgency of a gospel response, based on the evidences available, with which his ministry may be assessed.

His evangelistic preaching often had a real individual impact upon his hearers, some of whom experienced evangelical conversion through his ministry. For example, one writer referred to being 'aroused, I trust, by the Spirit of God, under the searching, winsome, and impressive preaching of Dr Kennedy, of Dingwall'.[124] Similarly, Rev. Donald Macfarlane recorded visiting a dying lady in Fodderty in 1907, stating: 'She mentioned that it was under the preaching of Dr Kennedy, from Revelation 3:20,[125] she was first moved to concern about her soul.'[126] Another sketch recounted how 'One man, burdened by sin, walked many miles to hear Dr Kennedy and said later, "He showed me all my heart and into its bleeding wound he poured the oil of consolation."'[127] These three accounts all emphasise how the two aspects of evangelistic preaching were present in Kennedy's sermons: the solemn exposure of sin, warning of the judgment of God; and the gracious offer of the gospel, promising salvation in Christ to all who come to Him. They are also indicative that many individuals came to know the comfort of assurance of salvation through his evangelistic ministry, and must therefore have felt deep gratitude towards him as an instrument in their personal experience of conversion.

In other cases, Kennedy's sermons led individuals through significant developments in their spiritual lives. A notable elder from Sutherland, Duncan Macrae, 'told a friend that when hearing the late Dr Kennedy at Creich he came to the decision to confess Christ before men by obeying the Saviour's dying command [to participate in communion]'.[128] Another kind of impact was recorded in the life of John Noble, then working in Dingwall as a draper's assistant, 'where, at the impressionable stage, he came under the influence of that prince of Highland preachers, Dr John Kennedy, with the result that eventually he decided to study for the ministry'; he subsequently became minister of Lairg Free Church.[129]

Kennedy's preaching also had an impact in the general encouragement of Christians throughout the Highlands, such that Auld remarks, perhaps with some hyperbole: 'We venture to affirm that there were few living Christians in the northern counties of Scotland who were not in their day indebted to Mr Kennedy for the reviving and strengthening of their spiritual life.'[130] One interesting case was that of Archibald Crawford, who testified to experiencing at one stage in his life a deep spiritual thirst, despite hearing many of the eminent preachers of the day, which troubled him particularly as he led a Friday night house meeting to which others came for spiritual guidance. His biographer recorded that at last he went to hear Kennedy at a communion:

> He was highly satisfied with the teaching that Dr Kennedy gave, yet he got nothing that touched the sore spot in his heart until the last service of the communion season on the Monday evening.
>
> As the preacher was drawing to a close, Crawford, as always, was sitting sedately, looking, not at the preacher, but, as it were, at a desk two or three seats in front of where he sat. Dr Kennedy said, 'You are here' – Crawford lifted up his head and their eyes met – 'you are here, and you have left your children at home crying for hunger, and you have nothing to give them. No, should you scrape the meal-chest you could not gather enough to colour the water. But wait; I hear a knock at the door. What is this? Here is a man with a sack of meal on

his shoulder. What is in the sack? "My grace is sufficient for thee, My strength is made perfect in weakness." Put that in your meal-chest and go and feed your children. But wait; I hear another knock. Who is this? Here is another man with a sack of meal on his shoulder. And what is in that sack? "I will never leave thee, I will never, never forsake thee." Go and put that in your meal-chest and feed your children.'

When the service was over, Dr Kennedy sat still in the pulpit, and Crawford remained in his seat until the way was open. Kennedy came down from the pulpit, and Crawford went up the aisle to meet him. They shook hands and kissed each other. That was their first introduction, and from that moment they were the closest of friends.[131]

This passage testifies to the vivid, rhetorical style of Kennedy's preaching, to its striking appropriateness to the felt needs of his hearers, and its basis in the application of appropriate passages of Scripture to answer their difficulties. A comparable account was given by a Lairg elder, Angus Gray: 'He spoke of the love of Christ, and so described my case that I was drunk with joy, and when I came out of the church I might as well have been in a foreign land for all I knew where I was [. . .] It was the greatest day I ever had in the world.'[132] Again, Kennedy had addressed specific concerns with such precision as to offer profound spiritual comfort.

Auld recorded a notable instance of such encouragement in a situation of spiritual difficulty, in the case of a young man who later entered the Free Church ministry.[133] The man was doubting the reality of his own salvation due to his perceived lack of spiritual mindedness, but went a distance to hear Kennedy preach, consequently arriving late:

Just as we entered the church, the preacher gave out the text (Isaiah 55:1): 'Ho! Every one that thirsteth, come ye to the waters', etc. He began by opening up the free and wide invitation of the Gospel to all classes of sinners; and I felt that though he was a most attractive speaker, and I could not help listening to every word he said, yet it was not the *proclamation* of the Gospel I was in quest of, but how to get the Gospel to *influence* my heart and life. At length, after showing the adaptation of the 'call' in the text to the various thirsts of mankind – their thirsts for happiness, for peace, for rest – he said, 'But there is one here today who says, 'You have not mentioned my thirst yet; my thirst is for *holiness*, for such a knowledge of Christ as would subdue sin in me and weaken my heart-corruption.' This arrested me, and I listened as if I were the person spoken to when he added, 'My dear, dear friend, if *that* is your case – if you do thirst for Christ in order to the crucifixion of all sin within you, and in order to your becoming conformed to His holy image – let me tell you, in His name, you shall yet be as free of sin as if you had never known it; yea, you shall yet be satisfied with the fellowship of Christ and with likeness to Him throughout the endless ages of eternity'!

> The glowing fervour, yet deep solemnity, with which he uttered these words quite overcame me, and as he went on to prove the *truth* of what he had stated, my enjoyment was such, that it was as a begun heaven.[134]

This account underlines the importance of Kennedy's preaching to particular individual cases, and the spiritual comfort he was able to bring through teaching Christian doctrine on the basis of thorough Biblical exegesis.

Equally, there were testimonies of special comfort received through his preaching on particular doctrinal subjects, as one biographical sketch attests:

> A Stornoway hearer testified, 'The manifestations I had that day of the glorious majesty, worthiness and suitableness of the Lord Jesus Christ in all His mediatorial offices, I never experienced before, nor indeed to the same extent since. I can never forget it.' [. . .] A Dundee man wrote to Dr Kennedy: 'I desire to bless God for having heard you. Your sermon on the electing love of God was a seasonable message to my soul, clearing difficulties and confirming me in the truth.'[135]

These statements indicate that Kennedy's didactic preaching was not stale or predictable, but fresh and vibrant, opening up new avenues of thought and addressing queries and problems in the minds of his hearers. The result, as in both of these cases, was a spiritual encouragement that was highly memorable, and again promoted a direct and personal gratitude to the preacher as the instrument of this felt blessing. David Budge, a Caithness man, experienced this preaching as the restoration of past spiritual comfort and expressed his gratitude, testifying: 'Mr Kennedy above others is a means of warming my cold heart and reviving something of the love of days gone by.'[136] Another to express this gratitude was Duncan Crawford from Oban, who was so disappointed with the succession of preachers in a period of vacancy in his congregation that he reportedly felt 'a suspicion of the ministry in general'. But he then heard Kennedy at a Greenock communion, and afterwards declared:

> I went to Greenock and heard Dr Kennedy, and as another said, 'whether in the body or out of the body I cannot tell'. From that day, the Gospel ministry was lifted for me out of the mud, and remained ever since what it ought to be in every Christian man's estimation.[137]

In this case, Crawford's gratitude extended to the whole ministry, as he recognised the value that preaching could have in the personal spiritual life; but it was obvious that the primary recipient of his appreciation was Kennedy himself.

Donald Munro of Lairg left a more traditional tribute to Kennedy, in his Gaelic poem, 'Lament on the Death of Dr John Kennedy who was in

Dingwall', which undermines many of the stereotypes of the Highland ministry. He wrote of Dingwall mourning Kennedy's

> comely handsome face
> Lit up with love
> Never to be seen there again.[138]

He went on to echo the impact felt on individual lives through his ministry:

> Many are the orphans that your death
> Left behind; and indeed they feel
> They have a reason to sorrow,
> For they have lost one who was blessed
> With gifts and grace, to speak
> To ones in bondage.
>
> Great indeed were the gifts
> And wonderful that were given to you –
> The strong natural parts,
> And also the graces:
> The abundant anointing,
> And also the acute reasoning,
> Made you special among your brethren –
> Even all your brethren.[139]

Such a lament indicated the intensity of the love for Kennedy, and especially the love for the benefit of his preaching ministry, both in its rhetorical power and in its depth and rigour of theological analysis.

Taken together, the testimonies above demonstrate that the significance and value of Kennedy's sermons were rooted particularly in the content of teaching they communicated. Yet this is the more remarkable given Kennedy's limited opportunity for serious theological reading. His divinity studies had been cut short by the Disruption, and thereafter he was thrown immediately into an exceedingly busy and demanding situation of ministry, which must have left him little time for focused preparation of sermons. As a result, he became known as a man who did his own thinking, as his colleague John Fraser stated:

> No characteristic of his mind is more marked than his reliance on his own resources in all his mental efforts. He seems to place little reliance on books, or on the thoughts and labours of others. He is not a learned man in the broad sense of that term; at least, with his many pulpit duties, he had no time to become an extensively read man, and, we believe, he lays no claim to this distinction. He works out his numerous discourses with little beside his Bible and Concordance to aid him.[140]

This assessment does require to be counterbalanced by Auld's reminder that the Bible he used was in the original languages, and that when so fatigued as to have to study in bed, he still required 'the standard authors on systematic theology' to be brought within his reach.[141] Auld was careful to ensure that no question can be laid against Kennedy's scholarly acumen, noting that his sermon manuscripts quoted from the Greek text, rendered with precision, extending to the smallest accent. Yet Fraser's basic point stands: Kennedy may have used reference works, but his serious study and engagement was with the Scriptural text itself rather than with human authors. The extant published sermons of Kennedy amply substantiate this point: they are careful and orthodox in exegesis of the text, but thoughtful and original in their application of the Scriptural message to the hearer.

Such a mode of pulpit preparation could only succeed based on a high view of the inspiration of Scripture, and this invariably marked his ministry. Barron observed:

> The complete submission of his intellect to authority – even though it be the authority of Scripture – is an uncommon spectacle. No one could question Dr Kennedy's intellectual strength or analytical power. Within the limits which he recognised as legitimate he could speculate with the most acute and soar with the most imaginative. But doctrines of profound import – doctrines which he believed to be revealed but which he could not comprehend – he was content to receive in the spirit of a little child. He always spoke with the accent of conviction.[142]

This was not intellectual obscurantism, but rather the outworking of a firm, settled conviction that the Scriptures were the only authoritative source for Christian doctrine, that they were the inspired Word of God, and therefore that their direct exegesis and application was the primary function of the Christian preacher.

In terms of actual preparation for the pulpit, Kennedy did not write out his sermons in full, but rather filled notebooks, of which several survive, with sermon skeletons varying substantially in length and detail.[143] These skeletons indicate well the themes, structure and development of the sermons, but give little sense of the passion and intensity which must have marked their delivery, or the quality and tone of language in which they were delivered. These were clearly worked out in the preacher's mind prior to entering the pulpit; where he did not make use of notes. He thus obviously followed the advice he received from a noted preacher of an earlier generation. As Barron records:

> On the day on which he was licensed the late Mr Stewart, of Cromarty, said to him: 'John, I think I know you now. Take one advice from me – don't write your sermons. Spend your time in thinking, for be assured, if you do not express clearly it will be because you have not thought sufficiently.'[144]

The disadvantage of his usually following this advice is the limited material extant to give a full sense of the style and character of his extemporaneous preaching.

The distinction between written remnants, or a corrected and subsequently published manuscript, and the actual sermon preached, is vital to remember. Extemporary preaching relied on the emotion and power of the preacher's oratory to attract a hearing, and this experience is not readily captured on the printed page. Indeed, Keith Francis has emphasised that both the purpose and the use of the printed sermon are quite different from those of the preached message.[145] Referring specifically to the Scottish context, Ann Matheson wrote:

> In nineteenth-century Scotland, the sermon continued to be the central tenet of worship in the Church of Scotland but more and more it was great oratory that drew the crowds. As the power of the evangelicals increased there was much greater emphasis on extempore sermons and as a result printed sermons no longer formed a very reliable source for the preaching of the day. For many, listening to great preachers was often the only form of entertainment available to them.[146]

These remarks undoubtedly apply to Kennedy, not least because his habit of preaching without any manuscript before him would have made frequent deviation from his prepared notes possible, and indeed probable. Matheson also stressed that the sermon structures were in any case not the most interesting aspect of the preached sermon: 'evangelical sermons followed a standard format comprising a number of heads which were subdivided in turn. Sermon style was cumbersome and prolix but the content could sometimes be dramatic and imaginative.'[147] The surviving outlines can give only the faintest impression of the actual experience of hearing Kennedy preach.

Nonetheless, the extant outlines have their own value in at least indicating Kennedy's general intentions for each sermon prior to entering the pulpit. An otherwise obscure Free Church minister, Murdoch Mackay (1852–1936),[148] ventured to publish a volume containing twenty-eight of these outlines, dated from July to November 1882, alongside 240 of his own, in 1927.[149] Further collections of extant outlines, from the years 1859 to 1874, have been published in full in recent years.[150] These sermon notes are generally more detailed and thus more useful than the later ones printed by Mackay. They vary considerably in length: for example, one outline from 5 June 1864 consists of short keywords, not always even forming sentences, and breaks off abruptly in the application as though the writer was interrupted before quite finished. On the other hand, the next sermon, dated a month later, is more complete in form, and includes far more detail under each heading. The sentences are fuller, and some could be read out as the final form of the oral sermon, while others were still evidently intended for extemporary expansion.[151]

Kennedy was generally a careful exegete in handling his text. As Ian Dickson writes of the evangelical sermon, 'The text acted as a controlling mechanism, setting the particular parameters for each message.'[152] However, several key themes can be identified in the messages, recurring repeatedly: the sovereignty of God, especially in the work of salvation; the gospel call to trust in Christ alone for salvation; and the need for serious self-examination for the marks that one has received God's grace in salvation. These three themes were repeatedly stressed and emphasised from a great variety of texts throughout the many sermons recorded from the fifteen years of ministry covered by these notebooks.[153]

For example, sovereignty was central to a sermon on Habakkuk 3: 2 from 11 December 1859, the first of three on that text, in which Kennedy discussed the work of salvation by grace as a work *of* the Lord, His will and plan; *by* the Lord, His achievement in commencing and progressing; and *to* the Lord, accomplished for His glory, satisfaction and love.[154] The same theme was repeatedly addressed: God as the only source of existence, of rational life and of the Moral Law; God as the One Who has willed and planned eternal salvation; God as He Who has sovereignly determined this salvation in the Covenant of Redemption from all Eternity.[155] In these, and indeed in all the sermon outlines, Kennedy emphatically proclaimed Divine sovereignty.

Equally, the gospel offer in Christ appeared consistently in the Application section of nearly every outline, whether by implication or in explicit statement. On occasions, it was the principal focus of the whole address, as on the text Luke 14: 23,[156] where the structure successively stressed the authority of the evangelistic call; the power in which that call must be given; the compelling urgency with which it must be pressed; and the on-going continuance of that call until the end of time.[157] The confidence in which Kennedy's own evangelistic call was given was indicated in the short sentences of application concluding a sermon on Isaiah 55: 1, doubtless to be expanded in the preaching:

But all are invited to come.
We are assured of a welcome.
All who come shall find this [salvation] to be waters indeed.[158]

However, a better sense of the potency of Kennedy's gospel call as actually preached from the pulpit is indicated in a passage from an 1865 sermon outline on Matthew 20: 30:

But Jesus is passing by. A brief and precious opportunity you get here. Oh, think of how you need salvation, and what the awful eternal consequences of being unsaved must be. Think of how good the opportunity is. Jesus passes by. He is near. He is near to you. His skirts are just to your hand. He is knocking at the door.[159]

The preacher's voice can practically be heard in these words, and the vividness and intensity of his evangelistic message on such an occasion. Furthermore, there is sometimes a gentleness in this evangelistic application that suggests a very compelling call, as in these notes from 1866: 'Are there any here who will come to this God for pardon? He is in Christ. He invites you to come and reason with Him. He is exalted in having mercy. He delights in mercy.'[160]

The subject of self-examination cropped up repeatedly as a vital element in Kennedy's ministry. The reason for this was his concern at the danger of false assurance of faith, and this concern was repeatedly addressed in the outlines. He warned, for example, that 'misrepresentations of faith are in fashion' and that the problem is 'a spiritual generation plague', pointing out that faith that consists of mere intellectual belief involves no personal Saviour, no change of soul, and no change of moral relationship to God.[161] Such a concern for accurate self-examination can be meaningfully understood only in the context of Kennedy's orthodox Calvinistic theology that viewed all mankind as inherently deserving of death and Hell forever, and of the substitutionary sacrifice of Christ, received by faith in Him, as the only alternative to this eternal sentence. Viewed in this context, Kennedy's concern that his hearers have a well-grounded assurance of salvation in Christ becomes comprehensible and meaningful. Therefore his vital concern is to distinguish true religion from false, by the careful identification of genuine 'marks', distinctive characteristics, of true saving grace. Examples would be the marks of 'fear of the Lord', 'thought on His name' and 'communing together', given on 1 January 1865; or the one 'great mark of all who are in Christ', identified in March of that year as 'evidence of living as new creatures', applied in six different respects.[162] The following year, he taught as marks that the true Christians are 'ashamed of their past life', 'desire to cease from sin' and 'desire to avail themselves of the security God has provided for a holy life in time to come'.[163] The accurate identification of true Christian experience was thus a central plank of Kennedy's ministry and fully evident in these sermon outlines.

Another important collection of manuscripts was published in 1910, under the title *Expository Lectures* and is a further valuable source for research into Kennedy's preaching ministry. This title indicated that these were not conventional sermons: hence, perhaps, why Kennedy had chosen to adopt a different mode of preparation, writing out fairly full notes in complete sentences, comparable only to the very fullest outlines included in the *Sermon Notes*. The 'lecture' was a form of pulpit address handed down from a prior generation, a consecutive exposition of Scripture carried on from week to week, usually at a fairly simple level. The lecture contrasted with the sermon proper, typically delivered at the other service of the Sabbath day, which would be deeper in content and more elaborate in composition, and usually on a different portion of Scripture each week. The practice was already dying out during Kennedy's lifetime, such that by 1911, the editor of the collection felt the need to explain the format of the lecture.[164] Given that none of the many assessments of Kennedy as a preacher from late in his ministry mention him following a practice of giving a lecture, and that the notebooks, all dating from after 1859, often give two detailed skeletons of sermons proper for each Sabbath, it seems likely that these full manuscript lectures were productions of his early ministry. Later, he seems to have abandoned both the format of the consecutive lecture and the preparation of full manuscript addresses.

Nonetheless, this volume gives a useful insight into Kennedy's expository ministry, as he led his congregation through several key chapters of the gospels, especially Matthew 5 and 9, John 5, Mark 1, Luke 4 and John 4, with other miscellaneous passages from the life of Christ. These addresses were logical and natural in structure, with a warm, devotional tone, and included natural and familiar illustrations, from the ministry of the well-known Highland preacher Lachlan Mackenzie, for example, to convey his point.[165] Yet within the refreshing simplicity of these lectures, the same three emphases identified above are clearly evident. Kennedy's gospel offer was plain and direct: 'There are those here who are afraid they are not blessed. Come with all your causes of fear to the fountain opened.'[166] His discussion of the examination of Christian experience was warm and pastorally encouraging. For example, he pointed out that some believers may be well advanced in holiness, yet be far behind lesser believers in their outward professions, illustrating the point in a homely manner: 'The man who tosseth a ball high into the air does not prove himself stronger than another who can scarcely move that stone to which he has set his shoulder.'[167] As always, he constantly stressed the sovereignty of God, emphasising that saving faith is 'something which one must owe to God' and that salvation is 'dependent on the sovereign will of God', albeit also warning against 'the extreme of ignoring man's will altogether and the important part it acts in the scheme of grace'.[168] He emphasised Divine sovereignty in discussing Christ's command to the paralysed man, 'Rise, take up thy bed, and walk,' comparing the man's paralysis to 'the spiritual impotence of the sinner'.[169] Kennedy pointed out that as the words of a man, the gospel call is 'the foolishness of preaching': as his own, 'it is weakness; but as spoken in the name, and in the faith, of Jesus it is warrantably, and wisely, and hopefully spoken'.[170] He later acknowledged the controversial nature of this teaching, that 'men are intolerant of the doctrine of God's sovereignty', adding that this is 'because it is a self-abasing doctrine, and because it seems to them, while they are under the power of unbelief, to shut them out from hope'. He concluded, however: 'But to this submission all who would know the Gospel must come.'[171]

Another vital source was the large volume of full-length sermons that Kennedy prepared for weekly publication during the last year of his life. However, these productions were patently written compositions rather than transcripts of oral addresses, and have features that could not have marked his spoken addresses. Auld remarked:

> Mr Kennedy's published sermons, excellent as they are, do not convey an adequate idea of his preaching. They were written in the cool retirement of his study when he was in delicate health, and were often penned on a sick-bed. They therefore, although exhibiting in the main his way of treating his subject, fall behind what was his wont in the pulpit, especially when fronting a large congregation, and all the powers of his mind raised to the fullest activity. His conceptions of truth were on such occasions clear and comprehensive, his grasp of mind sustained and mighty, and his powerful affections, all aglow, poured themselves forth in strains of unstudied eloquence, impossible to be attained in quieter hours.[172]

This rather apologetic defence suggested that the weekly sermons did not receive unstinting praise on their publication. However, that was by no means the only verdict. The noted church historian John Macleod included Kennedy last in his chronological study of Scottish theology:

> There is a book of his sermons to tell of the quality of his preaching. It is a massive volume and has been issued more than once, but it is exceedingly scarce. In it there are over 50 of his discourses. Almost all of these were written in the last year of his life when he was labouring under the malady that cut him off [...] But the written discourses, set down with the deliberate judgment of his fine mind, give us the doctrine, practice and experience that the preacher meant to lay stress upon. The English style has a decided distinction of its own. The inversion of sentences and the epigrams that often occur are marked features of it. The preacher was a special master in the field of delicate spiritual analysis.[173]

Certainly, Kennedy's *Sermons* is not a volume for light reading; the tone throughout was exacting and theological. In format and presentation, Kennedy followed the example set by his friend, the London Baptist preacher C. H. Spurgeon, whose weekly sermons were popular reading throughout Victorian Britain, but the level of theological understanding presupposed by Kennedy's discourses was substantially higher. He discussed the gender of Greek nouns, used without explanation theological terms like 'federal', 'types' and 'dispensations', and constructed complex arguments, regarding, for example, the nature of saving faith.[174]

This said, the same three emphases identified in the *Sermon Notes* and *Expository Lectures* come through with great clarity. The sovereignty of Divine grace was the subject of the very first message and Kennedy urged the preaching of this subject to all who will hear, to 'arouse them out of their lethargy'; to 'humble them before God'; and, for believers, 'to make them more thankful for His grace'.[175] Later, he used the analogy of Old Testament Israel, stating:

The whole course of His dispensation then was one continued display of His sovereignty, and of the difference, resulting from 'His purpose, according to election,' being carried into effect in behalf of 'a peculiar people'.[176]

This teaching led naturally to application for the present-day Church, that her hope must lie in God's sovereign rule on her behalf, and on that alone.[177] The teaching of Divine sovereignty was phrased in terms of a relationship of covenant, that God has freely chosen to elect some individuals to everlasting life, and entered into a covenant of grace that certainly secures their salvation, on the basis of Christ's work as mediator.[178] This covenant was not, however, presented as a dry legal arrangement, but as the fruit of Divine love, expressed in Jesus Christ's self-sacrifice for His Church.[179] Taking such a position, Kennedy was understandably critical of preachers who would 'separate the covenant from the gospel of grace, and who would ignore the sovereignty of the grace of God'.[180]

The gospel call to come to Christ was clearly given in the application of each sermon, which, as in the *Sermon Notes*, formed a distinct section of each published address. For example, Kennedy urged his readers to 'cry to Jesus', adding: 'O be not dumb before Him, who hath all that power, while thou art needy, while He is Jesus, and while His power is the might of saving grace.'[181] Kennedy never allowed the freeness of his gospel offer to be limited in any way by His stress on sovereignty. Indeed, such applications stressed Divine sovereignty rather as a positive ground for evangelistic urgency than for fatalistic inertia. He urged preachers to emphasise 'that the love of God to sinners is infinite, and that it is sovereign', and that this gives a solid basis on which the sinner may come.[182] In one sermon, he wrote with particular warmth:

> He can work in you both 'to will and to do', and you have a warrant to ask him to do so to you. If you will let Him do this for you, and leave yourself, with all your darkness and coldness, hanging on His grace, the Beloved is yours and you are His. If your objections to be His debtor are removed, then all is taken out of the way that could keep you from being His spouse.[183]

Kennedy passionately assured his readers that 'no fear is more groundless than that of not being received, with infinite gladness, when he comes'.[184] Throughout these *Sermons*, for all their theological depth, the gospel call was plain and unmistakeable.

Yet the *Sermons* also addressed the theme of Christian experience. As in his earlier notes, Kennedy warned repeatedly of the danger of false profession. For example, in one sermon he described the case of a false believer in searing terms:

> You know that you are not pained by a sense of your own unholiness, not anxious as to being sanctified. You cannot surely be on the way to

heaven if you care not about being made ready to enter it. And you know that you are not careful to examine the grounds of your hope that you may not be deceived. You hate the searching light of truth.[185]

This application identified a particular spiritual case and directly challenged such a person to serious self-examination. By the time of publication of the *Sermons*, Kennedy was plainly conscious of swimming strongly against the theological tide of his day. For example, on the subject of self-examination in general, he wrote:

> There is a kind of religion from which this duty is discarded, and which is assuming a pronounced position in these days. There are not a few who attain to an exercise of faith, because of the consciousness of which an assurance of being saved is enjoyed. This assurance they are anxious not to disturb. To maintain it the remembrance of their past faith and the bustle of what they call 'Christian work', are sufficient. To look within is decried as *legality*. To search for evidences of faith being genuine is denounced as mysticism. [. . .] But the text prescribes the duty, and none but those who deny the power of godliness will evade it.[186]

The whole area of Christian experience was therefore addressed in great detail throughout the *Sermons*, with applications following nearly every message addressed 'to the anxious',[187] intended to assist in determining whether or not the reader possesses the marks of a true believer in Christ.

From the various surviving evidences, therefore, it must be concluded that Kennedy's preaching ministry was characterised by three particular themes: Divine sovereignty in achieving salvation, the freeness of the gospel offer on that basis, and the need therefore for urgent and thorough self-examination to ensure that one possesses the reality of a work of sovereign saving grace. As Kennedy's contemporary, Robertson Nicoll, stated: 'The staple of his ministration was always the same – the greatness of God and the preciousness of His grace.'[188] Another colleague, John Fraser, concurred but discerned all three of the emphases identified above:

> He impressively sets forth the sovereignty of Divine grace, with the freeness and all-sufficing nature of Gospel salvation, and [. . .] Christ's divine authority, infinite readiness, and ability, to save sinners [. . .] His preaching, also, partakes largely of the experimental. [. . .] This gives additional interest and power to his ministry. It imparts a chastened and subdued feeling that is sometimes indescribably touching. It leads him to explore the recesses of the heart, to watch its varied workings, and study its manifold deceitful forms, and search into the foundation and evidence of Christian hope.[189]

From this tribute, it is plain that the experimental focus of Kennedy's preaching was its most distinctive quality within the context of the nineteenth-century Free Church.[190] That body was committed to confessional Calvinism, and Kennedy's emphasis on sovereignty, while pronounced, was wholly orthodox. Similarly, his strong evangelistic emphasis was exactly what would be expected in a thoroughly evangelical church, albeit that Kennedy probably expressed his preaching in a more powerful and winsome manner than was typical. It was his focus on identifying and describing Christian experience that tended to mark Kennedy out, even in his own day, as distinctive. Searching experimental preaching had undeniably been typical of the Puritan and seventeenth-century Scottish Presbyterian tradition, but was on the wane in the nineteenth-century Free Church. In this respect, Kennedy's ministry was unusual in the national Free Church, and underlined the differing trajectory of the Highland evangelicalism that appreciated preaching with an experimental emphasis.

Many other contemporary accounts of his preaching stressed this quality, one writer commenting, for example, 'Dr Kennedy was profound, deeply spiritual, experimental, and could deal with the various cases of exercised hearers in a way that very few others could approach.'[191] In his lament for Kennedy, Donald Munro apostrophised the late preacher:

> You were not proclaiming matters
> That you had never experienced
> But truths that you knew.
>
> For you were brought through waters
> That were indeed very deep
> [. . .]
> For you were able because of your own experience
> To deal with the wounds.[192]

Munro thus indicated that the experimental aspect of Kennedy's ministry was recognised as flowing directly from his own personal spiritual experience and that this was consequently highly valued. In similar terms, another writer praised the 'faculty of spiritual analysis' evident in his preaching,[193] while J. K. Cameron recalled his 'analytical and tenderly sympathetic treatment of Divine truth'.[194] John Macleod summed it up fairly: 'He was an experimental divine in the best sense of the word. The great Puritans had no more eminent successor in the Scottish ministry in the 19th century.'[195]

Appreciation for Kennedy's preaching ministry was therefore evidenced throughout the Highland Free Church. It was thus his work of preaching to an eager and receptive audience that gave Kennedy his unparalleled influence over the Highland Christianity of his day. While his principal aim was always the individual spiritual benefit of his hearers, he would also, as will be seen, weaponise this platform as controversy troubled the Free Church in the later years of his ministry.

Kennedy the Pastor

John Kennedy evidently exerted a powerful influence over the Highlanders of his day, and particularly over the Men. The Men were clearly defined by John Macinnes: 'They were an order of evangelical laymen venerated for their godliness, to whom alone was given the privilege of speaking at the Friday Question Meetings at a Highland sacrament'.[196] This quotation highlights both the healthy and the dubious aspects of the culture of the Men. On the one hand, it was good that there were Christian men of ability and spiritual experience to take a lead within the Highland Church. But, equally, the development of a self-selecting elite can be dangerous in any social grouping, and especially in churches. The Free Church had a Presbyterian structure of leadership by designated officers, elected by the congregational membership, according to clear criteria. The Men were not co-extensive with the eldership of the Highland Church; indeed, a few stood aloof from any church affiliation. The notion of a small elite possessed of unusual spiritual qualifications had not been part of the seventeenth-century Presbyterian heritage and was by no means a healthy innovation.

Kennedy himself was sensitive to criticisms of the Men, and tried to counter negative perceptions, claiming for the ministers a power over the choice of the Men:

> When a godly Highland minister discerned a promise of usefulness in a man who seemed to have been truly converted unto God, he brought him gradually forward into a more public position, by calling him first to pray, and then 'to speak to the question', at the ordinary congregational meetings. According to the manner in which he approved himself there was the prospect of his being enrolled among the Friday speakers on communion occasions. It was thus the order of 'the men' was established, and thus the body of 'the men' was formed.[197]

However, this passage of *The Days of the Fathers in Ross-shire* has been criticised as 'somewhat rosy' by a more recent writer.[198] The Men were highly selective in giving support to a minister, and the ministers who attained notability in the Highlands were those who held their esteem. Hence a minister approved by the Men, like Kennedy or his father, could exert this power of selection, while a minister subject to their disapprobation would be unable to do so, as the Men would not respect his judgment of a man's gifts.

In practice, the leadership of Kennedy and other ministers admired by the Men was exercised in a kind of arbitration of Christian experience. Where Kennedy's seal of approval was given to an account of experience, this was considered a strongly positive indication. For example, a posthumous sketch of one of 'the Men', William Murray, mentioned Kennedy's approval even as a young man:

Once at a Fellowship Meeting at Dornoch, the question was based on Isaiah 40, 31 – 'They that wait upon the Lord shall renew their strength, they shall mount up with wings as eagles.' Some of the speakers were dwelling on the flight of the believer as he ascends on the wings of faith and hope. When William was called, he remarked that there are times when some of the Lord's people cannot soar as the eagle, for they may feel themselves more like a roughly-treated dove with draggled plumage and bruised wings and its feet fixed in the mire so that it cannot rise as it desires to do. When Dr Kennedy, Dingwall, then a young man, closed the Question, he took particular note of William's illustration and said that the man whose case was represented by the sorely harassed dove was one that had made no mean flight in Christian experience.[199]

Such a passage indicated that Kennedy's endorsement of a description of experience, even while a young minister, was considered highly significant and indicative as an assessment.

Not all ministers enjoyed Kennedy's privileged status amongst the Men: Ansdell noted that where the tension between ministers and the Men became too great, it could lead directly to Separatism.[200] Kennedy himself stated that the enmity did not necessarily lie principally on the side of the Men, observing that 'They had bitter enemies at home, in the ungodly ministers of many Highland parishes' prior to the Disruption.[201] Nonetheless, he attempted to draw a sharp distinction, stating,

> There have been, in the north, for half-a-century at least, a few cliques of Separatists, quite distinct from the order of 'the men'. Specimens of the former have often been taken as if fairly representing the latter. Among these Separatists were men of eminent piety, and some of eminent gifts.[202]

Kennedy gave positive examples of these Separatists, John Grant and Sandy Gair, but warned of others who went to extremes in their censure of other Christians.[203] Kennedy was plainly anxious to underline the loyalty to the evangelical ministry that marked most of the Men. However, Paton observed that Kennedy's own description of the Men as those loyal to the ministers is plainly 'too restrictive' to work as a definition, since a number of widely acknowledged Men were prominent in leading separations from ministries that they considered unworthy.[204]

Significantly, Kennedy himself had a long association with one of these Men, Donald Duff, which helps to show the ambivalence of his position towards Separatism. Duff was described as 'one, especially, who had an abiding place in his affections', and served for some years as catechist in Dingwall Free Church. Duff certainly exemplified some of the faults of the Men, being described as using his opportunity to speak at the Friday Fellowship Meeting, to 'review the experimental quality and doctrinal soundness of the remarks made by the other speakers', though he also exhibited many of their better qualities.[205] Yet Duff was a Separatist, leading a secession from the ministry of Rev. John MacLean of Stratherrick Free Church in 1863, erecting a place of meeting in the district and keeping separate services, until the rift was healed in 1877. The *Free Church Annals* recorded that in the separation of 1893, 'The Duff party and their descendants again seceded.'[206] Significantly, a later writer echoed this analysis, noting the substantial movement in this area to the Free Presbyterian Church in 1893, 'as might be expected in a district where Separatism had been rife in earlier days'.[207] Norman Campbell rooted the initial separation in the attitude of the minister towards Duff personally, but suggested that the antipathy was not restricted to the Stratherrick minister. He pointed out how Kennedy had previously recommended Duff for a post as a Free Church catechist to the workers building the railway near Conon Bridge, but that the Presbytery had cancelled the appointment, due to the objections of the local minister, Malcolm Macgregor of Urquhart. Kennedy's subsequent appeal to the Ross Synod was rejected in April 1862.[208]

Plainly, with regards to Duff, Kennedy was unusual among the Highland Free Church ministers in regarding him as suitable for such public employment by the Church. It is worth noting that this case saw Kennedy very publicly siding with one of the Men in opposition to his own ministerial brethren. There was no sign that Duff's subsequent separation impaired his friendship with Kennedy, even given that this might reasonably be said to have substantiated the ministers' concerns about his suitability for work as a catechist. This may have been one basis for the criticism that Kennedy was too close to the Men. John Macleod tried to defend Kennedy from such a charge, describing him criticising one of the Men, Hector Jack: 'Dr Kennedy is sometimes said to have been too subservient to "the Men" and too lenient with them. This story shows that where there was a call for it, he could be firm.'[209] The defensive tone of this comment and the lack of substance to the example adduced – a vague criticism of a man not present hardly being evidence of firmness – tend to suggest that there may be more validity to the criticism than Macleod cared to admit.

The importance of the Men could hardly be overstated. They were part of their local communities in ways that transient ministers, however talented, were not. The ministers were usually natives of other parts of the country, and were consciously distinguished from their people by their education in Lowland cities, their higher social class and the fact that they were always subject to call elsewhere. The Men were permanent residents, respected in spiritual matters, and thus were often the true leaders of local opinion in the Church in the Highlands. Though they were not all elders in the Highland Free Church, some not even being formally members, enough of them were in office for the influence of the Men to be felt in church courts as well as in the fellowship meetings. But above all, this influence was exerted locally in the house gatherings and fireside discussions of Highland evangelical life. The leadership of the people in the later movements of separation in Highland communities in 1893 and 1900 was exerted not directly by the small and relatively undistinguished groups of ministers that separated, but by means of the Men in their local communities. Kennedy was greatly respected by the Men, but he also knew that his influence and leadership in the Highlands depended on that respect continuing, and it is likely that he was cautious not to jeopardise this relationship lightly. As it was, in ecclesiastical controversy, Kennedy knew that he had the loyalty of the bulk of the Highland Church behind him, through the support of the local leaders – the Men.

To gain, and retain throughout his ministry, this level of popular leadership was a significant achievement, indicating Kennedy's skills as a pastor. In particular, Kennedy was notable for acts of kindness that belied the stern reputation of the Highland ministry. Macfarlane recorded an amusing story of such an act:

> I knew a humble jobbing gardener who went in great trembling to see Dr Kennedy about joining the church. That is a big ordeal in the Highlands. When he painfully managed to tell his errand the Doctor threw his arms around his neck and kissed him. The gardener fearfully expected a bombardment of questions, and was bombarded with welcoming embrace and kiss. It was a heavenly surprise.[210]

Similarly, tributes recorded Kennedy's generosity with money, and also with time. Macfarlane comments how 'he was extraordinarily longsuffering with Naturals and Tiresomes', which he exemplified from Kennedy's patience in hospitality and correspondence with an indigent wanderer, Timothy Nathan. Macfarlane summed it up rather dismissively as 'his kindness to Feather-brains'.[211] This quality of kindness was recognised by Munro in his poetic tribute:

> You were a faithful pastor,
> And a gentleman, amiable, kind,
> Large-hearted and of great hospitality:
> A warm eye, and full of friendliness,
> With a genial countenance,
> Your generous hand stretched out to the poor,
> Your possessions scattered for them.[212]

When he felt it necessary, however, he could also be very blunt. A letter survives that he addressed to the classical scholar John Stuart Blackie, answering various questions regarding the basis for distinctive religious practices in the Highland Church. Having courteously addressed the queries, Kennedy went on to condemn Blackie's recent denunciation of the Free Church's discipline of the Biblical critic William Robertson Smith, and sharply critiqued his own personal religious conduct:

> The advocate of theatric exhibitions and of Sabbath amusements – the man whose code of morals seems to be 'the book of sports' and who once and again, has given from a pulpit, on a Sabbath evening, a sample of stage antics – cannot be tolerant of a religion marked by earnestness of feeling and by holy walking in the fear of God. Wiser far, than attempting to form, and venturing to publish an estimate of the state of religion in the Highlands, would it be, to devote the closing season of your life to [illegible] your hopes and aims to the test of scripture, to an absorbing desire to 'win' Christ, and to be found in him, and to intense and prayerful straining towards 'holiness without which no man shall see the Lord'.[213]

The tone of this communication was a good deal more combative than was conventional in Victorian letters, but interpreted within Kennedy's worldview, was wholly comprehensible and pastorally necessary. Blackie, as an individual whose public conduct was inconsistent with a Christian profession, in Kennedy's terms, needed to be warned of the solemn danger of this position, and Kennedy would be faithful to do so, even at risk of a damaged relationship.

The most constant and pressing pastoral problem was the lack of assurance, a very common concern in the Highland Church of this generation. In the Calvinist worldview of Highland evangelicalism, Christian conversion was a supernatural spiritual change, without which the individual would certainly be eternally lost, being subject to God's everlasting judicial punishment in Hell. This greatly enhanced the urgency of the question, while the tendency to a very elevated view of the evidence of this change heightened the uncertainty and anxiety over the issue. In this area, the Highland Church stood in the Puritan tradition, stressing texts such as 1 Corinthians 11: 28–9[214] to justify an extreme wariness of bold profession of faith. In practice, only a small minority of those attending worship in Highland congregations made public profession of faith, and sometimes individuals considered by all as Christians held back from the Lord's Table.[215] The fear of having experienced false conversion extended even to ministers. For example, John Macdonald, later Free Church minister of Helmsdale, delayed applying for licence after completing his divinity studies for two years, due to a lack of assurance.[216] Even the celebrated Finlay Cook, minister of Reay Free Church, was quoted as remarking, 'I am sometimes afraid I am not born again yet.'[217] Equally, warnings of the danger of false conversion featured largely in the writings of ministers of the period. John Macdonald of Ferintosh wrote very typically in his poem *The Christian* of this danger:

> Ah! My heart is full of pity for full many that profess
> Jesus' name and have not come to know their own heart's bitterness,
> Neither guilt nor yet the body of this death doth cause them groan;
> Satan leaves them free from trouble for he counts them still his own.[218]

Kennedy's sermons were full of such cautions; indeed, the warning against false hope of conversion was one of his most frequent points of application, appearing constantly throughout all the records we have of his pulpit ministrations.[219] Yet equally, alongside these cautions, were constant encouragements to those struggling with doubts. He repeatedly stressed that a sincere believer might not always be sure of the truth of their experience and tried to encourage doubters by giving marks of the experience of saving grace.[220] His message was plain:

> It is very difficult for [Christ's people] to form a true estimate of their condition. They are, at the same time, the most destitute and afflicted, and the richest and happiest, people in the world. They have sorrows which a stranger can know, and yet they have joys with which he cannot 'intermeddle'.[221]

Kennedy was emphatic that uncertainty was not a good thing, and that clear assurance should be sought – but only on the basis of the Scriptural marks identifying those who are the Lord's regenerate people.[222] Furthermore, he urged careful self-examination as the best route to true 'spiritual comfort', and as directly productive of 'liberty and boldness [...] as witnesses for God in the world'.[223]

While consistent with Calvinist theology, this teaching on assurance became increasingly controversial during Kennedy's lifetime. The American evangelist D. L. Moody taught that a true Christian should not be without assurance,[224] and Kennedy referred to this debate in his controversial pamphlet critiquing Moody's evangelistic campaign:

> Assurance is regarded [by Moody and his supporters] as the direct result of faith, or as essential to its exercise. A consciousness of faith is of itself deemed a sufficient ground of assurance. There is no place at all allowed to an attestation of faith by works.[225]

Kennedy considered this teaching to lead in an Antinomian direction, undermining the importance of the moral law in the life of the believer, with the consequent danger of encouraging those not truly converted to draw false hope that they had, in fact, been saved. Furthermore, it directly contradicted his pastoral experiences among multitudes of Highland believers wrestling with the question of assurance. A recent writer, Malcolm Maclean, has written in defence of Kennedy's teaching on assurance, arguing that his emphasis on the comfort to be drawn from marks of grace is consistent with the *Westminster Confession of Faith*,[226] and with the eighteenth-century Presbyterian tradition. Maclean noted especially how the Secession writer Ebenezer Erskine had similarly distinguished between the assurance of faith – the mental assent to the truth of the gospel – and the assurance of sense, which is the personal consciousness of having embraced the promised salvation. Much like Kennedy, Erskine used this distinction to bring pastoral comfort to those struggling with their own lack of felt assurance, pointing them to the assurance that they *did* possess, of the truth of salvation by Christ, and by emphasising the confessional teaching that the assurance of sense was not intrinsic to salvation.[227]

One of the most revealing passages of Kennedy's writing on the subject of false conversion is the autobiographical section of his second pamphlet on the Moody campaign, in which he describes his own painful experience of the ephemeral effects of religious revival in a past generation:

> I early found myself in the midst of a revival movement. It was in the Highlands, too. The preaching which was mainly instrumental in producing it was preaching which I greatly admired. [...] I went then to hear the gospel as one to whom the issue was to be life or death for ever. I craved with all my heart to share in the impression made on other hearts, if it verily resulted from the operation of the Spirit's power. But the greater the excitement, the less, to my consciousness, the power. [...] Those who knew the district well could tell of scarce any abiding fruit as the result of that remarkable movement.
>
> From this experience in the Highlands I passed to Aberdeen, and found myself there in the midst of the movement, in which William Burns was the leader. [...] I went to hear him with a fervent desire to be impressed; but, with all my reverence for the preacher, and my heart's hunger for the benefit of his services, I was constrained even then, young and inexperienced as I was, to conclude that his method was not judicious. [...] A year thereafter, I was present when Mr Burns asked those who were impressed during his former visit, to meet in a certain place at an appointed hour. I resolved to be, and I was, present there and then. Eleven young women appeared, and no more; and their cases, if one might judge by their demeanour, were not very hopeful. [...] How different this result, from the sanguine estimate of the year before, when Mr Burns, as he pointed to hundreds before him, declared his persuasion that they were all true converts! Mr Burns entered the place of meeting, looked down on the little group before him, crossed his arms on the book-board, bent his head on them, and wept. That most impressive scene I cannot forget. I learned a life-lesson then.[228]

Kennedy went on to describe further experience of revival during the same period in Ireland, where the apparent converts were reported subsequently to have 'gone back to the world'.[229] The obvious pain and disillusionment expressed in these passages may help to explain the tenacity with which Kennedy repeatedly reverted to the subject of false conversions. Furthermore, his pastoral concern for his congregation, and for his hearers across the Highlands generally, that they would have a well-grounded hope of salvation, left him unwilling to treat assurance as a light or easy thing.

The extent of the Highland difficulty with assurance was highlighted in the statistical disparity between adherents and communicant members in the congregations of the Free Church during the nineteenth century.[230] Adherents attended public worship, were usually themselves baptised persons and, on this basis, were considered to form part of the Christian Church. If they professed belief in the Bible as the Word of God, and Jesus Christ as the way of salvation, usually by repetition of answers from the *Westminster Shorter Catechism* before the Kirk Session, they could be granted the sacrament of baptism for their children. However, they did not make profession of personal experience of saving grace and so did not sit at the Lord's Table. As a result, there was a very sharp distinction in the practice of the Highland Church in the admission to the two sacraments, in total contrast to the situation that obtained in the Lowlands, where admission to the sacraments was generally one and the same, and included the great majority of people in regular attendance at public worship. Admission to baptism in the Highlands was, in practice, fairly general, such that even some Highland ministers criticised the perceived laxness of the administration of baptism. Unusually, one Highland minister, Roderick Macleod, parish minister of Bracadale in the 1820s, went further and aroused controversy by attempting to restrict the administration of baptism to the children of communicant members, and faced disciplinary proceedings before the General Assembly for his attempts to maintain this strictness of administration.[231] However, admission to communion was very strictly regulated, both by the set procedure requiring an interview before the full Kirk Session of the congregation regarding the individual's spiritual experience, and by a general culture that encouraged extreme caution regarding this step. The distinction in admission to the sacraments was, therefore, a pastoral situation that long predated the commencement of John Kennedy's ministry.

As a pastor, however, Kennedy set himself not to challenge this distinction but to defend and reinforce it. In the face of criticism of the longstanding Highland practice in this area,[232] Kennedy defended the distinction as pastorally necessary, and Biblically mandated. In this, he took something of a lonely stance, as other Free Churchmen, even from the Highlands, were reticent to endorse the Highland sacramental practice. A writer called 'Presbyterian', claiming to be from Creich, wrote to *The Scotsman* in 1878, strongly criticising the Highland Free Church for the limited participation in communion, claiming that people were frightened away from observance of the sacrament by 'the ministers and men', and personally blaming Kennedy by name for the continuance of this situation.[233] The later church historian Andrew Campbell concurred that the fear of man played a significant role in the fear of the communion in the Highlands.[234] Kennedy's longstanding fellow-minister Kenneth Macdonald of Applecross conceded the strictness of admission that prevailed in Highland communions, but argued that this had historical roots, being a reaction against the general participation in communion by the whole congregation prior to the penetration of Highland communities by evangelical preaching.[235] Furthermore, the later historian Leigh Schmidt noted that the communion season did engage the whole community in the observance of the sacrament.[236]

To one correspondent, Kennedy defended strict admission to communion as no innovation, but rather as 'the rule in the Lowlands in earlier times' and 'the primitive Scottish Presbyterian practice where there was an earnest ministry'.[237] Kennedy insisted that the purpose of this strictness was pastoral, noting that he had 'never been able to urge those who cannot discern the Lord's body to come to the Lord's table', and going on to add that 'zeal, according to knowledge, working in that direction, is mercy to those whom it would exclude, for it behoves to prevent their eating and drinking judgment to themselves'.[238] In a previous pamphlet, he wrote with evident horror of the practice of many churches regarding the Lord's Table, that 'it is, in many cases, almost as open to the profane and to the licentious, as to the most serious and virtuous of the people'.[239] He plainly regarded such a practice as a grave dereliction of duty on the part of the relevant office bearers. This said, Kennedy did not cut himself off from congregations following Lowland practices: for example, he served as a regular assistant at the communions at St Columba's Free Church, Aberdeen, where the minister followed the practice of examining intending communicants privately rather than requiring them to appear before the Session.[240]

In *Days of the Fathers*, he conceded that the strictness of admission was 'the most evident peculiarity' of the Highland Church.[241] However, here his principal defence was the assertion of a specific difference in the standard of admission to the two sacraments: baptism should be 'given on an uncontradicted profession of faith, while an accredited profession is required to justify the Church in granting admission to the table of the Lord'.[242] Citing the Dutch theologian Petrus van Mastricht (1630–1706), Kennedy argued that baptism marks the believer's admission to the benefits of the covenant of grace, while the Lord's Supper is the believer's sacrament of nurture, on the basis of 'the seeming fruits of his faith'.[243] He pointed out that those at the Lord's Table have 'the most conspicuous connection with the cause and glory of Christ', particularly as 'those who admit them point the eye of the world to them as the accredited children of Zion'.[244] Therefore, and on the basis of 1 Corinthians 11: 28–9, the Church must encourage solemn self-examination before this step is taken, and ensure that such a process has been followed.[245] Furthermore, he suggested, pastoral wisdom itself dictated that participation in the Supper should not be made a condition for a parent to receive baptism for their children, as this may place an undue pressure on an individual to go to the table while still unqualified.[246] Kennedy cited Biblical examples of instant administration of baptism from Acts to justify admission to that sacrament where no open contradiction existed between the parents' public life and a Christian profession, while retaining a higher view of the qualifications required for admission to the Lord's Table. In citing Scripture, the older Scottish Presbyterian practice and Continental theologians, Kennedy refused to defend the sacramental distinction as a local or regional peculiarity, but as normative Christian practice.

Kenneth Ross noted that Kennedy was not the first Highland minister to assert the distinction in admission to the two sacraments, but that he gave an important defence of the position on the basis of the distinct nature of baptism and the Lord's Supper. Kennedy thus bolstered confidence in the Highland practice, and Ross acknowledged 'the very small Communion rolls which have been a notorious feature of Highland Church life' since.[247] John MacLeod described Kennedy's defence of the Highland practice as 'more convenient than convincing', but admitted that his position has been highly influential in the Highland churches and holds near 'canon-law status' in the Free Presbyterian Church.[248] Donald Macleod recognised Kennedy's influence, but argued that on this point he and the Highland Church had diverged from the position of the *Westminster Confession of Faith*, and had adopted a 'pragmatic' distinction to allow baptism to be administered to infants other than the children of communicant members.[249] However, the *Confession* states only that 'the infants of one or both believing parents are to be baptised',[250] and it is a dubious step of interpretation to assert that this requires that they be communicant members of the Church. It is possible to be a true believer, while lacking the confidence to make profession of that faith by participation in the Lord's Supper, involving, as this did, an exacting interview before the Kirk Session. Furthermore, the Highland Church was maintaining continuity on this point of practice with the seventeenth-century Church of Scotland that adopted the *Confession*. Malcolm Maclean agreed on Kennedy's significance as a spokesman for the Highland Church on the Lord's Supper. In a cautious handling of the debate over communion, he stressed that any practice that saw 'true believers not communicating' was 'impossible to justify from Scripture', but equally rejected the Lowland practice of indiscriminate admission to the Table.[251] This suggests that his objection to the traditional Highland practice lay not with the principles of sacramental admission laid down by Kennedy but rather with the overly harsh criteria for admission to the Supper sometimes applied by individual Kirk Sessions. Other conservative authors from the Highland Church tradition have concurred in this assessment.[252]

Within the Free Church, Kennedy was often called upon to defend the distinctive sacramental practices of the Highland Church. For example, in 1870, he refused to sign a Report of Deputies to the Free Church General Assembly on the state of religion in Sutherland, in part due to the criticism it contained of the reticence of the majority in Highland congregations to participate in the communion. He wrote at the time of the Report:

> It was the result, I am persuaded, of a too favourable impression of the religious condition of the people. Judging by the strict morality and

> marked earnestness of the Highlanders, strangers are apt to think that a much larger proportion of them ought to be, and to search for some strong reason for their not being, communicants.[253]

Kennedy contended, not unreasonably, that those who did not know the local people well were hardly best placed to assess their fitness to sit at the Lord's Table. However, that such a report should be presented indicated the growing rift between the Highland and the Lowland Church over sacramental practices.

Two years later, this rift came to a head before the 1872 General Assembly. A controversy had developed over the election of a new minister to Killearnan Free Church, following the death of Kennedy's elder brother Donald, who had served his whole ministry there. The majority of the congregation's members wished to call Gustavus Aird of Creich, while a minority preferred a probationer, Neil Gillies. Normally, this would result in a call being moderated by the Presbytery to Aird. However, in this case, the great majority of adherents supported Gillies, and as Killearnan was a typical Highland congregation, with only a small proportion of the congregation in membership, the resolution of the case was not easy. The Chanonry Presbytery decided on a call to Gillies, which was duly signed by 400 of the 414 adherents in the congregation, but by only 24 of 66 members.[254] The Presbytery passed a majority motion to sustain this call, but this was appealed to the superior court, the Ross Synod, on which Kennedy sat as minister of Dingwall. The Synod overturned the Presbytery's decision by a vote of 9–2, declaring that, as the call had not been signed by a majority of members, it could not be sustained.[255] The case was then appealed to the General Assembly, and Kennedy was obliged to appear before the Assembly to defend the Synod's ruling.

Kennedy spoke strongly in defence of the Synod's action: 'From intimate knowledge of the parish, he could state that the dissentients represented the earnest spiritual life of the congregation.'[256] In terms of strict church law, Kennedy and the Synod were acknowledged to be in the right: the power of election of a new minister was vested in the communicant membership of the congregation. However, the leading ministers of the Assembly, Henry Moncrieff and Robert Rainy, noted that this law had been drafted with the Lowland situation in mind. In this situation, they proposed that the adherents should be treated as members, and therefore that the original decision of the Presbytery should be sustained. Moncrieff's speech was notable for the dismissive way in which he referred to the practice of the Highland Church:

> It was undoubted that the parties referred to were considered in the Highlands as entitled to baptism for their children, and allowed to remain in that position on account of peculiar views existing as to the ground on which parties might come to the Lord's Supper.[257]

Rainy concurred, noting that there was a lack of evidence of division in the congregation, in which case the requirement for majority support for the membership did not apply. However, he also condemned the Highland sacramental practice, publicly stating in his speech that the Killearnan adherents should be communicants, and even citing Kennedy's own statement against him, that 'the non-communicants of the north may compare favourably with the elders of the south'.[258] As a party to the case, Kennedy was not able to reply, but William Rose of Poolewe spoke for the Highland Church to insist on the superiority of the morthern sacramental practices: 'We in the Highlands must maintain the scripturalness of our own mode of administering the ordinances.'[259] An alternative motion, to uphold the Synod's ruling, was moved and seconded by Kennedy's Lowland allies on the Free Church's constitutionalist wing, Thomas Smith and James Begg. On a vote being taken, however, Moncrieff's motion carried by 155, against 56 for Smith's. The call was sustained, and Neil Gillies became minister of Killearnan Free Church later that year.[260] However, the significance of the case was much wider than one congregation. The General Assembly had decided to treat Highland adherents of the Free Church as members in all but name, granting them an equal voice in the choice of a minister. The implication was clear: the national Free Church would not interfere in local Sessional prerogatives to require mass admission to the Lord's Table in the Highlands, but it would not defer to the careful distinction between members and adherents in the Highland congregations that Kennedy and his colleagues were so anxious to maintain. Kennedy's Lowland colleagues did not share his concern to promote rigorous self-examination prior to participation in the Supper, nor did they emulate the experimental emphasis that marked his preaching. On these points, the Highland and Lowland sections of the Free Church were increasingly tending to diverge.

In 1879, the Highland Church faced a different challenge to their sacramental practice, in a request from the Ross-shire Farmers Club to the Free and Established Church Presbyteries of that county that communion weekends be co-ordinated to occur simultaneously throughout the bounds of each Presbytery. The farmers complained at the neglect of agricultural work as their labourers attended weekday communion services in other congregations. Kennedy used such strong language in denouncing this request at the Dingwall Presbytery that he was quoted in the national press:

[This is] the plan now followed in the South, of giving to the service of the Lord the driblet of time left by secular employment, and the remnant of strength of body and of earnestness of soul which survive the jading toil of the world [. . . It] is to be accounted for, mainly and only, by the desire to have all that pertains to the worship of God and to the eternal welfare of souls, subordinated to mere secular interests; it is the spirit of the world rebelling against the claims of God.[261]

Here, Kennedy treated the observance of the communion season as a sign of faithfulness to God, and thus as manifestly superior to Lowland practice. However, the press recorded that his response was mild in comparison to the strength of feeling expressed by the elders of Tain Presbytery. One elder threatened that if the farmers were even received, 'he would leave the Church, and worship on the hill-side', and others concurred. The Presbytery eventually agreed to give the delegation a hearing, but the request was entirely rejected in a strongly worded motion, carried unanimously.[262]

As a pastor, Kennedy earned the respect of the Highland Church, especially as a judge of Christian experience, and was thus able to exercise leadership over the Men. His pastoral concern was shown in his continued stress on the danger of experiencing false conversion, and the need instead for a well-grounded assurance of saving faith. To this end, he advocated the distinctive sacramental practices of the Highland Church, particularly the insistence upon an accredited profession of faith for admission to the Lord's Table. He defended the sacramental distinction in practice, crucially, not as a regional innovation of the Highlands, but as the historic Scottish Presbyterian practice inherited from the Free Church's seventeenth-century forebears.

Conclusion

John Kennedy did not have a peaceful ministry. His divinity studies were interrupted by the Disruption and his whole ministry was marked by ecclesiastical conflict. Yet in such conflict, he built a reputation as a bold and uncompromising proponent of evangelical Calvinism. He had weaknesses as a minister, such as apparent occasional tendencies to preach at too demanding a level for his hearers. In his pastoral leadership, he may have bolstered unhealthy aspects of the culture of the Men. He certainly recognised the established role of the Men in the question meeting, despite the distinction that sometimes obtained between the Men and the elected Presbyterian officers of the Highland Church, and may have sometimes withheld needed rebukes from the Men for the sake of preserving his close relationship with them. Nonetheless, he ministered effectively throughout the Highlands, and well beyond, and as a result of the popularity of his preaching, he exercised leadership over the trajectory of Highland Presbyterianism in the second half of the nineteenth century. His central emphases of Divine sovereignty, the gospel offer and the need for personal self-examination remained those of the Highland Church generally, while the benefit from his ministry in many individual lives is evident from extant personal testimonies. As a pastor, he encouraged a well-grounded assurance of faith, and insisted upon such an accredited profession of faith for admission to the Lord's Supper. Kennedy's ministry brought increased confidence and cohesion to the Highland Church in defence of its distinctive positions and principles, especially in the face of change in the Lowland Church, as Biblically mandated and historically precedented Scottish Presbyterianism. In the later years of his ministry, Kennedy came increasingly to view this as something that must be defended, even militantly, against perceived assault from without, and that same conflict would increasingly be taken up by the Highland Church as a whole. That conflict he fought with his pen, and so it is to Kennedy's writings that we now turn.

Notes

1. Andrew Mackillop, *'More Fruitful than the Soil': Army, Empire and the Scottish Highlands, 1715–1815* (East Linton, 2000), 234–44; David Taylor, *The Wild Black Region, Badenoch 1750–1800* (Edinburgh, 2016), 248–60.
2. Beith, *A Highland Tour*, esp. 102ff., shows the hazards of Highland travel in 1845. By 1884, Beith's tour would have been routine.
3. Ian R. MacDonald, *Aberdeen and the Highland Church, 1785–1900* (Edinburgh, 2000), 52.
4. For full discussion of terms based on original sources, c.f. C. W. J. Withers, 'The Historical Creation of the Scottish Highlands' (143–56), in I. Donnachie and C. Whatley, eds, *The Manufacture of Scottish History* (Edinburgh, 1992), 147–50.
5. 'Investigator', *The Church and Her Accuser*, 44.
6. 'Ian Maclaren', *Graham of Claverhouse*, quoted in J. H. Thorburn, *The Church of 1843 Versus a New Celtic Church* (Leith, 1908), 2.
7. Simpson, *The Life of Principal Rainy*, I, 429, 448.
8. John Kennedy, *The Days of the Fathers in Ross-shire* [first pub. 1861], [New and Enlarged Edition] (Inverness, 1897), 127, 144.
9. Kennedy, *Days*, 2–4.
10. Kennedy, *Days*, 4–8.
11. J. E. A. Dawson, 'Calvinism and the Gaidhealtachd in Scotland' (231–53), in A. Pettegree, A. Duke and C. Lewis, eds, *Calvinism in Europe: 1540–1620* (Cambridge, 1994), *passim*.
12. Kennedy, *Days*, 9, 13.
13. I. R. M. Mowat, *Easter Ross, 1750–1850* (Edinburgh, 1981), 113.
14. As described in Kennedy, *Days*, 215–16. Note that Scottish Episcopalianism grew significantly during the nineteenth century, but most of this increased support came from converts amongst the Anglicising upper and middle classes, not the Highland crofting communities that had retained a conjoint loyalty to Epicopalianism and the Jacobite monarchy in the wake of the Revolution Settlement. One recent study has stressed the wholly distinct development of these 'sub-cultures' of Scottish Episcopalianism over the nineteenth century; c.f. Rowan Strong, *Episcopalianism in Nineteenth-century Scotland* (Oxford, 2002), esp. Ch. 3.
15. Norman C. Macfarlane, *Apostles of the North* [first pub. 1931] (Stornoway, n.d.), 100.
16. Rev. John Macinnes, *The Evangelical Movement in the Highlands of Scotland, 1688–1800* (Aberdeen, 1951), 11.
17. Alan P. F. Sell, 'Kennedy, John (1819–1884)', *Oxford Dictionary of National*

Biography (Oxford, 2004), available at: <http://www.oxforddnb.com/view/article/15386> (last accessed 28 March 2022).
18. Stewart J. Brown, *Thomas Chalmers and the Godly Commonwealth* (Oxford, 1982), 50.
19. Macfarlane, 'John Kennedy', 100.
20. William Walker, *Additional Reminiscences and a Belated Class-book: King's College, 1836–40* (Aberdeen, 1906), 38.
21. Quoted in James S. Sinclair, ed., *Rich Gleanings After the Vintage from 'Rabbi' Duncan* (London, 1925), 7.
22. Macfarlane, 'John Kennedy', 100.
23. Quoted in Auld, *Life of John Kennedy*, 4–5.
24. John Kennedy, *The Union Question* (Edinburgh, n.d., c.1870), 2.
25. 'The Minister of Killearnan' (163–267), in *Days*.
26. Kennedy, *Days*, quoted in Auld, *Life of John Kennedy*, 5.
27. Macfarlane, 'John Kennedy', 100.
28. Auld, *Life of John Kennedy*, 7.
29. Auld, *Life of John Kennedy*, 8.
30. Quoted in Auld, *Life of John Kennedy*, 32 [emphasis in original]; the phrase appears to be a loose reference to *King Lear*, indicating Kennedy's poetic interests. *Annotationes Quotidianae* regrettably exists now only in Auld's quotations; Auld, *Life of John Kennedy*, 11–42. It covers dates from 24 September 1841 to a final date, presumably in 1843, referring to his imminent licensing. It is not clear whether this is a comprehensive transcription, as unfortunately it would be quite in keeping with nineteenth-century editorial practices for a biographer to censor such a source heavily in publication. The final date is a little mysterious: read in context, the diary concludes on 13 June 1842; this is deduced from its being headed '13th', directly following a run of apparently consecutive entries commencing from '1842 – January 1–8', with the penultimate entry being dated 'June 8th'. But this dating is impossible, concluding more than a year prior to Kennedy's licensing, which itself was already an expedited event, as noted above. The solution is probably a mistake in the transcription, whereby a year was lost at some point, either due to no entries being made or due to incomplete reproduction, but internal evidence is insufficient to establish where that break should occur. The last of the apparently consecutive chain of entries is on 4 February, almost certainly 1842; thereafter come three irregular entries, marked 'May 1st', 'June 8th' and '13th', one or all of which may refer to 1843.
31. Quoted in Auld, *Life of John Kennedy*, 6.
32. John Fraser, 'Rev John Kennedy, D.D.', in *Disruption Worthies of the Highlands* (1886), available at: <http://highlandchristianity.blogspot.co.uk/p/john-kennedy.html> (last accessed 22 May 2014). (Details in the text of this account, of Kennedy in the process of issuing a weekly sermon, indicate that it was written in its final form during the year 1883, while Kennedy was still living. Fraser himself also died in 1884: hence, presumably, why the text was not altered prior to publication; c.f. W. Ewing, ed., *Annals of the Free Church of Scotland, 1843–1900*, 2 vols (Edinburgh, 1914), 161.)
33. Quoted in Auld, *Life of John Kennedy*, 7.
34. John Kennedy, 'Donald Sage' (45–52), in J. Greig, ed., *Disruption Worthies of the Highlands* (Edinburgh, 1877), 50.

35. Callum G. Brown, *The Social History of Religion in Scotland Since 1730* (London, 1987), 65–7.
36. W. Taylor, ed., *Memorials of the Life and the Ministry of Charles Calder Mackintosh* (Edinburgh, 1870), 1ff.
37. John Kennedy, *The Establishment Principle and the Disestablishment Movement* (Edinburgh, 1878), 57. Note that his elder brother Donald (1813–71) succeeded their father as parish minister of Killearnan and remained as Free Church minister there until his death; c.f. Ewing, *Annals*, 198.
38. Norman L. Walker, *Chapters from the History of the Free Church of Scotland* (Edinburgh, 1895), 131–8.
39. This date has been the subject of some confusion, being given as September in Auld, *Life of John Kennedy*, 42–3, and even as August in Fraser, 'Rev John Kennedy'. The correct course of events can be confirmed from the Presbytery minutes, which indicate he was proposed for licence at the first Presbytery meeting after the Disruption, on 21 June; was set trials on 25 July; and presented his Divinity Hall certificates on 8 August. Having given a satisfactory performance in all the set trials, he was licensed on 3 October. For full details, c.f. MS Minute Book of Free Presbytery of Chanonry, 26, 28–9, 30–1. Note that Bertha Porter is therefore incorrect in stating that Kennedy was licensed in the Established Church; 'John Kennedy (1819–1884)', in *Dictionary of National Biography*, xxx (1885–1900), available at: <http://en.wikisource.org/wiki/Kennedy,_John_(1819–1884)_(DNB00)> (last accessed 16 May 2014).
40. Walker, *Additional Reminiscences*, 24–8.
41. Fraser, 'Rev John Kennedy'.
42. Thomas Brown, *Annals of the Disruption* (Edinburgh, 1884), 221ff., 238–40, 423–6.
43. Donald Macfarlane, *Memoir and Remains of Rev Donald Macdonald* (Glasgow, 1903), 28–31. After 1893, when he and most of his congregation in Shieldaig sided with the Free Presbyterian Church, Macdonald was again in the same situation for two full years, 34–6.
44. Brown, *Annals of the Disruption*, 310–13, 354–63.
45. Macleod, *By-paths of Highland Church History* (Edinburgh, 1965), 41.
46. Stewart J. Brown, 'Martyrdom in Early Victorian Scotland: Disruption Fathers and the Making of the Free Church' (319–32), in Diana Wood, ed., *Martyrs and Martyrologies* (Oxford, 1993), *passim*, esp. 331.
47. Ansdell, *People of the Great Faith*, 80–2.
48. MacKillop, *A Goodly Heritage*, 32.
49. MacLeod, *The Second Disruption*, 5.
50. Donald Macleod, 'Thomas Chalmers and Pauperism' (63–78), in Stewart J. Brown and Michael Fry, eds, *Scotland in the Age of Disruption* (Edinburgh, 1993), 72–3.
51. Innes MacRae, *Dingwall Free Church: The Story of 100 Years and More* (Dingwall, 1970), 7.
52. Ansdell, *People of the Great Faith*, 14.
53. James Sievewright, *Memoirs of the Late Rev. Alexander Stewart, D.D.* (Edinburgh, 1822), esp. 216–354.
54. Sievewright, *Alexander Stewart*, 261–2, 346.
55. MacRae, *Dingwall Free Church*, 10–12; Report, *Aberdeen Weekly Journal*, 3 May 1884.

56. John Noble, 'Memoir of the Rev John Kennedy, D.D.' (xxix–clxi), in Kennedy, *Days*, lii.
57. MacRae, *Dingwall Free Church*, 10–16. MacRae printed a handsome painting of this church building, executed by Kennedy himself, which now hangs in Dingwall Museum.
58. MacRae, *Dingwall Free Church*, 10–12.
59. C.f. Orr, *Scotch Church Crisis*, 85n.
60. MS Minute Book of Free Presbytery of Dingwall, 24.
61. Fraser, 'Rev John Kennedy, D.D.'.
62. Report, *Aberdeen Journal*, 9 September 1857.
63. Roberts, 'John Kennedy of Dingwall', 19.
64. MacRae, *Dingwall Free Church*, 10–20. MacRae thus corrects an erroneous estimate of 45 members on the roll in 1848, perhaps a misprinting of '145', published in Ewing, ed., *Annals of the Free Church of Scotland*, ii, 215.
65. MacRae, *Dingwall Free Church*, 12–13.
66. Donald Macleod, 'The Highland Churches Today' (146–76), in James Kirk, ed., *The Church in the Highlands* (Edinburgh, 1998), 154–5.
67. 'The Late Dr Kennedy of Dingwall', *The Signal*, iii, 6 (June 1884), 161–7.
68. MacKillop, *A Goodly Heritage*, 101.
69. Macfarlane, 'John Kennedy', 105.
70. MacKillop, *A Goodly Heritage*, 103.
71. MacRae, *Dingwall Free Church*, 16ff.
72. Report, *Aberdeen Journal*, 3 May 1884.
73. Roberts, 'John Kennedy of Dingwall', 19.
74. Report, *Caledonian Mercury*, 4 June 1849.
75. [Anon.], *In Memoriam, Rev John Kennedy, D.D.* (Inverness, n.d., 1884), 98. The metaphor is a telling one, referring to the Biblical account of Elisha succeeding Elijah as God's prophet in 2 Kings 2: 13–15.
76. Extract from the Register of Births, available at: <www.scotlandspeople.gov.uk> (last accessed 4 September 2021).
77. John Kennedy of Caticol, 'Mrs Kennedy, Craigroyston' (clxiii–clxxxvi), in Kennedy, *Days*.
78. *In Memoriam, Kennedy*, 54. This figure may not be much of an exaggeration; Kennedy's fellow-Highland minister Gustavus Aird assisted at twenty-three communions (out of fifty-two weekends) in 1887; cf. MacColl, *Crofting Community*, 185.
79. Archibald Auld, *Memorials of Caithness Ministers* (Edinburgh, 1911), 253.
80. Alexander MacRae, *Life of Gustavus Aird, A.M., D.D.* (Stirling, 1908), 137.
81. Report, *Glasgow Herald*, 29 April 1884.
82. Sell, *Defending and Declaring the Faith*, 228, n.7.
83. Porter, 'John Kennedy (1819–1884)'.
84. Ewing, *Annals*, I, 235.
85. Renfield had previously been pastored by a Highlander, Duncan MacNab, but following Kennedy's refusal of the call, the minister chosen was the English-born higher critic Marcus Dods; cf. Ewing, *Annals*, I, 53, 252. The fact that a congregation could extend consecutive calls to two ministers of such radically different views indicates how unapparent were the divergent trajectories in the Free Church in the early 1860s.
86. Report, *Aberdeen Journal*, 9 September 1857. The prior ministers were John

MacRae, who had retired – cf. G. N. M. Collins, *Big MacRae: Rev John MacRae, Memorials of a Notable Ministry* (Edinburgh, 1976); and Charles Calder Mackintosh – cf. Taylor, ed., *Memorials of the Life and the Ministry of Charles Calder Mackintosh*, who had accepted a call to Dunoon.

87. Greenock Free Gaelic Church instead called Kennedy's cousin, John Kennedy (1833–70), in 1859, and thereafter Murdoch MacAskill, later Kennedy's successor in Dingwall, cf. Ewing, *Annals*, I, 199, 214.
88. Report, *Scotsman*, 2 October 1871.
89. Roberts, 'John Kennedy of Dingwall', 30.
90. 'The Late Dr Kennedy of Dingwall', 161–7.
91. Report, *Dundee Courier*, 8 October 1883.
92. MacDonald, *Aberdeen and the Highland Church*, 270.
93. Auld, *Life of John Kennedy*, 126; 'The Late Dr Kennedy of Dingwall', 161–7.
94. Report, *Aberdeen Journal*, 27 August 1873.
95. Auld, *Life of John Kennedy*, 126–33.
96. As by the Ross Synod, to be Professor of Systematic Theology, Report, *Scotsman*, 19 April 1872; and by the Argyll Synod, to be Church History Professor, Report, *Scotsman*, 27 April 1872. Both vacancies were in the Free Church College, Glasgow, and were filled by J. S. Candlish and T. M. Lindsay, respectively.
97. Report, *Scotsman*, 18 November 1875.
98. Ewing, *Annals*, I, 44–5.
99. As asserted in John Kennedy, *Sermons* [first pub. 1885] (Inverness, 1888), viii.
100. In 1849 and 1863, cf. Ewing, *Annals*, I, 44–5.
101. Fraser, 'Rev John Kennedy'; William Robertson Nicoll, 'The Religion of the Scottish Highlands', *British Weekly*, lxxxiii 4 (1 June 1888); Auld, *Life of John Kennedy*.
102. Nicoll, 'Religion of the Highlands'.
103. John Macleod, *Scottish Theology in Relation to Church History Since the Reformation* (Edinburgh, 1943), 327.
104. K. Francis, W. Gibson, J. Morgan-Guy, B. Tennant and R. Ellison, eds, *The Oxford Handbook of the British Sermon, 1689–1901* (Oxford, 2012), xiii.
105. Keith A. Francis, 'Sermon Studies: Major Issues and Future Directions' (611–28), in Francis et al., *Oxford Handbook*, 611. Valuable examples of modern sermon analysis are found in J. N. Ian Dickson, *Beyond Religious Discourse: Sermons, Preaching and Evangelical Protestants in Nineteenth-century Irish Society* (Milton Keynes, 2007).
106. James Barron, 'Memoir of Rev John Kennedy, D.D., Dingwall', originally published in instalments in the *Inverness Courier*, 1893, available at: <http://nesher christianresources.org/JBS/kennedy/Memoir_of_Dr_Kennedy.html> (last accessed 17 November 2014).
107. Donald Beaton, *Some Noted Ministers of the Northern Highlands* [first pub. 1929] (Glasgow, 1985), 274.
108. Walker, *Additional Reminiscences*, 33–4.
109. Quoted in [Anon.], 'The Prince of Highland Preachers: A Sketch of Dr John Kennedy of Dingwall', available at: <http://reformedbooksonline.com/scotti sh-theology/free-church-of-scotland/kennedy-john-of-dingwall/the-prince-of -highland-preachers/> (last accessed 15 November 2014).
110. Macfarlane, 'John Kennedy', 104.

111. Roberts, 'John Kennedy of Dingwall', 13.
112. All three quoted in Roberts, 'John Kennedy of Dingwall', 2.
113. Barron, 'Memoir of John Kennedy'.
114. J. K. Cameron, *The Clerkship of the General Assembly of the Free Church of Scotland* (Inverness, 1938), 99.
115. Rev. Donald Munro, *Records of Grace in Sutherland* (Edinburgh, 1953), 44.
116. Neil Cameron, *Ministers and Men of the Free Presbyterian Church* (Glasgow, 1993), 109. Cameron records that the other aptly replied: 'There are men in Lochaber who will not leave a bait on his hook'!
117. Macfarlane, *Apostles of the North*, 93.
118. Anne MacLeod Hill writes of the 'poetic lexicon' of Scriptural and doctrinal knowledge which Gaelic evangelical poets shared with their audience; '"Pelican in the wilderness": symbolism and allegory in women's evangelical songs of the Gàidhealtachd' (Unpublished Ph.D. thesis, University of Edinburgh, 2016, 32–4). This knowledge was particularly rooted in the work of the Gaelic schools across the Highlands.
119. Donald Maclean, 'Memoir of Rev John Noble' (xvii–lxxv), in John Noble, *Religious Life in Ross* (Inverness, 1909), xxiii.
120. 'The Late Dr Kennedy of Dingwall', 161–7.
121. MacDonald, *Aberdeen and the Highland Church*, 271.
122. Letter, *Glasgow Herald*, 19 September 1892.
123. John Macleod, 'An Argyllshire Worthy' (231–85), in G. N. M. Collins, *John Macleod, D.D.* (Edinburgh, 1951), 262.
124. 'Mr Alex Ross, of Manchester and China', quoted in Sinclair, ed., *Rich Gleanings After the Vintage* (London, 1925), 6.
125. A classic text of Gospel invitation, 'Behold, I stand at the door, and knock: if any man hear my voice, and open the door, I will come in to him, and will sup with him, and he with me.'
126. Quoted in Donald Beaton, *Memoir and Remains of Rev Donald Macfarlane* (Glasgow, 1929), 122.
127. [Anon.], 'The Prince of Highland Preachers'.
128. George Macdonald, *Men of Sutherland* [first pub. 1937] (Dornoch, 2014), 141.
129. Munro, *Records of Grace*, 112.
130. Auld, *Life of John Kennedy*, 96.
131. Macleod, 'An Argyllshire Worthy', 250–1.
132. Ross, 'A Prince Among Preachers', xvii.
133. From dates and initials given by Auld, probably Henry Shepherd from Dundee, later minister of Cambuslang, a reminder that Kennedy's serious spiritual ministry was not restricted to Highlanders; cf. Ewing, *Annals*, i, 313.
134. Auld, *Life of John Kennedy*, 105.
135. [Anon.], 'The Prince of Highland Preachers'.
136. Quoted in Ross, 'A Prince Among Preachers', xvii.
137. Quoted in Cameron, *Ministers and Men*, 121; the quotation is from 2 Corinthians 12: 2, generally understood to refer to a spiritual experience of the Apostle Paul.
138. Donald Munro, 'Lament on the Death of Dr John Kennedy who was in Dingwall' (8–17), [translated by C. Johnston], in *Marbhrainn air Dr Begg, bha'n Dun-eidin; 's air Dr. Ceanadaidh bha'n Inbhirfeorathain; agus air daoinibh diadhaidh bh'anns an airde-tuath* (n.p., 1886), 8.

139. Munro, 'Lament on the Death of Dr John Kennedy', 9–10.
140. Fraser, 'Rev John Kennedy'.
141. Auld, *Life of John Kennedy*, 73.
142. Barron, 'Memoir of John Kennedy'.
143. Two of these notebooks, one for the years 1859–65 and another for 1866–74, held in private collections in the UK, have been published in full; cf. Kennedy, *Sermon Notes*. Another is held by Dingwall Free Church and has been consulted with permission, while a fourth, which has not been seen, is thought to exist in a private collection in the USA.
144. Barron, 'Memoir of John Kennedy'.
145. Keith A. Francis, 'Sermons: Themes and Developments' (31–43), in Francis et al., *Oxford Handbook*, 42–3.
146. Ann Matheson, 'Preaching in the Churches of Scotland' (152–66), in Francis et al., *Oxford Handbook*, 165.
147. Matheson, 'Preaching in the Churches of Scotland', 164.
148. Originally from Olrig, Mackay served brief pastorates in Kincardine and Croick (1910–13), and Kilmuir-Easter (1913–20). At the time of publication, he was supplying the pulpit of Dores Free Church.
149. John Kennedy (with M. Mackay), *Divine Religion Distinct from all Human Systems, 28 Sermons by the Late Rev John Kennedy and 240 by the Rev M. Mackay* (Dingwall, n.d., 1927).
150. Kennedy, *Sermon Notes*; cf. James Begg Society, available at: <http://easyweb.easynet.co.uk/~jbeggsoc/jbshome.html> (last accessed 15 October 2015).
151. Kennedy, *Sermon Notes, 1859–65*, 125–31.
152. Dickson, *Beyond Religious Discourse*, 64.
153. It should be stressed that the notes are not, of course, all, or anywhere near all, the vast number of sermons prepared and preached by Kennedy during this period. In total, there are 109 outlines in the first notebook and 96 in the second. The great majority of these date from the years 1864–7. There are no obvious criteria governing why particular sermons should be included in these as opposed to in other notebooks; many are from communion occasions in different places, especially across the Highlands, but there are also many from the regular weekly ministry in Dingwall. All the notes are in English, though it is not known whether Kennedy's written preparation for preaching in Gaelic would have been in that language; in any case, no such outlines are known to exist.
154. Kennedy, *Sermon Notes, 1859–65*, 1–8.
155. Kennedy, *Sermon Notes, 1866–74*, 145–9, 234–6, 81–8.
156. 'And the lord said unto the servant, Go out into the highways and hedges, and compel *them* to come in, that my house may be filled.'
157. Kennedy, *Sermon Notes, 1859–65*, 73–5.
158. Kennedy, *Sermon Notes, 1859–65*, 125.
159. Kennedy, *Sermon Notes, 1859–65*, 286.
160. Kennedy, *Sermon Notes, 1866–74*, 72.
161. Kennedy, *Sermon Notes, 1859–65*, 323–5.
162. Kennedy, *Sermon Notes, 1859–65*, 243, 268–9.
163. Kennedy, *Sermon Notes, 1866–74*, 3–4.
164. John Kennedy, *Expository Lectures*, J. K. Cameron, ed. (Inverness, 1911), vii.
165. Kennedy, *Expository Lectures*, 1–3, 20.

166. Kennedy, *Expository Lectures*, 30.
167. Kennedy, *Expository Lectures*, 77–8.
168. Kennedy, *Expository Lectures*, 76–7.
169. Kennedy, *Expository Lectures*, 94.
170. Kennedy, *Expository Lectures*, 95.
171. Kennedy, *Expository Lectures*, 174.
172. Auld, *Life of John Kennedy*, 95.
173. Macleod, *Scottish Theology in Relation to Church History*, 327.
174. Kennedy, *Sermons*, 1–11, 21, 41, etc.
175. Kennedy, *Sermons*, 8.
176. Kennedy, *Sermons*, 419.
177. Kennedy, *Sermons*, 425–8.
178. Kennedy, *Sermons*, 108–10.
179. Kennedy, *Sermons*, 143–54, a particularly fine sermon on Ephesians 5: 25–7.
180. Kennedy, *Sermons*, 457.
181. Kennedy, *Sermons*, 48.
182. Kennedy, *Sermons*, 547.
183. Kennedy, *Sermons*, 467.
184. Kennedy, *Sermons*, 547.
185. Kennedy, *Sermons*, 80–1.
186. Kennedy, *Sermons*, 122.
187. E.g., Kennedy, *Sermons*, 261.
188. Nicoll, 'Religion of the Highlands'.
189. Fraser, 'Rev John Kennedy'.
190. For further testimony to Kennedy's distinctively experimental ministry, cf. Kenneth Moody Stuart, *Alexander Moody Stuart, D.D.* (Edinburgh, 1899), 70. Moody Stuart himself was noted as unusually experimental in his emphasis for a Lowland minister, as, in a previous generation, had been John Love of Anderston. Both consequently attracted many Highland hearers who appreciated this form of ministry.
191. Macdonald, *Men of Sutherland*, 34.
192. Munro, 'Lament on the Death of Dr John Kennedy', 10–11.
193. Duncan Macgregor, *Campbell of Kiltearn* [Second Edition] (Edinburgh, 1875), 50.
194. Kennedy, *Expository Lectures*, viii.
195. Macleod, *Scottish Theology*, 327.
196. Macinnes, *Evangelical Movement in the Highlands*, 211.
197. On this basis, they were considered to form part of the Christian Church; Kennedy, *Days*, 94.
198. Paton, *Clergy and the Clearances*, 120.
199. Munro, *Records of Grace*, 39–40.
200. Ansdell, *People of the Great Faith*, 124.
201. Kennedy, *Days*, 90.
202. Kennedy, *Days*, 92.
203. Kennedy, *Day*, 92–4.
204. Paton, *Clergy and the Clearances*, 121.
205. Campbell, *Gleanings of Highland Harvest*, 94–103.
206. Ewing, *Annals*, ii, 210.
207. G. N. M. Collins, *Donald Maclean, D.D.* (Edinburgh, 1944), 31.

208. Norman Campbell, *One of Heaven's Jewels: Rev Archibald Cook of Daviot and the (Free) North Church, Inverness* (Stornoway, 2009), 183–4.
209. Macleod, 'An Argyllshire Worthy', 267.
210. Macfarlane, 'John Kennedy', 104.
211. Macfarlane, 'John Kennedy', 103–4.
212. Munro, 'Lament on the Death of Dr John Kennedy', 16.
213. National Library of Scotland, MS 2634 fo 74, Blackie Correspondence, Kennedy to Blackie, 25 July 1881, 8–10.
214. 'But let a man examine himself, and so let him eat of *that* bread, and drink of *that* cup. For he that eateth and drinketh unworthily, eateth and drinketh damnation to himself, not discerning the Lord's body.'
215. For fuller discussion, cf. Macleod, 'Highland Churches Today', 160–5. An example of a notable Highland Christian who never took communion was Annie Boyd of Dingwall (d.1915), whose death was marked by an obituary in the *Free Presbyterian Magazine*, reprinted in Cameron, *Ministers and Men*, 168–70.
216. J. Mackay, *Memoir of Rev John MacDonald, Minister of the Free Church at Helmsdale* (Edinburgh, 1861), 35.
217. Quoted in Auld, *Memorials of Caithness Ministers*, 48.
218. John Macdonald, *The Christian: An Elegy in 3 Parts* [trans. John MacLeod] (Glasgow, 1906), 9.
219. E.g., Kennedy, *Sermons*, 54, 80, 177, 307, 373; Kennedy, *Expository Lectures*, 76, 147–8, etc.
220. E.g., Kennedy, *Sermons*, 106, 178, etc.
221. Kennedy, *Sermons*, 94.
222. Kennedy, *Sermons*, 178.
223. Kennedy, *Sermons*, 307.
224. Alexander MacRae, *Revivals in the Highlands and Islands in the Nineteenth Century* (Stirling, n.d., c.1906), 121.
225. John Kennedy, 'Hyper-evangelism, "Another Gospel", though a Mighty Power' (12–36), in John Kennedy and Horatius Bonar, *Evangelism: A Reformed Debate* (Gwynedd, 1997), 28.
226. The relevant section reads: 'infallible assurance does not so belong to the essence of faith, but that a true believer may wait long, and conflict with many difficulties, before he be partaker of it', *Westminster Confession of Faith* (1–48), in *The Subordinate Standards and Other Authoritative Documents of the Free Church of Scotland* (Edinburgh, 1955), xviii.3.
227. Malcolm Maclean, *The Lord's Supper* (Fearn, 2009), 159–64.
228. John Kennedy, 'A Reply to Dr Bonar's Defence of Hyper-evangelism' (106–40), in Kennedy and Bonar, *Evangelism*, 112–13.
229. Kennedy, 'Reply to Dr Bonar's Defence', 114.
230. The proportion of adherents to members was reckoned to be eight to one, or even ten to one; cf. Orr, *Scotch Church Crisis*, 85n.
231. For a full account, cf. Roderick MacLeod, 'The Progress of Evangelicalism in the Western Isles, 1800–50' (Unpublished Ph.D. thesis, University of Edinburgh, 1970), 100–8.
232. The Established Church partisan 'Investigator' published strong criticism of the Highland communion practice as early as 1850; cf. *The Church and Her Accuser in the Far North*, esp. 28–38.

233. Letters, *Scotsman*, 8 April 1878.
234. Andrew J. Campbell, *Two Centuries of the Church of Scotland, 1707–1929* (Paisley, 1930), 241–2.
235. Macdonald, *Social and Religious Life in the Highlands*, 98–100.
236. Leigh Eric Schmidt, *Holy Fairs: Scotland and the Making of American Revivalism* (Grand Rapids, 2001), 218.
237. Kennedy to Blackie, 1–2.
238. Kennedy to Blackie, 5–7.
239. John Kennedy, *Signs of the Times* (Aberdeen, 2003).
240. MacDonald, *Aberdeen and the Highland Church*, 268–9.
241. Kennedy, *Days*, 139.
242. Kennedy, *Days*, 141.
243. Kennedy, *Days*, 142–5.
244. Kennedy, *Days*, 149, 152.
245. Kennedy, *Days*, 153.
246. Kennedy, *Days*, 155–58.
247. Ross, *Church and Creed in Scotland*, 242–3.
248. MacLeod, *Banner in the West*, 317–19, 373.
249. Macleod, 'Highland Churches Today', 152, 163–6.
250. *Westminster Confession of Faith*, xxviii.4.
251. Maclean, *Lord's Supper*, 160–5.
252. Macleod, *By-paths*, 32–3; G. N. M. Collins, *Men of the Burning Heart* (Edinburgh, 1983), 101–3.
253. John Kennedy, *Unionism and the Union* (Edinburgh, 1870), 35–6.
254. *Proceedings and Debates of the General Assembly of the Free Church of Scotland* [PDGAFCS], 1872, 120–2.
255. Report, *Scotsman*, 27 April 1872.
256. *PDGAFCS*, 1872, 125.
257. *PDGAFCS*, 1872, 125.
258. *PDGAFCS*, 1872, 131.
259. *PDGAFCS*, 1872, 131–2.
260. Report, *Glasgow Herald*, 30 May 1872; *PDGAFCS*, 1872, 120–32.
261. Report, *Scotsman*, 29 August 1879.
262. Report, *Scotsman*, 5 September 1879.

CHAPTER TWO

Writing

John Kennedy was a minister for ten years before he published his first work, and then it was only a single sermon printed as a pamphlet.[1] Amidst the demands of a busy pastorate, his free time for writing was very limited, and the preface to his first book is apologetic even by the standards of Victorian publishing:

> I might plead that I never wrote with care before, and that I had but little leisure for my first attempt, but if I did not do the best I could, I ought to have done nothing. Amidst my usual employment, when in health, I found no time for 'making books', and it was not, till laid aside by sickness from my wonted work, that the purpose of this book was formed. But health returned ere I had begun to write, and, being afraid to abandon my design, I gave to its execution such snatches of time as were left unoccupied by labours which I could not abridge.[2]

Writing, however, became an important part of his work as the years passed, and his total output was impressive for a man engaged in full-time ministry, suggesting that he gave an increasingly high priority in later life to the extensive readership that could be reached via the press in nineteenth-century Scotland. In particular, he wrote a volume of Highland church history, *The Days of the Fathers in Ross-shire*, published in 1861. In 1866, he published a full-length biography of a Highland minister of an earlier generation, John Macdonald of Ferintosh, *The Apostle of the North*. His third major work was a volume of theology, *Man's Relations to God*, published in 1869. He also produced a variety of shorter publications, including seventeen controversial pamphlets, some of them quite lengthy; many sermons; lectures on various subjects; a series of newspaper articles; and a couple of biographical sketches. This chapter focuses largely on his historical writings, particularly his first two full-length books. The third book will be addressed in Chapter Four, in the discussion of Kennedy as a theologian.

Kennedy the Historian

History, in a personal sense, is vital to evangelical Christians: they have a testimony, a historical account of personal transformation from an old life of sin to a new life of faith. Kennedy had such a history in the evangelical conversion he had experienced following his father's death in 1841. But he also had another very personal history: as a Highland evangelical reared in a Presbyterian manse, he embraced the historical narrative of the Presbyterian conquest of the Highlands. This history was a profound part of his identity and the recounting of it was no academic exercise, but rather an attempt to define and defend the character of the Highland Church against all critics. However, Kennedy did not write in a triumphalist spirit, but rather with a deep sense of foreboding, suggesting that he saw the Highland evangelicalism that he loved already in steep decline. His opening paragraph in his 1861 book, *The Days of the Fathers in Ross-shire*, used Biblical quotations to draw a direct parallel between his perception of the contemporary religious situation in the Highlands and the experience of Old Testament Israel:

> Wild and uncultivated as their native hills were the people of the north, when already, in some parts of the Lowlands, the desert was beginning to 'rejoice and blossom as the rose'. The winter of the north had lasted long, and dark and dreary had it been throughout. And when 'the time to favour', 'the set time,' had come, protracted and broken was the work of spring; but a genial summer followed, and a rich harvest was thereafter gathered. Cold and dreary, or dark and stormy, may be the winter that shall close this year of 'visitation'. The chill of its presence is already on the hearts of 'the living'; but who can tell, whether it shall continue to advance with the quiet of a blight, or yet burst upon us with the fury of a tempest?[3]

Kennedy's quotations were from Isaiah 35 and Psalm 102, passages describing spiritual blessing for the people of God after long periods of deadness, which he related to the advent of Protestant evangelicalism in the Highlands. To Kennedy's Biblically literate readers, the point was clear: just as God's blessing on His people was described in the Old Testament, particularly in the passages he quoted, as coming in cycles, with periods of blessing followed by long periods of spiritual decline and eventual rebellion against God, so the same could be expected in the Highlands, if present trends continued.[4]

This cyclical vision was in contrast to the conventional Victorian narrative of continual advancement and improvement. In terms of the Christian church, this was expressed as a conviction that the state of the nineteenth-century church represented substantial progress from the condition of the church in prior generations. Other contemporary Free Church writers usually spoke in optimistic terms regarding the prospects, both spiritual and temporal, of the young Free Church of Scotland. Gibb Mitchell, Free Church minister of Cramond from 1890, was typical of the attitude of most in his Church, regarding the Victorian era as a period of welcome progress and development in the Scottish Church:

> Old customs, habits, life, old religion, had to pass away; reminding us of the old lumber that we see lying in the corner of an old stock-yard

– the rusty scythe, the old harrows and the unused machine. [. . .] We were getting better revelations of God. Science had advanced, was advancing [. . . and] there has been a real moral advance.[5]

Kennedy's divergence from this narrative of continuing improvement was stark and emphatic. In a later pamphlet, he suggested that a spiritual decline had long been evident in the Free Church of Scotland, especially in the years after the Free Church had last re-affirmed the 'Claim of Right' of the Disruption era, in 1853.[6] The decline may have begun outside the Highlands, but inevitably it must affect all parts of the country eventually.

Kennedy was not alone in this concern regarding the direction of the Free Church of Scotland. About ten years previously, a theologically conservative Glasgow minister, Jonathan Ranken Anderson, had become convinced that there was a serious defection from the faith proceeding within the Free Church, which he began to denounce from his pulpit. He also began circulating privately, and later publicly, allegations of backsliding, never clearly substantiated, against other Free Church ministers. He resigned from the Free Church ministry in 1856 before he could be disciplined for this conduct, and subsequently ministered independently in Glasgow, while denouncing his former colleagues without restraint.[7] Even the young and relatively unknown Kennedy did not escape: Anderson denounced his first published sermon as 'rude and clumsy [. . . and] a total failure', and said of him personally 'that in divine things he has yet everything to learn'.[8] Anderson's behaviour made it impossible for loyal Free Churchmen to sympathise with him, but it also indicated that Kennedy was not the only minister discerning worrying trends within the Free Church. Furthermore, there was one definite point of correspondence between Anderson and Kennedy: while Anderson in one published attack on his former Church 'reserved [. . .] his most withering criticism for Thomas Guthrie', that same Edinburgh Free Church minister was the only one of Kennedy's colleagues singled out for explicit criticism in *Days of the Fathers*, for the apparent lack of gospel content in one of his books.[9]

A more substantial controversy occurred several years later, in 1856; this may be a more direct precursor to the publication of *Days of the Fathers*. James Gibson, a professor at the Free Church College, Glasgow, complained of serious doctrinal error amongst some of the divinity students at the College. Gibson charged seven of the students with, in the words of Drummond and Bulloch, 'virtually denying the doctrine of human depravity and attributing to the reason of fallen man abilities which it did not possess'. The students had 'openly laughed at the old-fashioned theology of Gibson'. However, despite pursuing the charges through church courts for three years, Gibson was wholly unsuccessful in making his charges stick or in preventing the students in question from moving to New College, Edinburgh, to complete their studies and, in due course, enter the Free

Church ministry.[10] Interestingly, a divinity student at New College named Alexander Ross, in a memoir of his studies from November 1856 onwards, revealed that the students then in the Theological Society were, in his view, 'borrowing from German writers of doubtful character, and also speaking nonsense, with disregard to Scripture and common sense'. It is conceivable, given the conjunction in dates, that the students to whom he referred were the exiles from the Glasgow College, but Ross also complained of the influence of German critical theories in the teaching of the New Testament Professor, George Smeaton.[11] Smeaton's later stance in church courts on the Robertson Smith case proved his opposition to the more radical conclusions of German Biblical scholarship,[12] but this testimony does suggest that the influence of broader theological perspectives was more widespread than among just a few individual students.

Mitchell again was no doubt typical of Free Church attitudes in glossing over the reported views of the students as 'the eccentricities of growing minds', the exact words that his subject Robert Rainy had used at the time in reference to the case to dismiss the suggestion of heterodoxy.[13] A later biographer of Rainy called it 'a tempest in a teacup'.[14] However, Rainy's assessment was somewhat disingenuous even then, and a good deal more so quoted in retrospect: the doctrine apparently being questioned by the Glasgow students, the strict Calvinist assertion of the total depravity of fallen man, was one from which the majority of Scottish Presbyterians would resile over the succeeding half-century.[15] There certainly is no indication that the Glasgow students embraced more strictly Calvinist positions later in their student careers; indeed, one former fellow-student noted that they were 'far from satisfied' with the teaching they received after moving to New College.[16] From a recent standpoint, Kenneth Ross has argued that the Gibson case was highly significant, indicating the early roots of the 'new evangelicalism' that he considered to have developed rapidly within the Free Church.[17] This he defined as an intellectual movement away from orthodox Calvinism, marked by a new view of the Bible, a new apologetics, a new epistemology and a new emphasis on the person rather than the work of Christ.[18] This analysis is very helpful, recognising that the various 'revolutions' of the nineteenth-century church, identified in such classic works of church history as Cheyne's *The Transforming of the Kirk*,[19] were really facets of a single mass movement that, over a period of several decades, drastically changed the face of Scottish Presbyterianism. But the significance of the Gibson case was more easily seen in retrospect, and there is no reason to suppose that Kennedy, or any other observer, discerned the scale of the movement it presaged.

For all that Kennedy seems to have shared some of Anderson's concerns, and strongly sympathised with Gibson in the students' controversy, ultimately his expressed concern in *Days of the Fathers* was not with students or ministers, or even with theology, but rather with the whole spiritual tone of the young Free Church, including the Free Church in the Highlands. In the 'Preface to the First Edition', he was quite explicit that his narrative had a didactic purpose, in the face of perceived spiritual declension:

> I saw that the righteous fathers of Ross-shire were already being forgotten, and that a lifeless formality was taking the place of their godliness. I could not therefore refrain from an effort, such as I could make, to revive their memory, and to turn the eye of a backsliding generation to their good old ways.[20]

The Days of the Fathers was thus expressly written to stir up the contemporaneous generation of Highland evangelicals to emulate the best of their spiritual forefathers, amid circumstances of apparent spiritual coldness. The term 'formality' should not be misunderstood here as a call to a more relaxed and irregular approach to worship, but rather as a criticism of Christian living showing more apparent concern for outward conformity than for inward spiritual reality. Kennedy was emphatic that in the best days of the Highland evangelical church, the lives of professing Christians had been marked by this reality, and not only in the lives of a few, but in the experience of many. The beginning of this period of widespread spiritual vitality, Kennedy argued, was the extended period of religious revival from the 1730s onwards known as the Evangelical Revival:

> It was after the first quarter of the eighteenth century had passed, that the best days of Ross-shire began. [. . .] Before the middle of the century the great revival of religion began, which spread its blessed influence alike over Highlands and Lowlands [. . .] The Lord's right hand wrought wonders of grace in 'turning' many 'from darkness to light' [. . .] Attaining to a clear view of the foundation, object, and warrant of the 'hope set before them' in the Gospel, they grew up, under the skilful tuition of godly ministers, intelligent, exercised, and consistent Christians.[21]

Thus Kennedy contended that the best days of Highland evangelicalism had involved ministers who were both godly in their private lives and effective in proclaiming orthodox doctrine, gaining many individual conversions to evangelical Christianity, and above all, acknowledging the power of God in salvation. Kennedy proposed a notable communion season at Kiltearn in 1782 as the 'culminating point of the spiritual prosperity of Ross-shire', and reckoned that 'such days of power as were formerly experienced have never yet returned'.[22] He thus considered the Highland Church to have experienced an extended period of spiritual decline over the eight decades prior to the publication of *Days of the Fathers*, and did not look to the immediate future with much optimism: 'Days of richer blessing shall verily be given; but ere they shall come the present generation may have passed, under "the shame of barrenness," from the earth.'[23] The trends that he saw at work in the Highland Free Church of the mid-nineteenth century were not leading back to the spiritual prosperity he discerned in Ross-shire in the late eighteenth century.

Having laid out his thesis in the first chapter of *Days of the Fathers*, entitled 'The Gospel in Ross-shire', Kennedy went on to argue his case in three further substantial chapters, entitled 'The Ministers of Ross-shire', 'The Men of Ross-shire' and 'The Religion of Ross-shire'. Appended to the book was a biographical sketch of his late father, John Kennedy of Killearnan. The basic argument of *Days of the Fathers* was plain: the Highland Church had prospered when it prized real godliness: that is, outward and inward conformity to the standards of Christian living inculcated in the Bible itself. Where this godliness was valued and experienced, the visible blessing of God was enjoyed; where it was not known, the blessing was absent. Kennedy suggested that the people really respected only those ministers marked by such piety of conduct, and that it was this respect that gave their preaching such influence in their communities.

This said, Kennedy asserted that the preaching, especially of the most eminent ministers of Ross-shire, was marked by a number of qualities, which helped to make it effective in directing the course of the Highland Church of the eighteenth century. In particular, such preachers were 'self-denied', 'earnest', 'faithful', 'powerful' and 'discriminating';[24] his obvious implication was that such qualities were needed again. But Kennedy emphasised one particular point: the ability of such preachers to address the 'cases' of individual hearers – that is, their own individual spiritual needs – which, he argued, was rooted in such ministers' depth of Christian experience.[25] Thus the personal piety of such ministers bore fruit in the value of their preaching to their hearers. As Kennedy noted: 'Words marvellously seasonable have been often thus spoken, to account for which no prophetic gift should be ascribed to the preacher,' although he did acknowledge that there may sometimes be a more direct 'guidance of the speaker's mind'.[26] Other strengths Kennedy highlighted, which he considered general amongst the pre-eminent Ross-shire ministers of the past, included careful preparation for the pulpit, much prayer for souls and watchful pastoral care.[27]

Kennedy's history proceeded with a series of concise biographical vignettes, carefully selected from the ministers of Ross-shire of the previous two centuries. He mentioned first the seventeenth-century Covenanters Thomas Hog and John M'Killigan, both of whom suffered severe persecution for maintaining Presbyterian principles after the Restoration, emphasising especially the respect they commanded from their own congregations.[28] He then proceeded to discuss the eighteenth-century ministers James Fraser, John Porteous, Hector M'Phail, Charles Calder, Lachlan Mackenzie and his predecessors in Lochcarron, Alexander Macadam, Angus Mackintosh and William Forbes, and closed with a mention of John Macdonald of Ferintosh, who was Kennedy's co-Presbyter until his death in 1849.[29] As a historian, Kennedy did not use footnotes and therefore his sources are usually unknown. Most likely, he drew his information from the manuscript records available to him, such as Presbytery minutes, from published sources and from oral accounts. In the sketches, he continually emphasised the personal piety of the ministers described, and the blessing that resulted from their preaching ministries.

Although Kennedy was careful not to sound any overtly critical note regarding his colleagues in the contemporary Free Church ministry in the Highlands, his inference was plain that such ministry as had been known in the eighteenth century was badly needed in his own day. His argument implied an evident deterioration in the quality of the Highland ministry, both in piety and in spiritual power, over the preceding eighty years. This was made explicit in his closing of the chapter 'The Ministers of Ross-shire', with a couple of pointed Biblical quotations: 'The "fathers, where are they?" "Woe is me! For I am as when they have gathered the summer fruits, as the grape gleanings of the vintage; there is no cluster to eat: my soul desired the first-ripe fruit."'[30] The first quotation is from Zechariah 1: 5, and in context referred to judgment: the fathers had perished because of their lack of repentance. Kennedy was obviously not suggesting a close parallel, but rather that the generation he had described had largely passed away and had not been replaced in his own day. The second was a complete quotation of Micah 7: 1, referring in context, by means of the analogy of fruit desired after the harvest has already been gathered, to the lack of good men in the prophet's generation. In Kennedy's use of this verse to close the chapter, he clearly asserted that ministers of the calibre of those pre-eminent in eighteenth-century Ross-shire were hard to find in his day.

Kennedy's third chapter, 'The Men of Ross-shire', directly challenged the stereotype of the Men of the Highland Church propagated by their critics, as, in Kennedy's words, 'superstitious and bigoted persons, who see visions and who dream dreams, and who think that their own straitened circle encloses all the vital Christianity of the Earth'.[31] Indeed, Kennedy specifically mentioned two of the most famous published critiques of Highland evangelicalism, that of 'Investigator'[32] and the subsequent similar journal article,[33] which Kennedy characterised as Investigator finding 'a lawyer who would write his paean in the Quarterly'.[34] He defended the Men by carefully distinguishing them from the Separatists, pointing out that there were very few separatists in Ross-shire, which he attributed to a succession of ministers in most parishes who commanded general respect.[35]

Kennedy was keen to stress the positive role played by the Men in the religious history of Ross-shire and his account had the ring of personal testimony: 'Valuable was the help and cheering the encouragement which a godly minister always received from their prayers, their counsels and their labours.'[36] Kennedy defended the value of the Men's contributions at the fellowship meetings in the Highlands, drawn from their own spiritual experiences. He noted that such services helped in the identification of suitably qualified men for the eldership and in exposing professing men who lacked Christian experience.[37] Kennedy was emphatic that no charge could be laid against the orthodoxy of the Men or their capacity in defending their convictions. However, he went on to assert their moral purity in particular, seen in their evident love for each other, which he asserted as the root of their influence over the Highland Church.[38] Just like their ministers, the Men wielded influence through the respect that their lives commanded within their own communities. Kennedy went on to give sketches of six notable Men of Ross-shire, emphasising their holiness of life: John Munro, Alexander Ross, Hugh Ross, Donald Mitchell, John Clark and Roderick Mackenzie.[39] His conclusion to this chapter was particularly significant:

> The time was when, in a single parish, twenty could have been found any one of whom would, in our day, be ranked among 'the first three' whom the whole county can produce. 'The king's mowing' has long since taken away the rich produce of the best days of Ross-shire. 'The latter growth' is rapidly disappearing; and desolate will be its spiritual aspect, and dismal the prospects of its future, if 'the men' shall be utterly removed from the north. Verily it is high time to cry '*By* whom shall Jacob arise? For he is small.'[40]

The Biblical allusions of this passage are telling: 'the first three' is a quotation from 2 Samuel 23: 19, referring to the most powerful warriors in the army of King David, his 'mighty men'. Kennedy thus acknowledged deterioration in the quality of the Men over the preceding decades, such that even the lesser Men of the eighteenth century would be outstanding in his day. The other three quotations are all from Amos 7: 1–2, and referred in context to the Lord's judgment on Old Testament Israel and the prophet's consequent appeal to God for mercy on His people. Kennedy's history of the Highland Church was therefore not just one of decline in ministry, but of internal spiritual decline, framed as a judgment from God against His people.

The assertion of decline became explicit in the fourth and final chapter of *Days of the Fathers in Ross-shire*, 'The Religion of Ross-shire'. This gave an idealised picture of the Church functioning in the eighteenth-century Highlands. He described the congregation, led by a godly minister and elders, and including many 'truly converted' people; the ordinary Sabbath, with spiritual feeding in the sermon, fellowship, evening worship and family worship; the weekly pattern of prayer meetings, fellowship meetings, catechising and pastoral visitation; and the traditional Highland communion season.[41] This section of *Days of the Fathers* was not at all critical in perspective and, indeed, could be aptly characterised, as by one recent commentator, as 'a warm and sometimes sentimental look at a bygone age'.[42] But Kennedy's argument was not that the Highland Church was perfect in eighteenth-century Ross-shire – he acknowledged that his description certainly did not hold for parishes where 'there was no evangelical ministry', for example – but that, at its best, Highland Christianity had a spiritual reality that commanded general respect, 'so as to win the esteem of the whole body of the people'.[43]

Kennedy directly defended the distinctive characteristics of Highland Christianity from the charges of Lowland critics:

> The Ross-shire preaching, they say, was too experimental, and in the religion of those who were trained under it, there was, in consequence, a faulty excess of subjectiveness. To the radical peculiarity thus indicated, whether it be accounted a defect or an advantage, may be traced all the developments of the religious spirit in the Highlands that form its distinctive character, as compared with the Christianity of the Lowlands.[44]

Plainly, Kennedy concurred with the identification of the root cause of difference between the evangelicalism of the Highlands and of the Lowlands: namely, the experimental focus that the preaching and spirituality of the Highland Church had retained. By this term, Kennedy meant Christian teaching that emphasised the subjective experience of the believer, which he considered rather a positive strength. Thus, to the charge that Highland Christians were marked by gloominess, he asserted rather that they engaged in serious self-examination to find evidence of true conversion; to the charge of pride, he asserted that in fact they were harder in their judgment of themselves than of anyone else; to the charge of 'closetism', which suggested a tendency to hide away their Christian faith in private, he asserted that Highland Christians were indeed zealous, but in pursuit of raising 'a godly seed', rather than of outward works in society; to the charge of holding improper fellowship meetings, he asserted that these are, rather, an indicator of 'lively spiritual feelings'; and to a charge of an undue paucity of professions of faith, he asserted at length that the Bible laid down a different standard of admission to the Lord's Supper than to Baptism, as discussed in Chapter One.[45]

The whole force of *Days of the Fathers in Ross-shire* was therefore both polemical and controversial. This publication was not intended as nostalgic local history, but as a manifesto of what the Christian Church should be. Throughout, Kennedy argued that a rare purity and clarity of Christian practice had obtained in the Highland Church, in Ross-shire particularly, in the late eighteenth century. He acknowledged that both amongst the ministry and amongst the people, there had been an evident decline since these days, but he continued to defend the distinctive characteristics of Highland evangelicalism as those that should characterise the whole Christian Church, and thus as highly worthy of emulation. In points of detail, he explicitly refused to permit his vision to be framed in parochial terms, citing Continental practices and theologians in defence of the Highland Church.[46] His work explicitly contradicted the general Victorian – and, it must be said, Free Church – assumption that the Church was making progress, and advancing towards a much improved state of piety and theological understanding, and the equally implicit supposition that the Highland Church would and should over time adopt the characteristics already adopted in Lowland evangelicalism. The importance of these assertions can hardly be overstated: prior to Kennedy's book being published in 1861, there was little evidence of either of these positions appearing in print. Within a few years of this publication, the divide on ecclesiastical questions between the Highland and Lowland sections of the Free Church began to open, eventually finding institutional expression, in the decades following his death, in the Free Presbyterian Church from 1893 onwards and the continuing Free Church after 1900.

The publication of *Days of the Fathers* was therefore a significant moment, both in Kennedy's life and in the history of Highland evangelicalism. Kennedy does not seem to have had any difficulty in getting the book published, in this first case with John Maclaren of Edinburgh, though he would work with many different publishers over the years. It was quite normal for Free Church ministers to publish books and pamphlets, and their publications were mainstream commercial ventures, accepted on the presumption of reasonable prospects of sales and profitability, given the high public profile of ministers in Victorian Scotland. As late as 1870, religious books dominated British publishing, forming the largest number of new books published that year, while works of fiction were only the fifth largest group.[47] Whether Kennedy made much money from the royalties of his works is not recorded, but he had a high reputation for generosity to those in need during his lifetime and it may have been a consequence that his estate at death was only £677, a modest sum for a man of his social standing.[48]

The reception of *Days of the Fathers* was predictably mixed. Its polemical force could not be missed and invited a strong response from a variety of critics. Tellingly, Kennedy remarked in the 'Preface to the Second Edition' that he 'anticipated all the censure and none of the praise, bestowed upon' his book, adding that he 'would have been quite as much disappointed, if it did not displease a certain class of readers, as if none at all had been found to commend it'.[49] The mere fact that Kennedy's 'Preface to the Third Edition' was dated 'October 1861' indicated the significant sales of the volume achieved within just a few months of publication – obviously greatly exceeding the expectations of the publisher.[50] Furthermore, a 'Preface to the Fourth Edition' was dated 'December 1866',[51] while a 'New and Enlarged Edition' was printed posthumously in 1897, incorporating biographical sketches of Kennedy and his wife, and testifying to an enduring popular demand for copies of this book.

Initial press reviews of the book were exceedingly negative. *The Glasgow Herald* printed an intensely hostile, scathing response, describing the volume as 'one of the most ridiculous productions that ever came into our hands'. Its accounts of piety were 'unctuous', the Men were a 'bigoted, tyrannical and impudent set', and altogether the work was found to be 'a most unsavoury and unprofitable mess of cant, ignorance, superstition, and presumption'.[52] The *Athenaeum* was equally cutting, finding in the work 'a superabundant and too officious zeal', with 'not a trace' of 'the savour of charity'.[53] The *London Review* was only marginally more favourable: the reporter noted that Kennedy was 'not a very amiable author' of 'hereditary partiality', albeit acknowledging that his faults were 'those of a vigorous and earnest man'.[54] Indeed, it seems the most positive initial notice of *Days of the Fathers* in the press was the inclusion of the occasional humorous extract as part of the miscellaneous notices of the papers.[55] One reviewer, in *The Inverness Courier*, did find some matter for praise, but only alongside copious criticism:

> At least one chapter of it (on the 'Religion of Ross-shire') contains most suggestive theological matter, and is written with a degree of metaphysical acumen which could not be acquired without the patient exercise of strong reasoning faculties, and constant analysis of the mental and moral condition of others. But the rest of the volume exhibits such an amount of simple credulity, superstition, piety, and intolerance, that it is hard to believe the two sections of the work come from the same hand.[56]

The argument for inconsistency of quality was clarified as the review progressed: the reviewer concurred in Kennedy's argument in the chapter, which highlighted that there were significant differences in religious outlook and practice between Highland and Lowland Presbyterian evangelicalism, and valued his historical descriptions. However, the reviewer strongly and explicitly rejected the broader thesis of the whole work, that there was an observable decline in the Highland Church of the nineteenth century, arguing rather that the older spirituality was 'rapidly giving way under the influence of another, and, as we believe, a better state of things'.[57] In other words, he acknowledged the distinctive characteristics of the Highland Church, but disagreed entirely with Kennedy's assessment of their worth.

Another mixed review was published later in the year in the *Stirling Observer* after the printing of the second edition, acknowledging the book as 'a curious but deeply interesting volume, whose merits and defects are alike conspicuous and characteristic'. The writer found in the biographical sketches 'the stamp of true manhood and true Christianity'; however, he added rather sardonically that, for Kennedy, 'the Ross-shire type of Christianity is the very highest and noblest', an assertion that he thought was conveyed in a tone 'defiant and domineering, not to say bullying'. This said, the work was nonetheless 'an able, though, as the author confesses, one-sided apology for the piety of the North Highlands'.[58] However, a retrospective report from many years later described the reception of the book by the general public in much more positive terms:

[Kennedy's historical writings] particularly illustrate romantic events, coupled with solemn seriousness, which occurring in that country sent a thrill of religious feeling, and gave birth to an assumption and assertion of independency throughout Scotland, an independency which has ever since maintained itself, and which has grown and flourished with the lapse of time.[59]

The writer considered the book not only to have found an appreciative readership, but especially to have stimulated a greater independence and self-assertion in the Highland section of the Free Church, which had continued and strengthened over the subsequent decades.

Certainly, many members of the Highland Church were pleased with Kennedy's publication. Duncan Macgregor, writing in a later ministerial biography, concurred in Kennedy's description of the piety of the Ross-shire ministers: 'The power and blessing that attended their preaching are touchingly described in the "Days of the Fathers".'[60] Similarly, Kennedy's friend Gustavus Aird, minister of Creich Free Church, sharing his love for the stories preserved by the oral culture of the Highlands of the religious life of previous generations, supported the project and reportedly supplied Kennedy with information for *Days of the Fathers*.[61] The additional fruits of Aird's own research into the Ross-shire Church of a previous generation were eventually published, in emulation of *Days of the Fathers*, albeit posthumously, under the name of a colleague who outlived him.[62] Furthermore, Kennedy's book was a more immediate template for others: his colleague Alexander Auld, minister of Olrig Free Church, published in 1869 a similar work, on the recent religious history of Caithness. Auld's Introduction showed the influence of his brother-minister, stating that in parts of the Highlands in the eighteenth century, 'Vital godliness then flourished as never before or since. Those "Days of the Fathers in Ross-shire" have passed away; but for our church and for our land, it is well that a "Son" has perpetuated the fragrance of their memory.'[63] The reference to Kennedy's recent publication was plain. Indeed, Kennedy's influence in stimulating the collection and publication of material on local church history continued. He oversaw the publication in 1868 of a volume of notable Gaelic sermons preserved by oral tradition, and wished that some of the addresses of the Men at question meetings could be published as well.[64] The simple comment in the preface to his published *Sermons* was apposite: 'Dr Kennedy's little book, "The Days of the Fathers in Ross-shire," unveils his heart, and shows the tradition in which he had been trained.'[65]

However, not all adherents of Highland evangelicalism welcomed Kennedy's work. One strong critic was the redoubtable Norman Macleod, now in advanced old age and ministering in New Zealand, who had led a separatist movement, while Kennedy's father was an assistant to the parish minister in Assynt, as described in *Days of the Fathers*.[66] Norman published a pamphlet in New Zealand, criticising Kennedy for associating his father with the likes of Thomas Hog, for claiming special revelation for some of the subjects of his sketches, for failing to criticise his father for having continued in communion with the 'drunkard' minister of Assynt, for treating seriously the religious profession of some he considered hypocrites, and for his uncritical treatment of Ross-shire in general, which he considered 'ridiculously proverbial for fruitfulness of invention'. The pamphlet closed with a short and contemptuous poem rejecting the work as 'lies' and its author as a 'profane and wretched son', who 'know[s] not God'.[67] However, as Norman had in previous writings been highly critical of notable Highland ministers, including John Macdonald of Ferintosh and Archibald Cook, such that John Macleod thought the tone of his response here to Kennedy showed that he had actually 'somewhat mellowed', it is unlikely that Kennedy gave much weight to his criticism.[68]

A much more important and balanced response came in a journal article by the noted Victorian lawyer Alexander Taylor Innes,[69] himself originally a native of Tain, and a member of the Free Church of Scotland. Innes, though he shared Kennedy's background in Highland evangelicalism and had originally intended entering the Free Church ministry, had eventually taken a different course in life, abandoning the study of theology for that of law, due to his openly admitted reservations regarding full subscription to the *Confession of Faith*. He was very plainly a convert from strictly orthodox Highland Presbyterianism to the broader evangelicalism – Lowland, urban and theologically more liberal – he found in Edinburgh.[70] He acknowledged *Days of the Fathers* as 'an able and powerful book', and acknowledged Kennedy and Auld as 'advocates and apologists' for Highland evangelicalism.[71] Though Innes plainly disagreed with Kennedy's attempt to distinguish between the Separatists and the generality of the Men, arguing that they shared the 'same spirit',[72] his overall assessment was markedly positive. He summed up his position: 'Highland religion was in its day a very powerful manifestation of Christianity – an intense and vivid illustration of vital piety,' though it may have become 'traditionary' in later years.[73] At root, he considered it a product of Puritan doctrine combined with the so-called 'Celtic temperament', and thus found both positive and negative characteristics to observe. Highland evangelicalism, or 'Highlandism', he found to be highly doctrinal and orthodox in teaching, strong on self-examination and giving great emphasis to preaching. However, he warned of a subjectivism that focused too much on individual experiences, including those of a mystical nature, rather than on practical Christian living, which could lead to inaction and undue melancholy. Interestingly, he concurred with Kennedy in acknowledging a decline in the Highland Church in recent decades, as the impetus of religious revival declined.[74] Therefore, the vital criticism of Innes's review was not directed against Kennedy's book as a broadly accurate historical account, but rather against the religious attitude it commended, most particularly with regard to mystical experiences.

It was a later generation of critics who directly challenged Kennedy's historical account of Highland evangelicalism. Keith Leask, for example, in his 1905 biography of Kennedy's contemporary colleague Thomas M'Lauchlan, minister of the Gaelic Free Church in Edinburgh, St Columba's, entirely rejected Kennedy's approach. He suggested that the status of the 'Fathers' reflected rather the religious poverty of the eighteenth-century Highlands, that they were elevated by idealism, and thus that the accounts by Kennedy and others served chiefly to undermine present-day Christians.[75] His implication was plainly that, in fact, the state of Christianity in the Highlands had been steadily improving under more modern influences. This same view was stated more boldly by Kennedy's former ministerial colleague Kenneth Macdonald, Free Church minister at Applecross, in his *Social and Religious Life in the Highlands*, published in 1902. He observed a tendency in the Highlanders over previous centuries to harbour zeal for the religion of a bygone day, and especially discerned from the early 1860s onwards 'croaking voices [that] were to be heard deploring the backsliding of the age'.[76] Kennedy, in particular, he thought very guilty of such living in the past, and of a consequent pessimism regarding the present religious situation. Macdonald himself argued that the advancing progress of education in the Highlands and the benefits of the modern age would yield a great improvement in the religious culture of the North.[77] Plainly, the attitudes of Leask and Macdonald were diametrically opposed to that of Kennedy. The differences in their account of nineteenth-century Highland church history can be adequately registered only in their differing view of what constituted improvement in evangelical piety and practice. For the former, improvement meant closer conformity to the development of modern liberal evangelicalism in the Lowlands, while for the latter, improvement meant a return to the distinctive characteristics of evangelical Presbyterianism, especially as seen in eighteenth-century Ross-shire.

Modern critics have generally read *Days of the Fathers* as what it undoubtedly is and confesses itself to be: a work of partisan church history, whereby the account of church developments is marshalled to serve a purpose. This is not to diminish the worth of the volume as a vital repository of local, albeit uncritical, church history, but rather to define accurately the purpose for which it was written. David Paton, for example, called the book 'in essence a sermon as much as a history', in which 'free use is made of drama and emotion to support and emphasise the inner truth'. But equally, he acknowledged the lasting importance of Kennedy's contribution as a local historian, pointing out that 'even now [*Days of the Fathers*] dominates discussion of The Men and the nature of Highland religion'.[78] Similarly, Douglas Ansdell noted that the early nineteenth century was seen 'as a golden age of evangelicalism' in the Highlands, and that those who appreciated this history desired it to live on in written accounts. However, he also recognised the polemical purpose of such accounts: 'In this view of history the participants were regarded as exemplary characters and the principles pursued were to serve as a standard for future generations and to encourage greater piety.'[79] Although Ansdell did not mention *Days of the Fathers* specifically in this context, his observations are an accurate summary of Kennedy's stated purpose for his own history of the Church in Ross-shire. Furthermore, the significance of *Days of the Fathers* is demonstrated by the fact that its publication preceded that of all the works that he did mention: *Disruption Worthies of the Highlands* (1877); *The Men of the Lews* (1924); *The Men of Skye* (1902); and *Ministers and Men of the Far North* (1869).[80] In his deeply appreciative account of the Highland Church of the past, Kennedy laid the template that many later writers would follow.

Donald Meek echoed this point in his thoughtful and balanced discussion of Kennedy's book, noting the tendency in a multitude of late nineteenth- and twentieth-century works of local church history to what he calls 'image-making', the propagation of an idealised view of historic Highland evangelicalism:

> Much of this image, which has achieved the status of an indelible stereotype – was created in the nineteenth century, chiefly in the second half, and twentieth century writings have been but a poor shadow of this. The archetype of such image-making is John Kennedy's volume, *Days of the Fathers in Ross-shire*.[81]

Meek acknowledged that, as history, *Days of the Fathers* was 'rather romantic and uncritical', and that its tendency to 'pious evangelical biography' bore comparison to the medieval tradition of hagiography. However, it was principally a polemical work, and thus both a product and a defence of a conservative Highland religious culture, demonstrating that 'cultural distinctiveness and religious conservatism went together in the Highlands'.[82] Its success as the 'archetype' for many other works, to use Meek's term, indicated how compellingly Kennedy articulated his vision of the past glories of the Highland Church.

More important than the many works that Kennedy's book fathered in the succeeding decades, however, were the attitudes it engendered, especially amongst readers in the Highlands. Allan MacColl suggested that the immediate purpose of the volume was very positive, that 'Kennedy was deliberately evoking the "days of the fathers" in order to preserve and recapture the spiritual energy which had once conquered Gaelic society', within a context of consolidation rather than growth in the Highland Free Church. In historical terms, Kennedy's writing was part of the growing alienation between the Highland and Lowland sections of the Free Church.[83] On this point, James Lachlan MacLeod was correct when he pointed out the 'Highland attitude' that helped to lead to the division of 1893:

> The Highlanders themselves were well aware of the distinction between 'the religion of the Highlands' and that south of the Grampians, and were not afraid to talk about it. There is ample evidence to suggest that

the Highlanders looked askance at the religion of the Lowland Free Church, considering themselves in many respects to be a separate and indeed superior denomination.[84]

Although he overstated the case slightly, as in this context 'Highlanders' referred only to conservative Highland evangelicals, MacLeod accurately described the attitude of those who formed the Free Presbyterian Church in 1893. This attitude echoed the argument of *Days of the Fathers*, and showed that the position that Kennedy espoused in his volume of church history in 1861 had become widespread across the Highlands, sufficiently to be considered a factor in a major church division by 1893, and an even greater one in 1900. The question that stands is whether this stance in the Highland Church preceded the publication of *Days of the Fathers* in 1861, or whether it rather resulted – at least to some degree – from Kennedy's book. The fact that Kenneth Macdonald dated the emergence in the Highlands of a deeply pessimistic view of the present-day Free Church in comparison with the piety of an earlier day – such a view as Kennedy's writing would foster – to 'the early 1860s'[85] may be highly significant, given the publication of *Days of the Fathers* early in 1861.

It is enlightening to compare Kennedy's book with prior publications on the church history of the Highlands. Angus Macgillivray certainly saw his own *Sketches of Religion & Revivals of Religion in the Highlands in the Last Century*, published just two years prior to Kennedy's volume, as an archetype, picturing in the preface his account as a mine opened and ready now for others to work it. Yet his approach differed starkly from that of Kennedy and from the writers who followed in Kennedy's footsteps. He emphasised the external influences that helped to bring the evangelical gospel to the Highlands, such as the return of soldiers to Ross-shire who had fought with the Swedish army in the Thirty Years War in the seventeenth century, while Kennedy's account exclusively focused on the work of the indigenous Presbyterian ministers. Macgillivray's tone in describing Highland religion was cautious and defensive, acknowledging some faults, especially of pride, and too much subjectivism, but arguing that such attitudes were comparable with those found in the popular religious writers John Bunyan and Jonathan Edwards. Unlike Kennedy, he did not emphasise or commend the Highland divergence from the evangelicalism of the Lowland Church, nor did he contend for any superiority in the Highland tradition. Only in one respect was his conclusion identical to Kennedy's: he asserted that 'Old Religion [was] to a large extent gone in the Northern Highlands,' that the contemporary Men were not of the same quality as in a past day, and that the consequent present need was for revival.[86] Macgillivray's book, in contrast to Kennedy's writings, has been largely forgotten.

John Mackay, in an 1856 biography of a noted Highland minister, John Macdonald of Helmsdale, demonstrated the same divergence from Kennedy's line of argument. He wrote of the qualities of the Men, while acknowledging faults in their tendency to a subjective emphasis, and to allegorising in interpreting Scripture. He also thought the name had been applied to some who were not worthy of it.[87] Furthermore, Macdonald himself, a Highland minister of the Disruption generation, plainly saw himself as part of a national movement of evangelicalism. In argumentation against the dissenters, as quoted in the biography, Macdonald himself cited the great past leaders of Established Church evangelicalism, 'Boston, Colquhoun, Love (Glasgow), Kidd (Aberdeen)', and then went on to cite the leaders of the Free Church movement: 'We have now a Chalmers, a Cunningham, a Candlish, a Gordon, a Guthrie, a Buchanan and others.'[88] The names cited are those of Lowland Church leaders, and plainly Macdonald saw himself at one with these men. There was no suggestion of meaningful divergence in the evangelicalism of the Highlands, and certainly not of superiority. These same attitudes, of caution and some criticism with regard to the Men, and of general identification with a national movement of evangelicalism, rather than with a Highland faction, were also reflected in the most famous Highland clerical memoir of the late nineteenth century, the *Memorabilia Domestica* of Donald Sage.[89] Although not published until 1889, twenty years after Sage's death, the memoir was apparently written in his younger years, the Preface being dated '25th May, 1840'.[90] Although it is not definitive evidence, as the finished text cannot be proven to predate Kennedy's work, on these points Sage's writing certainly reflected the characteristics of Highland church history prior to Kennedy.

A similar picture was painted in another clerical biography from the Highland, published in 1822s: that of Kennedy's noted predecessor Alexander Stewart, a famous evangelical minister of the pre-Disruption era, who pastored the Established Church in Dingwall from 1805 to 1820. Stewart's evangelical conversion was attributed largely to influences from outside the Highlands, and indeed from outside Scotland, particularly the visit of the Anglican minister Charles Simeon of Cambridge, and the writings of the English divines John Newton and Thomas Scott.[91] The *Memoirs* did note a high standard of spiritual life in the Highlands in the period in question, but this was counter-balanced by Stewart's own negative assessment of the state of religion in his own congregation in Dingwall and of the value of his own ministry there.[92] The account certainly does not suggest that the evangelicalism of the Highlands was signally different from that of England, nor superior in quality.

Perhaps most significant of all, because it is one of the earliest printed sources giving a detail account of Highland evangelicalism, is the anonymous *Account of the Present State of Religion Throughout the Highlands of Scotland*, published in 1827.[93] This is interesting because the tension that the author, 'Lay Member', identified in Scotland at this early stage was not a conflict between Highland and Lowland evangelicalism, but rather between evangelicalism and moderatism. This division did have a geographical fault line, but the author located it within the Highlands, between the East, with its more generally evangelical ministry, and the West, where the parish ministers were largely moderates. 'Lay Member' cited a speech to the 1824 General Assembly by the presumably moderate Rev. Norman Macleod of Campbeltown, who asserted that the western ministers were as earnest as those of Ross-shire, a claim challenged by the author of the *Account*. On the contrary, the 'Lay Member' pointed to the evidence of a lack of active support for Missions, Bible Societies and Education Societies from the ministers in the West, and characterised them as 'hostile to conscience and piety'.[94] In Easter Ross, he asserted, 'experimental religion is much attended to', whereas Argyllshire was characterised by ignorance and indifference to Christianity. He pointed to the recent change in the state of religion on Skye, from 1805 onwards, as proof of the improvement that could be effected by a sounder ministry.[95] Throughout, there was no suggestion of a meaningful difference between convinced evangelicals in the South and those in the North; the only difference was in the extent of the evangelical instruction of the population, albeit that this had so advanced in Easter Ross as to make its inhabitants 'singular and different from those of almost every spot in Britain' in discerning the quality of ministers.[96] In contrast to Kennedy's later writings, the 'Lay Member' saw evangelicals in the Lowlands and Highlands as natural allies. In a telling remark, he advised that 'those Christians in the low country or in England who wish to forward the cause of vital Christianity in the Highlands, may have an opportunity of doing so, by giving pecuniary aid', especially to support the Gaelic schools.[97] The divergence in tone from Kennedy and his successors was quite evident.

Undoubtedly, there was a marked change in the character of Highland evangelicalism during the second half of the nineteenth century, as the northern section of the Free Church became more overtly distinct, and more confident in this distinction. The Highland Church became simultaneously more assured that a valuable tradition was being preserved in their midst and that it was being lost elsewhere in the evangelical church. The question as to what extent this sea change in Highland attitudes towards Lowland and English evangelicalism was the product of Kennedy's historical writings may not be open to a decisive answer, but plainly Kennedy both bolstered such a view by his own authority, and supplied plenty of ammunition for those who wished to argue this case in the future. His book, *Days of the Fathers in Ross-shire*, far more than other works such as Macgillivray's *Sketches of Religion*, set the tone for future studies of Highland evangelicalism, and elevated what may before have seemed minor divergences in practice into vital points of principle. Its publication in 1861 marked a vital point of development in the history of Highland evangelicalism, after which it departed increasingly in its trajectory from the religious culture of the Lowlands and became a cohesive and confident force in internal Free Church controversies. Both in terms of texts and in terms of attitudes, Kennedy's historical writing heralded a sharp divergence in the course of evangelical Presbyterianism between North and South that would only increase in the decades ahead.

Kennedy the Biographer

As a historian, Kennedy's methodology was largely biographical. In its narrative, his one full-length historical work, *The Days of the Fathers in Ross-shire*, relied heavily on biographical sketches of notable ministers and Men, and indeed of some women, woven into a broader narrative. The work also included, as a lengthy appendix, a biographical account of Kennedy's father, John Kennedy of Killearnan.[98] These individual subjects were taken to epitomise the general character and development of Highland evangelical life. Following this initial publication, Kennedy became yet more focused on biography: his second full-length publication, *The Apostle of the North*, was a life of John Macdonald, the famous minister of Ferintosh; and he also contributed biographical sketches of fellow-ministers to the *Disruption Worthies of the Highlands* collection and to the Free Church *Monthly Record*.[99] The accounts of individual lives therefore formed a vital and influential portion of his published writings, as even his contemporaries observed. Discussing *Days of the Fathers* and other similar works, for example, Taylor Innes identified the element of 'hagiology' present. Indeed, he suggested that the reverential attitude towards individuals he observed was one of the distinctive features of Highland evangelicalism, which he saw as rooted in 'an attraction to powerful persons' characteristic of the 'Celtic race'.[100] But present-day critics recognise the consistency of this feature of Kennedy's work as well. For example, Donald Meek characterised his work as follows:

> Kennedy [...] provides a picture of the 'good old days' in Ross-shire – a region filled with solemn ministers, men and the occasional woman, who are intensely spiritual beings, with their minds firmly set on heavenly things, and spurning the things of the earth. The work is rather romantic and uncritical, a point illustrated by the portrayal of Kennedy's own father. This is a prime example of evangelical hagiography; Kennedy is doing for the ministers of Ross-shire what hagiographers did for the saints in the Middle Ages.[101]

The charge of hagiography is an interesting one, and in some respects must stand. In idealising his subjects, Kennedy's biographical practices were fairly standard for the nineteenth century, when Victorian biographers notoriously saw their role as ensuring for posterity the favourable reputation of the subject, with the biographer constrained to avoid or suppress information potentially damaging to the subject's character.[102] As Hermione Lee commented:

> The impulses of sympathy and veneration that dominated much 19th-century biography often solidified into hagiography. Though many

different kinds of Lives were being written between the 1830s and the 1890s, the period has come to be retrospectively caricatured for whitewashing and censorship. The hallmarks of Victorian biography [...] were morality and reticence.[103]

As a Victorian biographer, Kennedy sought to promote the reputation of his subjects; but, equally, he plainly wrote with a polemical purpose, setting out an ideal of what individual Christian and ecclesiastical community life should be. The point is not that his sketches in *Days of the Fathers* were drastically inaccurate, but rather that the subjects and narratives – and the specific details given – were carefully selected to bolster his account of the Presbyterian heritage of Ross-shire. In other words, his subjects were examples, whom his readers were urged to value as forebears and to emulate in practice. Of course, this is not strictly identical to medieval Catholic hagiography: Kennedy's subjects were not presented as objects of actual veneration, nor as proper recipients of the prayers of the living. But they were idealised, stripped of faults by a narrative that left only a record of their qualities and worth.

In the case of 'The Minister of Killearnan', this careful sanitising of the life, removing all traces of vanity, folly and hubris, was plainly a deliberate achievement, the work of a son determined to set forth his father as an exemplary minister. Inevitably, the result was adequate as a basic account but painfully lacking in the ordinary texture of human life. Thus, in his son's account, Kennedy the elder was found making it his habit to 'retire to some secret place to pray' from the age of three onwards, while no more usual childhood recreation reached the printed page.[104] As a young man, he was found on a deer-stalking expedition, but after a providential escape from an accidental shot, 'laid [his gun] aside, never to use it again'.[105] Instead, it was as a preacher that Kennedy exerted his energies and the account rapidly moved on to the blessed effects of his early ministry: two sisters converted in Lochbroom; a notable woman, Margaret M'Diarmid, in Eriboll; and several young men in Assynt.[106] The influence and success of his ministry were evident, especially after his translation to Killearnan,[107] but the most remarkable thing about this account is how little actual insight it gave into the character of the elder Kennedy himself. The following passage is as close as the narrative reached to any real analysis of its subject:

> Both outwardly and spiritually, his was a life of unusual happiness. Death had never visited his family till sent to summon himself to his home. The partner of his temporal lot was one who, by her watchfulness and wisdom, preserved him from many an annoyance that might have fretted his spirit and interfered with his work. His home life was indeed a holy life. Few ever spent more time in secret prayer, or more fully evinced that on communion with the Lord their happiness mainly depended. In anything connected with his temporal lot,

beyond its bearing on his work, and on the welfare of his family, he took no interest whatever.[108]

The force of the charge of hagiography against such an account should be sufficiently plain. Kennedy the elder was presented as both deeply pious and thoroughly unworldly. Beyond this, his personality remained a blank canvas: not a single defect of conduct was acknowledged; not a single peculiarity of character was identified. As presented in this account, he was an almost featureless ideal.

Having given the assessment above, the author turned entirely from his subject to discussing the congregation in Killearnan, the notable visitors who worshipped with them from other parishes, and the communion seasons.[109] Kennedy directly considered his father again only in describing his latter days and death, particularly mentioning his strong opposition to Catholic Emancipation, support for the evangelical party in the Ten Years Conflict, and negative assessment of the apparent revival movements of the late 1830s.[110] His death was recounted in sentimental, sanitised terms:

> Remaining in bed, he seemed lost in contemplation, an expression of placid joy resting on his countenance [. . . He] meekly submitted to the prescribed treatment, but the disease was quietly, though surely, making progress, and on Sabbath evening he fell asleep in Jesus.[111]

The gulf between this account and the ugly reality of fatal illness and death in an age without analgesics, doctors available on call or professional nursing care is perfectly obvious. This idealised depiction of death was typical of Victorian biography, as Pat Jalland has demonstrated,[112] but the account was still not creditable for honesty. This was biography from which everything unpleasant and unworthy had carefully been pruned; in many ways, it summed up the wider problem with Kennedy as a biographer. As Meek commented, 'Kennedy produced a romantic picture of evangelical idealism in eighteenth century Ross-shire,'[113] and this idealism was presented through the medium of biography, in the accounts of individual lives.

Furthermore, as mentioned above, Kennedy produced some individual biographical sketches of fellow-ministers. He wrote a kindly and affectionate obituary notice for Rev. William Macdonald, the otherwise obscure Free Church minister of Ballachulish, emphasising his diligent labours in a demanding charge. He described his subject's early death in typically warm, sentimental terms:

> His last words on the Saturday evening on which he died were, 'I am tired. Is it Sabbath?' The rest for which he pined his longing spirit found that night in heaven, and his worn and wearied body found it in the sleep of death.[114]

He also contributed two suitably adulatory chapters to the ornate memorial collection *Disruption Worthies of the Highlands*, sketches of the Free Church ministers Donald Sage and Mackintosh Mackay. Needless to say, with the text of each page surrounded by stylised interwoven thistles, with a burning bush at the top and a Covenanter banner at the bottom, these productions were idealised personal tributes, rather than anything approaching critical biography. Of Sage, he remarked on the quality of his sermons, adding, 'Few preachers have ever laboured more to exalt their theme and to abase themselves.'[115] Mackay he described powerfully addressing the 1849 Free Church General Assembly, of which he was Moderator and Kennedy a commissioner, on the needs of the Highlands: 'To a coterie of admiring Celts it gave no small joy to see some fussy prattling Southrons cower beneath the torrent poured forth upon them by the Highland chief.'[116] This passage, in its martial imagery and sharply drawn distinction between Highlanders and Lowlanders, was very typical of Kennedy. Mackay was praised highly, with particular regard to the quality of his preaching.[117] At the time of his death, Kennedy was still reportedly engaged in biographical work, preparing an account of his friend David Campbell, late minister of Tarbat Free Church.[118]

But it was in his second book, *The Apostle of the North*, that Kennedy undertook his most substantial biographical study, that of his friend and elder colleague in the ministry of the Free Church, John Macdonald of Ferintosh. Here, as the very title of the book suggested, Kennedy's interest was plainly and primarily the ideal of Christian piety in a Highland context, which he found in the life and ministry of his subject; thus the narrative was carefully selected and structured to convey this ideal. He first depicted the piety of Macdonald's father, the eminent catechist James Macdonald of Reay, whose character he described in glowing terms, as a father who set a vital example of spirituality for his son.[119] John Macdonald himself was set forth in Kennedy's account as an idealised Christian and minister from his young manhood. He experienced even in childhood conviction of his own sins, leading him to engage seriously in prayer even as a young boy, and as a young student to relinquish such levities as playing the bagpipes.[120] However, he had still to go through a full evangelical conversion: he so despaired of his sins as one day to contemplate suicide, walking towards the waves beating on the shore, only to find sudden and precious comfort in the thought of Christ as Saviour. As Kennedy wrote:

> Rushing at once from the danger which he had rashly provoked, and climbing up into a quiet cave in the rock hard by, he was there and then enabled to commit his soul to Christ. He went to the shore that day in the grasp of the destroyer; he returned from it in the arms of the Saviour.[121]

Kennedy's dramatic choice of words underlined the importance of this change to his narrative: as an evangelical convert, Macdonald would now live a whole new life, of service to God rather than to self.

Kennedy's narrative acknowledged that Macdonald's early efforts at preaching were not a great success, and that his hasty marriage, in 1806, was probably not a wise step at such an early and financially limited stage in life.[122] Interestingly, Kennedy's original draft text regarding the marriage was longer, acknowledged that 'in love' the step was taken and included the observation, 'Miss Ross of Gladfield proved to be an amiable wife, and his marriage was no drag on the progress of his work.'[123] The elimination of this matter, such that the published text does not even record Macdonald's first wife's name, indicated how little interest Kennedy had in the human details of his subject's life, especially those that were not useful in promoting his evangelical ideal. After brief service as a missionary in Berriedale, Macdonald was inducted to the Gaelic Chapel, Edinburgh, in 1807, where he began to acquire real eminence as a preacher to the Highlanders resident in that city, and further afield. Kennedy hinted at controversy and 'lines of section' in the Edinburgh congregation when Macdonald became its minister, but in fact his draft text noted direct opposition to Macdonald's induction, such that a separate congregation was formed in Edinburgh for a time.[124] Tellingly, this information was entirely omitted from the published work. Kennedy emphasised that Macdonald's preaching changed and markedly improved during this period, as he experienced what Kennedy calls 'a fresh baptism of the Spirit', but was at pains to assert that at all stages of his ministry he preached the gospel fully.[125] A lengthy section in the draft from the end of this chapter, describing Macdonald's regular pastoral visitation during the 'conflict portion of his ministry in Edinburgh', and the birth of the three children of his first marriage, was entirely omitted in the published book, again underlining Kennedy's desire to avoid recounting controversy and lack of interest in his subject's family life.[126]

In 1813, Macdonald was translated to the parish of Urquhart, in the Black Isle, where he ministered for the rest of his life, albeit latterly in the Free Church, in a congregation strategically situated to allow him to exercise his peripatetic evangelistic ministry far and wide. At this stage of Kennedy's narrative, his presentation of his subject as an ideal minister became blatant, exemplified in the following paragraph:

> He early acquired the habit of careful preparation for the pulpit. He laboured to apprehend his subject with definiteness, and to state his views with precision. His love of system moved him always to attempt an exact arrangement of his ideas. His acquaintance with the scheme of gospel truth enabled him to allocate its proper place to every doctrine which he handled. His power of illustration was sufficient to make his sermons interesting and clear. Always textual, he avoided the sameness which monotonizes their effusions, who discourse of a subject instead of expounding a text.[127]

While this paragraph was probably a largely accurate portrait of Macdonald, a preacher of high repute in his day, it nonetheless had less the ring of a critical biography, and more that of a homiletics textbook about it: the plain import of Kennedy's words, at least for ministerial readers, was 'Go thou, and do likewise.' The account that followed of the effects of his early ministry in Urquhart, especially in many apparent conversions,[128] bolstered the commendation of this character and quality of preaching. The value and accuracy of the account are not in question, but plainly Kennedy's account served a hortatory as well as biographical purpose.

This idealisation became plainer still in recounting Macdonald's wider missionary work, such as his memorable visit to the remote island of St Kilda in 1822, where he preached a series of sermons to the neglected islanders, who were, at that stage, without a regular Christian ministry.[129] Kennedy also recounted Macdonald's preaching tour in Gaelic-speaking parts of Ireland, his occasional sermons in London and his return visits to St Kilda, in addition to his regular preaching tours across the Highlands. As Kennedy commented, in typically idealistic terms, 'He preached upwards of ten thousand times during the last thirty-six years of his life; and never delivered an unstudied discourse.'[130] He praised Macdonald in his rigorously organised daytime routine, in his care of his family, in his mental abilities, in his depth of Christian experience and in his character, which combined humility and cheerfulness.[131] But he avoided obvious points of criticism: for example, Macdonald plainly could not have been the most devoted of pastors, as the sheer extent of his evangelistic labours must have been accomplished at some cost to his own local congregation, not to mention to his wife and family. Kennedy refused to mar the idealised portrait of Christian ministry he had produced, even where criticism was probably due; but, tellingly, his chief praise of Macdonald was as a preacher and as a theologian, rather than as a local parish minister.[132]

Where Kennedy did offer criticism, it was brief and incidental: 'Amiable though he was, and prone to too great facility, he could, when occasion required, hold his ground very firmly, and rise superior to all the influence which might be employed to sway him.'[133] This firmness he demonstrated by describing Macdonald's leaving a stately home late in the evening rather than remain where family worship was not permitted, but what Kennedy meant by his former hinted criticism of 'facility' was not explicitly clarified – presumably he meant the word in its sense of 'ready compliance', indicating Macdonald's willingness to associate in broader evangelical circles than Kennedy would approve.[134] He apparently disagreed with his subject's view of the apparent revival movement of the late 1830s, noting that while Macdonald 'was always sanguine of good results from such a movement as then waved over the land; [. . .] it cannot be said that his expectations were realized. Good was done, and abiding fruit remained; but many a bud of promise withered quite away'.[135] It is not at all clear that Macdonald would have agreed with this assessment; and certainly other participants in the movement of these years, such as the notable evangelical Horatius Bonar, remained highly positive about the effects of the movement even many years afterwards.[136] It is also interesting to see from the journal extracts included how comfortable Macdonald felt in English evangelical circles, staying, for example, with a family in Nottingham and preaching in dissenting meeting houses there.[137] It is hard to imagine Kennedy, with his rhetoric against 'Southrons', feeling equally comfortable about ministering in such broad evangelical company, notwithstanding his friendship with the conservative Baptist pastor C. H. Spurgeon.

The published reviews of *The Apostle of the North* were mixed at best, especially from critics directly opposed to the evangelical principles shared by Kennedy and Macdonald. *The Glasgow Herald* printed a hostile notice, entitled 'The Apostle of the North and his Dingwall disciple', dismissing Macdonald himself as a subject of whom 'no-one South of the Grampians has heard'. However, the reviewer reserved his strongest fire for Kennedy himself, arguing that Macdonald's friends should not 'have permitted "his life and labours" to be handled or mangled by this unique, this extraordinary and this incomprehensible Dingwall divine'.[138] The review in *The Scotsman* was a little more favourable, describing it as a 'curious and interesting work [...] lively, graphic, and abounding in anecdote'. Furthermore, the reviewer acknowledged that Macdonald was well known in the Highlands, and that Kennedy had not invented the appellation recorded in the title of the work. He gave a summary of the contents of the work, albeit interspersed with sardonic comments that suggested he was not greatly in sympathy with the evangelical creed of the subject, but concluding finally that the book was 'well worthy [of] a discriminating perusal'.[139] A fairly positive review in the *Inverness Courier* welcomed the biography, recognising Macdonald's stature as a preacher and evangelist in the Highlands and giving copious extracts from the text. The reviewer did note that Kennedy as a biographer 'appears to be too credulous' and doubted that many of his anecdotes would 'stand close examination'. Beyond the general remark that the author 'should re-consider some parts' for the second edition, the reviewer's assessment of the 'handsome little volume' was broadly commendatory.[140]

However, some commentators, even those sympathetic to Macdonald, considered that the divergence between Kennedy and his subject was greater than was immediately apparent, and hinted that his biographer had appropriated 'the Apostle of the North' as a subject in favour of his own agenda. For example, the writer identified only as 'A Highlander', who published a rather bitter reply to a pamphlet by Kennedy on the Disestablishment controversy, praised Macdonald warmly for the 'large and blessed results' that resulted from his ministry, but complained that Kennedy had written in his biography 'so miserable a caricature' of the older minister's 'life and labours'.[141] Patrick Carnegie Simpson, in his biography of Kennedy's colleague Robert Rainy, argued that Highland evangelicalism had noticeably changed during the second half of the nineteenth century. He asserted that the Highland section of the Free Church became increasingly hardened and dogmatic in its opposition to ecclesiastical and theological developments in the South, and that this was an unnatural transformation: 'The genuine Highland nature [. . .] found its truer expression in the warm evangelicalism of men like Dr Macdonald of Ferintosh, "the Apostle of the North," and others, before this blight arose.' The blight had come from 'those [ministers] who hardened the people in an irreconcilable hostility and fanaticised them against the south doctrinally as well as ecclesiastically'.[142] The reference to Kennedy is not explicit, but it is plain that he is the primary target here, as is underlined by the inclusion of the phrase he used as the title of his book. Simpson believed that Kennedy and allied ministers had led the Highland section of the Free Church into this increasingly reactionary position, ultimately under the power of an external influence, that of James Begg, who was always Simpson's *bête noire*.[143]

Perhaps most telling of all was the response from one of Macdonald's sons, Duncan, who publicly criticised the biography in extraordinarily sharp terms in a letter to the *Inverness Courier*:

> Whilst I most warmly thank the reviewer for his kind observations respecting my father, I cannot condemn the book itself too strongly. It is precisely what I had expected from the author of 'The Days of the Fathers in Ross-shire'. It smacks strongly of superstition and of whining mock-piety. It is disfigured, too, by blotches of bad taste and arrant bigotry. It is, in fact, nothing short of an attempt to expose to ridicule a departed champion of true religion, and to blacken the memory of one of the most charitable of men.[144]

He went on to suggest that the biographer had deliberately suppressed some of his father's views; that he had done wrong in transcribing extracts from his subject's manuscript diaries; and that he had failed to represent the elder Macdonald's sociable character and love of music accurately. He added cuttingly that he had 'strongly protested against Mr Kennedy having anything to do with a memoir of my father', though to whom this protest was directed is not clear; presumably other members of the family did not share his aversion to Kennedy.[145] This criticism is so sweeping as to seem somewhat suspect. John Macdonald and John Kennedy had been co-Presbyters and personal acquaintances, such that Macdonald had officiated at his biographer's wedding; it is therefore a little unlikely that the gulf between their attitudes was quite so gaping as this letter would suggest. Furthermore, the published text of *The Apostle of the North* had indeed included long passages of direct quotation from Macdonald's own journal, which were very illuminating regarding the nature and extent of his ministry, not at all discreditable to their author, and served to render the accusation of wholesale misrepresentation of his father's character and outlook simply untenable. The younger Macdonald was a noted agricultural engineer, who worked extensively in London and Canada, with a number of publications to his credit, all of a secular nature; he was also apparently a Freemason, having been presented in 1858 with a testimonial 'by a few friends and masonic brethren', which would suggest a religious outlook a good deal broader and more syncretistic than that of his father.[146] It may well be that the son was reflecting in this criticism how far he had moved in his attitudes from the position of his late father, and that it was the extent of this divergence – his own rather than his father's – from the views expressed in the biography, that gave such sharpness to his criticism.

An intriguing passage in Kennedy's private notebook may shed more light upon this remarkably hostile response. The passage has no heading and appears to be a draft for some kind of public statement or letter; if it was ever actually printed, then it has not been located.[147] The draft appears to be a response to public criticism of Kennedy's biography by the Macdonald family, very likely the letter in the *Inverness Courier* quoted above. The censure particularly answered in the draft was of Kennedy's handling of a sensitive matter, an accusation of adultery levelled at Macdonald late in his life by a woman who bore a child out of wedlock. In the biography, Kennedy discussed the matter at some length, explaining that the slander had been very widely circulated, to the great distress of Macdonald and greatly to the detriment of his reputation, until circumstances had at last vindicated him from any involvement in the case. He did, however, intensely spiritualise the case as an assault of the Devil upon Macdonald's ministry,[148] which may not have been appreciated by his subject's professionally successful son. Duncan Macdonald wrote in his letter to the *Courier*: 'The unkindest cut of all was to have given space to an atrocious local scandal.'[149] The subject was taken up in a letter published in a later issue of the *Courier* from 'An Old Ferrintosh Man', protesting against Kennedy's assertion that the later misfortunes of Macdonald's slanderers in the case were due to Divine judgment. Alongside this critical letter was printed a humorous extract from *Punch* praising the 'becoming and filial demonstration' of the younger Macdonald's letter. Kennedy gave no response in this or later issues of the *Courier*, but the Editor added below the critical letter and extract the following comment: 'We have heard that Mr Kennedy was induced to write the memoir out of kindness to the family of Dr Macdonald – a circumstance which should not be forgotten by critics.'[150]

In the untitled draft response, Kennedy wrote:

> It is due to the public and to myself that I should explain the very unreasonable position in which I am placed as Dr Macdonald's biographer. After several others had been requested to write a memoir, I for lack of better was applied to.

He then went on to explain that he had postponed the writing of the work for some years, partly because the records given by the family were very limited, and partly due to 'a threat of legal proceedings to prevent my publishing any memoir from a member of his family'.[151] This latter remark would tend to suggest that the objection of a member of Macdonald's family, presumably Duncan, against the work was so strong as even to precede its composition. The letter cited above, in its strongly personal criticism of Kennedy, would tend to suggest that the ground of the objection was the choice of the biographer to accomplish the work, given the tenor of Kennedy's previous publication.

In the draft, Kennedy explained the motivations that led him to proceed with the work:

> Ascertaining at last that the unappearance of a memoir occasioned surprise, considering that the proceeds of the sale were intended for the benefit of the family, and knowing that the only prospect of their being helped in that way was dependent on my making the attempt I began the labour of love in spring of last year. No one can be more sensible than I am of the unsatisfactoriness of the memoir, but of this I feel assured that I have not misrepresented the character nor misstated events of the life of Dr M'Donald, and that there was nothing in all the papers given to me which should have been published beyond what has appeared.[152]

This passage certainly tended to suggest that, at least in Kennedy's assessment, any real divergence had been between the historical Macdonald and the views and attitudes of one or more of his own family in their adult years. Nonetheless, the issue was a sensitive one. Kennedy's difficulty in writing this response is quite evident from the extant draft, with many words and phrases scored out, and the sentence, left tantalisingly unfinished, immediately following the paragraph quoted above, 'But his family is' . . .

Perhaps the most difficult issue was that addressed in the following section of the draft text:

> I applied myself to the work under the conviction that a biographer undertakes to give the remarkable events in the life of him whose memoir he is writing, and that to withhold one of these is virtually to lie. An event occurred towards the close of his life so remarkable that I could not ignore it. I recorded it, and by doing so have given offence to those whom I intended to benefit and wished to gratify. It was not without the most careful consideration I referred to the great trial of his life. Could I have avoided doing so, no mention of it would have appeared but I felt shut up to giving some comment of it on the following grounds.[153]

He then proposed four numbered reasons why the incident should have been addressed: that it was remarkable; that the churches needed to hear of his innocence; that the public needed that vindication; and that the event's occurrence, in the Providence of God, and in fulfilment of the Biblical text 'Blessed are ye when men shall revile you,' justified its inclusion.[154] To a modern biographer, the idea of attempting to suppress such a widely known scandal would be inconceivable. Even by nineteenth-century standards, there does not seem anything very exceptionable in Kennedy's account of the case, which clearly asserted throughout Macdonald's entire innocence of any impropriety. Kennedy was undoubtedly open to the charge of idealising his subject in *The Apostle of the North*, but it is intriguing to note that he was strongly criticised at the time of his book's publication for his frankness.

Undoubtedly, there were differences of outlook between John Macdonald and John Kennedy. Some of these, in the very occasional hints of criticism, can be discerned even in the biography itself: Macdonald's comfortable association with a variety of English and Irish evangelicals; his positive assessment of the revival movement of the late 1830s; and his warmth of emotion, that led him into a marriage that Kennedy thought imprudent. Furthermore, historians have identified differences in practice. Ian R. MacDonald notes that Macdonald was careful to respect the prerogatives of ministers in their own parishes, even when these were moderates, while Kennedy did not always accord his evangelical colleagues in the Free Church the same respect.[155] John MacLeod claims that Macdonald was known to play the pipes after officiating at weddings and to permit dancing at his home;[156] and while these assertions are based on questionable sources, written long after his lifetime,[157] the mere fact that they could be averred with any credibility indicated the great difference in character and repute between Macdonald and his more strait-laced biographer. But all of these differences, even if entirely true, did not add up to any really substantive divergence, and certainly nowhere near enough to justify Duncan Macdonald's full-scale assault on Kennedy as a biographer.

Like any writer, Kennedy approached the task of biographical writing with his own purposes and priorities. He wrote in a different historical context from that in which John Macdonald had lived, and faced different controversies from those that had troubled his ministry. Believing, as he had written in *Days of the Fathers*, that the Highland Church was declining and under threat, he chose the very finest of its ministers – in his estimation – and presented his life and conduct as a compelling model. In this idealised presentation, Kennedy's biographical practice was fairly standard for the nineteenth century; indeed, he received his honorary doctorate, a D.D. from Aberdeen University in 1873, presumably in part as an acknowledgment of his achievements as a biographer and historian. It would, therefore, be ahistorical to censor him too heavily for his tendency to smooth over the less praiseworthy aspects of his subject's character or those areas where he disagreed with him. Indeed, as noted above, Kennedy was criticised by at least one contemporary for too great frankness in discussing an allegation of misconduct levelled against Macdonald. Kennedy's purpose in writing the book was not to undertake a critical biographical appraisal, in the modern understanding of biography, but rather to commemorate a notable minister, and, while doing so, to bring a hortatory challenge to the Highland Church of his day on the basis of this idealised account of one of its finest ministers. Broadly speaking, this was what he achieved.

Kennedy the Mystic

There was one major charge against Kennedy as a biographer and historian of which discussion has been deferred until now: the accusation of superstition. In giving his idealised defence of the Highland Church of a past generation, and of some its more notable members, Kennedy frequently recounted instances of supernatural insights by individuals whom he considered well advanced in godliness. These incidents were presented as certified occurrences, which supported Kennedy's thesis of the special spiritual power and maturity of the Christians of the Highland Church. No aspect of Kennedy's historical writing was more controversial, both in his own day and in the present, and many commentators were none too careful to reflect the nuance of his position. All too frequently, he was termed a believer in the supposed natural gift of the second sight, of which stories were frequent in Highland tradition.

His obituary in one newspaper was quite typical in commenting on this aspect of his writing: '[*The Days of the Fathers in Ross-shire*] has acquired some notoriety from the sort of back-handed support it gives to the Highland superstitious notions on "second sight".'[158] In similar terms, a newspaper correspondent identified as 'Presbyterian', apparently from Creich, wrote in *The Scotsman* in 1878 of the Highlanders' 'infatuated belief in the "second sight"' and of the popularity of Kennedy, whose 'immense influence he has gained by pandering to this degrading superstition'. He added that *Days of the Fathers* was 'full of the most childish tales of the second sight', and expressed disbelief that 'such rubbish could, without a blush, be penned by an educated man in the nineteenth century'.[159] Interestingly, the letter was answered in a subsequent issue by one who identified himself as 'A Native of the Parish of Creich', who rebutted some criticisms of Kennedy, but suggested that even some Highlanders sympathetic to Kennedy's ecclesiastical views considered his book to be indefensible in certain particulars. Further publications repeated the charge of believing in the second sight, including a posthumous magazine article,[160] a memoir by one of Kennedy's friends from university days,[161] and one rather lurid work, entitled *Highland Second Sight*, which had the temerity to use Kennedy's name and some of the narratives from his writings as evidence to support the traditional belief in this phenomenon.[162] A modern journal article has repeated the allegation in scholarly terms, that Kennedy, 'a Free Kirk minister and gatherer of folklore [...] regarded second-sight as hierophany',[163] even though close reading of Kennedy's works reveals the sharp distinction between traditional folklore and the kinds of spiritual experience he described and defended.

Most seriously, Kennedy's ministerial colleague Horatius Bonar, while writing in defence of the evangelistic campaign of D. L. Moody, referred to Kennedy's supposed belief in second sight, and its absence in Moody's evangelistic campaign, as a reason for Kennedy's negative view of that campaign. Giving eight examples from *Days of the Fathers*, Bonar insisted that Kennedy accepted 'second-sight as a reality', and therefore that his judgment of Moody's campaign must be suspect.[164] In context, the argument was a little strained, but it indicated that many in the Lowland Free Church disagreed with Kennedy's views on supernatural occurrences, and believed that such views undermined his credibility as a commentator on other issues. In his subsequent reply, Kennedy did demur from the term Bonar used:

> What he quotes as instances of 'prophetic discernment,' or 'second-sight,' as he chooses to call it, is a mere narrative of facts, given on the authority of men who were never known to lie, or according to evidence furnished by my senses, with some corroborating testimony from consciousness. In writing this, I knew that I would expose myself to sneers not a few; but I also knew that, if I did not write it, those who came after me would not be likely to do so, and that this feature, be it a defect or the reverse, would be awanting from the portrait left to the generations to come, of the religion that spread its blessed influence, with unique effect, over the Highlands of Scotland.[165]

This paragraph is significant in showing that, far from the supernatural accounts being a reluctant addition, they were of the very substance of the *Days of the Fathers*. It is a tribute to the success of his book in this respect that it was followed by a number of volumes that recorded the spiritual experiences of Highland evangelical believers.[166] While Kennedy rejected Bonar's use of the phrase 'second-sight' to describe these spiritual experiences, he did not labour the point. He argued that Bonar had only mentioned these incidents in order to undermine the credibility of his own opposition to the Moody campaign and 'to give [Bonar] an opportunity of exciting a feeling against the author of "Hyper-Evangelism"'.[167]

In fact, the charge that Kennedy advocated belief in second sight was false: Kennedy did not believe in a natural gift of second sight, and strongly condemned such claims. Even in his very first book, recounting how his father lay sick as a young child, and a local man 'who had the reputation of a seer' was consulted, this action was attributed by Kennedy to the mother's 'superstition'. Furthermore, the seer's gloomy prophecy of the child's imminent death was characterised as coming from 'a messenger of Satan', indicating that Kennedy considered that the man's claims of foresight were not merely fraudulent, but actively malignant. Kennedy's grandfather indignantly dismissed the supposed seer, and, as Kennedy notes, the child lived, in contradiction of the supposed prophecy.[168]

What Kennedy did believe, and recorded in his publications, were many stories of apparently supernatural insights experienced by those who were mature and experienced Christian believers. His argument was for the reality of mystical insights as the fruit of some individuals' particularly close walk with God. For example, writing of Hector M'Phail, a former minister of Resolis, Kennedy described the following incident:

> Seated, on one occasion, at dinner, in the house of one of his parishioners, along with some of his elders, he rose suddenly from the table, and, going out of the house, was seen by those whom he left behind walking hurriedly towards a wood not far from the house. There was a small lake in the wood, on the margin of which he found a woman just about to cast herself into the water. She had come from the parish of Alness, and, distracted and despairing, was driven by the Tempter to suicide. Mr M'Phail arrived just in time to intercept her from her purpose, and, preaching Christ to her disconsolate soul as 'able to save to the uttermost,' this poor sinner was then and there disposed and enabled to 'flee for refuge to the hope set before' her.[169]

The implication of this account was evident: Kennedy believed that God had communicated to M'Phail some feeling, at the least such a sense of urgent need as to make him walk out unexpectedly to the lake in time to prevent the suicide. In his view, God had used the minister to fulfil his salvatory purpose. Another incident concerned Kennedy's own father:

> Once, while preaching there [at Killearnan] on a Sabbath, he said, in a very marked and emphatic way, 'There is one now present who, before coming into the meeting, was engaged in bargaining about his cattle, regardless alike of the day and of the eye of the Lord. Thou knowest that I speak the truth, and listen while I declare to thee that if the Lord ever had mercy on thy soul, thou wilt yet be reduced to alms as thy daily bread.' The confidence with which this was said was soon and sorely tried, and he passed a sleepless night under the fear that he had spoken unadvisedly. At breakfast next morning in my father's house several neighbouring farmers were present, one of whom said to him as they sat at table, 'How did you know that I was selling my heifers yesterday to the drover?' 'Did you do so?' my father quietly asked him. 'I can't deny it,' was the farmer's answer. Directing on him one of his searching glances, the minister said, 'Remember this warning that was given you, for you will lose either your soul or your substance.' 'But will you not tell me how you knew it?' the farmer asked. The only reply to this was in the words of Scripture, 'The secret of the Lord is with them that fear him.' Some of those who heard the warning given to him were often applied to for alms by that farmer during the latter years of his life.[170]

This account is interesting because a measure of uncertainty is acknowledged on the part of the recipient of the apparent communication. He was not certain that he had been correct in his statement, and he did not know the identity of the individual whom it concerned until he identified himself. In both cases, these incidents concerned individuals who, despite their sins, were to be eternally saved, if the accounts are accepted as true. Other such communications, however, concerned judgment, such as the elder Kennedy's prophecy of the death of a reputedly immoral woman in a house fire, and Mary Macrae's vision of the approaching death of a nearby minister of questionable character.[171] The former communications had an apparent purpose of salvation, to warn of danger and to bring to repentance before it was too late; but these latter communications served rather as warnings to others, of the danger of dying without preparation for eternity. The secret purposes of God were, in these very limited respects, allegedly being revealed, to support the testimony of the visible church.

The criticism incurred by such narratives has already been indicated above in the deeply hostile reviews of *Days of the Fathers* in the public press. Secular journalists were not persuaded by the veracity of Kennedy's claims and considered the accounts to undermine the credibility of the book as a whole. Indeed, not all Kennedy's colleagues in the Free Church ministry sympathised with his interest in these accounts of supernatural insights. The noted Highland minister, Alexander Beith, wrote critically of Kennedy's friend Isaac Lillingston of Lochalsh that 'he delighted in the marvellous, in superstitious religious anecdotes', and that after an evening of hearing these retailed, 'one felt as if breathing in an infected atmosphere'.[172] Another former colleague, Robertson Nicoll, commented of Kennedy's handling of such accounts:

> [He] tries to vindicate himself from the charge of superstition in telling [these stories]. In this, he is perhaps not very successful, for the knowledge of the future is in itself not a grace. What all believing souls join in desiring is not an intimation of God's purpose concerning others, but of His will with them.[173]

Kennedy sought to respond to these critiques in prefaces to subsequent editions of the book. In particular, in the 'Preface to the Second Edition', he remarked on the mixed response:

> I therefore feel that I have no cause to complain of the reception it has met with; for by those whose censure I would reckon praise, it has been most heartily abused; and some friends of Christ have been moved to say of it, 'The Lord bless it,' and to say to me, 'Be of good courage'. [. . .] I expected that many would count me credulous, some call me superstitious, and a few denounce me as fanatical, because of some anecdotes I gave, to prove how near to God were the godly men of former days.[174]

This passage is particularly noteworthy as it indicates that Kennedy considered such accounts as supporting evidence in favour of his general thesis of decline from a past time of more notable spiritual prosperity in Ross-shire. Significantly, he treated the opposition to such accounts as itself indicative of the low spiritual state of his critics: 'The rarer attainments of the godly [. . .] are more offensive to them, merely because they are more palpable evidences of the reality of communion with God.'[175] These experiences were known only to those 'peculiar' in godliness, circumstanced 'such as to allow of their devoting themselves to closet intercourse with God, as other Christians could not, who were placed in a busier sphere'. The experiences themselves were therefore 'veritable proofs' of 'the reality of [the spiritual Christian's] communion with God, and of the gracious condescension' of God. In an amusing reversal of his critics' arguments, Kennedy suggested that if indeed Highlanders were naturally superstitious, then these experiences were indications of God condescending to such a weakness. These experiences, he asserted, 'are at least as true as they are strange'.[176]

The criticism continued, and Kennedy acknowledged in the 'Preface to the Third Edition', dated October 1861, that on the subject of supernatural experiences, 'there is almost nothing bearing upon it in the former Editions, either in the way of explanation or of defence'.[177] Consequently, he appended to that edition the full text of a sermon of his own on the relevant Biblical text, 'The secret of the Lord is with them that fear him' (Psalm 25: 14), in which he attempted to give a fuller Scriptural basis for his position on supernatural experiences.[178] Much of this discourse is uncontroversial to those of confessional Reformed views: Kennedy opened by considering the individuality of Christian experience, that each believer is 'peculiar', and then discussed in detail the fear of God as a mark of His people, and how this fear entails that His people will be earnest in seeking Him, and as they do so, 'may expect his secret to be with them'. In the second half of the discourse, Kennedy turned more directly to address this 'secret', acknowledging that, in the first instance, it refers to the Scriptures and to the covenant of grace. But, more specifically, he argued that it also refers to assurance of salvation, to the answer to prayers by special application of the words of Scripture, to the application of Scriptural texts to the spiritual cases of others interceded for at the throne of Grace, and to the understanding of His Providence.[179] This argument has considerable force, as plainly, for any Christian to claim assurance of salvation is to make a claim of insight beyond the direct teachings of Scripture, and indicates that that person considers the Scriptural identifications of the true believer to apply to them. Kennedy suggested that those who denied such insights indicated their own spiritual poverty and their lack of any real communion with God. He went on to lay down several guiding principles: the secret is only with those who fear, and therefore none can claim any natural gift; the secret is a precious thing, indicating the ambition to high spiritual attainments that must motivate the Lord's people; and the secret must be governed in all cases by the actual plain meaning of the Scriptures.[180]

Although Kennedy's writings made no claim of unusual supernatural communications for himself,[181] he did, as a biographer acknowledged, sometimes preach 'under the mantle of a prophet'. When he did so, 'his words were well weighed', especially in his solemn warnings against the declension in the church of his day, as many of his hearers evidently considered him to benefit from a particularly close relationship with the Lord.[182]

For example, John Macleod wrote of Kennedy's friend Archibald Crawford as follows: 'Sometimes when he [Crawford] spoke of Kennedy, he would say, "He was a curious man, the Doctor." "Curious" here stood for unusual, out of the ordinary.' Crawford found a close spiritual unity with Kennedy, such that they seemed on a couple of occasions to be pre-empting one another's thoughts in preparing lectures on passages of Scripture, in a manner that seemed to suggest a supernatural communication at work.[183] Furthermore, one of Kennedy's biographers recorded that he had intimated on a communion Sabbath in Stornoway: 'I feel oppressed in my spirit. I fear some immediate calamity impends.' The foreboding was considered justified, as an old woman was run down immediately after the service by one of the carts carrying worshippers home, and died shortly afterwards. Kennedy referred to the tragedy in the evening service but added that he was 'glad it was not worse'.[184] A later historian recorded an incident of Kennedy experiencing apparently supernatural insight with regard to one of the Men of Sutherland, George Grant:

> Dr Kennedy was the preacher [at a Creich communion], and in the course of his sermon, he said, 'You are here before me of whom it is true', and then, though he knew nothing of George's circumstances at the time, he described his case so minutely, and even pointed with his finger to the spot where our worthy sat among the assembled hundreds, that he felt the address contained a special message for himself. He returned from the Communion like the Ethiopian who went on his way rejoicing.[185]

The parallels with the kind of incidents recorded in *Days of the Fathers* are striking, and would, if true, indicate that Kennedy knew of what he wrote with regard to such insights. Interestingly, the same historian records, of the same Man, another occasion when Kennedy was actually the bearer of such an insight, but in a dream rather than in reality! George Grant dreamed that Kennedy appeared to him, asking after a neighbour of his, Robert Hamilton, one of the Men, who was at that time suffering from spiritual depression. Grant responded that Hamilton was still distressed and dreamed that Kennedy then replied: 'In eight days Robert will be quite well.' Sure enough, the depression began to ease, and eight days later, on 5 June 1866, Robert 'was called away to his everlasting rest'.[186] Another of the Men, James Matheson, apparently had an extraordinary vision while he sat listening to Kennedy preaching, again at a Creich communion, seeing him even while he stood there preaching in the open air, surrounded by an angelic host.[187] Similarly, one of the notable women of the Highland Church, Marion Macleod, told Kennedy after hearing him at a communion that he would not long be with them, as she considered his preaching had become so like that of his late father in his last days. She never heard him preach again, as he died shortly afterwards.[188] The association of such experiences with Kennedy's ministry suggests not only that the apparently supernatural aspect of Highland evangelicalism was much in evidence during Kennedy's own lifetime, but also that he himself, particularly in his preaching, had become a central influence upon the spiritual life of many people.

Just as Kennedy's contemporary reviewers struggled with his uncritical acceptance of supernatural incidents, so later historians, even when theologically sympathetic to Kennedy, sometimes have difficulty with this aspect of Highland spirituality. Conservative and confessional Presbyterians must acknowledge the absolute sovereignty of God over the affairs of men, and thus His ability to intervene supernaturally if He chooses to do so. The *Westminster Confession* undoubtedly states the completeness of God's revelation in Scripture:

> It pleased the Lord, at sundry times, and in divers manners, to reveal Himself, and to declare that His will unto His Church; and afterwards for the better preserving and propagating of the truth, and for the more sure establishment and comfort of the Church against the corruption of the flesh, and the malice of Satan and of the world, to commit the same wholly unto writing; which makes the Holy Scripture to be most necessary; those former ways of God's revealing His will unto His people being now ceased.[189]

However, this is not strictly germane to the matter at hand, as the closure of the canon of Scripture after the inspiration of the New Testament is not in question. The sort of communications Kennedy described were, at most, insights into God's providence; indeed, they were usually transitory and fragmentary, and sometimes regarded with suspicion even by the recipients of them. They were not authoritative words of prophecy to be placed on the level of Scripture, but rather indications of the individual circumstances of other believers, and of the will of God with regard to them. All professing believers claim such indications with regard to themselves, in their own individual assurance of faith; the only difference is that the indications that Kennedy described had regard to the cases of others.

Within the Puritan tradition, which Kennedy explicitly embraced,[190] such experiences had been accepted as valid, and indeed the standard Puritan work on providence, John Flavel's *The Mystery of Providence*, described something nearly identical to some of the experiences above as an example of God's providential dealings:

> Souls after their first awakening, are apt to lose the sense and impression of their first troubles for sin; but providence is vigilant to prevent it; and doth effectually prevent it sometimes, by directing the minister to some discourse or passage, that shall fall as pat, as if the case of such a person had been studied by him, and designedly spoken to. How often have I found this in the cases of many souls, who have professed that they stood amazed, to hear the very thoughts of their hearts discovered by the preacher, who knew nothing of them?[191]

The recent historian Norman Campbell agreed that the view of Divine providence as allowing for 'special impressions about future events being made on the minds' of Christians was widely defended in the Highland Church. However, he added the useful observation that even those who reportedly experienced such impressions 'never claimed that this was a true mark of grace. They did not insist on this phenomenon as a normal part of every believer's experience, or claim it was a gift of the Holy Spirit.'[192] The Highland evangelicals accepted that such experiences could happen but did not expect them, and certainly did not require, or even accept, such instances as proof that one was regenerate. And above all, regardless of the value placed upon the experiences of believers, 'For them, the Bible, as the Word of God[,] was also the last word.'[193] The canon remained closed.

The twentieth-century Free Church minister Murdoch Campbell strongly concurred with Kennedy's views, quoting at length from his writings on the subject,[194] and argued for this aspect of Highland evangelicalism as being a sign of the closeness of many Highland believers to the Lord. He wrote: 'The Bible makes it clear that God has access to our minds at all times, and that in every age He has instructed many of His people in this mysterious way.'[195] Elsewhere, he argued at length that there was no ground to consider that dreams were no longer used by the Lord: 'He keeps all His doors open, this one included.' He went on to list Christians who had enjoyed such spiritual experiences, showing that they came from a broad variety of geographical backgrounds and denominational affiliations, mentioning Kennedy alongside the English Puritans John Howe and John Bunyan, the Welsh Baptist Christmas Evans and the French mystic Madame Guyon. All were at one, he asserted, in their subjection of their visions and experiences to Scripture, but welcomed the Lord's immediate 'guidance and care':

> Were we to say that he has closed this door, we should not only deny that the Christian believer is spiritually in touch with the supernatural world of glory, but we should also contradict the overwhelming consensus of belief within the Christian Church.[196]

Kennedy himself later cited the Glasgow minister John Love (1757–1825) as evidence that such experiences had been known in Lowland evangelicalism in a better day.[197] The twentieth-century historian and minister John Macinnes observed that the reports of such occurrences linked Highland evangelicalism with the Celtic Church, and he gave numerous examples of such instances, from Kennedy's writings and from many other sources.[198] He summed up by remarking:

> We are convinced that a few men, Thomas Hog and Lachlan Mackenzie for instance, did possess a prophetic insight which was other and beyond the prescience born of a shrewd appreciation of events. Lesser men, desirous of the popular reverence which the gift evoked, assumed a mantle which was not theirs by right. But even if we regard 'The secret

of the Lord' merely as the tribute which popular piety pays to eminent godliness, its historical significance is unaffected. With a people especially sensitive to the supernatural, it invested the more intense evangelicalism with the manifest stamp of heavenly authority.[199]

Kennedy would surely have agreed with this assessment, and especially that such occurrences served to corroborate evangelical teaching and spirituality, and to commend it to the wider population of the eighteenth- and nineteenth-century Highlands.

Recent historians have been much more cautious in handling accounts of supernatural events. Douglas Ansdell considers the attitude to such occurrences in the Highland Church to be 'ambivalent':

> In a number of forms, supernatural events were accommodated within the church and attributed to divine intervention. If, however, supernatural events were associated with catholicism or with some vestige of a pre-Christian past they would be shunned along with the beliefs with which they were linked.[200]

As a historical observation, this comment is certainly accurate. However, it carefully avoids the vital point at issue, whether such supernatural occurrences are indeed credible within a confessional Presbyterian context. Interestingly, though, Ansdell does relate a number of reports of supernatural events, which he appears to accept as valid.[201]

John Macinnes goes further than Ansdell, asserting a continuity that Kennedy would certainly have rejected between pre-Christian folk beliefs and the supernatural accounts characteristic of Highland evangelicalism. He considers that the Highland Church retained medieval influences, accommodated the older tradition of the second sight in Reformed terms as 'sanctified foreknowledge', and gave expression to many of the positive qualities of medieval community life within the structures of Scottish Presbyterianism.[202] More negatively, James Hunter describes Highland evangelicalism as 'combining a harsh and pristine puritanism with a transcendental mysticism that had less to do with nineteenth-century Protestantism than with an older faith'.[203] Hunter explains the reported supernatural events in sociological – indeed, Marxist – terms as an assertion of spiritual autonomy by a crofter class subject to disempowerment by the dominant social classes.[204] However, this interpretation relies on dubious psychological analysis, rather than on close study of the actual testimonies of supernatural experience in the Highland Church. A more constructive sociological approach is that of Steve Bruce, who notes that religious assertions were supported in a culture by 'resonance' with accepted beliefs, and thus Highland evangelicalism's heritage of supernatural events gave it plausibility as a belief system in a superstitious society.[205]

But none of these rather sweeping points of interpretation should be allowed to blur the vital distinction between pre-Christian traditions of the supernatural and the accounts of Christian experience typical of Highland evangelicalism, such as those included in Kennedy's books. In fact, there are several important points of difference: Highland evangelicals considered spiritual insights to be the fruit of a close relationship with God, in a mature and seasoned Christian, not any kind of natural gift with which a person had been born;[206] they regarded such insights as uncertain, sometimes even dubious, until later events verified them, unlike pre-Christian traditions of prophecy; and, above all, they always made these records subject to the overarching authority of Scripture. In other words, if Highland evangelicals are allowed to speak for themselves with regard to these experiences, the parallels with older traditions in the Highlands seem more incidental, and the distinctions more marked and evident, than some social historians would allow. Kennedy's publications were an endeavour so to give a record of supernatural experiences, in terms of Reformed Protestant Christianity, by a convinced Highland evangelical, whose testimony would support belief in the reality and validity of such experiences.

Conclusion

As a historian, Kennedy wrote with an eye to the present, delivering a narrative of general decline from a perceived high point of spiritual blessing in the late eighteenth-century Highland Church, with an explicit purpose of summoning the Church of his day to recover the values and practices typical of that older Highland evangelicalism. In particular, he saw this as a church culture that prized godliness above scholarship, that expected preaching that offered clear discrimination between the true believer and the hypocrite, and that respected and valued Christian experience. More than an account of the past, *The Days of the Fathers in Ross-shire* was a manifesto for the future of the Church. Kennedy used the lives of individual believers as exemplars of the ideal of Christian piety that he advocated, drawing biographical subjects from the recent past of Highland evangelicalism, effectively as illustrations for his didactic argument. Furthermore, he supported his argument for the superiority of the piety of these older believers by including accounts of their dramatic and unusual supernatural experiences. The whole of his historical work therefore served to exhort Highland evangelicals of his own generation to maintain the piety and practices of a former generation, and to contend for those points that distinguished the Highland Free Church from the Lowland Free Church as vital points of principle.

Truthfully, in this endeavour Kennedy was far from a model historian. Quite apart from his over-reliance on biographical sketching in his methodology, his lack of references and his explicit didactic purpose, his historical writing was marred throughout by a lack of critical edge. His historical narrative would have been more persuasive had he given a realistic and unsentimental portrayal of the church in eighteenth-century Ross-shire.

His biographies would have been more convincing had he been less selective, and incorporated more of the texture of real life into his writing. His accounts of supernatural experience would have been more persuasive if he had openly evaluated the credibility of the testimonies he recounted. But ultimately, none of these legitimate defects hindered his work from reaching its intended readership. The reviewers may have disdained his work, but its pervasive influence over subsequent generations of Highland evangelical writing and thought is hard to overstate. This chapter has shown that writings on the Highland Church that predated its publication differed significantly from its major emphases: in particular, its emphasis on the quality of the indigenous Presbyterianism of Ross-shire that could be traced back into the seventeenth century and earlier, in contradistinction to external influences; its sharp distinction between Highland and Lowland evangelicalism; and its assertion of the superiority of the piety and the practices of the former. On these points, Kennedy's historical writing was hugely influential on the subsequent development of the Highland Church in the decades after 1861, and on its literature in which it defined and defended itself: above all, in its growing divergence from the evangelicalism of the Lowlands. This departure became most clearly evident in ecclesiastical controversy and was seen as plainly as anywhere in the published writings of Kennedy himself from the late 1860s onwards, as he turned his attention from historical subjects to address directly the central ecclesiastical controversy of his day.

Notes

1. John Kennedy, *The Lord's Controversy with his People* (Edinburgh, 1854).
2. John Kennedy, 'Preface to the First Edition' (ix–xi), in *Days*, x.
3. Kennedy, *Days*, 1–2.
4. The cycle described was evident in the Old Testament Book of Judges, which structures its narrative of the early centuries of Israel's possession of the land of Canaan in terms of repeated seasons of blessings followed invariably by progressive stages of rebellion. A similar literary structure was used for the historical narrative of Psalm 78. The specific quotations in the paragraph were from Isaiah 35: 1 and Psalm 102: 13. However, the phrase 'year of visitation' did not occur in these chapters, and was invariably used in the Old Testament of approaching judgment (e.g., in Jeremiah 23: 12), further underlining the sense of foreboding.
5. D. Gibb Mitchell, *Life of Robert Rainy, D.D.* (Glasgow, n.d.), 14–16.
6. John Kennedy, *The Disestablishment Movement in the Free Church: An Address to Free Churchmen in the Highlands* (Edinburgh, 1882), 10–11.
7. A very full account, sympathetic while unsparing regarding the defects in Anderson's conduct, is provided by Roy Middleton, 'Jonathan Ranken Anderson and the Free Church of Scotland – Part I' (135–274), *Scottish Reformation Society Historical Journal*, iv (2014); 'Jonathan Ranken Anderson and the Free Church of Scotland – Part II' (211–318), *Scottish Reformation Society Historical Journal*, v (2015); and 'Jonathan Ranken Anderson's Critique

of the Free Church of Scotland in the 1850s' (321–51), *Scottish Reformation Society Historical Journal,* v (2015).
8. Quoted in Middleton, 'Anderson's Critique of the Free Church', 348–49; the reference is to Kennedy, *The Lord's Controversy.*
9. Middleton, 'Anderson and the Free Church, II', 329; Kennedy, *Days,* 22.
10. Drummond and Bulloch, *Church in Victorian Scotland,* 19, 301; James Strahan, *Andrew Bruce Davidson, D.D., LL.D., D.Litt.* (London, 1917), 57; cf. Kennedy's own account of the case, wholly favourable to Gibson: John Kennedy, *Signs of the Times,* 39–40.
11. Quoted and cited in Stewart J. Brown, 'The Disruption and the Dream: The Making of New College, 1843–1861' (29–50), in David F. Wright and Gary D. Badcock, eds, *Disruption to Diversity: Edinburgh Divinity, 1846–1996* (Edinburgh, 1996), 47.
12. John W. Keddie, *George Smeaton* (Darlington, 2007), Ch. 9.
13. Mitchell, *Robert Rainy,* 100; quoted in Strahan, *Davidson,* 60–1.
14. Simpson, *Life of Principal Rainy,* i, 142.
15. Cheyne, *Transforming of the Kirk,* Ch. iii.
16. James Duguid, quoted in Strahan, *Davidson,* 57.
17. Ross, *Church and Creed,* 170–4.
18. Ross, *Church and Creed,* 154–70.
19. Cheyne, *Transforming of the Kirk,, passim.*
20. Kennedy, *Days,* ix.
21. Kennedy, *Days,* 14–15.
22. Kennedy, *Days,* 16.
23. Kennedy, *Days,* 17; the phrase in quotation marks is a loose reference to Isaiah 54.
24. Kennedy, *Days,* 24–5.
25. Kennedy, *Days,* 27.
26. Kennedy, *Days,* 27–8.
27. Kennedy, *Days,* 28–30.
28. Kennedy, *Days,* 30–7.
29. Kennedy, *Days,* 37–84.
30. Kennedy, *Days,* 84.
31. Kennedy, *Days,* 86.
32. 'Investigator', *The Church and her Accuser in the Far North.*
33. The reference is undoubtedly to [Anon.], 'Puritanism in the Highlands', lxxxix 178 (September 1851).
34. Kennedy, *Days,* 91.
35. Kennedy, *Days,* 91–4.
36. Kennedy, *Days,* 95.
37. Kennedy, *Days,* 94–101.
38. Kennedy, *Days,* 101–4.
39. Kennedy, *Days,* 104–20.
40. Kennedy, *Days,* 120.
41. Kennedy, *Days,* 121–6.
42. Iain D. Campbell, quoted in Finlayson, *Unity and Diversity,* 264.
43. Kennedy, *Days,* 126–7.
44. Kennedy, *Days,* 127.
45. Kennedy, *Days,* 129–61.

46. Kennedy, *Days*, 138–9, 142–5.
47. Iain H. Murray, *The Undercover Revolution* (Edinburgh, 2009), 5.
48. 'Dr Kennedy was never rich, and he had the gift of making himself poor'; Macfarlane, *Apostles of the North*, 104; Sell, 'Kennedy, John (1819–1884)'. Kennedy's estate may be compared to the £15,269 left the previous year by his friend and colleague James Begg, who, despite energetic philanthropy, had a reputation as a shrewd investor of his money; cf. John Wolffe, 'Begg, James (1808–1883)', *Oxford Dictionary of National Biography* (Oxford, 2004), available at: <http://www.oxforddnb.com/view/article/1959> (last accessed 7 January 2017).
49. 'Preface to the Second Edition' (xiii–xix) in Kennedy, *Days*, xiii.
50. 'Preface to the Third Edition' (xxi), in Kennedy, *Days*, xxi.
51. 'Preface to the Fourth Edition' (xxiii–xxiv), in Kennedy, *Days*, xxiv.
52. Review, *Glasgow Herald*, 7 March 1861.
53. Review, *The Athenaeum*, 24 August 1861, 245–6.
54. Review, *London Review*, xvi 31 (April 1861), 261–7.
55. E.g., in 'Miscellanea', *Dundee Courier*, 1 April 1861.
56. Literature, *Inverness Courier*, 14 February 1861.
57. Literature, *Inverness Courier*, 14 February 1861.
58. Review, *Stirling Observer*, 8 August 1861.
59. 'Death of Rev. Dr Kennedy', *Aberdeen Weekly Journal*, 3 May 1884.
60. Macgregor, *Campbell of Kiltearn*, 168.
61. MacRae, *Life of Gustavus Aird*, 260, 286.
62. Noble, *Religious Life in Ross*, v–vi.
63. Alexander Auld, *Ministers and Men of the Far North* [first pub. 1869] (Inverness, 1956), 24.
64. [Anon.], *Dioghlum o Theagasg nan Aithrichean* (Edinburgh, 1868), the title meaning 'Gleanings from the Teachings of the Fathers'; Munro, *Records of Grace in Sutherland*, 27–8, 34.
65. 'Biographical Sketch' (vii–viii), in John Kennedy, *Sermons* [first pub. 1885] (Inverness, 1888), viii.
66. Kennedy, *Days*, 200–2.
67. Reproduced in full in Macleod, *By-paths*, 148–61.
68. Macleod, *By-paths*, 146–8.
69. Innes, 'The Religion of the Highlands' (413–46).
70. Gordon F. Millar, 'Innes, Alexander Taylor (1833–1912)', *Oxford Dictionary of National Biography* (Oxford, 2005), available at: <http://www.oxforddnb.com/view/article/41289> (last accessed 5 July 2016).
71. Innes, 'Religion of the Highlands', 415–16.
72. Innes, 'Religion of the Highlands', 416.
73. Innes, 'Religion of the Highlands', 419.
74. Innes, 'Religion of the Highlands', 416–44.
75. W. K. Leask, *Dr Thomas M'Lauchlan* (Edinburgh, 1905), 17–18, 43–4.
76. Macdonald, *Social and Religious Life in the Highlands*, 70, 135–6.
77. Macdonald, *Social and Religious Life*, 169ff., 247, 299, etc.
78. Paton, *Clergy and the Clearances*, 123.
79. Ansdell, *People of the Great Faith*, 86–8.
80. Ansdell, *of the Great Faith*, 86. Many more publications could be added to Ansdell's list.

81. Meek, *The Scottish Highlands*, 61.
82. Meek, *The Scottish Highlands*, 35–7, 61; for the same argument from a psychological perspective, cf. Alistair McIntosh, *Island Spirituality* (Kershader, 2013), 51–3.
83. MacColl, *Crofting Community*, 85–8.
84. MacLeod, *Second Disruption*, 165.
85. Macdonald, *Social and Religious Life*, 135–6.
86. Angus Macgillivray, *Sketches of Religion & Revivals of Religion in the Highlands in the Last Century* (Edinburgh, 1859), esp. Preface, 23–6, 47.
87. Mackay, *Memoir of Rev John MacDonald*, 22–3.
88. Mackay, *Memoir of Rev John MacDonald*, 74–5.
89. Donald Sage, *Memorabilia Domestica, or Parish Life in the North of Scotland* [Second Edition] (Edinburgh, 1889), 98–9, 239ff.
90. Sage, *Memorabilia Domestica*, viii.
91. Sievewright, *Alexander Stewart*, 87, 94ff.
92. Sievewright, *Alexander Stewart*, 227, 263, 346.
93. 'Lay Member', *An Account of the Present State of Religion Throughout the Highlands of Scotland* (Edinburgh, 1827).
94. 'Lay Member', *Present State of Religion*, 1–3, 10.
95. 'Lay Member', *Present State of Religion*, 19, 28–30, 47ff.
96. 'Lay Member', *Present State of Religion*, 41.
97. 'Lay Member', *Present State of Religion*, 98.
98. John Kennedy, 'The Minister of Killearnan' (163–267), in *Days*.
99. John Kennedy, 'Mackintosh Mackay' (79–88) and 'Donald Sage' (45–52), in J. Greig, ed., *Disruption Worthies of the Highlands* (Edinburgh, 1877); John Kennedy, 'William MacDonald' (300), *Monthly Record of the Free Church of Scotland*, 173 (December 1876).
100. Innes, 'Religion of the Highlands', 435ff.
101. Donald E. Meek, 'Saints and Scarecrows: The Churches and Gaelic Culture in the Highlands since 1560' (3–22), *Scottish Bulletin of Evangelical Theology*, xiv (1996), 6–7.
102. Note the specific examples given of biographers incurring public opprobrium for overly frank revelations in their works, in Nigel Hamilton, *Biography: A Brief History* (Cambridge, MA, 2007), 109ff.
103. Hermione Lee, *Biography: A Very Short Introduction* (Oxford, 2009), 57.
104. Kennedy, 'The Minister of Killearnan', 168.
105. Kennedy, 'The Minister of Killearnan', 175.
106. Kennedy, 'The Minister of Killearnan', 178–9, 188, 199–200.
107. Kennedy, 'The Minister of Killearnan', 210–11.
108. Kennedy, 'The Minister of Killearnan', 212.
109. Kennedy, 'The Minister of Killearnan', 212–32, 232–45, 245–58.
110. Kennedy, 'The Minister of Killearnan', 258–61.
111. Kennedy, 'The Minister of Killearnan', 265–6.
112. Pat Jalland, *Death in the Victorian Family* (Oxford, 1996), Ch. 1, esp. 26.
113. Donald E. Meek, *The Quest for Celtic Christianity* (Boat of Garten, 2000), 229.
114. Kennedy, 'William MacDonald'.
115. Kennedy, 'Donald Sage', 52.
116. Kennedy, 'Mackintosh Mackay', 83–4.
117. Kennedy, 'Mackintosh Mackay', 88.

118. Obituary, *Scotsman*, 29 April 1884.
119. Kennedy, *Apostle*, Ch. 1.
120. Kennedy, *Apostle*, 25–6, 31.
121. Kennedy, *Apostle*, 36.
122. Kennedy, *Apostle*, 22–5.
123. Kennedy, MS Notebook, 53.
124. Kennedy, *Apostle*, 48–9; Kennedy, MS Notebook, 55; the additional text is heavily stroked out in the draft, presumably to ensure that it was not included in the printer's copy.
125. Kennedy, *Apostle*, 53; the sentence is a late addition to the draft text, cf. Kennedy, MS Notebook, 57.
126. Kennedy, MS Notebook, 58.
127. Kennedy, *Apostle*, 76–7.
128. Kennedy, *Apostle*, Ch. v.
129. Kennedy, *Apostle*, Ch. vi.
130. Kennedy, *Apostle*, 188.
131. Kennedy, *Apostle*, 234–6, 328–30.
132. Kennedy, *Apostle*, 330–1.
133. Kennedy, *Apostle*, 194.
134. 'Facility', in Dictionary.com, available at: <http://www.dictionary.com/browse/facility> (last accessed 4 August 2016).
135. Kennedy, *Apostle*, 232.
136. Horatius Bonar, *Life of the Rev John Milne of Perth* [Fifth Edition] (New York, 1870), Ch. v; Horatius Bonar, 'The Old Gospel: Not "Another Gospel" but the Power of God unto Salvation' (38–104), in Kennedy and Bonar, *Evangelism: A Reformed Debate*, 46–9.
137. Kennedy, *Apostle*, 249.
138. Report, *Glasgow Herald*, 7 February 1866.
139. Report, *Scotsman*, 2 April 1866.
140. Review, *Inverness Courier*, 14 December 1865.
141. 'Highlander', *The Disestablishment Movement in the Free Church* (Edinburgh, n.d., c.1882), 4.
142. Simpson, *Principal Rainy*, I, 448–51.
143. Simpson, *Principal Rainy*, I, 451.
144. D. G. F. Macdonald, Letter, *Inverness Courier*, 21 December 1865; quoted in MacLeod, *Banner in the West*, 163–4.
145. Macdonald, Letter, *Inverness Courier*, 21 December 1865.
146. [Anon.], 'Macdonald, Duncan George Forbes', in *Dictionary of National Biography*, xxxv (1885–1900), available at: <https://en.wikisource.org/wiki/Macdonald,_Duncan_George_Forbes_(DNB00)> (last accessed 4 August 2016).
147. The most natural place for such a response would have been a subsequent issue of the *Inverness Courier* but no answer to the younger Macdonald's letter appeared in that periodical. Kennedy presumably decided that no purpose would be served by prolonging the dispute.
148. Kennedy, *Apostle*, 289–300.
149. Macdonald, Letter, *Inverness Courier*, 21 December 1865.
150. Letter, *Inverness Courier*, 18 January 1866.
151. Kennedy, MS Notebook, 62.

152. Kennedy, MS Notebook, 62.
153. Kennedy, MS Notebook, 62.
154. Kennedy, MS Notebook, 62–3; Matthew 5: 11, Authorised Version.
155. MacDonald, *Aberdeen and the Highland Church*, 85–7.
156. MacLeod, *Banner in the West*, 164.
157. Duncan Macdonald does, however, confirm that Macdonald 'loved musical instruments, and played the bagpipes within recent years'; Macdonald, Letter, *Inverness Courier*, 21 December 1865.
158. Obituary, *Scotsman*, 29 April 1884.
159. Letter, *Scotsman*, 8 April 1878.
160. 'Highland Seers' (196–200), *Good Words*, xxxiv (December 1893), 198.
161. Walker, *Additional Reminiscences*, 35.
162. Norman Macrae, ed., *Highland Second-Sight* (Dingwall, 1909).
163. Deborah Davis, 'Contexts of Ambivalence: The Folkloristic Activities of Nineteenth-century Scottish Highland Ministers' (207–21), *Folklore*, ciii 2 (1992), 214; but note that other ministers cited did seem to accept it as valid; cf. Macinnes, *Evangelical Movement in the Highlands*, 56–7.
164. Bonar, 'The Old Gospel', 48–55.
165. John Kennedy, 'A Reply to Dr Bonar's Defence of Hyper-evangelism' (106–40), in Kennedy and Bonar, *Evangelism*, 121.
166. Comparable experiences of Highland evangelicals of a later generation were recorded, e.g., in Beaton, *Memoir and Remains of Rev Neil Cameron*, 19–20, 22–4, 25–6; Murdoch Campbell, *Memories of a Wayfaring Man* (Glasgow, 1974), 51–5; and in many other similar books.
167. Kennedy, 'A Reply to Dr Bonar's Defence', 120–1.
168. Kennedy, *Days*, 169–70.
169. Kennedy, *Days*, 53–4.
170. Kennedy, *Days*, 207.
171. Kennedy, *Days*, 207–8, 231–2.
172. Beith, *A Highland Tour*, 83.
173. Nicoll, 'Religion of the Scottish Highlands'.
174. Kennedy, 'Preface to the Second Edition', xiii.
175. Kennedy, 'Preface to the Second Edition', xv.
176. Kennedy, 'Preface to the Second Edition', xv–xix.
177. Kennedy, Preface to the Third Edition', xxi.
178. 'Appendix' (271–92), in Kennedy, *Days*.
179. Kennedy, 'Appendix', 271–83.
180. Kennedy, 'Appendix', 283–92.
181. He did, however, adopt the conceit of a prophetic dream as a literary device for one of his pamphlets, a critique of the ecclesiastical trends of his day under a rather Bunyanesque allegory; John Kennedy, *A Visit to Leper Isle* [Second Edition] (Glasgow, 1892).
182. Campbell, *Gleanings of Highland Harvest*, 79.
183. Collins, *John Macleod*, 255–7.
184. Macfarlane, *Apostles*, 104–5.
185. Munro, *Records of Grace*, 44–5.
186. Munro, *Records of Grace*, 38–9.
187. Macdonald, *Men of Sutherland*, 99–100.
188. Macdonald, *Men of Sutherland*, 147–8.

189. *Westminster Confession of Faith*, i.1.
190. See, e.g., John Kennedy, 'Preface' (iii–v), in John Owen, *On Communion with God* [subtitled *Air comh-chomunn nan Naomh ri Dia*, Gaelic trans. by A. Macdougall] (Edinburgh, 1876).
191. John Flavel, 'Divine Conduct, or The Mystery of Providence' (336–497), in *The Whole Works of the Rev Mr John Flavel*, 6 vols (London, 1820), iv, 384.
192. Campbell, *One of Heaven's Jewels*, 116.
193. Campbell, *One of Heaven's Jewels*, 116.
194. Campbell, *Memories*, 55.
195. Campbell, *Gleanings*, 122.
196. Campbell, *Memories*, 53ff.
197. Kennedy, *Evangelism*, 120.
198. Macinnes, *Evangelical Movement*, 191–4.
199. Macinnes, *Evangelical Movement*, 194.
200. Ansdell, *People of the Great Faith*, 136.
201. Ansdell, *People of the Great Faith*, 134–6.
202. Macinnes, 'Religion in Gaelic Society', 228–30, 239–41.
203. Hunter, *Making of the Crofting Community*, 151–2.
204. Hunter, *Making of the Crofting Community*, 151–2.
205. Steve Bruce, 'Social Change and Collective Behaviour: The Revival in Eighteenth Century Ross-shire' (554–72), *British Journal of Sociology*, xxxiv 4 (1983), 567.
206. An exception to this rule is found in a recent publication, in the editor's 'Biographical Notes', in David Campbell (ed.), *The Suburbs of Heaven: The Diary of Murdoch Campbell* (Kilkerran, 2014), 154–5. A claim here is made that Murdoch Campbell's 'clairvoyance was not religious in origin', with the implication that this was some natural gift, which may 'call into question ordinary beliefs concerning the relation between mind and body'. This assertion approaches much closer to the traditional belief in second sight, and differs strongly from John Kennedy's reports of specifically spiritual experiences. It is not typical of Highland evangelical literature.

CHAPTER THREE

Constitutionalism

John Kennedy did not initially play much of a role in the wider affairs of the Free Church. Although ordained early in 1844 and attending the General Assembly as a commissioner about once every three years, he took no prominent role in Assembly proceedings until the 1870s. He did not deliver his maiden speech to the Assembly until 1872, when he was fifty-two.[1] As one of his biographers wrote:

> On the public questions of the day he had held his peace for years, and did not seem to care for platform speaking. It was only when forced in the interests of the truth he held so dear that he reluctantly entered the turbulent arena of controversy.[2]

In the latter years of his ministry, he began to contribute significantly to the internal debates of the Free Church, first by the publication of a substantial theological work, relevant to broader contemporary discussions, in 1869, and thereafter through a steady flow of controversial pamphlets from 1870 onwards, through addressing public meetings, and increasingly through contributions in church courts, including the Assembly.

By these means, he helped to mobilise the majority of Highland evangelical opinion on his own side in the central controversy of the nineteenth-century Free Church, which concerned the constitution of the Free Church of Scotland, and its consequent relation to the other major Presbyterian denominations in Scotland – the Established Church and the United Presbyterian Church. This controversy commenced in the mid-1860s over proposals for a full incorporating union with the United Presbyterian Church, which were successfully resisted by a minority within the Free Church, Kennedy included, on the grounds of theological divergence between the churches over the doctrine of the atonement and especially over the Establishment Principle. For taking this ground the minority became known as the constitutionalist party. Following this setback, the controversy continued in a new form, as the majority party sought to vitiate the latter ground of separation by challenging the privileged position of the Established Church in Scotland, leading eventually to the controversial majority decision of the Free Church General Assembly to call for full disestablishment in Scotland. This call was strenuously resisted and opposed by a minority within the Free Church, located chiefly in the Highlands, and led by Kennedy and his friend, James Begg.

Kennedy and the Atonement

The atonement, the concept of an absolute reconciliation achieved between a just God and sinful human beings, has always stood at the centre of evangelical theology and preaching. Thomas Chalmers wrote:

> The doctrine of the atonement, urged affectionately on the acceptance of the people, and held forth as the great stepping stone, by which one and all are welcome to enter into reconciliation and a new life [. . .] I hold to form the main staple of all good and efficient pulpit work.[3]

Scottish Presbyterians of the nineteenth century inherited from their forebears a rigorously defined Calvinistic doctrine of atonement as codified in the *Westminster Confession of Faith*. The *Confession* taught that the atonement was achieved by Christ's sufferings and death on the Cross, accepted in place of His people, whereby God's wrath was propitiated and the sins of Christ's chosen people were expiated forever.[4] The ministers of the Free Church of Scotland licensed prior to 1892 swore that they 'sincerely own[ed] and believe[d] the whole doctrine of the Confession' without reservation.[5]

But the Westminster doctrine was increasingly questioned in the changing theological climate of the nineteenth century. In particular, the Scottish theologian John McLeod Campbell rejected the Calvinistic formulation of the doctrine, arguing that the atonement was incorrectly described by Reformed theology in legal rather than familial terms. He argued for the universal Fatherhood of God, and for the atonement of Christ as consequentially universal rather than limited to His chosen elect.[6] He was convicted of heresy by the General Assembly in 1831 and deposed from the ministry of the Established Church, by mutual consent of evangelicals and moderates alike. He ministered independently in Glasgow thereafter, but his writings were hugely influential in later decades, especially his 1856 book *On the Nature of the Atonement*.

The Established Church minister James Cameron Lees was typical of many, as he 'read and reread McLeod Campbell', embracing the 'realisation of the Fatherhood of God which transfigured life for him'. Its effect was that 'he was delivered from the shadow of that Calvinism which darkened the lives of his fellows'.[7] This intense admiration, and consequent influence, were shared by the more liberally inclined ministers of the Free Church of the rising generation, such as Donald John Martin (1847–1913), minister of the Free English Church, Stornoway, and a rare Highland supporter of the liberalising trend in evangelical theology, who was 'profoundly glad' to be a relative of McLeod Campbell.[8] Alec Cheyne describes the theological change of the middle years of the century in gradual terms: 'The old emphasis upon election and reprobation slipped further and further into the background, and the tone of Scottish theology became gradually more liberal and charitable.' By the 1860s, the 'gradually accelerating transformation [had] become apparent'[9] and the pace of change did not slacken. By the first decade of the twentieth century, there could be no doubt that a revolution had occurred in Scottish Presbyterian theology, such that in the major denominations, as J. H. Leckie observed in 1907, 'The central thoughts [...] of the Confession are no longer the central thoughts of living faith. [...] The idea of the Divine Fatherhood [...] is the centre of real faith today.'[10] In other words, far from concurring in the General Assembly's condemnation of McLeod Campbell, the great majority of Scottish ministers came to share his conclusions. As Cheyne wrote: 'He is now generally regarded as his country's greatest modern theologian and the forerunner of a milder, more loving, more truly evangelical understanding of the faith.'[11]

Changing attitudes concerning the doctrine of the atonement first became evident in the United Presbyterian Church. One of the denominations that came together in 1847 to form the United Presbyterian Church was the United Secession Church; it had held several key heresy trials over the doctrines of traditional Westminster Calvinism in the 1840s. James Morison, a United Secession minister in Kilmarnock, was suspended in 1841 for advocating a universal atonement; then, two of the denomination's professors who had taught him, Robert Balmer and John Brown, faced similar charges. Balmer died before the conclusion of his case but Brown was formally acquitted in 1845, having argued that the language of the *Westminster Confession* could accommodate his view, which he defined as the 'double reference theory' of the atonement. Thereafter, he exercised a leading role within his church, and from 1847 in its successor, the United Presbyterian Church.[12] Cheyne emphasised the significance of this case:

> There seems to be no denying that from then onwards it was the love of God to all men which occupied the central place in the teaching and preaching of the United Secession and (after 1847) the United Presbyterian Church, and that the old emphasis upon election slipped further and further into the background.[13]

The double reference theory was, strictly speaking, distinct from an unqualified theory of universal atonement. Brown and his supporters argued that the death of Christ had a 'general reference' to all mankind: He died for all, but His atonement was only effectual to the salvation of some, the elect, who will have faith in Him. Thus Christ's atonement had both a general reference, which, in the words of Brown, was 'to lay a foundation for unlimited calls and invitations to mankind to accept salvation in the belief of the gospel', and also a particular reference, restricted to those specifically elected to salvation.[14] In practice, contemporary observers noted that the rather fine, and indeed rather questionable, distinction between this teaching and a direct assertion of universal atonement was increasingly lost as the years passed.[15] In any case, in 1879, the United Presbyterian Church passed a Declaratory Act that removed the obligation on all ministers to defend the confessional doctrine in every point, meaning that the fiction of unchanging adherence to the strict wording of the Confession no longer required to be maintained.

Ian Hamilton, whose postgraduate research addressed the change in credal subscription in the United Presbyterian Church, has traced the beginning of the 'erosion of Westminster Calvinism' in that Church directly to the Brown case of 1841–5. The outcome 'resulted in the sanctioning of Amyraldianism within the United Secession Church', which 'undermined the specific particularism of the [Westminster] Standards in their exposition of Christ's atonement'.[16] This dealt a 'body blow' to Westminster Calvinism, Hamilton argues, and was an indication that 'a climate of thought was evolving' in Scotland, increasingly open to a new theology.[17] It was undeniable that, as John Macleod noted, the Brown 'decision left ambiguous the relation of the largest body of the Secession to the Confessional teaching' on the Atonement.[18] The case, however, did not hinder the union of the United Secession Church with the Relief Church in 1847 that produced the United Presbyterian Church. Some United Presbyterians continued to adhere to Westminster Calvinism and to the limited atonement. However, as Alexander Stewart has observed, it was clear that there were 'two schools of thought' within that Church, one of which was 'inclining to a more or less modified form of Arminianism'. Soon, he noted, 'a theology of a more Arminian tendency prevailed within the U.P. Church than had yet found acceptance in the Free Church'.[19]

For Kennedy, as for many in the Free Church, the toleration of what they considered gravely erroneous teaching on the atonement within the United Presbyterian Church rendered any proposal for union highly questionable. Kennedy was firmly within the older category of Calvinist evangelical, for whom the Westminster formulation of the doctrine of the atonement was central and vital. His preaching centred upon Christ in His work as mediator between God and man, and on the absolute necessity of this work being applied to the soul of the believer. In this regard, he was entirely consistent with the theological orthodoxy of the Free Church from its formation in 1843. In the 1840s, there had been no distinction between Highland and Lowland evangelicalism on the atonement: for example, the early New College theologians, such as William Cunningham, had insisted on the absolute necessity of holding to a particular atonement.[20] Furthermore, the Free Church was prepared to defend this orthodoxy, and when, in 1845, William Scott, minister of Free St Mark's, Glasgow, was charged 'with teaching Morisonian views of man's natural inability', the Free Church General Assembly deposed him from the ministry.[21]

However, the Free Church was not immune to the broader trends of theological thought, and the next generation of teachers at the Free Church divinity colleges had to address the changing climate. Cunningham's successor as Principal of New College, Robert Candlish, delivered a course of public lectures on the fatherhood of God, challenging the increasingly popular notion of the universal fatherhood of God defended by McLeod Campbell, by the lay theologian Thomas Erskine of Linlathen and by the liberal Anglican theologian F. D. Maurice. He argued instead that the redeemed enter into a whole new relation of sonship with God through adoption, incomparable with their relationship to Him, even prior to the Fall: that only then do they become His sons and He their Father.[22] However, Candlish's vigorous denial of God's universal fatherhood, and corresponding denial of the Divine sonship of man, ignited some controversy. Thomas Crawford, an Established Church minister and Professor of Divinity at the University of Edinburgh, published a critical response to Candlish's lectures, defending a form of universal Divine fatherhood, though he distanced himself from heterodox authors like Maurice.[23] Even some of Candlish's friends disagreed with assertions made in his work, especially his controversial teaching that the redeemed become, by virtue of their union with Christ, sharers in the everlasting sonship of the Lord. On the key question addressed by the work, it was Candlish who was more in continuity with traditional Westminster Calvinism, as later theologians have recognised.[24] Still, the theological mood in Scotland was changing. As the contemporary scholar Andrew Fairbairn observed, 'it was Crawford, not Candlish, who appealed more strongly to Scotsmen of the eighteen-sixties'.[25]

In the Highlands, evangelicals had a history of contending for the limited fatherhood of God. As early as 1753, the evangelical minister Aeneas Sage of Lochcarron brought a charge of heresy against his colleague Aeneas Macaulay of Applecross, for a sermon the latter had preached on the text 'For we are also his offspring'.[26] The charge was eventually dismissed at the General Assembly of 1758, but John Macinnes noted that the controversial sermon was significant as 'premonitory of the direction taken by liberal evangelicalism in after ages', and gave a lengthy summary.[27] To a strict Calvinist evangelical like Sage, the teaching was evidently highly offensive. William Enright's research on nineteenth-century evangelical sermons showed that evangelicalism largely developed into liberal evangelicalism in Scotland between the years 1855 and 1880, and that one of the key themes evidencing this transition was the new emphasis in preaching on the fatherhood of God.[28]

Kennedy's 1869 treatise on the doctrine of adoption, *Man's Relations to God Traced in the Light of 'the Present Truth'*, was therefore a highly topical work, addressing both the contemporary theological trend towards assertions of universal Divine fatherhood, and the specific theological debate between Candlish and Crawford. As the later critic Donald Beaton observed:

> In this work, [Kennedy] deals with the question of the Fatherhood of God, and endeavours to take up a middle position between Dr Candlish's as set forth in his Cunningham Lecture [...] and the modern universalistic views of the doctrine of the Fatherhood.[29]

Above all, it was a critique of the theology permitted within the United Presbyterian Church, and thus, by implication, an argument against the proposal for union, on the basis of the constitutional stance of the Free Church. Kennedy structured the work in four substantive chapters, in a structure very comparable to that of the seventeenth-century Scottish theologian Thomas Boston in his famous work, *Human Nature in its Fourfold State*. Boston considered man in his states of 'primitive integrity, entire depravity, begun recovery, and consummate happiness or misery';[30] Kennedy, given his specific focus on adoption, addressed man in his relationship with God 'as created', 'as fallen', 'as evangelized' and 'as in Christ'.[31] In comparison with Boston's structure, Kennedy's approach particularly focused on the change in man's relationship with God in this world, rather than in its eternal fulfilment. However, Kennedy acknowledged in his Preface that the work had not entirely achieved his original aim as expressed in the title, comparing it to the body of a statue 'utterly dwarfed' by its head. Nonetheless, he expressed confidence in the argument of the work, asking only that his 'views be judged, not according to [his] design or execution, but as they appear in the light of Scripture'.[32]

Kennedy began with an assertion of God's creative work, of the trustworthiness of His record of it, and of the uselessness of attempting to ascertain it by speculation or by geological investigation.[33] His opening passage must be read in the light of the growing popularity of the theory of evolution as explanatory of human origins. For Kennedy, one seeking understanding of creation 'must occupy the standpoint which has been assigned to faith' and seek it 'in the light of Scripture', as its 'meaning is plain, and its authority is divine'.[34] Any theory of 'development' was, he argued, rendered untenable by the instantaneous character of the creation of man described in the Bible, and evolutionary theory downplayed the role of God in creation so that 'man can stand erect in his pride'. Kennedy's assertion that he and his readers 'stand on the further side of about six thousand years from that act of creation', based on 'Scripture history, and the steps of Scripture genealogy', was an explicit rejection of the geological timescale already widely accepted by nineteenth-century science, and by previous scientific commentators from the Free Church, such as the late Hugh Miller.[35] Kennedy's point was that man was a 'mere creature' of God, yet was also 'a thinking being', and 'as a soul, [. . .] in closer alliance to God than other creatures'.[36]

However, Kennedy argued, the unique nature of man implied a unique relation to God, that man required the direction of the moral law, but that this was exercised through conscience, so that the responsibility for obedience was his alone.[37] Equally, however, this law reflected the character of God and His justice: 'Man's relation to God as judge, is thus normal and necessary, and therefore everlasting.'[38] Therefore His absolute justice in dealing with sinners is essential to God: 'were he less rigorous I could not revere Him'.[39] The specific form of this relationship of law was stated by Kennedy as the 'Adamic covenant', with God's promise to Adam of life being conditional on Adam fulfilling his promise of obedience. Therefore to man's relations with God as his creator, sovereign and judge was added the additional relation of covenanted obedience, with Adam, 'constituted the federal head of all his seed', giving 'an epitome of the whole – a perfect sample of the wise and holy government, which shall finally be wound up in a consummation'.[40]

This conclusion led on, however, to Kennedy posing the crucial question arising from contemporary theological debate: that is, whether God had a relationship of fatherhood to man in his created state. Kennedy answered it decisively: 'It is impossible to reconcile what has been done by God, as Sovereign and Judge, with what should be expected from Him, as Father.' Indeed, he described this conclusion as 'one of the outworks of Calvinism which has not hitherto been sufficiently strengthened'.[41] On the theological debate on God's fatherhood, Kennedy asserted that first 'It is necessary to determine what such a relation implies, ere we enquire whether it exists. His not doing so, at the outset, is a marked defect, in the first part of Principal Candlish's remarkable work on "the Fatherhood of God".'[42] Kennedy argued for two conclusions: first, that the relationship of creation was different from that which would later be established by Divine adoption; and second, that it was not analogous to human fatherhood. While he acknowledged that 'Creation did constitute such a relationship as subsists between a parent and his offspring', he distinguished this from fatherhood as a purely genealogical relationship. Kennedy recognised that human parenthood necessarily implied the moral responsibility of fatherhood, but he denied that this could apply to God:

> What law could impose an obligation on Jehovah to act the part of Father to his creature? Did he not create him with a view to the manifestation of His own glory[?] Is He not free to deal with him in order to that end, without being restricted by any such conditions as fatherhood would impose[?]
>
> The relation of fatherhood would impose conditions which cannot consist with the free exercise of God's sovereignty.[43]

Kennedy argued that any claim of universal fatherhood would require that God exercise His sovereignty in fatherly love to His children, thus rendering it 'utterly impossible that His child can die'. By instead placing man 'under trial', by permitting the serpent's temptation, the Fall and death, God had not demonstrated fatherhood. While God has provided 'instances of goodness', yet these 'fall short of a full expression of a human father's love'.[44] Furthermore, God cannot be considered a Father to fallen man, given their 'eternal woe', yet the Fall of man could not logically terminate a relation inherent in man's creation.[45] If God's fatherhood were indeed a relation terminated by the Fall, then salvation would be merely a restoration to the original state. However, in Kennedy's view, the New Testament evidence suggested that the new relationship secured by adoption was far superior, 'more secure than Adam's was, and more elevated than his would have been, even if he had never fallen'.[46]

Furthermore, as Kennedy argued from specific examples, the Scriptures usually cited in favour of universal Divine fatherhood, supported instead only parenthood.[47] Moreover, there was a fundamental contradiction between universal fatherhood and limited atonement: 'A Father, as such, loving all His family, and providing salvation only for some of them'. Instead, he stated, in conclusion to his first chapter:

> [The Bible] plainly teaches, that God saves sinners, not because He was the Father of any or of all; but because, as the great 'I am,' He will have mercy on whom He will. Salvation flows to men, not necessarily out of the divine nature, nor as a natural result of previous divine procedure, nor as a fitting expression of fatherly affection, but from the good pleasure of the sovereign Lord of all; because He loves, not because He is love; because He is the Lord and has willed to love, and not because He is a Father and is bound to love.[48]

The theory of universal Divine fatherhood thus entailed serious difficulties for the goodness of God as a father, and for the freedom of God in the exercise of salvation.

In the second chapter, Kennedy addressed the relations of God to man in his fallen state. He emphasised that sin commenced 'as an act, in him', and though Satan tempted man to fall, the deed was that of man, without any external compulsion.[49] The result was deadness, enmity to God and the entire loss of the image of God in man, a subject so tragic that Kennedy expressed it in uncharacteristically poetic terms:

> That temple is now an utter ruin. True there is still some light – 'the work of the law written in the heart,' – but, like a lamp, hung from the broken vault of a ruin, its flickering glimmer only makes more manifest the wreck on which it shines. True, there is a conscience still in that fallen soul, which seems as if it were a living thing amidst the dead; – the one survivor of those who once worshipped in that temple. It is there, and it speaks; but its cry, like the screech of the owl amidst the desolation of the ruin, only serves to make the place more dismal. It befits the ruin; it is no exception to its utterness. Or, if a survivor, it is so only as that maniac is, to whom the fall of the temple was the death of his reason; and who, with the life of an animal only, still haunts the scene of ruin, finding nought to feed on but the putrid carcases of the dead, and making with his shrieks, which express alike his madness, his hunger, and his loathing, the place more dismal than if all were still.[50]

This succession of images conveyed the starkness of the doctrine of man's fall, that the lost sinner's ruin is complete, and the presence of conscience only emphasised the utter destruction of his moral character. In the face of a theological trend towards mitigating the extent of the Fall through teaching God's universal fatherhood, Kennedy was determined to establish the opposite, the total depravity of fallen man.

The misery of man's situation was exacerbated, Kennedy argued, by his status, being 'a dependent creature and, at the same time, a guilty sinner', enjoying God's temporary forbearance, yet hating His holiness and dreading His coming judgment.[51] Man's status remains under the covenant of works, broken on man's side but not on God's, and therefore God remains committed by His covenant to punish sin and to demand perfect obedience to His law. Under this relation, Kennedy stated, 'there is a strong tendency to hide the stern aspects of our state, as sinners, in relation to God' because men will 'cleave to self and cling to hope' and thus choose a standard 'that shall not disturb their self-complacency'.[52] Thus, said Kennedy with regard to the then current theological debate, 'they cast the veil of universal fatherhood over the stern aspect of God's character and relation as Judge'[53] – a metaphor with the obvious implication that what was being concealed was nonetheless real. God showed mercy in forbearance, in His ongoing providence and especially in His provision of a covenant of grace; but Kennedy insisted that in none of these arrangements did He contravene His first covenant or provide any basis for an assertion of universal fatherhood.[54] Taking the same analogy as before, Kennedy expressed more bluntly his objection to a theological teaching he saw as deceitful:

> The fiction of a universal fatherhood of God, expressed to all in the kindness of providence, has been woven by the imagination of sinful men, as a veil by which to hide the stern glory of God's name and throne as Judge. They like to think of Him as a Father, who is indulgent to His foolish children, and to whose pity their helplessness can effectually appeal. He seems to them a Being in whom compassion is a weakness, of which advantage may be taken; instead of being regarded as a Sovereign, who, in order to the fulfilment of His purposes, and in perfect consistency with all His rigorous righteousness as Judge, is extending mercy for a season to sinners, who shall all the more miserably perish, if His goodness shall not lead them to repentance.[55]

The change in relation that granted to some the hope of eternal salvation was their free election in Christ to eternal life: this choice, Kennedy said, rendered their salvation 'infallible; while the salvation of all others, appears, to the divine mind, an utter impossibility'.[56] For these elect, Christ was their incarnate brother, and their redeemer before God; for their sake only, the world continued and the grace of God was at work.[57]

Kennedy's third chapter addressed God in His relations to man 'as evangelized'. He emphasised that this relation must be consistent with man's fallenness; with His purpose in election; and with the revelation of His covenant in the Old Testament. The fuller light of the gospel was not new, Kennedy argued, in being revealed through a Mediator, because God's revelation was always by Christ; in superseding the Old Testament revelation, because it was consistent with it; or in undermining the covenant of works or the moral law, which still stood.[58] However, he stated that 'the gospel dispensation is *brighter, freer, more catholic,* and more *spiritual* than that which preceded it', and went on to expand on each of the italicised terms.[59] Kennedy then addressed the relation of sinners to whom the gospel is preached – to God, Christ, the atonement and salvation.[60] The gospel revealed God in His character of absolute truth and justice, as well as of love, and of sovereign grace that achieved fully His purpose of love in the salvation of His elect people. In Kennedy's view, it was only pride that brought forth the contradiction, which he described as 'the anxiety to evade the truth that electing love is the source of all salvation'.[61] He rejected the view that there was another, more general love of God that did not lead to salvation, and emphasised that such love, in any case, could be no of comfort to the unconverted sinner: 'To tell him that God loves him as He hath loved millions who are already in hell, is but to dishearten him, and it dishonours God.'[62] He strongly defended the preaching of the gospel to all men without distinction because it was God's grace alone that could bring forth a response, and that an earnest call could be addressed to all, because it was the genuine and authoritative summons of the sinner to glorify Christ as his saviour.[63]

Kennedy wrote further that Christ Himself was the great theme of the gospel, and the great need of the sinner was nothing less than living union with Him, a true saving faith in the Person of the Son, rather than merely in some statement about Him.[64] Specifically, the message of the gospel was Christ as crucified, in Whose death an interest was 'essential to safety'. Kennedy conveyed the necessity of Christ by using a very topical illustration, drawn from the extreme difficulties in laying the first transatlantic telegraph cables over the preceding fifteen years:

> It is along the line of divine intention the current of saving grace flows forth to men through Jesus Christ. It is along the wire that the electric current passes through the ocean; but the wire must be hid ere it can conduct the subtle stream. It must be carefully covered, and all the wrapping which conceals it, must extend to the further shore. The current is stopped when the covering is pierced. It is when the section of the whole cable has reached, that the message can be carried to, the further shore; and only then can the wire be denuded and exposed to view. Thus is the chain of love from heaven to earth covered with the design of salvation to sinners.[65]

Thus Kennedy argued that the 'personal reference' could not be separated from 'the gracious design of the death of Christ'; the death could not be dissociated from the person of Christ; nor could the Spirit be ignored in the free sovereignty of His working.[66]

At this point, Kennedy addressed the double reference theory of the atonement, explained above, making his view of this theory plain: 'There are some who, Calvinists in their vows and Arminians in their tendencies, teach the doctrine of a double reference of the atonement.'[67] He pointed out the incompatibility of believing that a universal reference of Christ's atonement made salvation possible if it did not make it certain:

> How can the possibility of my salvation be before the mind of God, unless He sees my sins atoned for in the death of Christ? How could they be atoned for unless they were imputed to Him? And how could they be imputed to Him unless He was my surety?[68]

In fact, if strict definitions were adhered to, Kennedy insisted, this general reference 'is after all no reference of the atonement. There is no atonement that does not imply satisfaction to divine justice.'[69] Rather, while there were benefits to all mankind from the death of Christ, these benefits were not a reference of the atonement, but 'merely an accident of the process, whereby all good is conveyed to some'. The actual work of Christ was, Kennedy insisted, directed to the salvation of the elect. Therefore, he reached a strongly worded conclusion on the double reference theory:

> The doctrine of the double reference is an oil and water mixture; – it is opposed to Scripture; – no one who has subscribed the Confession of Faith can consistently hold it; – it adopts the practical bearing of Arminianism; – it endangers the doctrine of the atonement; – and it is quite unavailing for the purpose to which it is applied.[70]

In the succeeding pages, Kennedy amassed evidence in support of each of the statements of this paragraph.[71] This was a theological conclusion, but its implications for the Free Church of Scotland were evident, though not stated. It would have been quite obvious to Kennedy's readers that his words called into question the wisdom of the Free Church pursuing union negotiations, given that the double reference theory was explicitly tolerated in the United Presbyterian Church.

Kennedy went on in the work to defend the free offer of the gospel, arguing that it could be maintained consistently with Divine sovereignty, 'if we viewed salvation *as embodied in the Christ whom the Gospel reveals, and as embosomed in the promise given to all who believe in His name*'. Salvation was freely offered to all in Christ but would be accepted only by those whom the Father drew, and he argued that this should be the content of gospel preaching, on the basis of exegesis of Christ's sermon from John 6.[72]

In his fourth and final chapter, Kennedy discussed 'Man, as in Christ, in relation to God'. Such a man, he argued, is born again into new life by the Spirit of God dwelling and working in him, is now the seed and member of Christ, and is thus truly of God.[73] He is justified by a sovereign and just God, securing entire remission of his guilt, because of the love of God, through the work of Christ, securing eternal life.[74] Kennedy defined the Reformed doctrine of justification as resulting in actual entitlement to life for the believer, and thus in a new relation to God, superior to that even of Adam before the Fall.[75] This new relation is the act of adoption, whereby God becomes a Father to the believer through the work of Christ, following in due succession from his regeneration and justification.[76] At this point, Kennedy addressed the debate between Candlish and Crawford, in addressing the bearing of the Christ's sonship 'on the sonship of the adopted': 'They differed from each other, but they both differed from the truth.' Candlish had argued that the adopted shared Christ's sonship, while Crawford had denied any connection at all; but Kennedy argued rather that Christ's sonship *cannot affect the sonship of the adopted, except so far as it affects His own relations and power, as the Christ of God*.[77] Thus he described Christ's humiliation in His life and work in the flesh, and His subsequent exaltation in His human nature into His place as Son in Heaven, bearing His people with Him in His relation to them as their covenant Head. The result was that 'the Sonship of Christ, as exalted in human nature, represents His Kingly power, as His people's Head'.[78] Kennedy described the effect of this relation as follows:

> Now I cannot trace the course of Christ from His place as servant and surety in the flesh on earth, up to His position of power and glory as the Son on high, and keep in view throughout His relation to His people, without expecting as the result, an analogous transition of all His members, from bondage and insecurity, as the servants of sin, into the liberty and steadfastness of the position of sons in the Father's house.[79]

Thus, he argued, the sonship of believers was because of Christ's sonship but was not identical to it, being necessarily subordinate, a position distinct from both that of Candlish and that of Crawford:

> The Spirit of adoption is the spirit of the Son. He hath power to send Him, now that He is in the Son's place on high, and the Spirit comes to give to them the enjoyment of what is theirs in union with the Son.[80]

Kennedy quoted John 20: 17 in support of his view, 'I ascend unto my Father and your Father, and to my God and your God,' emphasising the connection and yet distinction implied in these words. He went on to describe the new relationship established with the Father by adoption, in its privilege, in its chastisement but in its ultimate safety; with the Son, as their first-born brother, redeemer, living head, and model to which they shall be conformed; and with the Spirit, as the one effecting this change and, as the comforter, the one granting foretastes of their eternal privilege.[81]

Inevitably, the popular reception of the work was more limited than for Kennedy's two previous historical publications, as Alexander Auld acknowledged:

> The circulation of this book, though fairly good, could not be expected to be extensive, on account of its severely logical structure and conden-

sation of truth. It would make an admirable text-book for a teacher of theology, but it would receive, as it did receive, a cold reception from those who cannot deal with God's universal call in the Gospel without endeavouring to trench on His eternal purpose to save an elect people.[82]

The uncompromising nature of the book, rejecting as it did the whole trend of contemporary theological thought, was hardly such as to command unstinting praise. A dismissive notice in *The Glasgow Herald* commented: 'We are by no means satisfied that all the theology of the book is Biblical, but it is more than orthodox, and unmistakeably "dogmatic",' adding that the author 'makes some statements that to us sound rather like unconscious and unintentional profanity'. However, the reviewer acknowledged that Kennedy's name was 'highly respectable' and that his work displayed 'considerable ability'; it would 'no doubt prove very acceptable fare in the North'.[83] The *British and Foreign Evangelical Review* did not welcome the work either, acknowledging 'acuteness, energy and skill in dialectics' in the volume, but regretting its publication, as 'we were flattering ourselves with the idea that evangelical divines were beginning to come to a better mutual understanding'.[84] In theology, Kennedy's work was wholly out of touch with the spirit of the times. A Free Church periodical, *The Presbyterian*, which openly campaigned for union with the United Presbyterians under Rainy's editorship, gave the book a more nuanced reception, praising Kennedy's reputation and the 'condensation and rapidity of treatment' of the work. In particular, 'he presents us with a great deal of fresh and vigorous thinking, and exhibits many aspects of the truth with great force'. The reviewer went on:

> If we were to select any feature of the book for especial mention, it ought to be, perhaps, the sense and recognition of the majesty of God which appear throughout [. . .] We would direct attention also to the power with which Mr Kennedy grasps and wields the whole connection of the positive Calvinistic theology. We are not sure that he always observes the limits which a wise discretion would impose on the argumentative use of so great an engine; but we admire the insight and cogency with which he argues.[85]

The reviewer recognised the quality of Kennedy's reasoning, even while rejecting his principal theological assertions relevant to the union controversy.[86]

Kennedy's book is rightly characterised by Alan Sell as his 'most sustained and least controversial piece of theological writing', and as a work that 'expose[d] the kernel of Kennedy's theology'. Sell does not accede to Kennedy's principal argument, but instead follows Kennedy's younger contemporary, the Free Church theologian A. B. Bruce, in asking, 'may we not hold that God *is* Father of all by virtue of creation, but that not all are true sons?' Kennedy certainly would not consider that proposition to answer his objection to the Fall of man as inconsistent with the care that might be expected of God for His children, but it does indicate the trend of response to the fatherhood debate that developed in evangelical theology in the latter half of the nineteenth century. But despite this demur, Sell recognises the 'practical and experimental interests' of Kennedy's Calvinist theology, 'in the line of the best of the Puritans', and defends him against the charge of 'Hyper-Calvinism'.[87] David Bebbington points out that Kennedy had resisted the developing trend in evangelical theology, in common with the Anglican theologian and Bishop of Liverpool, J. C. Ryle, noting of *Man's Relations to God*: 'It is clear that Kennedy felt the force of the cultural trend towards reformulating the conception of deity in terms of fatherhood, but was steeling himself to resist it.' Nonetheless, the teaching of universal fatherhood prevailed and, just as Kennedy predicted, led to a general modification of the doctrine of the atonement in evangelical theology in a universalist direction.[88]

But Kennedy's work was more than a theological treatise; it was also a challenge to the developing progress of the movement for union between the Free Church and the United Presbyterian Church. Historians have rightly identified the doctrine of the atonement as key to Kennedy's opposition to the union, especially Kennedy's conviction that the United Presbyterian Church was tolerating heterodox views on the subject within its ranks.[89] The publication of *Man's Relations to God* seems to have been a crucial moment for Kennedy, as his absolute rejection of double reference theory as unscriptural and unconfessional left him with no logical alternative other than outright opposition to a union with a church that permitted the view amongst its ministers. Contemporary responses to the work were therefore shaped by the union debate, with Kennedy's unionist colleague Thomas M'Lauchlan considering him to have taken an objectionably 'high ground' on predestination in the volume, adding that Kennedy had 'found few to follow him' in his position.[90] On the other hand, the anti-unionist periodical *The Watchword*, edited by Kennedy's close friend and ally James Begg, welcomed the work 'as an able and seasonable contribution in the defence of present truth'. The review expressed some caution: the writer, 'without being committed to all the views put forth in the volume', commended the book for its opposing the double reference theory of the atonement 'with much ability, force, and decision'; a later issue of *The Watchword* carried a lengthy extract. Interestingly, the publication was taken as indicating that Kennedy 'himself can take no part in the union' given his rejection of the double reference theory, suggesting that this had not previously been known to the anti-unionist leaders.[91] A favourable quotation from *Man's Relations to God* in the letters page of a later issue indicated that at least one 'Free Church Minister' had appreciated Kennedy's writing on the atonement.[92]

However, despite this appreciation, it is possible that Kennedy did feel some later dissatisfaction with *Man's Relations to God*. A reference to the volume is found in the biography of Kennedy's contemporary and close friend, the Highland elder Archibald Crawford:

> As soon as he could, Archie got a copy and read it. There was one criticism that he felt disposed to pass upon it – that it did not hold the balance between the claims of God's Sovereignty and man's responsibility, the latter being too lightly stressed. This was a matter on which Crawford laid great emphasis, that men must have brought to their own door the full tale of their responsibility for how they treat both Law and Gospel.[93]

The author went on to describe how Kennedy was apparently brought round to Crawford's way of thinking through an experience of illness that convinced him of his fault, such that 'The new note that was to be detected in his subsequent teaching was the emphasis that he laid on the hearer's responsibility for receiving the Gospel.'[94] The narrative does not directly assert that Kennedy acknowledged a defect in his volume, and, in fairness to him, Crawford's concern was plainly only for balance rather than regarding any explicitly unorthodox statement. The freeness of the gospel offer and its necessity in preaching were both clearly stated in Kennedy's volume,[95] albeit its principal concern was with the matters directly at stake in the relevant contemporary debates.

Later assessments of the work from strictly confessional Calvinist writers have been positive. The publisher's 'Introduction' to a new edition of the work in 1998 by the James Begg Society, an organisation dedicated to the propagation of the Westminster Calvinism typical of Begg and Kennedy, commends the work to its readers as 'a heavenly blend of doctrine and devotion, a fine example which refutes the idea that doctrine is dry and lifeless'.[96] Similarly, the twentieth-century Free Church minister John Macleod writes of Kennedy as a theologian: 'In doctrine he was clear and powerful and at the same time practical: He was tender and judicious in his application of his message and he was an experimental divine in the best sense of the word.'[97] Both writers therefore concur that Kennedy's theology was not abstract or disengaged from the reality of life, but was directed to Christian experience.

As Kennedy's most substantial work in theology, *Man's Relations to God* defended a rigorously confessional Calvinistic theology that, however in keeping with the constitutional basis of the Free Church of Scotland, was increasingly out of favour in Scotland of the 1860s. Tellingly, the writer in *The Glasgow Herald* anticipated that Kennedy's book would find a more favourable reception in Highland than in Lowland Scotland, as there was more sympathy for such theology in the Highlands. Kennedy's rejection of universal fatherhood defied the rather sentimental trend of nineteenth-century thought, as he insisted on the rigorous logic of the limited atonement. His careful definition of the adoptive sonship of believers as distinct from but based upon the Divine Sonship of Christ improved upon the rather loose formulations of the doctrine by both Candlish and Crawford in their debate earlier in the same decade. But Kennedy's work was especially important because he discerned the direct logical link between assertions of universal fatherhood and of universal atonement, and identified both as heterodox teachings, leading in a gravely erroneous direction. On the basis of this conclusion, he had no logical alternative but to engage more directly in ecclesiastical controversy.

Kennedy and the Union Controversy

By 1863, the leadership of the Free Church of Scotland was increasingly interested in exploring the possibility of union with the United Presbyterian Church, a denomination formed in 1847 by a union that brought together the principal remnants of the eighteenth-century Secession Churches into a third national Presbyterian Church in Scotland. The Free Church General Assembly of 1863 appointed a large Union Committee of representatives of all parts of the Free Church to discuss the prospects of union. This Committee made slow progress, attempting to identify the key points of difference between the two churches in terms of history and constitution. In particular, the Committee acknowledged that the United Presbyterian Church diverged from the Free Church in that it largely rejected the principle of church Establishment by the State, permitted theological divergence on the double reference of the atonement, and sanctioned the use of hymns in public worship.[98] By the 1865 Assembly, Julius Wood, a former Moderator, had heard enough and argued that negotiations be discontinued. In 1866, a motion to that effect was moved on the floor of the Assembly, but although the commissioners divided heavily against it, 439 to 7, it was an indicator of underlying concern.[99] Discussions continued, but it was evident that the differences were real, and could be resolved only by leaving the issues as open questions, which was inconceivable to those who considered them vital points of principle. In 1867, a group of six resigned from the Union Committee, led by James Begg, and now strongly opposed continuance with the discussions. The significance of Begg's leadership was plain from the sudden growth in the anti-unionist vote, with the commissioners dividing 346 to 120 in support of Robert Rainy's motion that there was 'no bar' to union, and with Begg tabling a protest against the finding.[100]

However, in reconstructing the events that led up to this first vote, which indicated a major divergence of opinion within the Free Church on the question of union, there is an important difference between the standard church histories and the account suggested by the available evidence. Drummond and Bulloch assert that Begg persuaded Kennedy of the impossibility of a union consistent with the principles of the Free Church, with the assertion that this persuasion was effected prior to the vote of 1867:

[Begg] looked round for allies, found none worth having in the south, and decided that he must find his army where Prince Charles Edward had found it, in the north. In 1866 Begg had two wars on his hands. The other was against the introduction of hymns, and by happy coincidence his prospective allies were of one mind with him on this also. Dr John Kennedy, a man of strong Christian devotion and unyielding Calvinist principles, was the leader of the Free Church in the Gaelic north, deeply respected by the Highlanders, and not without cause. Begg communicated with Kennedy and persuaded him that the United Presbyterian Church was unreliable at a most sensitive point, the doctrine of the atonement [...] From now on Begg could rely on the backing of a solid phalanx from the north who would support him through thick and thin. The result was seen at the Free Church Assembly of 1867.[101]

As evidence for this paragraph, Drummond and Bulloch cite the accounts from Simpson's biography of Rainy, from MacEwan's life of Cairns and from the memoir of Kennedy by John Noble. Yet even granted a bit of dramatic licence for an engaging piece of writing – for example, Begg had quite a number of prominent allies in the South, especially amongst the older and more robustly Calvinistic ministers, though admittedly probably not enough to succeed in preventing the union – this account does founder on the detail. There is no evidence to suggest that Kennedy was persuaded by Begg, or indeed at all, of the anti-unionist cause prior to 1867, either in the cited sources or elsewhere.

Undoubtedly, Begg's leadership was vital to the anti-unionist cause. He brought skill and confidence in Assembly debate, vigour in public speaking, and a willingness to engage in the controversy through every available medium. He founded a monthly magazine, *The Watchword*, as early as 1866, and maintained its publication throughout the controversy, as well as establishing a Free Church Defence Association to rally public support against the union. Contemporary sources from both sides of the partisan divide concurred that his leadership was vital in these respects in building the strength of anti-unionist feeling and, ultimately, in preventing the union from taking place.[102] Subsequent historians have concurred with this assessment.[103] Furthermore, it is true that in the later stages of the controversy both Kennedy and Begg were united in their opposition to the union. Kennedy was, as his biographer noted, 'one of those who perceived that the Churches differed radically, especially on the questions of "the Atonement" and of "the relation of the civil magistrate to religion and to the Church of Christ"', and who could not permit these to be left open questions.[104]

Yet the assertion that Begg personally persuaded Kennedy of the need to resist the union prior to the first crucial vote of 1867, and thus benefited from the outset from Kennedy's advocacy of his cause, holds no water. Kennedy was not a commissioner in 1867, and the record showed that of the six commissioners from his Presbytery, two did not register a vote on the union, and the other four voted in favour of continuing the negotiations. Of the commissioners from the whole Synod of Ross, eight voted in favour of the unionist motion and only four against, with five not registering votes. The 120 commissioners who supported Begg's opposition to the union were from Presbyteries throughout the Free Church, with no remarkable concentration in the Highlands.[105] Furthermore, Kennedy apparently did not support the action of Begg and his immediate allies in resigning from the Union Committee in 1867, as he allowed his own name to be nominated for the Committee the following year, was duly appointed, and in fact continued to serve on the Committee until its discharge in 1873.[106] That Kennedy actually joined the Union Committee in 1868, a fact which appears to have escaped the notice of every previous writer on the controversy, should be sufficient to show that his eventually decided opposition was the fruit of serious reflection over a period of years and, more to the point, of actual engagement in the negotiations with the United Presbyterian delegation. Kenneth Macdonald, minister of Applecross Free Church, recorded a significant conversation with Kennedy, probably from the year 1868:

> Shortly after that I met Mr Kennedy of Dingwall, afterwards Dr Kennedy, and as he was a member of the union committee, I asked him his opinion as to the outcome of the negotiations. His calm reply was 'Union is sure to take place, the leaders are committed to it.' What concerned him most was the question of doctrine, and he believed the United Presbyterians were safe on that point. He was satisfied from his intercourse with their representatives in the committee, that they were thoroughly sound as a Church, and that it would be unfair to blame the denomination for the stray utterances of some of its members. The prospect of union did not alarm him.[107]

If this testimony is accepted, then Kennedy did not become a convinced opponent of union until some time after joining the Committee in 1868. As Macdonald observed, it was only 'later on' that Kennedy would help to form 'a strong anti-union party in the Highlands'.[108]

In fact, it can be definitely demonstrated that Kennedy did not reject outright the possibility of continuing union negotiations in 1868, as at a meeting of the Ross Synod in that year he moved an amendment 'that if the negotiations between the two churches were to be continued, there should be no ambiguity on the doctrine of the atonement'. He did, however, on that occasion, express grave concern regarding the double reference theory. His motion was overwhelmingly defeated, in favour of unqualified support for the union negotiations to proceed.[109] At the Assembly of that year, when Kennedy was again not a commissioner, his elder brother Donald, minister of Killearnan Free Church, actively opposed Begg, voting in favour of progress towards union, and would do so again in 1870.[110] As late as May 1869, Begg was calling upon Kennedy by name to come out against the union publicly: 'Have Dr Duff, and Mr Kennedy of Dingwall, considered the matter?'[111] Yet that same month, Kennedy himself failed to vote either way on the union question as a commissioner in the General Assembly.[112] And, as mentioned above, in June 1869, *The Watchword*, under Begg's editorial control, responded gratefully to the publication of *Man's Relations to God* as evidence that Kennedy would not enter the union,[113] even though Kennedy had not directly referred to the union question in the text. The evidence suggested that he carefully worked his own way through the question, over a period of two or even three years, before committing himself to the anti-unionist cause. There was no basis for the portrayal of Kennedy as a man swayed by the direct personal influence of Begg right at the beginning of the controversy.

Indeed, Kennedy does not seem to have publicly expressed direct opposition to the proposed union earlier than 1870, when he began to address public meetings and to publish pamphlets in opposition to it.[114] One biographer wrote of the effect of his early campaigning:

> Many will still remember the remarkable speech which Dr Kennedy delivered at an anti-Union meeting in the Inverness Music Hall in September 1870. It roused an immense audience to the highest pitch of approval and admiration, and, being circulated in thousands, had a great effect throughout the Highlands.[115]

Kennedy informed the Presbytery of Dingwall, at its meeting of 8 August 1870, that when the question of union was taken up for discussion, he would move that 'the reports do not evince the existence, on the part of the churches represented in the joint Union Committee, of such unity in principle, as would warrant an incorporating union on the basis of the Westminster Standards'.[116] At the meeting of 21 December, he accordingly moved in these terms but was opposed by Malcolm Macgregor, minister of Urquhart Free Church, who moved 'that there is no difference of principle between the negotiating churches, which should prevent an incorporating union'. The Presbytery narrowly passed Kennedy's motion, by 5 votes to 3.[117] The result was reported in *The Scotsman*, as was Kennedy's more convincing victory in the Ross Synod, which in 1872 opposed union by 12 votes to 7.[118] Evidence suggests that it was after 1870, when Kennedy took a clear and outspoken stance against it, that opposition to the union became general in the Highland Free Church.

Ulrich Dietrich, in a postgraduate dissertation from 1974, has undertaken a detailed analysis of the geographical distribution of votes in the successive Assemblies in the union controversy, and found that the anti-union movement, while always stronger in the North, only reached a majority among the Highland commissioners in 1871–2.[119] This suggests that, apparently like Kennedy himself, Highland ministers and elders may have taken time to reach a settled view on the subject. It may also indicate the importance of Kennedy's leadership and persuasion in particular, in coming out very strongly and publicly against the union in 1870, in persuading a majority of Highland commissioners eventually to oppose the union. In a helpful series of tables, Dietrich shows that the Assembly commissioners from the Synod of Glenelg had moved to a heavily anti-unionist position from 1870 onwards, and those of Sutherland and Caithness to the same position from 1871. Those from Kennedy's own Synod, Ross, were by a majority against union in 1871, and more firmly still in 1872. Commissioners from the more peripheral Highland Synod of Moray were in the majority against union in 1872, and those from Argyll in 1871, though just short of a majority in 1872. While the minority opposition to union in the Lowland synods remained generally consistent in proportion through the years 1867–72, the opposition grew dramatically in the Highlands, and by 1872 included the overwhelming majority of commissioners from the North.[120] These tables suggest that the constitutionalists won the union controversy in the Highlands – and therefore that the role of the leading Highland ministers, of whom Kennedy was pre-eminent, was crucial. As a contemporary correspondent observed, the 'Highland segment' proved sufficiently strong to prevent the union.[121] In fairness to Drummond and Bulloch, on this, the central point, their analysis was borne out by the evidence.

Drummond and Bulloch's error with regard to the chronology of Kennedy's involvement in the union controversy seems to have come from a misreading of Simpson, whose biography of Rainy, though exceedingly partisan, is nonetheless a valuable historical source. Simpson argued that the anti-unionist leaders, chiefly Begg, had imported their opposition to the union into the Highlands, exploiting the pre-existent division, which he considered to be 'racial'. In particular, the anti-unionists achieved their purpose, he argued, by winning over the leading ministers, Kennedy in particular:

> Immediately after the critical Assembly of 1867, Dr Begg went north and stayed a week in Ross-shire, and there he won the adherence of the most influential Highland preacher of the time – Dr John Kennedy of Dingwall. Dr Kennedy was a really eminent and, in many ways, a noble man. [...] Undoubtedly Dr Kennedy was an extraordinary preacher, and even a reader of his *Days of the Fathers in Ross-shire* can feel something of his literary and religious power. But, by general testimony, he seems to have been impressionable and impulsive, and a man who could be led by natures more commonplace than his own. Dr Begg, a far less spiritual and less noble but a far more forceful man, could lead him and use him. The combination of these two men meant an immense advantage for the anti-union party in the north. It did not mean that the Highlands were completely brought under it; for many ministers and congregations in the north – including some of the very best – stood staunch against anti-union tactics and refused

to follow Begg or even Kennedy. A truer Highland churchmanship was there all the time and was gradually extricating itself. But Begg and Kennedy [. . .] were able to carry conflagration through the Highlands and make the problem for the whole Church a very serious one.[122]

Disregarding the partisan shots, Simpson's testimony here is most important: Begg had actively pursued Kennedy's support, but after, rather than before, the 1867 vote. In one respect, the account is defective: namely, the implication that a week's contact with Begg was sufficient to turn Kennedy into a fervent opponent of union. But there is no real contradiction between Simpson's information and the other sources that suggested that Kennedy gradually came to oppose the union entirely between 1867 and his final emergence as a vigorous public campaigner on the point in 1870. Begg may have stimulated Kennedy to consider the question afresh but the evidence suggests that he did his own thinking.

Yet, despite the evidence, the assertion that Kennedy's opposition to the union was due to Begg's influence has been repeated consistently in the literature of the union controversy. In part, this must be attributed to partisan feeling against the anti-unionists, who were seen by their opponents as having obstructed an important step of progress in the nineteenth-century Free Church. As Kennedy was remembered so widely with evident affection, it was easier to undermine the significance of his inveterate opposition to the union as the result of a baleful external influence. Begg, while grudgingly admired for his gifts, seems to have commanded no such affection, and could therefore be portrayed as the malignant adversary responsible for the stalled progress: Rainy caricatured him as 'the evil genius of the Free Church'.[123] A good example of this was in the biographical sketch of Kennedy by Norman Macfarlane, a minister of the United Free Church, and therefore bound to register his demur from Kennedy on this point:

> He kept company with that gentle warrior, Dr Begg, who was hatched from an egg that differed much from the Kennedy egg. Dr Begg was gentle in the respect that he never lost temper, kept calm as a pond, and threw into his speeches humorous stories. He had granitic hardness and was as dogmatic as a timetable. Controversy makes strange beds! How Dr Kennedy, with all his spiritual instincts in bloom, could lie in the bosom of Dr Begg was one of the stupefying problems of the Highland mind.[124]

The choice of language here, 'lie in the bosom', redolent of the lamb belonging to the poor man in the parable of 2 Samuel 12, subtly suggested a lack of power or responsibility on Kennedy for his part in the union controversy, which was, of course, wholly denied by the historical evidence.

Other writers from the United Free Church wrote in similar terms: Kenneth Macdonald blamed Begg's influence on Kennedy for the union controversy troubling the Highland Free Church at all: 'The demon of dispeace crossed the Grampians in one of her Majesty's mailbags.' Kennedy was, he thought, 'easily led by a man of Dr Begg's plausibility and pretensions'; thus, in his view, 'Dr Begg [was] responsible for all the commotion of that time, and for the ecclesiastical disturbances that troubled the Church in the Highlands since.'[125] W. K. Leask insisted that Begg had 'imported' the feeling on the subject into the North; Alexander MacRae complained that bitterness had been 'introduced' into the Highlands.[126] Only William Ross seemed to blame Begg and Kennedy equally.[127] Later historians have been too much influenced by these writers, whose works were, despite their value, marked by the remains of party feeling: they condescended to the Highland anti-unionists or excused them as ill-led, rather than recognising their concerns as genuinely held. J. R. Fleming thought that Begg, being 'strongly Celtic in his sympathies, [. . .] could make a special appeal to the peculiar mentality and limited outlook of Highland Free Churchism'.[128] He later added that the Highlanders were 'preyed upon'.[129] Even Drummond and Bulloch retain more than a trace of this patronising attitude:

> Flattered at times by the leadership, the Gaelic ministers grew more and more out of touch with the south, where they were spoken of as 'the Highland Host'. Isolated and on the defensive, misunderstanding and misunderstood, they came to see themselves as defending the last bastion of the true faith.[130]

For Kennedy's case at least, this was far from an accurate depiction: he was an anti-unionist through conviction, not isolation, whether geographical or intellectual. James Lachlan Macleod may have overstated the importance of anti-Highland racism to the controversies of the nineteenth-century Free Church, but he has certainly shown that it did exist, and one manifestation of it was the prevalent view that the Highlanders venerated their 'leaders' and were 'easily led'.[131]

In fact, too much emphasis on leadership as an explanation in church controversy can obscure the real facts. Evidence suggests that even before Kennedy declared his own position on the union question, there was a widespread and growing opposition to the proposal in some parts of the Highlands, especially in the North-West. The Presbytery of Lochcarron carried a resolution against the union in 1867, and the Assembly commissioners from the Synod of Glenelg were found in the majority against the union from the very first significant division in 1867 onwards.[132] A correspondent from the Isle of Lewis, writing in *The Watchword* in 1869, claimed that opposition to the proposal was very widespread amongst the Free Church people in his community, and that a minister had denounced the proposals during a recent communion season, to the satisfaction of the majority of his hearers.[133] Certainly, the opposition to union in the Highlands, and especially the East Highlands, grew dramatically after 1870, but it is probably wiser to link this opposition to the force of the arguments that Kennedy and other Highland constitutionalists deployed. The suggestion that Begg led Kennedy, and that Kennedy in turn led the Highlanders, without reference to the actual substance of the debate, is to deny the force of the evidence.

Nonetheless, the close alliance formed with James Begg, of which the week in 1867 mentioned above seems to have been the beginning, was very important to Kennedy's later ministry. There was a personal friendship forged, such that the Edinburgh minister, despite his lack of Gaelic, was frequently invited to assist Kennedy at communions in the Highlands, even at the memorable communion held at Obsdale in 1880, to commemorate the 200th anniversary of the Covenanting communion held there during the 'killing times'.[134] In turn, Kennedy assisted annually at the Newington communions and stayed with Begg when in Edinburgh, including during a major time of illness in 1875[135]; he eventually was invited to preach Begg's funeral sermons, after his friend's death in 1883.[136] Though they came from entirely different spheres within the Free Church, Begg, one of the last representatives of the older, strictly confessional, Lowland Presbyterian tradition, and Kennedy, leader of the younger and by then more vibrant Calvinist strain in the Highlands, found a harmony of outlook. Begg's biographer wrote of them: 'Their similarities and their dissimilarities combined to establish a friendship of no ordinary strength between them,' and went on to compare their bond to the Biblical friendship between David and Jonathan.[137]

But, though friends, Begg and Kennedy were not identical in outlook. Begg shared the desire of the Highland evangelicals to uphold the Westminster Standards in theology and practice. But he was not a Highlander, and differed from the emphases of Highland evangelicalism. Even in the midst of controversy, and at risk of offending much-needed allies, Begg gave only a cautious welcome to the Free Church minister Alexander Auld's *Ministers and Men in the Far North*, a book that followed much in the mould of Kennedy's writings, albeit focused on Caithness, with many accounts of supernatural experiences. Begg published a review of the work in *The Watchword*, generally commending the work, but adding that 'we decidedly differ' from some of Auld's views.[138] Begg had, however, given a highly positive review of Kennedy's *The Apostle of the North* in *The Watchword* in 1866.[139]

Kennedy and Begg evidently shared a real friendship but it was also an important alliance in terms of the Free Church. If Begg was the unquestioned leader of the anti-unionist forces on the floor of the Assembly, it was Kennedy's influence that provided an increasingly large proportion of his support, and of the votes at his command, from 1870 onwards. As Noble acknowledged of Kennedy:

> The Southern brethren [...] naturally looked to him as a powerful ally in the rapidly-approaching contest, and hailed with satisfaction the acquisition of a champion, whose distinguished eminence and

commanding influence had by this time become paramount through the northern counties.[140]

Noble was honest enough as a biographer to concede that Kennedy was not universally admired as an ecclesiastical controversialist, with some considering him too impulsive or too sensitive; though others, even opponents, expressed admiration of Kennedy's conduct in public debate.[141] It may have been that his skill and confidence in this area grew over time. However, Kennedy's real strength in controversy was that he undoubtedly commanded the confidence of the majority of Free Church Highlanders. By this leadership, as one newspaper observed after his death, even more than Begg, it was Kennedy who 'prevented the union' from taking place.[142]

But a further vital distinction between Kennedy and Begg was their principal focus in the union controversy. As has been noted above, there were three key issues in the United Presbyterian Church that concerned the constitutionalists: the failure to uphold the Establishment Principle, the toleration of the double reference theory of the atonement, and the use of uninspired hymns in public worship. Of these points, the third was the least significant to the controversy, as it was evident that there was a strong appetite for hymns in the Free Church, and the legislation permitting their use proceeded concurrently with the battles over union, receiving final approval in 1872 at the same Assembly as finally abandoned the quest for union.[143] Of the two that were decisive,[144] there was no question which was more significant for Begg: he still held passionately to the old vision of the 'godly commonwealth', a national Established Church, working in every parish for the good of the whole community, and was horrified at the thought of this being abandoned in the toleration of the 'voluntaryism' of much of the United Presbyterian Church.[145] Andrew Campbell observed that Begg was deeply motivated in the union controversy by the Church of Scotland's decision to demand an end to patronage in 1869, believing that this may yet lead to a reconstruction of the divided Church of Scotland.[146] By contrast, Kennedy was deeply concerned about the atonement issue, which he saw striking at the heart of the gospel. As Sandy Finlayson writes: 'He wanted to preach and teach that Christ's death actually saved people from their sins, and not just that it made salvation possible.' Kennedy's concern was 'that this view was gaining ground in the United Presbyterian Church, and that it had not been condemned by their General Assembly [*sic*]'.[147]

It quickly became clear that the United Presbyterian tolerance of the double reference theory of the atonement would make the union proposal problematic for many in the Free Church. Early Free Church leaders like Cunningham and Candlish were on record as strongly condemning the theory, and Julius Wood strongly denounced attempts by the Union Committee to gloss over the point at the 1865 General Assembly.[148] The Professor of Systematic Theology at New College, James Macgregor, came out strongly against the union on the atonement question from 1870 onwards, publishing pamphlets and speaking against it on the floor of the Assembly in 1871.[149] Kenneth Ross has rightly stressed the significance of theology to understanding the controversies of the nineteenth-century Free Church:

> The tensions between metropolis and provinces, between contrasting social contexts, between differing forms of piety and between conflicting practice in public worship could probably have been contained within one ecclesiastical communion, had there not been more fundamental division.[150]

Hamilton has concurred, emphasising that the union controversy is too easily reduced to personalities, and needs to be considered with regard to the actual issues at stake.[151]

Hamilton notes that 'a sizable proportion of those who opposed union did so, at least in part, due to their belief that the United Presbyterian Church had departed from some of the teachings of the Westminster Standards'.[152] Undoubtedly, Kennedy fell into this category. At a key public meeting in Inverness, Kennedy explained his own involvement with the union question, claiming that he had been suspicious of the movement from the start as expressing 'indiscriminating charity'. He saw the debate's effects as causing division, as encouraging doctrinal inexactness even amongst the Free Church leaders, and as promoting 'the revolt of proud intellect against authority in matters of religion'.[153] Crucially, Kennedy stated emphatically the significance of the atonement question to his own engagement in the public debate: his interest did not lie 'in the discussion of the question of the doctrine of the civil magistrate'. Rather, he took his 'stand in opposition to this Union on the ground of the differences existing regarding the fundamental doctrine of the Atonement', and asserted the prevalence of 'Amyraldism' in the United Presbyterian Church. This he saw as damaging to the gospel, as leading inevitably to sinners hoping in the 'good will of God', rather than in Christ. But equally, he demanded that the Free Church uphold the duty of the civil magistrate to support the Church – the Establishment Principle – as nothing less than 'her testimony in behalf of Christ as King of nations', and on this basis stated it as his duty to oppose the union.[154] Kennedy warned that, far from needing greater size, the Free Church was 'too large already' and had 'more need of sifting than of heaping', an obvious deprecation of the quality of the Lowland Free Church's membership. He noted that the union could be approved in principle as early as 1872 and warned that the Free Church could be looking very soon at another 'disruption'.[155]

Significantly, though Kennedy clearly mentioned the issue of the atonement, it was the Establishment Principle that he emphasised, and indeed, the main issue raised throughout the union controversy was undoubtedly the question of establishment. Hamilton has estimated that 'probably over

90 per cent of the speeches' on the union question in the Free Church Assembly 'were taken up with the two Churches' attitude towards the State'.[156] Kennedy's new emphasis in the controversy was also reflected in his preaching, as the theme of Christ's Kingship, reflected in the duty of the State, became an oft-repeated theme of his later sermons.[157]

Kennedy's first substantial controversial pamphlet, *Unionism and the Union*, was a direct reply to criticism of his public speech of October 1870, printed as *The Union Question*. He criticised the overly political manner in which the union movement had been instigated, linking it to the support of the same individuals for the disestablishment of the Church of Ireland, which had been legislated in 1869 and was still a matter of contemporary controversy. Kennedy denied that there was any spirit of revival in the union movement, and regarded the claims of revival to have led to doctrinal indifference.[158] He saw the same spirit at work in the Evangelical Alliance, which the Baptist preacher C. H. Spurgeon, 'that outstanding witness for the truth', had left, but which still included 'one who denies the eternity of future punishments'. The Establishment Principle had separated churches before, and remained a fundamental barrier of principle: Kennedy described how he had tried to explore the United Presbyterian view of the State in the joint committee, and found no clarity:

> Their Union bias produced mist over every question that was discussed [. . .] This was my experience of the Union Committee [. . .] I found that the determination to effect a Union made those, from whom I expected light, more busy in raising clouds over emerging differences, than in discovering the exact state of opinion, and securing harmony according to the truth.[159]

The result of his discussions was a multiplication of questions rather than answers and the realisation that the United Presbyterian Church had no position at all on the issue, but that one could hold any view on the Church and State question and hold office within that denomination. A union with such a basis would, in Kennedy's view, bring to an end the Free Church of Scotland as he knew it.[160]

He also addressed the atonement question, pointing out that the United Presbyterians were equally confused and contradictory on that subject, such that 'we pay them an undeserved compliment, when we credit them with anything so systematic and self-consistent as Amyraldism'.[161] If all sources, and especially the records of the heresy trial of Brown, were admitted as evidence, 'it would not be difficult to prove, that doctrinal views, in opposition to the Confession of Faith, are avowed in the United Presbyterian Church, and that on that ground there is an insuperable bar to union'. He described how he had worked to reach agreement on a clear statement on the atonement in the Union Committee, to no avail.[162] Rather, as he demonstrated from the statements of leading United Presbyterians regarding their own doctrine, some in that Church were teaching a universal reference to the atonement as a source of gospel comfort, rather than the sufficient atonement of the Saviour.[163] Kennedy asked if there would be a disruption, something he predicted would be a 'catastrophe', but emphasised that if union was concluded, some were 'resolved not to forsake the banner of the Free Church' and thus the disruption would be the responsibility of those who left that position to enter such a union.[164]

As these contributions reflected, 1870 was a very heated year in the union controversy: the 'agitation reached its climax of fierceness', Simpson remarked, as the prospect of union became more immediate.[165] The Assembly of that year witnessed a notable intensification of the conflict, as anti-unionist speakers 'began to mention the possibility of seceding from the Free Church, should it pursue union at all costs'.[166] The concerns of men like Begg, Kennedy and Macgregor were emphatic and deeply held; but there was no attempt made by the unionists, as Hamilton observed, to answer the charge of doctrinal unsoundness regarding the United Presbyterians. In fact, there was no easy answer that they could make, as it was evident that there was greater latitude in theology permitted amongst United Presbyterian ministers than a strict reading of the Confession would permit, but the unionists' silence on the point had the inevitable result of fuelling concerns and suspicions.[167] A second disruption no longer seemed a remote prospect, as the Free Church seriously considered entering a union from which many ministers and elders would undoubtedly stand apart.

In 1871, Kennedy was not a commissioner to the General Assembly, but the union battle was again keenly fought. The formal proposal had been sent down to Presbyteries the previous year, and while a majority of these courts had supported the union proposal, a significant minority, especially in the Highlands, had expressed opposition.[168] Robert Buchanan, Convenor of the Union Committee, urged the Assembly to continue the progress towards union, but Sir Henry Moncrieff, a prominent Edinburgh minister and clerk of Assembly, who took a centrist position in the Free Church constitutional debates, moved rather that the Committee direct their attention for the present towards whatever means might 'draw the negotiating Churches into closer and more friendly relations to one another'. Robert Candlish, as leader of the unionists, reluctantly supported this as the only feasible way forward for the present: he recognised, as Simpson later wrote, that 'to press on the union immediately meant a new division'.[169] Meanwhile, William Nixon, a close ally of Begg, moved for the constitutionalists to terminate the matter. The final vote was closer than prior votes on union, 435 to 165, with substantial opposition in the Highlands, and many Highlanders amongst the names signing a protest against the decision.[170] For the first time, the commissioners from Kennedy's own Synod of Ross divided against the Union Committee's proposals.[171]

Kennedy wrote a further, rather heated pamphlet early in 1872, *Reply to the Ten*, in answer to a 'Statement and Appeal' privately circulated by ten

Free Church ministers in favour of the union.[172] This statement had claimed credit for the unionist party in dropping the immediate prospect of union, but Kennedy warned that the proposed alternative scheme, mutual eligibility between the two churches, whereby ministers of either denomination could be called to vacant congregations of the Free Church, involved 'as thorough a sacrifice of principle' as the union itself.[173] The scheme would inevitably 'lead to a gradual fusion of the Churches', Kennedy asserted, and involved dishonesty in permitting men to take the vows of Free Church ministers, without any examination to see if they repudiated the erroneous views tolerated in the United Presbyterian Church. He pointed out that the Free Church had contended clearly for the Establishment Principle and limited atonement before, and added that many were 'grieved' that the ten authors had 'begun to waver' and had become 'inconsistent'. The statement warned that the anti-unionists were teaching that 'disruption is a reasonable and incumbent course' should mutual eligibility be enacted, and urged that even opponents of the union must not take this course. Kennedy, by contrast, urged strict adherence to 'the truth' as the only way forward for the Free Church and its office bearers.[174] In a more specific appendix, he noted that under the Scheme being proposed, a United Presbyterian probationer being inducted as a minister need not sign the Free Church formula until after his induction, and then would be free to give whatever qualifications he wished, substantiating these assertions with reference to Assembly legislation.[175]

In 1872, the Union Committee indeed returned to the Assembly with firm proposals for a scheme of mutual eligibility between the Free and United Presbyterian Churches. The constitutionalists opposed the proposal vigorously, fearing that it would serve, as indeed it was explicitly intended to serve, as a vehicle towards an eventual union.[176] For the first time, Kennedy broke his self-imposed silence and addressed the Assembly in a memorable speech. Though he professed 'great diffidence' and stated that he had risen only 'at the urgent solicitation of his friends', he did so because 'no one had risen from the north to represent the views and feelings of the people there'. In his view, the proposal involved 'compromise of principle', as it suggested that there was no good reason for the churches remaining separate, and would likely lead to a union eventually anyway. To accept the proposal would, he argued, lead to 'further division and strife'. He and his allies on the question were not those calling for change and innovation; those who desired such things were free to depart but he would 'cling' to 'the old ship'. He concluded by insisting that he harboured no feeling to any brother in the Church except 'hearty good-will'. The following speaker, William Arnot, though of a different outlook, complimented Kennedy on his speech, saying, 'it did my heart good to hear' it.[177] The eventual vote of 369 to 172 to send the proposals down to Presbyteries for consideration, though a decisive majority in favour, indicated that an increasingly substantial minority saw danger in proceeding further with mutual eligibility.[178]

Such was the danger perceived that, for the first time, Kennedy decided to address his own congregation on the subject of ecclesiastical controversy, an address later published in pamphlet form.[179] He explained that with the Assembly approaching, a 'crisis' might soon be reached. If the 'bastard charity' that lay behind the union movement achieved its objective, it would only 'add dishonesty to division'. He denied that there was any true spirit of religious revival behind the union movement, and traced its history down to the proposal for mutual eligibility of 1872.[180] In justifying the rejection of union, he argued that the United Presbyterians were 'avowed voluntaries' and quoted Candlish, Chalmers and Hugh Miller on the importance of maintaining the Establishment Principle. In contrast, he quoted the United Presbyterians' statement on voluntaryism, showing the serious implications: not only was State funding for the Church prohibited, but also any legislation for the teaching of Christianity, an implication he called 'infidel and even atheistic'. Equally, the Protestant succession to the throne, Sabbath observance, the judicial oath and any other State acknowledgment of Christianity were incompatible with the voluntary principle. Kennedy stated his own opposition forcefully: 'With the Voluntaryism of the manifesto, there can be no compromise without shameful apostasy. I would rather die than help to admit and foster it within my Church.'[181]

As a second ground for rejecting union, Kennedy pointed out the Amyraldism of the United Presbyterians, noting that 'at first [he] took comparatively little interest' in the establishment question, as the atonement issue was a deeply held concern. He noted that at one time he 'adopted this doctrine; and it was one of the most critical periods of [his] life', as he was 'led to see its falseness, and the dangerous results to which it leads'. The logical conclusion of the doctrine directly contradicted the Biblical and confessional standards of the Free Church.[182] He added that a third barrier to the progression towards union had emerged: namely, the decision of the United Presbyterian Church to allow liberty to her congregations to introduce organs into public worship. This Kennedy deplored as rejection of confessional principles of worship, as an indulgence of the desire for the 'new and sensational', and as a breach of the principle of uniformity in worship. Crucially, however, he admitted that the Free Church was 'passing through the same course by which the other reached its present state of feeling'.[183]

Kennedy identified mutual eligibility as the 'last phase' of the union movement, as the proposal practically declared that there was no difference between the standards of the two churches. Its practical effects would be to eliminate the constitutional distinction of the Free Church. It would be union in effect, without a basis.[184] His crucial challenge to his congregation came in the conclusion:

That the Mutual Eligibility Overture shall be passedinto [*sic*] a law, is the loudly declared resolution of those who speak for the majority of the Assembly. We must reckon on that event. *And it shall rend our Church.* In that event you and I shall have to choose our position and to act our part. Till the crisis comes let our place be at the feet of Jesus, praying that we may know His will, and obtain strength to do it.[185]

Kennedy's meaning was plain: in the event of the proposals being enacted, he would seek the support of his congregation in separation from the majority of the Free Church. His conduct in the months leading up to the crucial Assembly supported this assessment of his position, as he addressed meetings on the subject all over the country and engaged in tense discussions with colleagues.[186]

The General Assembly of 1873 therefore met in an atmosphere of gravely heightened tension over the mutual eligibility proposals. As these had received approval from a large majority of Presbyteries, it seemed inevitable that they would be enacted, but equally, the opposition of the constitutionalists had been so emphatic that it seemed unlikely that the unity of the Church would survive. Begg had taken legal advice, and obtained opinions that the property of the Free Church would belong to the minority in the event of a change to the constitution of the Free Church.[187] By the time of the Assembly, many feared that a second disruption was imminent, and indeed a hall had been hired to which the minority could withdraw.[188] Candlish moved that the Assembly enact mutual eligibility and discharge the Union Committee. Nixon moved for the constitutionalists that an additional stage was necessary in the process of calling a United Presbyterian minister, to ensure his full adherence to the Free Church standards. Eventually, a compromise motion was negotiated behind the scenes, providing for mutual eligibility while ensuring that the ministers admitted under the measure would take the same commitments as were required of Free Church ministers, and was allowed to pass without a vote, provided the constitutionalists could record their dissents.[189] Neither party desired a division and the resolution was met with general relief. Hugh Martin remarked afterwards on his 'fatigue of body, and especially of brain, induced by ten days, and I may say ten nights, of conference and extreme anxiety to prevent disruption, now, by God's great goodness to the Church, averted'.[190] The Free Church had narrowly escaped the threatened division.

The First Union Controversy was intriguing as the victory of a determined minority, who succeeded in frustrating the will of a formidable majority. Kennedy's significance to that anti-unionist success could not be denied: while he was not one of the leaders of the party on the floor of the Assembly, his powers of influence were exerted in the Highlands, to considerable effect. As Finlayson wrote, 'opinion in the Free Church had changed, at least in part through Kennedy's writing on the subject'.[191] Statistical analysis shows that the growth in anti-unionist support as the controversy developed was largely in the Highlands, underlining the significance of Highland leaders of the opposition to union, such as Kennedy and

Gustavus Aird. It was in deference to the resolve of the opponents of union that the proposals were dropped. Some were inclined ultimately to ascribe the exercise of this influence to James Begg, as Douglas Ansdell observed:

> He has been accused of single-handedly provoking the constitutionalist reaction in the Highlands and nurturing it for his own ends. It has been claimed that this was achieved by Begg's influence over Kennedy of Dingwall, and that from Dingwall Begg's influence spread and came to disturb the whole of the Highlands.[192]

However, the evidence shows that Kennedy's views on the union question were the product of a long period of reflection, of involvement at Committee level and of writing, before he publicly committed himself against a union that he had concluded was incompatible with the constitution of the Free Church of Scotland. This must be seen as more than just the result of his friendship with Begg. If he did help to mobilise Highland opinion against the union, it was because of the depth of his convictions and the force of his arguments he utilised in that cause. But what was also evident, though only reluctantly acknowledged, was the inherent contradiction of the anti-unionist position: Kennedy and Begg were mobilising to defend distinctive principles of the Free Church position, despite the fact that many in the Free Church were evidently moving towards conformity with the United Presbyterians on these precise points. On worship, on the atonement and on the establishment question, the differences were already eroding in practice, if not yet in terms of constitutional statement. The anti-unionists had erected a temporary bulwark against the tide but events would soon prove that it was made of sand.

Kennedy and the Establishment Controversy

The union controversy was not even concluded when it was overtaken by the next phase of the Free Church constitutional controversy, which was fought over the immediate application of the Establishment Principle in nineteenth-century Scotland. The new phase of the controversy was no less heated, and raged without abatement for the rest of Kennedy's life, and indeed for more than two decades thereafter. Churches had been established by law in all four constituent nations of the United Kingdom since the sixteenth-century Reformation, but from the 1830s their status became the subject of intense controversy. In an era when, as one history noted, 'individualism reigned supreme in the economic life and social order' of the country, it was probably inevitable that the older parish structure would tend to disintegrate into a multiplicity of competing churches and charitable institutions.[193] In practice, the debate on the subject became an intense and heated conflict – in Bebbington's view, 'the sharpest fissure that divided Evangelicals one from the other during the nineteenth century'.[194] The point at issue was fundamental; as Drummond and Bulloch point out, what was involved was not a matter of payments to a rival Church but the nature of society. Was the Church to be a private religious society unrelated to the State or was the State to be guided by Christian moral principles?[195]

The controversy, though it had its beginnings in Scotland, involved the whole United Kingdom, and by the late 1870s had become a central issue in national as well as ecclesiastical politics.[196]

The renewed controversy over Establishment commenced in 1869, when the Established Church in Scotland decided to petition the Government to repeal the laws instituting ecclesiastical patronage. This was the issue over which the Disruption had originally occurred, and the Church of Scotland leaders made clear that they had in view the removal of a barrier to reunion with the Free Church.[197] In practice, the issue presented the Free Church with considerable difficulty. For constitutionalists like Begg and Kennedy, who still harboured a vision for a united national Presbyterian church, founded on the constitutional basis of the Westminster Standards and supported by the State, the development was welcome. But the unionists in the Free Church were attempting to achieve a union with the United Presbyterian Church, which rejected State Establishment as a matter of principle, and the development therefore aroused their determined opposition. Robert Rainy and the Free Church majority well knew that if patronage was abolished with their support, then the distinction between the Free Church and the Church of Scotland would be weakened, the impetus towards national reunion would strengthen and ties with the United Presbyterians would be threatened. Members of the Free Church would, they feared, be tempted to return to the Establishment rather than continue to bear the heavy demands of the sustentation fund.[198] The Church of Scotland of 1869 was in any case a much more vigorous and pastorally engaged denomination than the remnant from which the Free Church had separated in 1843. Led by popular, nationally respected preachers and writers like Norman Macleod and A. H. Charteris, the Established Church had recovered something of the vision of Chalmers for a parish church at the heart of the community; and consequently had significantly expanded its adherent base.[199] This recovery underlined the threat to the Free Church that the leadership perceived.

Rainy claimed to support the principle of Establishment, but he denounced the Scottish Established Church as unsound in its constitution and subject to undue state interference.[200] Ministers of the majority rejected out of hand any talk of efforts towards reunion, and some began to demand disestablishment as 'the necessary sequel of the Disruption'.[201] In practice, there was no doubt that during the 1870s the Free Church was moving away from Chalmers's vision of the 'godly commonwealth' with a territorial church in every community, coming rather to see itself as a gathered body of individual believers. As Stewart Brown has noted, this trend was accelerated by the individualistic focus of the evangelistic campaign of D. L. Moody in 1874, which was hugely influential in moving the Free Church in a voluntaryist direction. The number of Free Church territorial missions steadily declined, even while the rhetoric of the leadership became more defensive.[202] As Ian Machin has noted, whatever their professions of principle, 'Rainy and his followers were ardent Voluntaries in their attitude to the existing Establishment.'[203]

The first round in the establishment controversy was fought at the 1870 Free Church Assembly, over the national education question. This concerned the progress of legislation through Parliament, eventually enacted in 1872, to provide a system of national education in Scotland, which previously had largely been the province of denominational schools, including those founded and run by the Free Church, albeit with substantial financial support from the State.[204] For strict voluntaries such as the United Presbyterians, the State must not favour any denomination, and some questioned the propriety of any Christian instruction at all in State schools. By contrast, the Free Church constitutionalists desired the schools to be dedicated to the instruction of pupils in Westminster Calvinism, still by law the creed of the Church of Scotland. Negotiating a balancing act between these two poles, Sir Henry Moncrieff moved in terms of broad support for the proposals of William Gladstone's Liberal Government. James Begg counter-moved that the Assembly additionally commend the 'use and wont' of Establishment in Scotland, the house dividing 223 to 154 for Moncrieff.[205] At the Assembly a year later, with a specific bill published by the Government, Moncrieff moved successfully in support, while Thomas Smith for the constitutionalists argued that the Free Church should demand greater confessional safeguards.[206] In 1872, with the Bill in final form ready for enactment that year, Robert Elder moved in support, while the constitutionalist Hugh Martin moved against, expressing concerns regarding the provisions for religious education. The vote was a decisive 325 to 156, with Kennedy, a commissioner that year, amongst the minority.[207] In practice, the significant concern over the provision of religious education in schools quickly died down, as it became clear that 'use and wont' would prevail generally. However, Stevenson has rightly observed that the churches' acceptance of the looser system, without specific credal safeguards, was itself an indicator of the changed 'climate of opinion' in Scottish Presbyterianism from previous decades.[208]

In a further round of the controversy that year, the Assembly noted and criticised the demand of the Established Church for an end to patronage, and asserted the separate stance of the Free Church, on the motion of Robert Rainy. A counter-motion by James Begg, not criticising the Established Church but explicitly asserting the Establishment Principle, was rejected by 239 to 62.[209] The Free Church majority was not explicitly rejecting the Establishment Principle but did not desire to emphasise it. Rainy and other Free Churchmen went on to campaign vigorously against the abolition of patronage, and were instrumental in persuading Gladstone to oppose it in the House of Commons as a measure supposedly intended to strengthen Conservatism.[210]

Later in 1872, the full campaign for the disestablishment of the Church of Scotland commenced at a mass meeting in Edinburgh addressed by the United Presbyterian leader John Cairns; its influence on the Free Church was soon to be felt.[211] At the 1873 Assembly, for the first time, a motion was tabled explicitly demanding the disestablishment of the Church of Scotland. A counter-motion, by Moncrieff, directly opposed that outcome. Tellingly, both were rejected in favour of John Adam's compromise motion that declared the present situation indefensible but stopped short of calling for disestablishment.[212] But the crucial development came in 1874, with Parliament that year finally enacting the abolition of patronage in the Church of Scotland. Robert Rainy moved a formal protest against the legislation in the Free Church Assembly, while the constitutionalists, led in the debate by William Nixon, welcomed it. In a vote on the Free Church response, the Assembly backed Rainy by an overwhelming majority, 433 to 66. A further debate on Establishment saw an even more direct position being adopted, as the Assembly largely backed John Adam in denouncing the present connection between the State and the Established Church, against an establishmentarian motion by Moncrieff.[213] It was evident that the great majority in the Free Church were unwilling even to consider any efforts towards reunion with their old foes in the Church of Scotland, unless the national church was first disestablished.

In the years following, a vote on Establishment was taken at each Assembly, with a large majority consistently favouring strong criticism of the present settlement. At last, in 1878, the Free Church voted, on the motion of Adam, to call for the disestablishment of the Church of Scotland. Just five years after the same call had been decisively rejected, it was now supported overwhelmingly, by 404 to 134. Kennedy was a commissioner, delivered a speech against disestablishment and voted against the majority. He was recorded as a teller for one of the constitutionalist motions – indicating his prominent support for it – and added his name to a protest against the Assembly receiving the overture for disestablishment.[214] After the 1878 Assembly, the lines of the controversy were clearly drawn, and an annual Assembly debate and vote on the subject were invariably held, and invariably won by the supporters of disestablishment, for the rest of Kennedy's life.[215] Beyond the bounds of the General Assembly, Rainy and his colleagues engaged in an intense political agitation to bring down the Established Church, in the name of the Free Church, and in alliance with Cairns and the United Presbyterians.[216] In large part through their efforts, disestablishment 'became the leading political question in Scotland', as Machin observed, and the campaign was stronger in Scotland than anywhere else.[217] In 1880, the issue was prominent in the general election, with candidates repeatedly challenged to declare a decisive position, and the

1885 election, as Brown has remarked, 'was fought largely on the issue of disestablishment'. However, no legislation was enacted to change the relationship of the Church of Scotland to the State, and from 1886 onwards, the issue was largely superseded by the more pressing question of Irish home rule.[218]

Repetitive and inconclusive though the Establishment debates were, the internal significance of the controversy lay in the differing visions of the future of the Free Church being presented. In this respect, the debate over Establishment was a proxy dispute, for later and more immediately consequential controversies over the terms of confessional subscription and church union. The vision of the constitutionalists was a return to a purified Established Church, in which all Scottish Presbyterians of unqualified confessional commitment could be united upon the foundation of Westminster Calvinism, with the support of the State, both moral and financial. For the majority party, the favoured vision was an end to State connection for the Established Church, and a loosening of confessional subscription all round. In the short term, they desired union with the United Presbyterian Church, but ultimately such a situation could eventually allow for a general reunion of Scottish Presbyterians in a large disestablished church, without strict confessional subscription, incorporating a broad spectrum of opinion. To Kennedy, this latter vision was wholly repugnant. As Drummond and Bulloch observe, Kennedy saw that the Free Church leadership 'had reacted to the end of patronage by abandoning their former principles', in using the occasion as an opportunity to secure the disestablishment of a rival church.[219] Furthermore, as a Highlander he felt a particular indignation at seeing the property and endowments of the Established Church being used to maintain tiny skeleton congregations since 1843, while the bulk of the Highlanders, adhering to the Free Church, derived no benefit from them, and had to rely on the charity of the Free Church sustentation fund to sustain ministries in the impoverished North. As a consequence both of principle and of practical concern, the Establishment Principle was 'not only worth living for, but worth dying for'.[220] He had decisively identified with the constitutionalist party in the Assembly from 1870 onwards, and became increasingly active in the establishment controversy as the years advanced. As well as delivering numerous speeches in various forums addressing the subject, he published six substantive pamphlets on Establishment in the last decade of his life.

The first was an 1875 address, 'published by request', based on an exposition of Isaiah 60: 1–12, which proclaimed a vision of the people of God renewed, blessed and defended from their enemies.[221] Especially, as Kennedy emphasised, the kings of the nations would 'minister unto' the Lord's people. Kennedy went on to apply this to the New Testament Christian Church, drawing out the duty of 'civil rulers' to acknowledge the Church, to respect her spiritual independence, to give her aid in the spread of the gospel, and to remonstrate in regard to unfaithfulness on her part. He went on to condemn the new 'disestablishment alliance', combining 'the Voluntaries of Scotland with the leaders of the Free Church', and to commend the recent Act abolishing patronage. However, he argued against any suggestion of return to the Establishment until the Church of Scotland's spiritual independence was specifically enshrined in law, until that Church ceased to tolerate serious doctrinal error, and until the Church ceased permitting divergence from 'the simplicity of New Testament worship'. He rejected voluntaryism as an intellectual novelty; as historically ineffective in evangelising the Highlands, due to the poverty of the people; as undermining the Disruption position; as a force of enmity against the Established Church in the days of evangelical ascendancy prior to 1843; as transforming Free Church leaders into politicians; as disadvantaging both Church and State; and because the best days in the Highlands were known under evangelical ministers of the Established Church. Most importantly, Kennedy went on to demand that the endowments of the Establishment in the Highlands be put at the service of the Free Church, given that the vast majority of the people, for whose benefit they were provided, adhered to her. He even hinted that, were such a demand made and definitely refused, he would be open to a separate 'Celtic Church of Caledonia' – that is, a separate Highland Established Church – to benefit from the endowments in the northern parishes. But he especially condemned the disestablishment movement as destructive to Church and State alike.[222]

In January of the following year, Kennedy addressed a published *Letter* to the Highland Free Church.[223] He wrote in the wake of the Uig case, in which a strongly constitutionalist Free Church congregation, that of Uig on Lewis, shocked the wider church by dividing, with the majority leaving the Free Church *en masse* in late 1875 and returning to the Established Church of Scotland, on the ground that the abolition of patronage had removed the barrier between the churches. The majority of the congregation, now benefiting from the local teinds, called a Free Church minister, Angus Maciver, to become their parish minister, and he duly accepted. The Free Church Presbytery was left impotently to express its 'disapprobation' of the action, in a motion carried by a large majority, opposed only by the strict constitutionalists on the Presbytery.[224] The news caused widespread alarm within the Free Church, though in fact the case was entirely exceptional[225] and was never replicated in any other congregation.[226] Kennedy wrote to defend the Free Church position, carefully defining the Establishment principle, and emphasising the failure of the State to recognise in statute the spiritual independence of the Established Church. He defended the Free Church as superior in faithfulness to the Established Church. He admitted that the leaders of the Free Church were now campaigning for disestablishment, and that the Established Church's constitutional position was greatly improved by the abolition of patronage, but asserted that without legislative protection, it remained vulnerable to State intrusions upon its spiritual independence. He added that Free Church members must judge the churches with respect to the evidences of purity and piety that they discerned, and adhere to the church that they judged to be more consistent and faithful. That said, he also urged the Highlanders to petition the Government to grant the teinds to the Highland Free Church congregations.[227] From the evidence available, it is not possible to assess what effect the letter had on popular opinion in the Highlands, but it is worth noting that no other congregation succumbed to the temptation of the endowments, and Kennedy's letter may have helped shore up the support for his church.

Kennedy's pamphlets, given their controversial content, inevitably attracted critical responses. In particular, James Macgregor, Professor of Divinity at the Free Church's New College in Edinburgh, published two pamphlets on disestablishment, defending the Establishment Principle but insisting that, as the Free Church majority believed, the only proper course for the future in the Scottish context was the disestablishment of the Church of Scotland, as a church unworthy of that privilege. Macgregor was courteous towards Kennedy but he called his pamphlet on the *Distinctive Principles of the Free Church* 'imprudent'.[228] Another pamphlet, published under a pseudonym, also adopted a respectful tone towards Kennedy but rejected the argument of his *Letter*, instead maintaining that the Free Church constitutionalists should now return to the Establishment.[229] Another colleague, the older Highland minister Alexander Beith, issued a much more direct challenge to Kennedy in an alternative *Letter* to the Highland Free Church, urging acquiescence in the disestablishment policy of the Free Church majority.[230] He scornfully described Kennedy as assuming the position of 'a Master in Israel', based on the supposedly superior authority of Highlanders to determine ecclesiastical questions, and added that Kennedy's *Letter* had 'excited much indignation in the minds of many'. Beith suggested that Kennedy secretly desired a return to the Establishment, and used Biblical metaphors, such as the Israelites desiring to return to slavery in Egypt, to characterise and reject Kennedy's suggestion that the Highlanders should seek to regain the teinds and other endowments of the Establishment. Beith argued that the Free Church had much common ground with the voluntaries of the United Presbyterian Church, and denied that Kennedy was 'a Free Churchman of the true stamp'.[231]

Kennedy responded to some of the negative criticism, the 'virulence and unfairness' his writings had elicited, in his next pamphlet, published that same year.[232] He rejected with indignation the insinuation that he was tempted by the emoluments of the Establishment, and warned of the growing voluntaryism in the Free Church. He recognised that some of the barriers between the Establishment and the Free Church had been removed by the abolition of patronage, but he asserted that other barriers still remained. The Patronage Act had rendered the parish churches immune from interference by the courts in the process of calling and inducting a minister, but this did not undo the erroneous course of the

Established Church in the years after 1843 in submitting to unwarranted State interference. The Established Church remained subject to the court of teinds with regard to the erection of new parishes, it was unsatisfactory in the calibre of its ministry, tolerated preaching that diverged from the *Westminster Confession* and was permitting change in worship in a ritualistic direction. For these four reasons, Kennedy could not agree to return to the Establishment.[233]

In 1878, Kennedy addressed the developing controversy in two public lectures, subsequently published as a single pamphlet.[234] In his first lecture, he urged the positive embrace of the Establishment Principle, and the duty of the Free Church to contend for it, quoting from the Disruption leaders Thomas Chalmers and Hugh Miller in support of the principle. He defined voluntaryism, describing its dangerous implications, and cited Biblical passages such as Isaiah 60 and Psalm 2 in rejection of it. In particular, he pointed out that the evangelical advance in the Highlands during the eighteenth century was largely achieved through the endowments of the Established Church, as the people were, in these days of severe poverty, wholly unable to support a ministry without aid. In the second lecture, Kennedy argued, based on a rather laboured analogy with a ferryboat company, that the disestablishment outcry was mean-spirited and inconsistent, and that principle demanded the support of a continuing Establishment in Scotland, even from those who could not conscientiously enter it. He particularly emphasised that disestablishment would be final and irrevocable, and that there could be no possibility of re-establishment thereafter. He predicted that 'if there is a future of blessing in store for our land', it would come 'in connection with an Establishment'. Crucially, he identified as a vital strength of an Establishment 'the fixity of its Standards', an indicator of Kennedy's very different vision for the future of the Church in Scotland from the majority even in the Free Church. He denied harbouring any desire to return to the Establishment 'till the constitution [. . .] is first thoroughly adjusted', but he nonetheless urged his hearers to support and defend the principle of an Established Church.[235]

At that year's Assembly, Kennedy spoke to second Begg's motion against disestablishment. In a short but vigorous speech, Kennedy remarked that 'To kill off a man who was sick was not the prescription to follow', and therefore, although there were unscriptural aspects to the current Established Church's relations to the State, the Free Church's duty was to seek the adoption of the Claim of Right by Church and State alike.[236] Later in 1878, Kennedy addressed a *Plea in Self-Defence* to the Free Church leadership, in which he openly acknowledged himself to be a member of 'the constitutional party' in the Assembly, and admitted the increasing numerical weakness of that grouping. He criticised the pro-disestablishment majority, as motivated by an un-Christian hostility to their brethren in the Established Church, as disingenuous in professing adherence to the Establishment Principle, yet seeking union with voluntaries, and as pursuing policies that would make any future re-united established church impossible. He urged instead that the Free Church should return to the position of 'the Claim of Rights' of 1843, asking that these rights be granted by the State so that the breach of the Disruption could be healed.[237]

In 1879, Kennedy accepted an invitation to publish a series of eight articles in the *Perthshire Courier*.[238] He urged the importance of a recovery of confessional commitment and solid doctrinal teaching, and he deplored the recent proposal for a Declaratory Act in the United Presbyterian Church, which was devised to ease the terms by which ministers subscribed to the *Westminster Confession* (and which was passed later that year). According to the Declaratory Act, ministers simply had to declare that the *Westminster Confession* contained the essence of the true faith, without having to subscribe to every doctrine. Kennedy argued at length against the terms of the proposed Act, which effectively meant that ministers could pick and choose which doctrines they believed and would preach.[239] In considering the Free Church, Kennedy directly connected the disestablishment movement to the growing approval of radical Biblical criticism, and with the move to loosen confessional subscription in the United Presbyterian Church, as just different aspects of the same movement of declension. Regarding the Church of Scotland, he praised the fact of Establishment itself but not the Church as then constituted, and regarding the Scottish Church as a whole, his counsel was for her to 'be steadfast and unmoveable' in commitment and practice.[240]

By the early 1880s, the agitation on the subject had reached its peak in Scotland: disestablishment seemed 'at the door', being held back chiefly by the lack of enthusiasm of the Liberal Prime Minister, Gladstone.[241] Kennedy's final pamphlet in the establishment controversy was published in 1882 and was specifically addressed to 'Free Churchmen in the Highlands'.[242] He identified this new burst of agitation for disestablishment and determined to answer it, largely by repeating the arguments he had used previously, including the stated pro-Establishment positions of the original Disruption leaders, the pro-Establishment language of the Claim of Right of 1843, and the grave implications of disestablishment for Scottish Presbyterianism. He warned against the 'unsteadfastness' of the Free Church, as recently seen in 'the cry of incipient rationalism against orthodoxy', in the increasing rejection of Sabbath observance and in the demand for innovation in worship. He remarked that in the three decades since 1853, 'the change is so marked, that it requires an effort to identify the later with the earlier body'. This whole change in the Free Church he identified with the effects of the 'disestablishment movement'. With regard to the condition of the Established Church, he agreed that it was unsatisfactory, but he also observed that the Established Church did 'not present the same measure of decline since 1843' as did the Free Church. He critiqued the voluntary movement, especially in its claim to be demanding only the disestablishment and disendowment of the Established Church, when in truth this would also remove all State recognition of, and support for, the Christian faith. He also described, with evident horror, the prospect of a general reunion in disestablishment of the Presbyterian churches on a foundation of doctrinal 'indifferentism', and predicted that such would lead to the growth of the Episcopal and Roman Catholic Churches and eventually to the ascent of 'Popery' over Scotland.

In this situation, Kennedy urged that the Free Church 'stand fast on Disruption ground', and especially urged Highlanders, who had disproportionately supported that stand, to defend the Establishment Principle and to demand as their own the endowments of the Highland parishes. In an appendix, Kennedy proposed as an alternative to disestablishment the use of the teinds and endowments to support ministries of any denomination fully committed to the confessional position. This he saw not as a new or radical proposal, but as a continuance of the constitutional settlement of the Scottish Church in her relationship to the State. Indeed, Kennedy's constitutionalism applied equally to the State, as was seen in his spirited defence of the British constitution as a guarantor of liberty in an address in 1880.[243]

Kennedy's 1882 pamphlet elicited a substantial critical response. His colleague John MacTavish wrote *An Address to Free Churchman*, partly in response to Kennedy, defending the pro-disestablishment majority in the Free Church. He challenged Kennedy by name on whether indeed the Established Church was any better in its constitution as a result of the abolition of patronage.[244] MacTavish also published a more direct response to Kennedy, professing respect for his brother-minister, and 'extreme regret' that he felt compelled to criticise his recent contribution to the disestablishment debate.[245] MacTavish argued from the conventional Free Church position of professed adherence to Establishment as a principle, alongside entire opposition to the continuation of the present Scottish Establishment, to which, he hinted, Kennedy was showing far too much sympathy. In particular, he characterised as an 'astounding statement' Kennedy's argument that the constitution of the Established Church, 'in respect of its Erastianism', was previously far worse than at the present. In truth, circumstances since have tended to justify Kennedy's position on this matter – that the days of State interference in the life of the Church of Scotland were past. MacTavish disclaimed any interest in the endowments of the Established Church's parishes in the North, and urged his fellow-Highlanders likewise to reject any scheme of wider union urged on the basis of these incentives.[246]

An equally unsympathetic response came from an anonymous 'Highland Minister' who included 'Animadversions on Dr Kennedy's Address' in a postscript to his pamphlet on the controversy, which otherwise recycled the familiar arguments for a Free Church position of supposedly establishmentarian opposition to the contemporary Established Church. Like MacTavish, 'Highland Minister' had apparently supported Kennedy in his anti-unionism, but now parted with him over disestablishment. The author rejected Kennedy's demand that the present Establishment be continued as being as much as 'to say, "Let us do evil that good may come."'[247] An anonymous pamphlet by a 'Highlander' was a good deal less respectful: the author wrote to Kennedy, 'you assume the possession of a power and influence that entitle you to speak *ex cathedra* on these subjects', an obvious reference to the claims of the Papacy. The writer went on to question the fruits of Kennedy's ministry and the worth of his previous writings, and to call his position on Establishment 'semi-Erastian'. In his argument for a reconstructed Establishment, Kennedy was, the writer asserted, 'attempting to hoodwink the unwary, and to debauch the consciences of the simple'.[248] The language was overblown but indicated the strength of feeling that the establishment controversy, and Kennedy's part in it, provoked in the early 1880s.

One of the ironies of the establishment controversy was the new alliances it created, especially that between the Free Church constitutionalists and the principal defenders of the Established Church from within its ranks. Kennedy formed a particular friendship with A. H. Charteris, a committed Church of Scotland minister, a leading defender of the Established Church and Professor of Biblical Criticism at Edinburgh University: they shared an aversion to radical Biblical criticism, but, more importantly, a profound commitment to the Establishment Principle. Together, ministers of the Establishment and of the Free Church constitutionalist party travelled the country campaigning on the issue, and found a surprising degree of unity in a day of very sharply drawn denominational lines. Some Church of Scotland leaders were even prepared to state publicly that in Highland parishes where there was no meaningful congregation of the Established Church, the teinds rightfully belonged to the local Free Church.[249] As Charteris's biographer has observed, 'it was no small concession and condescension for Dr. Kennedy, who carried the keys to the Highlands at his belt, to seek intercourse on equal terms even with Dr. Charteris', and yet they enjoyed congenial discussions when Charteris was in Dingwall to assist at communions in the Established Church and when he holidayed at Strathpeffer.[250] Inevitably, Kennedy's opponents in the Free Church seized upon such associations as a ground for questioning his denominational loyalties.[251] Kennedy himself was quoted as addressing an 1872 meeting in Edinburgh pointing out that his supposed 'Establishment leanings' were solely the result of the changed position of the Free Church majority: 'we stand where our whole Church stood ten years ago'. Truthfully, however, he did seem to prioritise his Establishment Principles over his denominational connection, as he wrote to Charteris in 1879 that he would even 'sacrifice my present Church connection' to safeguard the Establishment, if only the latter Church was 'thoroughly adjusted' in its constitution.[252]

One of the criticisms of Kennedy was the unlikely allegation that he was working with the Lord Advocate to smooth the passage of Free

Churchmen into the Establishment.[253] The suggestion of such a motivation, however, had been given weight by the Uig case, mentioned above. Some blame was attached to Kennedy for the action in Uig, as he was rumoured to have hinted at a Stornoway communion in February 1875 that the barriers between the churches were gone with the abolition of patronage. An anonymous pamphlet also alleged that Kennedy had met with the leader of the secession prior to its instigation, and had been understood 'on the whole as encouraging' such a move.[254] Kennedy later used strong language in criticism of the Established Church in its then form, possibly to remedy the impression that he supported the action in Uig.[255] John Smith has rightly observed that plans for a reconstruction of the National Church on strictly confessional lines by the 1870s were unrealistic and probably unachievable, given the strongly liberal trend of theology in the Victorian Established Church. The Free Church itself was increasingly 'an unsustainable coalition', and the inherent contradictions of a reconstructed church would only have been greater still.[256] Even Kennedy's contemporary critic, Kenneth Macdonald, acknowledged that there was no actual prospect of him joining the Established Church in its then present form.[257] Kennedy's alternative proposal, for a separate Highland Established Church, was never more than a pipe dream, though his successors in the Highland evangelical leadership continued to advocate it, and as late as the 1920s, the continuing Free Church claimed that some of the endowments of the northern parishes should be allocated to her by right.[258]

Kennedy was also criticised, probably fairly, for some of his actions in the disestablishment campaign. In particular, he agreed to an intrusion, apparently encouraged by Begg, into the congregation of Urquhart Free Church, where his fellow-minister held differing views, to hold an anti-disestablishment meeting. Mrs Kennedy is alleged to have expressed vehement disapproval of Begg's influence on her husband's conduct in this case, exclaiming 'I hate him for it!'[259] This kind of conduct must have greatly undermined the confidence between Free Church ministers in the Highlands. Macfarlane also criticised Kennedy's tendency to carry his disestablishmentarianism into his preaching:

> I well remember when Dr. Kennedy closed the Monday services of Communions with sermons on Christ as King of Nations. It seemed a very innocent theme, but it was a shelving beach that sloped rapidly to a deep sea! I was only a stripling but I felt this was a different note from the previous sweet and sacred hours on the mount. Somehow this was a somersault in which a lurid ray fell on the pulpit.[260]

Kennedy also referred directly to the establishment question in his published sermons.[261] The introduction of such a subject into worship, controversial both in ecclesiastical and national politics, may have been questionable in its propriety but no one could deny the effect.

Kennedy's influence on the disestablishment question was not particularly seen on the floor of the Assembly, where only small minorities of commissioners supported the constitutionalist motions. Rather, his leadership was evident on the ground in the Highlands. As a letter to *The Glasgow Herald* put it: 'Whenever Dr Kennedy gives forth a voice [...] on any of the great questions agitating the Presbyterian Churches, Dr Kennedy is followed by about nine tenths of the people of the North.'[262] The strength of the support he was able to mobilise was seen not in the Assembly, but in the transmission of a memorial against disestablishment to the House of Commons in 1882, publicised largely through Kennedy's efforts, which attracted a truly remarkable 80,000 signatures.[263] It is no wonder that, at a major conference on disestablishment held at Inverness earlier that year, it was admitted that while the Highland ministers were divided on the question, the Highland people were generally opposed.[264]

By the 1885 general election, after Kennedy's death, the disestablishment question had come to dominate Scottish politics. A Conservative candidate in the Highlands claimed Kennedy's posthumous support as a fellow-establishmentarian, and a Liberal candidate with strong links to the Free Church constitutionalists, Robert Bannatyne Finlay, was elected for Inverness Burghs on a platform of defending the Establishment.[265] However, the moment for disestablishment soon passed: the Liberal party split in 1886 over the more pressing matter of Irish home rule, and, with all prospect of legislation gone under a Conservative government, enthusiasm for Scottish disestablishment declined in the late 1880s. A further period of Liberal government produced only more disappointment; by the late 1890s, the disestablishment campaign had reached a natural end. It was not until 1921 that the connection of the Established Church to the State was adjusted in law, and the enactment did not include disestablishment.[266] But the damage had been done within the Free Church, in the deep division that had opened between the Lowland leadership and the Highland people:

> By 1886 the split in the Free Church had become so pronounced that those who favoured the original position of the Free Church would not go to hear ministers of the Rainy party, neither would the followers of the Rainy party go to hear ministers of the Constitutional camp. They were really even then divided into two opposing camps.[267]

Over the preceding twenty years, a gulf had opened between the popular Calvinist evangelicalism in the Highland Churches and the more liberal evangelical theology in the Lowland Free Churches, and it was never to close. For the Lowland liberal evangelicals, Establishment was a thing of the past, ill suited to the diversity of modern religious life, and, in practice, a barrier to union and to the adjustment of confessional commitments. But for the Highlanders, support for Establishment was a matter of Biblical and theological principle, part of Scotland's Reformation and Covenanting traditions, and of real practicality as the ideal means for the support of a local ministry in an impoverished part of the country, where local donations were usually inadequate for the purpose. Establishment seemed to offer the prospect of grounding a church on an unchanging confessional foundation settled in law, and to defend the Christian character of society amid the changes of rapid modernisation, through which it seemed increasingly under threat. Between these two visions, there was no common ground: the two groups had adopted wholly different trajectories, and the divergence would only increase, until institutional unity became impossible.

Conclusion

This chapter has charted three controversies that affected the Free Church during the later decades of the nineteenth century, over the doctrine of the atonement, the proposal for union and the prospect of disestablishment; but the three were directly connected. Really, the controversy was one: it concerned the relationship of the Free Church to the other Presbyterian churches in Scotland, and especially its relationship to its own constitution. Ultimately, it concerned the whole vision of the future of Church and State in Scotland. As indicated above, Kennedy discerned a significant movement of doctrinal declension in the Scottish Presbyterian Churches in the Victorian age, and dedicated himself to resisting the process of change. Many dismissed the worth of Kennedy's independent judgment in ecclesiastical controversy, as previously quoted from Ansdell:

> [James Begg] has been accused of single-handedly provoking the constitutionalist reaction in the Highlands, and nurturing it for his own ends. It has been claimed that this was achieved by Begg's influence over Kennedy of Dingwall and that from Dingwall, Begg's influence spread and came to disturb the whole of the Highlands.[268]

However, this chapter has demonstrated that Kennedy reached his major conclusions on the atonement debate, and subsequently and consequentially on the union debate, through lengthy and independent study over a period of several years. This period produced his most extended theological work, *Man's Relations to God*, and demonstrated that his stance on the questions troubling the wider Free Church was both coherently reasoned and based on principle. Kennedy's treatise was an important defence of Westminster Calvinism as a system of logical yet experientially relevant theology. His argument for the confessional doctrine of limited atonement, his opposition to union and, in the longer term, his advocacy for the retention of the Scottish Establishment on a confessional basis all followed consistently from his argument in this treatise.

However, Kennedy's position was undermined by the inherent contradictions within the Free Church of Scotland itself. He defended confessional theology, yet knew that many of his Free Church colleagues were rapidly departing from it; he opposed union with the United Presbyterians on the basis of differences in worship and theology and on Establishment, yet acknowledged that all three positions were increasingly being adopted in his own church; he opposed disestablishment, in the face of the great majority of the commissioners at his own General Assembly. Increasingly, Kennedy appeared to be defending the Free Church as it had stood in the immediate aftermath of the Disruption, not as it existed in the rapidly changing climate of late nineteenth-century Scotland. By his death, he was part of a small party able to command the support of only a few tens of the many hundreds of commissioners at the Free Church General Assembly. However, Kennedy's influence was rather seen in his ability to command the loyalty and confidence of the majority of members and adherents of the Highland Free Church, such that 80,000 joined their names to his petition to Parliament against disestablishment in 1882. To those who claimed that he had lost the respect of his fellow-Highlanders, it was a powerful and effective rebuttal.

Twenty years of controversy had opened a widening gulf in the Free Church, especially between the people in the Highlands and the rest of the Church. Kennedy's writings, sermons, lectures and contributions to debate in church courts all helped to broaden this gulf, as hearers and readers, especially in the Highlands, embraced the principles and vision for which he contended. There was undoubted irony in an alliance that joined Kennedy to such champions of the Established Church as A. H. Charteris, and indeed there was never much prospect of an Establishment reconstructed, as Kennedy would wish, on a basis of sincere confessional commitment. To belong to a church with that basis, it would later prove necessary for the Highland evangelicals to separate from the national denominations, bearing the whole cost of such action themselves, as they did in 1893 and again in 1900. The greater irony was that the successors of Kennedy's opponents in the Free Church were those who returned in 1929 to a national Church with a State connection, while his own heirs, still committed to the Establishment Principle, stood apart in practice from the Establishment, in continuing protest against its loosened confessional basis.

Notes

1. This may be contrasted with the maiden speech of his more confident and combative friend, James Begg, delivered before the Assembly of the Established Church in 1832, when he was just twenty-three; Thomas Smith, *Memoirs of James Begg*, 2 vols (Edinburgh, 1885, 1888), i, 235ff.
2. John Noble, 'Memoir of the Rev John Kennedy, D.D.' (xxix–clxi) in Kennedy, *The Days of the Fathers in Ross-shire* [first pub. 1861], [New and Enlarged Edition] (Inverness, 1897), lxiii.
3. Quoted in Iain H. Murray, *The Old Evangelicalism* (Edinburgh, 2005), 104–5.
4. *Westminster Confession of Faith*, viii.
5. *Subordinate Standards of the Free Church*, 462.

6. David W. Bebbington, *The Dominance of Evangelicalism* (Leicester, 2005), 157. This should not be misunderstood as an assertion of universal salvation, which was not widespread in Scottish Presbyterian theology until the twentieth century. Under a theory of universal atonement, faith in Christ was still requisite to the efficacy of the atonement for the individual.
7. Maclean, *Life of James Cameron Lees*, 82.
8. Norman C. Macfarlane, *Rev Donald John Martin* (Edinburgh, 1914), 15.
9. A. C. Cheyne, *Studies in Scottish Church History* (Edinburgh, 1999), 25.
10. Quoted in Cheyne, *Studies*, 213.
11. Cheyne, *Transforming of the Kirk*, 61.
12. Cheyne, *Transforming of the Kirk*, 63–5.
13. Cheyne, *Transforming of the Kirk*, 65.
14. John Brown, quoted in Ian Hamilton, *The Erosion of Calvinist Orthodoxy* (Fearn, 2010), 58.
15. Cf. Alexander Stewart and J. Kennedy Cameron, *The Free Church of Scotland 1843–1910* (Edinburgh, 1910), 42–3.
16. Hamilton, *Erosion of Calvinist Orthodoxy*, 162; 'Amyraldianism' is a theological term for a theory of universal atonement, derived from the name of an early advocate, Moses Amyraut (1596–1664).
17. Hamilton, *Erosion of Calvinist Orthodoxy*, 162.
18. Macleod, *Scottish Theology in Relation to Church History*, 244–5.
19. Stewart and Cameron, *Free Church of Scotland*, 41–2. Arminianism was a theological system based on the thought of Jacobus Arminius (1560–1609); the term is sometimes used broadly, as here, to refer to Christian theology that rejects key tenets of Calvinism.
20. William Cunningham, *Historical Theology*, 2 vols (Edinburgh, 1864), ii, 323ff.
21. Ewing, *Annals*, i, 312.
22. Robert S. Candlish, *The Fatherhood of God* (Edinburgh, 1865).
23. Thomas J. Crawford, *The Fatherhood of God* (Edinburgh, 1867).
24. Macleod, *Scottish Theology*, 272–5; Cheyne, *Transforming of the Kirk*, 71–2.
25. Cited in Cheyne, *Transforming of the Kirk*, 71–2.
26. Acts 17: 28, Authorised Version.
27. Macinnes, *The Evangelical Movement in the Highlands of Scotland*, 194–6.
28. Enright, 'Preaching and Theology in Scotland in the Nineteenth Century', 283–6, 355–61.
29. Beaton, *Some Noted Ministers*, 275.
30. Thomas Boston, *Human Nature in its Fourfold State* [first pub. 1720] (Glasgow 1830), title page.
31. Kennedy, *Man's Relations to God*, vii–viii.
32. Kennedy, *Man's Relations to God*, v–vi.
33. Kennedy, *Man's Relations to God*, 1. This passage in Kennedy's rough draft text is, if anything more defensive, indicating that he knew that his assertions on this subject could be considered contentious: 'The account of man's creation in the Scriptures must be accepted as it is given', etc.; cf. MS Notebook of John Kennedy, from the collection of Dingwall Free Church, and used by permission, 141.
34. Kennedy, *Man's Relations to God*, 1–3.
35. Kennedy, *Man's Relations to God*, 3–5; cf. Hugh Miller, *The Testimony of the Rocks* (Edinburgh, 1857).

36. Kennedy, *Man's Relations to God*, 8–9.
37. Kennedy, *Man's Relations to God*, 11–15.
38. Kennedy, *Man's Relations to God*, 15.
39. Kennedy, *Man's Relations to God*, 18.
40. Kennedy, *Man's Relations to God*, 20.
41. Kennedy, *Man's Relations to God*, 22.
42. Kennedy, *Man's Relations to God*, 22.
43. Kennedy, *Man's Relations to God*, 25.
44. Kennedy, *Man's Relations to God*, 25–8.
45. Kennedy, *Man's Relations to God*, 28.
46. Kennedy, *Man's Relations to God*, 31.
47. Kennedy, *Man's Relations to God*, 32–4.
48. Kennedy, *Man's Relations to God*, 38.
49. Kennedy, *Man's Relations to God*, 39–41.
50. Kennedy, *Man's Relations to God*, 42–3.
51. Kennedy, *Man's Relations to God*, 43–5.
52. Kennedy, *Man's Relations to God*, 45–9.
53. Kennedy, *Man's Relations to God*, 49.
54. Kennedy, *Man's Relations to God*, 49–54.
55. Kennedy, *Man's Relations to God*, 51.
56. Kennedy, *Man's Relations to God*, 56.
57. Kennedy, *Man's Relations to God*, 56–8.
58. Kennedy, *Man's Relations to God*, 59–66.
59. Kennedy, *Man's Relations to God*, 66–72.
60. Kennedy, *Man's Relations to God*, 72.
61. Kennedy, *Man's Relations to God*, 75–81.
62. Kennedy, *Man's Relations to God*, 82–5.
63. Kennedy, *Man's Relations to God*, 85–90.
64. Kennedy, *Man's Relations to God*, 91–4.
65. Kennedy, *Man's Relations to God*, 97.
66. Kennedy, *Man's Relations to God*, 96–100.
67. Kennedy, *Man's Relations to God*, 100–1.
68. Kennedy, *Man's Relations to God*, 102.
69. Kennedy, *Man's Relations to God*, 103.
70. Kennedy, *Man's Relations to God*, 104.
71. Kennedy, *Man's Relations to God*, 105–16.
72. Kennedy, *Man's Relations to God*, 116–20.
73. Kennedy, *Man's Relations to God*, 121–31.
74. Kennedy, *Man's Relations to God*, 131–5.
75. Kennedy, *Man's Relations to God*, 135–47.
76. Kennedy, *Man's Relations to God*, 147–52.
77. Kennedy, *Man's Relations to God*, 153.
78. Kennedy, *Man's Relations to God*, 153–9.
79. Kennedy, *Man's Relations to God*, 159–60.
80. Kennedy, *Man's Relations to God*, 163.
81. Kennedy, *Man's Relations to God*, 166–75.
82. Auld, *Life of John Kennedy*, 136.
83. Review, *Glasgow Herald*, 17 June 1869.
84. [Anon.], 'Kennedy on Man's Relations to God' (796–809), *British and Foreign*

Evangelical Review, xviii (1869), 796. Typically of the *BFER,* the review is unsigned; the editor at the time was Thomas McCrie 'the younger', who was representative of mainstream Lowland evangelicalism.
85. Quoted in Noble, 'Memoir of John Kennedy', xcix–cii.
86. Review (121–6), *Presbyterian,* v (September 1869).
87. Sell, *Defending and Declaring the Faith,* 34–7, 231–3.
88. Bebbington, *Dominance of Evangelicalism,* 156–8.
89. Cf. Drummond and Bulloch, *Church in Victorian Scotland,* 324–5.
90. Leask, *Dr Thomas M'Lauchlan,* 229.
91. Review (142–3), *The Watchword,* iv 39 (June 1869); 'The Double Reference of the Atonement' (227–30), iv 41 (August 1869). This uncertainty will be addressed further below. Kennedy was not a commissioner at the 1867 or 1868 Assemblies, when, for the first time, significant minorities began to vote against progressing the union debate, and in 1869 failed to register a vote on the union question. Kennedy campaigned vocally against the union from 1870 onwards; cf. Kennedy, *Unionism and the Union.*
92. Letter (187–8), *The Watchword,* iv 40 (July 1869).
93. Macleod, 'An Argyllshire Worthy', 261–2.
94. Macleod, 'An Argyllshire Worthy', 262.
95. Kennedy, *Man's Relations to God,* 116–20.
96. 'Introduction' (v–vi), John Kennedy, *Man's Relations to God* [first published 1869] (Trowbridge, 1998), v.
97. Macleod, *Scottish Theology,* 327.
98. Drummond and Bulloch, *Church in Victorian Scotland,* 318–23. At the same time, union negotiations proceeded between the Free Church Union Committee and the Reformed Presbyterian Church. This latter body, however, was not found to diverge from the Free Church on these points, or on any other significant question, and a successful union was concluded to general satisfaction in 1876. The controversy was exclusively with regard to the United Presbyterian Church, and exclusively on the Free Church side of the proposed union. The United Presbyterian perspective on the controversy was detailed in A. R. MacEwen, *Life and Letters of John Cairns, D.D., LL.D.* (London, 1895).
99. Drummond and Bulloch, *Church in Victorian Scotland,* 318–23.
100. Ross, *Church and Creed in Scotland,* 22–3.
101. Drummond and Bulloch, *Church in Victorian Scotland,* 324–5.
102. Stewart and Cameron, *Free Church of Scotland,* 24–41; Simpson, *The Life of Principal Rainy,* i, 440–52.
103. Ross, *Church and Creed,* 19–21; Finlayson, *Unity and Diversity,* 174–5.
104. Auld, *Life of John Kennedy,* 134ff.
105. *Proceedings and Debates of the General Assembly of the Free Church of Scotland,* 1867, vii–xx.
106. *The Principal Acts of the General Assembly of the Free Church of Scotland* (Edinburgh, 1868), 587; *The Principal Acts of the General Assembly of the Free Church of Scotland* (Edinburgh, 1872), 516. Kennedy appears to have been nominated due to the depletion of the Committee through resignations and deaths, perhaps especially that of Roderick Macleod of Snizort (1794–1868), whom he seems to have directly replaced as a leading Highland representative in the union negotiations.
107. Macdonald, *Social and Religious Life,* 141.

108. Macdonald, *Social and Religious Life*, 141.
109. Noble, 'Memoir of John Kennedy', cx; Barron, 'Memoir of John Kennedy'.
110. *PDGAFCS*, 1868, vii–xx; *PDGAFCS*, 1870, ix–xxii.
111. 'National Education and the United Presbyterians' (49–61), *The Watchword*, iv 38 (May 1869), 59; the reference in context was to the implications of voluntaryism for the question of National Education, as a ground for rejecting the union.
112. *PDGAFCS*, 1869, vii–xx. The *Proceedings* made no distinction between an unavoidable absence and a deliberate abstention, but the former is unlikely, as the commissioners were under obligation to attend Assembly sederunts and Kennedy recorded votes on other questions. It is undeniably curious, and contrary to the accepted narrative of Begg's influence over Kennedy, that as late as 1869 Kennedy did not actively vote against the union.
113. Review (142–3), *The Watchword*, iv 39 (June 1869), 142–3.
114. He published two pamphlets at that stage of the controversy: the first was the transcript of his anti-union address delivered at an Inverness meeting, from the *Inverness Courier*, 6 October 1870; in it Kennedy remarked that he had not 'taken finally and publicly my position on the Union Question up till now'; Kennedy, *The Union Question*, 1. Kennedy, *Unionism and the Union* was a more substantial publication from later the same year. By December of that year, he was being advertised as the speaker at a public meeting in Glasgow on the subject; Advertisement, *Glasgow Herald*, 30 December 1870.
115. Barron, 'Memoir of John Kennedy'.
116. MS Minute Book of Free Presbytery of Dingwall, 332–3.
117. Minute Book, 339–41.
118. Report, *Scotsman*, 23 December 1870; Report, *Scotsman*, 19 April 1872.
119. Ulrich Dietrich, 'Church and State in the Free Church of Scotland Between 1843–73' (Unpublished M.Th. dissertation, University of Glasgow, 1974), 141.
120. Dietrich, 'Church and State', Tables 1–5.
121. Report, *Liverpool Mercury*, 12 February 1877.
122. Simpson, *Principal Rainy*, i, 440–3.
123. Quoted in Simpson, *Principal Rainy*, ii, 50.
124. Macfarlane, *Apostles of the North*, 103.
125. Macdonald, *Social and Religious Life*, 139–46, 169.
126. Leask, *Thomas M'Lauchlan*, 210ff.; MacRae, *Life of Gustavus Aird*, 163.
127. J. M. E. Ross, *William Ross of Cowcaddens* (London, 1905), 296ff.
128. Fleming, *History of the Church in Scotland, 1843–1874*, 180.
129. Fleming, *A History of the Church in Scotland, 1875–1929* (Edinburgh, 1933), 78.
130. Drummond and Bulloch, *Church in Victorian Scotland*, 322.
131. MacLeod, *Second Disruption*, 152–9.
132. Macdonald, *Social and Religious Life*, 140; Dietrich, 'Church and State', Table 1; the only exception was in 1869, when the Synod's commissioners were marginally in favour of union, 11 to 9.
133. Letter (378–9), *Watchword*, iv 44 (November 1869).
134. Report, *Dundee Courier*, 5 August 1880. Begg preached in English and Kennedy in Gaelic; the symbolism of claiming the mantle of the Covenanters was evident.
135. 'The Late Dr Kennedy of Dingwall' (161–7), *Signal*, iii 6 (Jun 1884); Report, *Dundee Courier*, 12 November 1875; Auld, *Life of John Kennedy*, 172–3.

136. In accordance with the *Directory of Public Worship*, these were delivered not at the funeral proper, but on the Sabbath following, in the deceased minister's church; cf. John Kennedy, *Sermons Preached in Newington Free Church, Edinburgh: On Occasion of the Death of James Begg, D.D.* (Edinburgh, 1883).
137. Smith, *Memoirs of James Begg*, ii, 538; 'The Late Dr Kennedy of Dingwall', 161–7.
138. Review (44–5), *The Watchword*, iv 37 (April 1869), 45; the authorship of the review is not given but was likely Begg himself; in any case, as Editor, he was responsible for it.
139. Review (19–22), *The Watchword*, i 1 (April 1866); Review (36–40), *The Watchword*, i 2 (May 1866).
140. Noble, 'Memoir of John Kennedy', lxii.
141. Noble, 'Memoir of John Kennedy', cv, cxvii–cxviii.
142. Obituary, *North-Eastern Daily Gazette*, 1 May 1884.
143. Ian Hamilton notes that hymn-singing was only once mentioned in the Free Church Assembly debates on union; Hamilton, *Erosion of Calvinist Orthodoxy*, 85–6n.
144. The two points were identified by Begg as the vital ones as early as 1868, 'Our New Arrangements' (213–15), *The Watchword*, iii 31 (October 1868), 213.
145. Alasdair J. Macleod, 'James Begg (1808–1883) and the Death of the Godly Commonwealth: Social Vision and Theological Principle in Nineteenth-Century Scotland' (Unpublished M.Litt. dissertation, University of Glasgow, 2009), *passim*.
146. Campbell, *Two Centuries of the Church of Scotland, 1707–1929*, 300.
147. Finlayson, *Unity and Diversity*, 276; the supreme court of the United Presbyterian Church was, rather, a synod.
148. Ross, *Church and Creed*, 76–81.
149. John W. Keddie, *James MacGregor* (n.p., 2016), Ch. 5.
150. Ross, *Church and Creed*, 253–4.
151. Hamilton, *Erosion of Calvinist Orthodoxy*, 105–6.
152. Hamilton, *Erosion of Calvinist Orthodoxy*, 86.
153. Kennedy, *The Union Question*, 1–2.
154. Kennedy, *The Union Question*, 2–3.
155. Kennedy, *The Union Question*, 3–4.
156. Hamilton, *Erosion of Calvinist Orthodoxy*, 85n.
157. The shift is especially marked in the later outlines in Kennedy, *Sermon Notes, 1866–1874*, e.g. 253.
158. Kennedy, *Unionism and the Union*, 3–7.
159. Kennedy, *Unionism and the Union*, 8–14.
160. Kennedy, *Unionism and the Union*, 14–19.
161. Kennedy, *Unionism and the Union*, 19–20.
162. Kennedy, *Unionism and the Union*, 20–4.
163. Kennedy, *Unionism and the Union*, 24–35.
164. Kennedy, *Unionism and the Union*, 37–8.
165. Simpson, *Principal Rainy*, i, 180.
166. Hamilton, *Erosion of Calvinist Orthodoxy*, 96.
167. Hamilton, *Erosion of Calvinist Orthodoxy*, 103ff.
168. The figures were 49 Presbyteries in favour, 14 definitely against and 12 expressing reservation; Norman L. Walker, *Chapters from the History of the Free Church of Scotland*, 246.

169. Simpson, *Principal Rainy*, i, 182–3.
170. *PDGAFCS*, 1871, 85–198.
171. Dietrich, *Church and State*, Table 2.
172. Robert S. Candlish et al., *Statement and Appeal: Private Letter to a Minister* (Edinburgh, 1872).
173. Kennedy, *Reply to the Ten*, 1–2.
174. Kennedy, *Reply to the Ten*, 3–7; Candlish et al., *Statement and Appeal*, 2–3.
175. Kennedy, *Reply to the Ten*, 7–8.
176. *PDGAFCS*, 1872, 133–98.
177. *PDGAFCS*, 1872, 183–4.
178. *PDGAFCS*, 1872, 196.
179. John Kennedy, *Unionism and its Last Phase* (Edinburgh, 1873).
180. Kennedy, *Unionism and its Last Phase*, 3–8.
181. Kennedy, *Unionism and its Last Phase*, 8–15.
182. Kennedy, *Unionism and its Last Phase*, 16–17. The personal reference was cryptic but presumably referred to Kennedy's unconverted days.
183. Kennedy, *Unionism and its Last Phase*, 18–19.
184. Kennedy, *Unionism and its Last Phase*, 19–23.
185. Kennedy, *Unionism and its Last Phase*, 23.
186. E.g., Report, *Aberdeen Journal*, 18 December 1872; Report, *Dundee Courier*, 8 February 1873; Report, *Glasgow Herald*, 28 February 1872.
187. Later published as James Begg, *Memorial with the Opinions of Eminent Counsel in Regard to the Constitution of the Free Church of Scotland, and Remarks on our Present State and Prospects* (Edinburgh, 1874).
188. Simpson, *Principal Rainy*, i, 192.
189. *PDGAFCS*, 1873, 123–89; Simpson, *Principal Rainy*, i, 194–7.
190. *PDGAFCS*, 1873, 232.
191. Finlayson, *Unity and Diversity*, 277.
192. Ansdell, *People of the Great Faith*, 190.
193. Drummond and Bulloch, *Church in Victorian Scotland*, 328.
194. D.W. Bebbington, *Evangelicalism in Modern Britain* (London, 1989), 136.
195. Drummond and Bulloch, *Church in Late Victorian Scotland*, 95; cf. Ross, *Church and Creed*, Ch. iii, for a full discussion of the significance of the question.
196. Ian Machin, 'Voluntaryism and Reunion, 1874–1929' (221–38), in Norman MacDougall, ed., *Church, Politics and Society: Scotland, 1408–1929* (Edinburgh, 1983), 221–3.
197. Drummond and Bulloch, *Church in Victorian Scotland*, 335–6.
198. Ross, *Church and Creed*, 121ff.
199. Cheyne, *Transforming of the Kirk*, 160–1; Stewart J. Brown, 'Thomas Chalmers and the Communal Ideal in Victorian Scotland' (61–80), *Proceedings of the British Academy*, lxxviii (1992), 74–8.
200. Simpson, *Principal Rainy*, ii, 22ff.
201. Sell, *Defending and Declaring the Faith*, 26–7.
202. Brown, 'Chalmers and the Communal Ideal', 72–4.
203. Machin, 'Voluntaryism and Reunion', 222.
204. For a full discussion, cf. John Stevenson, *Fulfilling a Vision: The Contribution of the Church of Scotland to School Education, 1772–1872* (Eugene, OR, 2012), ch.5.
205. *PDGAFCS*, 1870, 77–92.
206. *PDGAFCS*, 1871, 208–34; the vote was 316 to 136. These debates were highly

consequential: as one of the main providers of education in Scotland, the Free Church's cooperation would be needed if a national system of State education were to be created.
207. *PDGAFCS*, 1872, vii–xx, 206–31.
208. Stevenson, *Fulfilling a Vision*, 152–5.
209. *PDGAFCS*, 1872, vii–xx, 238–62. In this division, Kennedy did not record a vote.
210. G. I. T. Machin, *Politics and the Churches in Great Britain, 1869 to 1921* (Oxford, 1987), 90–1.
211. Cheyne, *Studies*, 150–2.
212. *PDGAFCS*, 1872, 222–36; in the voting, Moncrieff's motion narrowly outpolled Smith's, 153 to 144, but was decisively defeated by Adam's, 244 to 134.
213. *PDGAFCS*, 1874, 172–225.
214. *PDGAFCS*, 1878, vii–xxi, 163–200.
215. The only exception was at the 1883 Assembly, when it was agreed not to take a vote, but simply to record the dissents of the opponents of disestablishment; *PDGAFCS*, 1883, 141–6.
216. Stewart J. Brown, *Providence and Empire: Religion, Politics and Society in the United Kingdom, 1815–1914* (London, 2008), 262–7.
217. Machin, *Politics and the Churches in Great Britain*, 92, 111.
218. Machin, *Politics and the Churches in Great Britain*, 119–22, 145ff.; Brown, *Providence and Empire*, 312.
219. Drummond and Bulloch, *Church in Late Victorian Scotland*, 108.
220. Quoted in Smith, 'Free Church Constitutionalists and the Establishment Principle', 103–4.
221. John Kennedy, *The Distinctive Principles and Present Position and Duty of the Free Church* (Edinburgh, 1875).
222. Kennedy, *Distinctive Principles, passim.*
223. John Kennedy, *Letter to the Members of the Free Church in the Highlands* (Edinburgh, 1876).
224. Report, *Aberdeen Journal*, 22 December 1875.
225. Some individuals were, however, reported to have left the Free Church in Arran in disgust at the disestablishment movement in the wider Free Church, John Kennedy Cameron, *The Church in Arran* (Edinburgh, 1912), 130.
226. A popular summary of the Uig case is found in MacLeod, *Banner in the West*, 179; cf. [Anon.], *The Uig Challenge to be Free* (Glasgow, 1876), a contemporary defence of the local action. The Church of Scotland congregation in Uig again proved exceptional in 1929, when the then minister and half of the congregation declined to enter the union with the United Free Church and instead joined the Free Presbyterian Church of Scotland. Following his ministry in Uig, Maciver joined the post-1900 continuing Free Church, underlining the fact that, like his congregation, he remained a constitutionalist; G. N. M. Collins, ed., *Annals of the Free Church of Scotland 1900–1986* (Edinburgh, n.d.), 21.
227. Kennedy, *Letter to the Members of the Free Church, passim.*
228. James Macgregor, *Notes on the Disestablishment Question* (Edinburgh, 1875); James Macgregor, *Disestablishment and the Highlands* (Edinburgh, 1875).
229. 'A Highlandman', *A Voice from the Pew: Being a Reply to Dr. Kennedy's Letter to the Members of the Free Church in the Highlands* (Edinburgh, 1876).

230. Alexander Beith, *To the Men of the North, A Letter* (Edinburgh, 1876).
231. Beith, *To the Men*, passim.
232. John Kennedy, *The Constitution of the Church of Scotland and her Relations to other Presbyterian Churches as Affected by the Anti-Patronage Act* (Edinburgh, 1876); also published in Gaelic, John Kennedy, *Air comh-shuidheachadh Eaglais na h-Alba, 'agus a daimhibh ri eaglaisibh cleireach eile, ann an coimh-cheangal ris an Achd leis an do chuireach a' phatronachd air chul* (Edinburgh, 1876).
233. Kennedy, *Constitution of the Church of Scotland*, passim.
234. Kennedy, *The Establishment Principle and the Disestablishment Movement.*
235. Kennedy, *Establishment Principle*, passim.
236. *PDGAFCS*, 1878, 183–4.
237. John Kennedy, *A Plea in Self-Defence Addressed to Leaders of the Disestablishment Party in the Free Church* (Edinburgh, 1878), passim.
238. Kennedy, *Signs of the Times.*
239. Kennedy, *Signs of the Times*, 7–8, 13–16, 21–36.
240. Kennedy, *Signs of the Times*, 37–44, 45–9, 61.
241. Campbell, *Two Centuries of the Church of Scotland*, 302.
242. Kennedy, *Disestablishment Movement in the Free Church*; the inclusion of a Gaelic proverb without translation on page 22 underlined the impression that Kennedy felt himself now to be writing chiefly for a Highland readership. The pamphlet was also published entirely in Gaelic; John Kennedy, *An gluasad air son an Eaglais a dhealachadh o'n Staid: earail do mhuinntir na h'Eaglais Shaoir anns a Ghaidhealtachd* (Edinburgh, 1882).
243. John Kennedy, *An Address to Volunteers Delivered at the Opening of the New Drill Hall, Bonar Bridge, in April 1880* (Edinburgh, 1886), 3–7; later published in Gaelic, along with a sermon, in John Kennedy, *Searmon agus Oraid* (Edinburgh, n.d.).
244. John MacTavish, *An Address to Free Churchmen* (Inverness, 1882), esp. 9.
245. John MacTavish, *Remarks on Dr Kennedy's Pamphlet on Disestablishment* (Inverness, 1882), 3.
246. MacTavish, *Remarks on Dr Kennedy's Pamphlet*, 4–12. 'Erastianism' was the view that the State should rule over the Church in spiritual matters, or as in the case of the Church of Scotland after 1843, the tacit acceptance of a measure of such interference, at least for a time.
247. 'Highland Minister', *Disestablishment on Free Church Lines* (Oban, n.d., c.1882).
248. 'Highlander', *The Disestablishment Movement in the Free Church*, 3–5, 15. It is possible that the author was Kennedy's old adversary Duncan Macdonald, as 'Highlander' used exactly the same phrase, 'so miserable a caricature', to describe Kennedy's biography, *The Apostle of the North*, as Macdonald had used in his criticism of it; Letter, *Inverness Courier*, 21 December 1865.
249. Drummond and Bulloch, *Church in Late Victorian Scotland*, 95.
250. Arthur Gordon, *The Life of Archibald Hamilton Charteris* (London, 1912), 300–3; cf. Maclean, *James Cameron Lees*, 238–43.
251. E.g., Macdonald, *Social and Religious Life*, 178–82.
252. Both quoted in Gordon, *Life of Charteris*, 144, 302.
253. Report, *Dundee Courier*, 21 March 1878. Earlier that year, he had been part of a constitutionalist delegation to the Lord Advocate; Report, *Scotsman*, 9 January 1878.
254. 'Highlander', *Disestablishment Movement*, 8–9.

255. Smith, 'Free Church Constitutionalists', 106–7.
256. Smith, 'Free Church Constitutionalists', 115.
257. Macdonald, *Social and Religious Life*, 182–3.
258. Ross, *Church and Creed*, 141–2; MacLeod, *Banner in the West*, 235.
259. Macdonald, *Social and Religious Life*, 168–9.
260. Macfarlane, *Apostles of the North*, 103.
261. E.g., Kennedy, *Sermons*, 168, 325–6.
262. Letter, *Glasgow Herald*, 27 February 1882.
263. Auld, *Life of John Kennedy*, 196–201.
264. Report, *Scotsman*, 15 February 1882.
265. Report, *Scotsman*, 19 August 1884; Smith, 'Free Church Constitutionalists', esp. 112–13.
266. Stewart J. Brown, 'The Social Vision of Scottish Presbyterianism and the Union of 1929' (77–96), *Records of the Scottish Church History Society*, xxiv (1992), 80ff.; Ross, *Church and Creed*, 125–6.
267. Alexander McPherson, ed., *History of the Free Presbyterian Church of Scotland, 1893–1970* (Inverness, 1973), 34.
268. Ansdell, *The People of the Great Faith*, 190.

CHAPTER FOUR

Controversy

John Kennedy's ministry divides very naturally into two stages. The first, to 1870, was the ordinary life of a rural Free Church minister: his principal focus was on fulfilling his regular duties of preaching, and pastoring his own congregation, to which he had added the writing of some books. These had not, as Chapter Three has noted, proved universally popular, and they were historical and theological rather than controversial writings. However, from 1870 onwards, Kennedy was actively engaged in the major public controversies of the Free Church. Given his retiring disposition, it is unlikely that Kennedy relished this role, but he clearly felt that the issues at stake required him to put aside his native sensitivities. The first significant controversial speech Kennedy gave, in October 1870, addressed the union question, and he continued to engage actively in that and in the closely related disestablishment question until his death, as was discussed in Chapter Three. However, other public questions soon engaged his attention as well. Kennedy proved adept at using the medium of the controversial pamphlet in particular to argue his case, and he wrote numerous such publications over the last fourteen years of his life, on many subjects. But although the issues on which Kennedy engaged in controversy were superficially disparate, in fact his public stance was both consistent and coherent. In the 1860s, Kennedy had published books describing the traditional Calvinistic Presbyterianism of the Scottish Highlands; from 1870 onwards, he contended vigorously for this Calvinistic Presbyterianism.

Kennedy and Worship

The subject of the public worship of God was central to John Kennedy's whole adult life from the time he was ordained to the full-time ministry at the age of twenty-four. He routinely conducted five services a week in Dingwall and was frequently engaged in leading worship elsewhere. For Kennedy, worship was nothing less than the practical expression of one's view of God. For this, the *Westminster Confession* taught, one day in seven was set apart as a Sabbath 'to be kept holy unto him' by all people, involving 'an holy rest all the day from their own works, words, and thoughts about their worldly employments and recreations'. Instead, they are to spend 'the whole time in the public and private exercises of His worship, and in the duties of necessity and mercy'.[1] General observance of the Sabbath was therefore part of Scotland's Presbyterian heritage, and was largely unquestioned at the time of the Disruption in 1843. This was especially the case in the Highlands, where zealous evangelical religion, including strict Sabbath observance, had taken firm root only in the eighteenth century.[2] For Highland evangelicals, the urging of the strict obligations of Sabbath observance upon all reflected the conviction that the whole community was duty-bound to give obedience and worship to God. But a revolution in worship was to come, and one aspect of that movement was a changed view of Sabbath observance.

Instruction on Sabbath observance was a normal aspect of Kennedy's ministry, as evidenced, for example, in the notes for a sermon in Dingwall on 'Remember the Sabbath day to keep it holy' (Exodus 20: 8) on 3 January 1864, defending the traditional doctrine, both negatively, as 'a day of rest from all such employments and recreations as are lawful on other days', but also positively, as 'a day of rest with God [for] having communion with God and doing His will' and 'a day of rest in Christ'. Under this latter heading, Kennedy emphasised the evangelical purpose of the day, that the right use of the Sabbath entailed faith in Christ: 'You come into his rest, you cease from works, you take the finished work of Christ [and] you rest thereon.'[3] Later that year, he returned to the same subject on the Sabbath morning of the Dingwall communion, on 7 August, when he challenged his hearers in the 'fencing' address, traditionally intended to distinguish between those who should participate in the Lord's Supper and those who should not: 'Do you love the Sabbath?' To this he added the headings 'trains, papers, letters . . .', obviously intending to expand on some contemporary temptations to breach of the Sabbath.[4] The brevity of these references suggested that the doctrine of the Sabbath was not an area of particular controversy in Kennedy's own congregation, though it remained one aspect of his regular pulpit instruction.

But in wider Scottish society, views on the Sabbath were changing rapidly. In February 1865, the North British Railway publicly defended its decision to run trains on Sundays, the directors arguing that these were essential in an industrialised age. Furthermore, a prominent Established Church minister, Norman Macleod of Glasgow's Barony Church, broke ranks to defend the decision, arguing for a more liberal interpretation of the obligations of Sabbath observance, and there was no appetite for action against him within his Presbytery.[5] More disturbing still for Kennedy, ministers of other churches rallied to support the liberal approach, including John Eadie of the United Presbyterian Church and, shockingly, W. C. Smith of the Free Church, and no discipline was enacted in either case.[6] The latter, though not named, was plainly the subject of Kennedy's criticism in a newspaper article from 1879, when he wrote of 'a new style of dealing with nascent heresies [that] was inaugurated in the course taken in the case of [. . .] a minister, in Glasgow'. He described the outcome of the case in terms of grave disappointment:

The blossoming antinomianism of the minister was scolded at, and he himself allowed to preach as much or as little to the dishonour of the divine law as he pleased. Practice of this kind strengthened the feeling of indifferentism which it expressed.[7]

Kennedy believed in the duty of the Free Church to contend vigorously for the perpetual obligation of strict Sabbath observance, but it was clear that his views were not universally shared in the Lowland Free Church. Even in the Highlands, there were occasional complaints at the rigour of Sabbath observance expected in the community. 'Presbyterian', an anonymous individual who wrote letters critical of Highland evangelicalism to *The Scotsman* in 1878, asked rhetorically: 'Do people within the jurisdiction of the Dingwall Presbytery never receive public reprimands or have Baptism refused their children on account of frivolous complaints of Sabbath-breaking?'[8] Similarly, a Free Church member from Gairloch, Osgood Mackenzie, complained in his memoirs of the excessive strictness of Sabbath observance that was taught in his congregation.[9] However, these were the views of individuals only; the community as a whole in the Highlands remained strongly committed to Sabbath observance. When a pleasure-steamer was sailed on Loch Shin on the Sabbath in 1888, the Free Church people in Lairg were deeply offended, gathered for a protest meeting and sent critical resolutions to the wealthy holidaymakers responsible, arousing a storm of controversy in the national press.[10] Kennedy himself became known nationally as a staunch Sabbatarian and was mocked in a *Scotsman* editorial in 1881, being caricatured as 'view[ing] with more profound contempt and pity than ever those "conceited Lowlanders" who assume the right of questioning the Kennedian interpretation of the fourth commandment'.[11]

In 1883, a storm of protest erupted in Wester Ross when a special train was put on to run from Strome Ferry to Inverness for the benefit of east-coast fishermen landing their catch on that day. The action caused great offence, not least because the Sunday landing would have contravened regulations in these days even at major ports like Leith, but was apparently considered legitimate by the authorities at Strome. On Sunday, 3 June, the local people gathered in force and prevented the landing, withstanding the forces of railway officials and police present. They remained in occupation of the pier and station, praying and singing psalms, until midnight. The authorities arrested and prosecuted ten of the men, sentencing them to four months' imprisonment apiece, but for many in the Free Church they were heroes.[12] Though they would not condone violence, ministers like Alexander MacColl of Lochalsh and George Mackay of Inverness expressed sympathy for the men, both in their objection to Sabbath-breaking and in their harsh sentence, as did Spurgeon, and even John Cairns of the United Presbyterian Church. On their eventual release from Calton Jail in Edinburgh, James Begg entertained them to tea, and organised the collection of £500 to compensate the men for their lost earnings.[13]

John Kennedy, however, went a good deal further. Not only did he personally stand surety for £100 bail for the men after they were charged, but he also raised money for their legal expenses, and organised public meetings in their support across the Highlands.[14] At the rally in Dingwall, speaking in support of a memorial calling for the release of the men, Kennedy remarked, 'I feel so warmly towards the poor prisoners in the Calton Jail, that I cannot speak coldly regarding their case – so strongly that I may find it difficult to speak calmly. I regard them as specimens of the most law-abiding community in this country.' He declared the Sabbath activity of the fishermen and Railway Company itself to have been illegal, and comparing the local men's conduct to that of Nehemiah in the Bible, forcibly preventing mercantile activity in breach of the Sabbath. If the men were guilty of 'indiscretion', the real blame lay on those who failed to enforce the laws of the land against Sabbath desecration. Furthermore, by despatching troops to Strome Ferry in the wake of the disturbance, the Government had risked inciting bloodshed:

> Rather than that a few herrings should lose a little of their flavour before reaching London – let human blood be shed! This was the remorseless behest of the Railway Company, and to fulfil it the executive and the Government proved themselves quite ready to help them.[15]

Kennedy was strongly criticised in the national press for expressing such support for the men: his conduct, said *The Scotsman*, proved him rather 'a genuine priest than [...] a true Christian'.[16] But he earned praise from many fellow-Highlanders. The Gaelic poetess Mary MacPherson wrote a song, *Gaisgich Loch Carunn* (the Lochcarron heroes), in sympathy with the local men, praising those who had supported them, but with particular mention of Kennedy, by then deceased:

> The soldier
> Who often gladdened the flock
> Who was generous to the Sabbath
> May he have an eternal Sabbath.[17]

Kennedy delivered a substantial lecture in his own congregation on the subject of Sabbath observance on 16 September 1883, in the wake of the Strome Ferry case, and subsequently printed the text as one instalment in his run of printed sermons that year.[18] He considered first 'The Divine authority and perpetual obligation of the fourth commandment', then 'What is required by the fourth commandment?', and finally, 'How is the Sabbath observed in Scotland, and by each one of ourselves?' Under the final heading, Kennedy especially highlighted the widespread running of Sunday trains as a grievous breach of the Sabbath, and addressed the Strome case in very blunt terms:

> A wanton and flagrant desecration of the Sabbath, by railway officials and their servants, occurred, and not only was there no interference on the part of the executive to put down the excuseless traffic, but all exertions were put forth, by those who should be 'a terror to evil-doers', to protect it, and arrangements made for shooting down the men whose only crime was a pronounced expression of zeal in behalf of the Sabbath law of heaven and of Scotland.[19]

The Government he criticised in scathing terms, for permitting and protecting Sabbath work at Strome and elsewhere, but also its defenders in the print media. *The Scotsman*, in particular, he termed 'an organ of infidel Liberalism', the adjective 'infidel' being especially telling, as that which Kennedy habitually used to describe the call for disestablishment (cf. Chapter Four), thus implying that desecrations of the Sabbath came from exactly the same movement for change as that which demanded ecclesiastical disestablishment. In closing, Kennedy applied the obligation of the Sabbath very pointedly to his own hearers, warning against loose or casual observance, and even cautioning parents against allowing Sunday schools to become a replacement for church for their children, as he rather urged families to attend public worship together. The Sabbath, he argued, was a day for communal worship.[20]

But the content of worship was also vital. Kennedy's concern on the subject was evident as early as 1865, when he introduced a sermon on Psalm 149: 2 on 10 December to his own congregation, as recorded in his own preparatory notes, with a defence of psalm-singing in public worship:

> The psalms were inspired and recorded with a view to their being a perpetual vehicle of the church's praise on earth. As such were they intended for Old Testament times, and as such they were then used. But they have not been laid aside by God. They are still in His book. In the New Testament there is nought to take their place. We have no prepared New Testament psalmody. Is it not manifest therefore that the Lord regards the psalms of David as never out of date, whatever men in whom carnal sentiment takes the place of genuine godliness may regard them [*sic*]. And do these inspired songs not suffice? What do we need besides them, but that New Testament light should shine upon them? Is there a phase of spiritual feeling not expressed in them, from a despairing groaning of an Asaph to the highest raptures of triumphant faith? Is there an aspect of Christ, divine, incarnate, humbled, crucified, buried, raised, reigning, giving, pitying, washing, not presented to us?[21]

Kennedy clearly wished to ground his own people firmly in a love for the Psalms as the sole materials of sung praise for the Christian Church, and to bolster them against any arguments advanced for the introduction of any other materials of praise. This had, in fact, been the practice of all the congregations of the Free Church since the Disruption, albeit with occasional supplementary use of 'paraphrases' (metrical renderings of other passages of Scripture) in some congregations, chiefly in the Lowlands. Again, this reflected the position of the Westminster Assembly: the *Directory for Public Worship*, formally accepted by the General Assembly of the Church of Scotland in 1645, prescribed only psalms in worship.[22] The *Directory* continued to be recognised by the Established and Free Churches, though some of the secession Presbyterian churches had begun to use hymns in worship.[23] The Psalms in question were those from the metrical version, published in 1650 by the Westminster Assembly, together with a direct Gaelic translation of the same for Highland congregations. Kennedy's own practice was strict exclusive psalmody in public worship, although it is true that he was once persuaded by his friend, the Baptist pastor C. H. Spurgeon, to give out a paraphrase, when the latter was preaching for him in Dingwall in 1870. The anonymous writer 'Presbyterian' described the incident in humorous terms: 'Dr Kennedy was once imposed upon by the waggery of Spurgeon, and read out a paraphrase, but his face on that occasion was an index of the misery it caused him.' Otherwise, however, Kennedy's practice was unvarying, as the same writer asked rhetorically whether Kennedy, or any of the other prominent Highland ministers, had ever been heard to 'give out a paraphrase or hymn to be sung on a Sabbath in Church at public worship?'[24]

A. C. Cheyne warns, however, against imagining that Presbyterian worship was therefore unvarying; he identifies 'diversity and development' as characterising worship in all periods of Scottish church history, and observes that, in practice, the *Directory* was 'to experience all the vicissitudes of approbation, emendation, neglect and even obloquy'.[25] In the mid-nineteenth century, this especially involved an increasing use of ritual in Presbyterian worship, with the gradual introduction of read prayers, choirs, and greater ceremony in the administration of the sacraments; in fact, the Established Church was, by the 1860s, experiencing what some termed a 'Renascence of Worship'.[26] Such a movement could be satisfied only for a time with superficial changes, and more radical innovations were bound to come. In 1861, the Church of Scotland published the first small selection of hymns for congregational use, and in 1863, more controversially, Robert Lee of Old Greyfriars Church introduced a harmonium into worship services.[27]

The increasing availability of inexpensive musical instruments, the greater frequency of musical concerts, and of opportunities for attendance at professional musical performances, and observance by travellers of the more musically sophisticated worship of the Church of England all added to the pressure for change in the worship of Victorian churches in Scotland. But above all, David Bebbington has pointed out a 'drive towards respectability' that characterised much change in Victorian society, and that this was especially relevant to changes in worship. The perception of organ music as dignified and cultured meant that, with regard to the introduction of instrumentation, 'the predominant tendency of change was towards catering for the growing respectability of the worshippers'.[28] The tribute that John Caird, while minister of Park Church (1857–62), 'infused "a new note of reverence, good taste, and culture" into the services' is very telling: the latter two were not terms that would be applied by a connoisseur of orchestral music to the plainness of unaccompanied congregational psalm-singing.[29] The standards by which worship was judged were changing, and the change that began in the Established Church quickly became manifest in the Free Church. By 1886, the Free Church Moderator felt free to criticise the unaccompanied psalmody he heard while touring the Highland congregations of the Free Church, on the grounds of musical quality.[30]

The progress of this change was rapid. In Canada, a Free Church introduced an organ in 1855; the Presbytery immediately ordered its removal.[31] But the 1860s saw growing pressure in the Free Church to introduce hymns. In 1866, there were twenty-one overtures on the subject before the General Assembly, including eight clearly in favour, all from the Lowlands, and six clearly against, all from the Highlands. On the subject of worship, as Kenneth Ross observes, 'the Church was divided, and the division, to a striking degree, was between Highlands and Lowlands'.[32] By 1869, a committee reported to the Free Church Assembly, recommending that the Church prepare the way for the introduction of hymns. Kennedy registered his vote against, alongside conservative leaders like James Gibson and James Begg, but a growing number of Free Church ministers were prepared to argue the opposite case, and the proposal carried by a large majority.[33]

By 1872, matured proposals were tabled in the Assembly to permit a small number of approved hymns. Kennedy had already broken his life-long silence on the floor of the Assembly earlier that week with a speech against the union, and again spoke in the hymns debate, in support of the motion of his friend Hugh Martin against the approval of hymns in worship.[34] Interestingly, Kennedy had registered his own strong feelings on the subject by drafting a lengthy speech in his notebook on the subject of psalm-singing in worship, commencing 'Moderator, this is the first time I have ever sought a hearing in the Assembly,' which indicated the importance with which he regarded the question, as he obviously prepared this before deciding to speak to the union debate also.[35] In delivery, the speech was condensed and a good deal more polished than in this draft, unsurprisingly given Kennedy's vast experience as an extemporaneous speaker. A later Free Church writer termed it a 'masterful oration',[36] and it is certainly a clear and coherent contribution to the debate. Kennedy's argument followed similar lines to his sermon extract above, noting that sung praise requires a manual available to all, that such has been provided in the Psalms, and that no manual or instruction to prepare one being included in the New Testament, there is no need for any supplement. Furthermore, his opponents were obliged to prove 'that the Old Testament Psalmody was not intended for the New Testament Church', which Kennedy wholly denied:

> Could not the Lord then give what would be suitable for all ages[?] Can men uninspired do now better than he did then? Does not the completeness of it prove that it was not to be superseded? What view of God's character is not unfolded in the Psalms? What aspect of His providence is not presented in them? What special dealing with His Church, individually or collectively, is not celebrated? What phase of spiritual feeling, from the deepest groan of agony and hopelessness to the highest ecstasy of triumphant joy, is not expressed? And have we not in the Psalms the grand facts of the redemption in the historic form? The coming, the death, the resurrection and the ascension of Christ are set before us in the form in which it is meet the New Testament Church should sing of them. If we have this psalmody from the Lord's own hand, if it be complete, and if it presents the materials of praise in the form best adapted to our circumstances, what more do we require? This sufficed for the Old Testament Church, and with all the light of the New Testament shining on its songs, it ought surely to suffice for us. In heaven the song of Moses is also the song of the Lamb.[37]

He went on to urge that as no human composition could be put on a level with the Psalms, so no hymn should be introduced alongside the Psalter. He argued that the desire for hymns came from the desire for the artificial excitement such songs could produce in evangelistic campaigns, which he rejected as a legitimate use. However, the vital point of Kennedy's argument lay in the following remark:

> To my mind, this Hymn movement seems a side current of a stream which, if it continues to increase in volume and in force, shall ere long carry down before it all that is definite in our system of doctrine, and all that is simple in our mode of worship.[38]

The introduction of hymns was part of a far greater revolution, theological as well as liturgical. In this assertion, Kennedy was undoubtedly correct: the adoption of hymns as worship material was a decisive step away from the Westminster Confessional model of worship, and therefore from the traditional worship of Scottish Presbyterianism. The motion permitting the use of hymns in the Free Church carried overwhelmingly, by 213 votes to 61.[39]

The organ question had not been raised, and defenders of the hymns had even argued, whether disingenuously or myopically, that permitting hymns was 'the best way to shut out any chance of such things occurring'.[40] In hindsight, of course, Kennedy was perfectly correct, anticipating accurately that the desire for organs in worship would only be fuelled by the introduction of hymns. He remained, however, resolutely opposed, and raised the issue the following year as a point of argument against the proposed Mutual Eligibility Scheme with the United Presbyterian Church, as its Synod introduced permissive legislation for instrumental accompaniment in 1872. Kennedy argued that such worship was a departure from the *Confession*, the heritage and even the Presbyterian polity of that Church, by leaving the question open for individual congregations to decide:

> The first organ peal that awakes an echo in a U. P. Church, shall sound, in the ears of any in whom the spirit of the Erskines still survives, as a wail over the grave in which the last relics of their labours have been buried out of sight.[41]

The following year, Kennedy wrote his controversial pamphlet *Hyperevangelism*, which warned of the dangers of the evangelistic campaigns of D. L. Moody, particularly criticising the addition of 'musical practisings' to prayer meetings. This referred to the habitual use of a harmonium to accompany singing at the meetings connected with Moody's campaign, and the solo performances of his colleague Ira Sankey. These innovations, Kennedy argued, had helped to foster an unhealthy expectation of instant results: 'From both the addresses and the music, much was expected, when the evangelistic deputies arrived.'[42] He went on to highlight a number of 'unscriptural devices' used to promote the evangelism, of which the first two were hymn singing and instrumental music. Regarding the former, he contended that 'singing the gospel to men has taken the place of singing praise to God'. This, he thought, indeed 'produced an effect', especially when the singing was good; his implication was evident that such conversions were not necessarily any true work of God.[43] Instrumental music only added to this effect, he argued: 'The organ sounds effectively touch chords which nothing else would thrill.' He objected to instrumental music in worship as unconfessional, as an aspect of Old Testament ceremonial worship that was not warranted in New Testament times, and as equivalent in its purely sensual appeal to 'crucifixes and pictures, and [. . .] all the paraphernalia of the Popish ritual'. Against these innovations, Kennedy presented three arguments: such things are 'not prescribed in New Testament Scripture'; 'they are incongruous with the spirituality of the New Testament dispensation'; and they 'help to excite a state of feeling which militates against, instead of aiding, that which is produced by the word'. For these reasons, he urged the entire abandonment of hymns and instruments in worship.[44]

In his reply to Kennedy's pamphlet, Horatius Bonar acknowledged the use of hymns and of the harmonium, but did not mount a direct defence of these aspects of Moody's campaign, rather urging his colleague to see 'enough of excellence behind [the innovations] to warrant our rejoicing in the work as genuine'.[45] Undoubtedly, however, despite Bonar's reticence, Moody's campaigns were significant in preparing the way for the introduction of musical instruments into the worship of the Free Church. Free Church ministers and elders were active in supporting the meetings of the campaign, many Free Church people attended, and all therefore became used to the solos, choruses and the harmonium, and to associate these innovations with evangelistic success. Indeed, Sankey's hymn book was so popular that messenger boys reportedly sang his songs in the street, and the publication earned the men £7,000 in royalties while they were in Britain, though it only cost sixpence.[46] Inevitably, the campaign helped to encourage the embrace of hymns, and fed the popular demand for instruments to be introduced into the regular Sabbath worship of the Free Church. Kennedy, from the perspective of Highland evangelicalism, was therefore right, and indeed far-sighted, to criticise this aspect of its influence.

Kennedy remained prominent in the Free Church as an opponent of hymns, and in the 1878 General Assembly seconded a motion of Begg's against the approval of the Free Church's own Hymnal, though he acknowledged that he spoke with no expectation that the motion would carry, but 'simply with the view of clearing his own conscience and preserving consistency in relation to this matter'. Again, he urged the sufficiency of the Psalter as a manual of praise, and insisted that his opponents in the debate were obliged to produce proof that it required supplementation. As Kennedy had anticipated, the motion was decisively defeated.[47]

Predictably, the supporters of change soon brought the demand for the introduction of instruments into public worship before the courts of the Free Church. As Ross pointed out, this was more controversial in the nineteenth century than the hymns issue, as it marked a more decisive break with the past. Paraphrases had always been used in some congregations, but never any form of instrumentation. Organs would arguably contravene the confessional regulative principle in worship, that only what was specifically warranted in Scripture should be included in worship, and would also contravene the 'uniformity of worship' stipulated in the Revolution Settlement of 1690. When the issue was raised in the 1882 Assembly, James Begg argued strongly that it was an unconstitutional proposal, and thus beyond the powers of the Assembly to legislate. Again, the overtures that supported this position came from the Highlands.[48]

Kennedy, though not a commissioner, was equally steadfast in opposition, and delivered a memorable speech before his own Presbytery on the subject, later published as a pamphlet.[49] He stressed the importance of the regulative principle of worship from the *Confession*, 'that nothing should be introduced into the practice of worship which is "not prescribed in the Holy Scripture"'. Under this principle, instruments should be excluded, he contended, arguing in detail that the use of instruments specified in the Old Testament was ceremonial and typical: that is, prophetic of New Testament spiritual realities. He went on to discuss the New Testament evidence, which he found to support the view that instruments had been abolished from the use of the Christian Church. Historically, he pointed out, instruments had been introduced into the worship of the Catholic

Church only in the seventh century, which he saw as a time of 'decay'. In the Presbyterian Church, instrumental accompaniment had been excluded for three centuries:

> What have we now, in respect of intellect, or of godliness, or of wisdom, that can possibly accredit, or make even respectable, any movement that differs in its direction from the practice with which these worthies of other days are associated. A long pause, at least, is due to these men of God ere we venture to differ from them. We have reaped in blessing the fruits of their labours. What is likely to be the harvest to be reaped by those who come after us, if views, and practices, in opposition to theirs are to obtain the ascendency? I protest, in the name of all the grand Scottish worthies of the three past centuries, against being drawn into the adoption or tolerance of an innovation against which they unanimously revolted.[50]

Even in the present, Kennedy found that 'some of the most devout and intelligent' of the members of the Free Church objected very strongly to the introduction of instruments. He later quoted from some of the founding fathers of the Free Church to show that they had not anticipated or desired such a change. He also denied that it was constitutional for the Church to permit instruments without revision of the *Confession of Faith*; without this, he insisted, it was a straightforward breach of the ordination vows of the office bearers supporting such a development. However, his most important objection was what he anticipated the permission of instruments would lead to. For Kennedy, it was merely the thin end of a 'rending wedge', and formed one part of the same movement that introduced hymns, the agitation for union and permitted 'reckless assaults upon the Word of God', by which he evidently referred to the Biblical higher criticism being promoted in Scotland by William Robertson Smith. It was Kennedy's contention that the revolutionary changes in the Free Church of Scotland in the nineteenth century formed a single interconnected movement for change, and one from which he entirely demurred.[51] His stance was that of an older evangelicalism that saw itself in direct continuity with the simplicity of the New Testament, and it was telling that his final argument was from that simplicity:

> I cannot conceive how one can, in faith, enter one Synagogue congregation after another, following Jesus, reach one hill-side gathering after another, and realise Jesus as there, and then join the little assembly, in the upper chamber, where Jesus was present, and thereafter visit the worshipping assemblies of the early Christian Church, and mark the utter absence of all that was demonstrative and sensuous in the mode of worship, appointed by the authority and sanctioned by the example of the Lord, and by the practice of those who believed in His name, and then arise to propagate a movement for the introduction

of organs into a church whose form of service was hitherto according to the pattern, thus so fully accredited – the gift, to His church, of Him who declared, that they who 'worship the Father must worship Him in spirit and in truth'.[52]

This was a theologically conservative argument, but one that found its basis for conservation not in church tradition, but in the Scriptural model of New Testament worship. Kennedy was certainly defending the principles of Highland evangelicalism in contending for exclusive psalmody, but he defied any attempt to bracket his position as merely local or sentimental. As Alan Sell observes, Kennedy sensed that 'the foundations were being undermined', in worship, in doctrine and in practice, and his opposition to the innovations was therefore implacable.[53]

Kennedy even addressed the issue in the pulpit. In a sermon dated 2 July 1882 and marked 'Inverness', on Proverbs 23: 10–11, especially on the words 'Remove not the old landmark', Kennedy prepared in his notes to address 'The landmark between the scriptural and the unscriptural'. Under the heading, he particularly noted the new demand for instrumental music, remarking, 'This arises from a desire to fashion and worldly society'; he went on to cite the New Testament description of worship as 'the fruit of our lips' (Hebrews 13: 15).[54] The fact that Kennedy would use what was almost certainly a Saturday communion preparatory service, when one of the largest congregations in the Highlands would be further multiplied by large numbers of visiting worshippers from elsewhere, to address the issue of instrumental music in worship showed the seriousness with which he viewed the issue and condemned the innovation. Similarly, in the tenth of his run of weekly printed sermons in 1883, Kennedy scathingly condemned the call for instruments:

> O! the drivelling folly of those who, under the name of Christians, are clamouring for the sounds that come from dead matter in the house of God, in stead of praying to the Lord for broken, believing hearts [...] What a fit of spiritual madness has seized the churches of Scotland when, instead of seeking and commending the praise that springs from prayer, they are seeking to please carnal worshippers by the sounds that are pressed from an organ![55]

Kennedy went on to urge his hearers not to follow such a course but to direct their attention to giving worship from the heart. He made further applications in the same vein in subsequent printed sermons, continuing to condemn the demand for instrumental accompaniment and urging worshippers to focus on personal spiritual participation.[56] While he did not mention it from the pulpit, he also organised a petition to the 1882 General Assembly from the members and adherents of the Free Church, and managed to amass a remarkable 53,000 signatures in opposition to the approval of instrumental music in public worship.[57]

The issue was formally decided at the Free Church General Assembly in May 1883, in Kennedy's absence, in a heated debate. The petition Kennedy had organised was presented, and before the debate even began, Begg and others tabled a formal protest against the issue being raised. Henry Moncrieff moved against the introduction of instruments, Rainy moved in favour and the house divided, 390 to 259 in favour of instruments, with many dissents recorded.[58] Though the conservative position was decisively beaten at Assembly level, the issue remained highly controversial. The battle over worship continued at a congregational level, as the issues of the constitutionalist magazine *The Signal* from the 1880s recount, with attempts to introduce hymns, instruments or both in individual Free Churches leading to local ructions and realignments.[59] For example, George Smeaton, the eminent New Testament Professor at New College, Edinburgh, left his eldership in Grange Free Church over a change in the worship, moving to the conservative Buccleuch congregation.[60] The constitutionalist magazine *The Signal* recorded a meeting of elders co-ordinating their opposition to instrumental music in April 1884, the month of Kennedy's death.[61] Conflict over worship was thus exacerbating the division in the Free Church.

For the Highland Church, the issue of worship was fundamental. In his Gaelic elegy for Kennedy, Donald Munro praised Kennedy as an opponent of error, directly linking his opposition to foreign heresy (presumably German higher criticism) with his opposition to change in worship:

You were a faithful watchman and soldier, in all things;
To erroneous beliefs you would not yield,
Nor have respect to them.
Against the stream of ungodliness,
You often wrote and spoke powerfully.

And against such heretical teaching you stood boldly,
A teaching which came from overseas
And was contemptible —
Against those who sang hymns instead of
The songs of Zion.[62]

Like Kennedy, Munro saw the revolution in worship and the revolution in Biblical criticism as two aspects of the same movement of 'erroneous' and 'heretical' instruction. For Kennedy, worship and doctrine always went hand in hand. He connected the legitimisation of Sabbath work with the 'infidel' call for disestablishment, and the demand for hymns and instruments with the desire to please men rather than God. In the trend of rejection of the Westminster model of worship, manifested in different ways, Kennedy saw a single movement at work, and it seems that many in the Highlands shared this outlook. Tellingly, the 1905 Assembly of the continuing Free Church, the minority who had stayed outside the union of 1900, not only repealed the Declaratory Act, which permitted divergence in doctrine from the Westminster Standards, in matters such as Biblical inspiration and the obligations of Sabbath observance, but also repealed the acts permitting hymns and instruments in worship. This latter action proved controversial in several Lowland congregations, notably Leith and Kinglassie, which desired to practise diverse worship, and led to several ministers and elders resigning from the Church, but the Assembly was not to be dissuaded.[63] The Free Church minority did not merely re-affirm their subscription to Westminster Calvinism; they also re-affirmed the Church's commitment to the unaccompanied psalmody advocated in the *Westminster Directory of Public Worship*. Like Kennedy, their desire was to return to the practice of an older evangelicalism in worship.

Kennedy and Mass Evangelism

As a preacher, Kennedy was constantly engaged in evangelism throughout his ministry, and his published sermons evidence throughout that frequent and urgent evangelistic application was a staple of his pulpit ministry. He was an evangelist, but he also wanted to see evangelism consistent with Biblical and confessional theology. When this consistency was lacking, he had no hesitation in offering criticism. As early as 1862, long before Kennedy became known as a controversialist, he publicly criticised, though not by name, a wealthy English lady called Laura Thistlethwayte, on holiday in Garve, who had begun delivering evangelistic addresses in church there.[64] The sensation of a 'lady preacher' attracted great crowds, but Kennedy pointed out that for a woman to preach was not Biblical, stating that he did not wish to 'repress the Scriptural development of a Christian lady's zeal' but did not want it 'misdirected'.[65] Mrs Thistlethwayte disregarded his concerns, replying publicly in a letter to *The Scotsman*.[66] She went on to address many revivalist meetings in England and France in later years, and most notably expressed her defiance of Kennedy by conducting meetings in Dingwall on the 'fast day' of the Free Church communion there in August 1866.[67] A recent research paper has suggested that she later had an extended affair with the Victorian statesman William Gladstone.[68]

In his sermons, Kennedy consistently expressed concern at superficial evangelism, noting in a very characteristic warning in an 1859 sermon that 'An increased activity may accompany a waning spirituality in the case of an individual, and also of the church at large, and may serve to hide the decay that has verily taken place.' He foresaw this kind of shallow work leading to supposed converts falling away; so, for example, in notes for an 1864 sermon warning against false faith, he wrote 'no wonder in Ireland', presumably intending to illustrate the point by highlighting the converts who abandoned their professions after evangelistic work there.[69] In an 1866 sermon, he warned against 'some who claim a monopoly of preaching a free gospel', yet whose 'idea of the gospel is that it is a revelation of God's willingness to save sinners, and that the faith of this good will to men is all that is required in order to salvation'. Such preaching, which demanded neither repentance nor faith in Christ, 'must produce marked results' because the faith demanded could 'be exercised by anyone', without any renewal by the Spirit. But evangelism that proceeded in such a manner would not, in Kennedy's view, produce true converts.[70]

In 1874, this issue became the ground for a major controversy over the merits of the evangelistic campaign that the American preacher Dwight Lyman Moody was leading in Scotland, and which we have already discussed in relation to the organ controversy. Moody was already an experienced evangelist in his native USA, but his extended mission to Britain in 1873–5 became a major national event.[71] Moody attracted support from many leading preachers across all the major Protestant denominations. The Free Church, in particular, gave massive, if informal, backing: many of its ministers sat on the platform at Moody's meeting, they encouraged their congregations to attend, they helped to counsel his converts and they obtained the use of the Free Church Assembly Hall in Edinburgh for his meetings. In publishing a critique of this campaign, albeit without naming Moody specifically, in his 1874 pamphlet *Hyper-evangelism*, Kennedy knew that he was breaking with friends like Spurgeon, with former allies in the union controversy like Horatius and Andrew Bonar, and with the majority view in his own denomination. Many evangelicals believed the Moody campaign to be a genuine religious revival, and Kennedy must have known that they would not welcome his criticism.

Kennedy could not be accused of mere prejudice with regard to Moody: when the American evangelist first came to the Highlands, Kennedy himself preached preparatory to him in Thurso, on the 'bread of life'.[72] His experience was therefore personal, and he no doubt felt burdened by this early association, which made him look like an endorser of Moody's campaign. However, there was a further prequel to the controversy that reflected far less credit upon Kennedy, which seems to have escaped every prior academic commentator on the Kennedy–Bonar debate. In 1873, while in America to attend the meeting of the Evangelical Alliance, Kennedy met a Scot named John Mackay of Chicago.[73] In February 1874, some months after his return to Scotland, Kennedy received a letter from Mackay, purporting to give him some information about Moody. The letter alleged that Moody had been dismissed by his employer in Chicago for divulging confidential information to the opposing side in a legal case. The letter further alleged that Moody denied the doctrines of election and eternal punishment: 'Mr Moody is too shrewd, however, to make his real tenets known in Scotland until he has first found he has got a foothold among the people; then shall the cloven foot be made manifest.'[74] Without further verification, Kennedy began to circulate this information in Scotland, passing on the manuscript itself to unnamed persons in Inverness. By May of that year, the letter had come to the attention of the committee overseeing the Moody campaign in Scotland, and had caused distress to Moody himself. Rev. John Kelman of

Leith sent a copy to John Farwell, a known associate of Moody's in Chicago, asking him to ascertain the truth.[75] Farwell obtained an emphatic denial from the claimed source of the allegation, the employer in question, who denied that Moody had been responsible for any such conduct while with his firm, and indeed had intended in the conversation in question with Mackay 'to raise [Moody] in his estimation'; Mackay reportedly still refused to retract even in the light of this decisive testimony. Farwell even proposed libel action against him: 'I really think it would be a charitable act to make him pay $5,000 or $10,000 for his slanders to be expended in evangelizing Dr Kennedy's district in Scotland, or some other good work.'[76]

Kennedy made no mention of the false allegations in his pamphlet *Hyperevangelism*, either of misconduct or of concealed doctrines, but the incident does explain the lengthy testimonial to Moody's character from many eminent citizens of Chicago included at the end of Horatius Bonar's pamphlet in reply to Kennedy. It is to Bonar's credit that he did not comment on Kennedy's circulation of the letter earlier in the year, which did little credit to Kennedy's judgment. It is fair to suggest that in the months following his receipt of Mackay's letter, Kennedy was unfairly biased against Moody, and if this period was when Kennedy wrote *Hyper-evangelism*, it may account for the sometimes sweeping judgments against Moody in that pamphlet. The pamphlet was published reasonably early in 1874,[77] early enough that before the end of the year it had run through seven editions and had received a reply from Bonar. Certainly, it is unlikely that Kennedy knew that the allegations of Mackay were false when he wrote the text, though he did not have sufficient confidence in them to reproduce them in print here or anywhere else. However, what is clear is that Kennedy stood by the main thrusts of his argument in his reply to Bonar the following year, long after Mackay's allegations had been decisively and publicly refuted in print. The light that the incident throws upon Kennedy is not creditable, but it was separate from his doctrinal criticisms of Moody, which must stand or fall upon their own merits.

Whatever the validity of this critique, Kennedy was certainly correct in identifying the significance of the Moody campaign: historians concur that the Moody campaign had a transformational effect on nineteenth-century Scottish Presbyterianism. Undoubtedly, Moody promoted change in worship, as discussed above, but more importantly he popularised a new theological emphasis. Drummond and Bulloch acknowledge that Moody and Sankey had brought 'into the Free Church a more emotional, warm hearted expression of the faith'.[78] But the theological shift was more radical than a mere change of presentation: Patrick Carnegie Simpson considered Moody's ministry to have helped vitiate 'the old hyper-Calvinistic doctrine of election and [...] what theologians call "a limited atonement" and to bring home the sense of the love and grace of God towards all men'.[79]

Moody effected change not by challenging or dogmatically rejecting accepted doctrine, but rather, as Bebbington has observed, he 'avoided controversial topics' in his preaching, such as election and perdition.[80] Many ministers followed his example, in Scotland especially, and the inevitable consequence was that such doctrines were neglected in the Churches and eventually largely abandoned. Indeed, the debate over Moody's campaign chiefly concerns not the nature of the revolution effected in Scottish theology, at least in part through his influence, but whether or not it was a change for the better.

Kennedy began his pamphlet by acknowledging the scale of the movement in Scotland, while stating that to him it 'hitherto yielded more grief than gladness'.[81] He was cautious not to deny that there may be true converts arising from the movement, but urged that the cases were premature for judgment, and the movement must rather be judged on the means employed. His first condemnation was directed against the religious teaching of the movement, which he termed 'hyper-evangelism', and called 'another gospel'. His attempt to coin a term undoubtedly drew from the frequent characterisation of traditional Free Church preaching as hyper-Calvinistic: that is, going beyond true and historic Calvinism. Kennedy reversed the phrasing, suggesting that Moody was going beyond the true gospel and teaching error. His main polemic was divided into two sections, entitled 'Another Gospel', which addressed Moody's alleged doctrinal errors, and 'A Mighty Power', which addressed the means utilised in the campaign.

In the first section, Kennedy maintained that Moody failed to stress 'the character and claims of God as Lawgiver and Judge' or 'to bring souls in self-condemnation'. He accused Moody of ignoring 'the sovereignty and power of God' and failing to show 'how God is glorified in the salvation of the sinner', or to offer any caution 'against the tendency to antinomianism in those who profess to have believed'.[82] These were serious charges, and perhaps a little sweeping, with only the occasional brief quotation from Moody's sermons to substantiate the points in question. Undoubtedly, some doctrines historically prized by Calvinistic Presbyterians were not taught in Moody's 'stripped-down kerygma'; as Coffey noted, 'Moody's theology, like his style, was simple and anti-intellectual.'[83] However, even if Kennedy was highlighting omissions of doctrine in Moody's preaching rather than emphatically false doctrinal assertions, the list was still a formidable one, and from a perspective of strict confessional adherence, a sobering critique.

In the second section, Kennedy condemned, as addressed above, Moody's use of hymns and instrumental accompaniment; he further challenged the introduction of an 'inquiry room' into his meetings. These gave opportunity for individuals to be 'pressed and hurried to a public confession', which Kennedy considered wholly unwarranted, as it involved no trial of time or experience. More to the point, the light and easy presentation of conversion in Moody's teaching appeared to Kennedy to show a profoundly irresponsible care of souls. As Ross noted: 'He was aghast that people were accepted as converts simply upon an affirmation of faith at the close of an evangelistic meeting.'[84] Equally, Kennedy condemned the 'open prayer-meetings' which accompanied the campaign, where anyone could stand and pray without being called; these Kennedy called 'factories of sensation'.[85] In an intense illustration, Kennedy likened the movement he was witnessing in the Church to his experience at the bedside of his dying daughter, when 'convulsions of life' only indicated the approach of death. He concluded by prophesying confusion and decline in the Scottish Church if the trends continued: 'a negative theology will soon supplant our Confession of faith, the good old ways of worship will be forsaken for unscriptural inventions, and the tinsel of a superficial religiousness will take the place of genuine godliness'.[86]

Kennedy's publication created an immediate storm of controversy, not least because of the immense popularity of the movement he was criticising and the implied censure that his brother-ministers in the Free Church felt from it. It was an index of Kennedy's influence on the Highland Church by the early 1870s that his condemnation in *Hyper-evangelism* was considered single-handedly to have led the 'Highland Host' to distrust Moody.[87] Perhaps as a consequence, Moody did not exercise the same influence in the Highlands that he did in the rest of Scotland. As Donald Meek notes, effectively 'he did not penetrate the Gaelic-speaking Highlands', despite holding a few well-attended meetings in the region, notably at Inverness, Tain and Strathpeffer.[88]

But the Lowlands were different. Even many years later, an obituary recalled unfavourably Kennedy's 'somewhat bitter pamphlet' against Moody, and this feeling was evidently widespread.[89] By far the most important answer to Kennedy was that of Horatius Bonar, the prominent and respected minister of Grange Free Church, Edinburgh, which he entitled, rather pointedly, 'The Old Gospel: Not "Another Gospel" but the Power of God unto Salvation'. Bonar and Kennedy were longstanding colleagues, who had stood together in opposition to union with the United Presbyterian Church and had cooperated in advancing the Free Church cause: they had jointly opened the new Free Church at Avoch in 1863, for example.[90]

Bonar therefore began graciously, acknowledging the 'honoured name of Dr John Kennedy', but rejecting his pamphlet as based on 'anonymous hearsay' in contrast to Bonar's own personal experience of the whole campaign from the beginning.[91] He was prepared to grant that there were 'blemishes' in the work, but urged that these were no greater than those that had accompanied revival movements in Ross-shire in previous generations. Kennedy had, he remarked, denied prior revival movements in the South in his previous publications, such as that associated with William Chalmers Burns in the late 1830s, in the face of eminent witnesses to the contrary, while describing Highland revivals in a favourable light.[92] Interestingly, Bonar chose to frame the debate in terms of the distinction between Highland and Lowland evangelicalism: it was, he asserted, 'the theology of the Lowlands that Dr Kennedy has summoned to his tribunal'.[93] He denied that Moody failed to preach repentance from sin; defended the many sudden conversions that had been professed as a result of the campaign, pointing out that Kennedy was happy to record such occurrences favourably when they occurred in the Highland Church; and urged that all connected with the campaign were convinced of the necessity of the work of the Holy Spirit to the success of the movement.[94] He stressed the care with which the work was managed by a large committee of ministers and other workers, and the prayer and seriousness with which it proceeded, and concluded by pointing out that if the work were truly of God, Kennedy's opposition would constitute 'contending against Him'.[95]

Another response to Kennedy was that of the noted Edinburgh theological scholar Robert Young, who wrote very heatedly against Kennedy, comparing him contemptuously to the Biblical character Elijah in his despondency. Unlike Bonar, Young defended hymns and instruments vigorously, and brought a charge of 'pure formalism and legalism' against Kennedy. He went on to surmise, not very charitably, that 'Highland zeal, Highland whisky', a deceitful heart and even 'Satanic influence' were responsible for the 'folly and malignancy' of Kennedy's pamphlet.[96] A much kinder and more gracious answer was that of Spurgeon, a mutual friend of both Moody and Kennedy, who addressed the issue in his church magazine, the *Sword and the Trowel*, strongly recommending Bonar's pamphlet 'as amply meeting Dr Kennedy's strictures, and needing no supplement'. He went on to express his disappointment at reading from others 'the most bitter reflections on Dr Kennedy, as though he were an enemy of the gospel'. Rather, Kennedy was, in his view, 'one of the best and holiest of men' and 'jealous of Divine sovereignty'; the controversy should end with both sides seeking to learn from the other.[97]

Kennedy replied in print to Bonar in 1875, indicating that his concerns with the Moody campaigns were undiminished, though he expressed 'respect and love' for Bonar himself.[98] He strongly defended himself against the charge of being opposed to revivals, pointing out that he had early experience of revival in the Highlands in boyhood, personally attended the meetings of Chalmers Burns in Aberdeen in his student days and went to Ireland to see the revival meetings there. In each case, he argued, the results were largely evanescent: there was 'a genuine work of grace' in some but the bulk of the work was mere 'superficial excitement'. The need was for teachers to bring 'searching doctrine to bear on the impressed', so that excitement would be calmed and the true fruit thus be made evident.[99] He strongly denied Bonar's allegation that he lacked evidence for his negative conclusions regarding Moody's teaching, noting that he himself had heard the principal quotations he gave from Moody's own lips. Furthermore, he absolutely denied harbouring any 'anti-Lowland prejudice', and pointed out that Lowland ministers of a previous generation like John Love shared the supernatural experiences of 'prophetic discernment' that he in his writings had identified in the Highlands. Kennedy's standard for judging whether a conversion experience was genuine was, he insisted, that of Scripture.[100]

However, Kennedy went on to show that there was a fundamental gulf between his gospel and that which Bonar was defending: he urged the importance of preaching the law, while Bonar appeared to deny it; he urged the setting forth of Christ as the object of saving faith, which included trust in Him, while Bonar seemed content to recommend 'mere belief'; Kennedy urged self-examination on new converts but Bonar appeared to teach assurance, regardless of a lack of evidence of change.[101] Kennedy reiterated his concerns at the innovations in worship of the Moody campaign, especially the 'inquiry room', which by its busy and superficial nature, 'cannot admit of due care being taken in dealing with souls individually, as to their eternal interests'. In closing, he vehemently defended himself against any suggestion of a charge of hyper-Calvinism in opposing the campaign, insisting that his gospel concerns were those of Christ in John 6, in contrast to the Moody campaign: 'No one, who ignores the sinner's need of regeneration in order to faith, can fully preach "the gospel of the grace of God".'[102]

Kennedy's strong words against campaign evangelism were some of his most controversial in his own lifetime and have continued to divide critics since. In his biographical sketch of Kennedy, James Barron was carefully neutral on the subject:

> He was not in sympathy with the revival movements which characterised the religious activity of the time. He believed that they wanted thoroughness. He had a marked preference for what may be called the subjective, experimental religion of his own north countrymen.[103]

This was undoubtedly true, though, as mentioned above, Kennedy objected to the debate being framed in regional terms. Norman Macfarlane was more pointed, calling it 'one spot in his fine mind which went lame'. He was, however, unreasonable in marvelling that Kennedy 'should oppose and almost scoff at Revivals', scarcely a fair representation of his position in the debate. Reluctantly, Macfarlane acknowledged that the Highlanders largely followed Kennedy's view on this point: 'He moved like a great ship, and hundreds of smaller craft were affected by his wake.'[104] The historian John Kent was simply factually incorrect when he denounced Kennedy's opposition as that of 'a hyper-Calvinist leader in the Highlands': Kennedy's fervent evangelistic preaching and commitment to the free offer of the gospel were well known in Scotland and easily verified from his publications.[105]

But other writers were more favourable. Stewart and Cameron, writing more than thirty years later, concurred very firmly with Kennedy's assessment of the campaigns:

There can be no doubt that the teaching and methods of the American evangelists had a lasting influence upon the religious life of Scotland, and especially of the Free Church. On the spiritual results of their work it would be unwise to pass any judgement. It is best to leave the fan in the hand of him whose winnowing alone is sure, because his discernment is unerring. But there is reason to fear that in several directions their influence was the reverse of salutary. They gave a decided impetus to the spread of Arminian teaching in Scotland. They helped to give the doctrine of a universal Atonement an almost unchallenged place in its theology. They lowered the conception of conversion until it came to be well nigh emptied of spiritual significance. They did much to eliminate the element of healthy, godly fear from our modern religion, giving currency in its place to a certain jauntiness of assurance which too often reared its head from a very slender basis of experience.[106]

The early Free Presbyterian leader Neil Cameron plainly shared Kennedy's concerns; a colleague wrote of his 'abhorrence of the decisionist evangelism associated with Moody and Sankey'.[107] Donald Beaton called *Hyper-evangelism* 'one of the ablest of [Kennedy's] pamphlets', noting that it 'reveals an acuteness of mind and a cautious judgement that give incisiveness and impressiveness to his criticisms'.[108] The theologian John Macleod agreed with Kennedy's concerns, and especially identified the influence that the Moody campaign had on Presbyterian theology:

> The definite out-and-out Calvinism of another day was going out of fashion and yielding place to a presentation of the gospel which, without being pronouncedly Arminian, avoided the emphasis which the older Evangelicals laid on the New Birth as a Divine intervention.[109]

Other twentieth-century Free Church ministers, like Kenneth MacRae, George Collins and Hugh Cartwright, concurred that history had wholly vindicated Kennedy's concerns at the Moody campaign.[110]

Furthermore, historians have not always been kind to Moody's supporters in the Free Church. William McLoughlin pointed out how such ministers 'blandly denied that they found anything contrary to the *Westminster Confession* in Moody's preaching', while going on to cite the contemporary Evangelical Union pastor George Craig, 'who regarded such explanations as mere sophistry. He believed the revival would make it obvious to all that the *Westminster Confession* had been abandoned by those Presbyterians who supported Moody.' McLoughlin concluded that Moody and Sankey 'undoubtedly deserved credit as a catalytic agency in the modification of the Westminster Confession' in the various churches, and gave examples of ministers acknowledging how Moody's influence had changed their theological outlook.[111] Donald MacLeod has demonstrated how Moody appealed to Christian businessmen like the Free Churchman Charles

Cowan as 'a gifted salesperson, a no-nonsense raconteur', yet pointed out that, in practice, his ministry was a 'challenge to the Free Church', both in worship and in theological emphasis: 'Kennedy did have a point.'[112] Similarly, Kenneth Ross, in a thoughtful journal article on the Kennedy–Bonar debate, notes that subsequent developments undermined the latter's position:

> Historically the judgment of Bonar that Moody's teaching was thoroughly Calvinistic may well seem naive since the campaign now appears to have been a turning point in the transition from the old Calvinism to a less doctrinal Evangelicalism with quite different emphases.[113]

Other writers have attempted to defend Moody's ministry. George Adam Smith was glad that Moody came before the higher critical debates, as he saw the campaigns as bolstering the evangelical faith of the Scottish Church in preparation for the challenge of accepting a revised view of the Bible, and the later historian Fleming concurred with this interpretation.[114] However, their view both acknowledged the change in Scottish theology that was in process, and gave Moody a place in the development of that change; far from contradicting Kennedy, such an interpretation would seem wholly consistent with his critique of the Moody campaign. The only difference was that Smith and Fleming regarded the changed face of Scottish Presbyterianism in the early twentieth century, in its embrace of universal atonement and the main conclusions of higher criticism, with approval, while Kennedy anticipated such changes with abhorrence.

Seen in a wider context, Kennedy was more far-sighted than many who shared his Calvinistic convictions. One biographer of Spurgeon, Iain Murray, called Kennedy's *Hyper-evangelism* 'a stirring pamphlet', and suggested that Spurgeon 'missed the main thrust of Kennedy's evaluation of the American's evangelism':

> Kennedy did not believe there is such a thing as a simple gospel, halfway between Calvinism and Arminianism; rather, a man in teaching the centrality of salvation must be either Calvinistic or Arminian even though he might appear to be neither. Kennedy opposed Moody, not merely because Moody left out certain truths, but because in doing so he was quietly yet inevitably promoting a type of Gospel preaching which in its general tendency was bound to weaken both the orthodoxy and the evangelism known to Scotland since the Reformation.[115]

Murray pointed out that Spurgeon in his later years did come to criticise some of Moody's practices, including his demand for an immediate public response, and the inquiry room. Murray charged Bonar with equal shortsightedness in a thoughtful and balanced summation of the debate:

> My own tentative impression of this disagreement is that Bonar was indisposed, on account of the fruitfulness of the missions, to coun-

tenance theological criticism, while Kennedy probably did not give sufficient weight to the immediate benefits attending Moody's work in Scotland. Bonar looked at the immediate blessings and saw no need for caution; Kennedy looked first at the long-term doctrinal implications and in so doing he arrived at far more critical conclusions.[116]

In a more recent discussion in 2006 of the same debate, in the context of a commendatory biographical sketch of Bonar, Murray has been more favourable to his side of the debate, arguing that Kennedy was 'seriously wrong in characterising the evangelistic movement of 1873–4 as the product of "another gospel"'. In particular, he considers Kennedy wrong to deny that there was indiscriminate love to humanity expressed in the gospel offer, in addition to the more specific love for the elect alone, and that 'the element of God pleading with men [...] was necessarily overshadowed, to the extent that Kennedy was consistent with his principles'. Murray still concurs with Kennedy's opposition to the inquiry room and with 'his fears over the entry of an "easy believism" in the south'.[117] Truthfully, the recent discussion by Murray is not easy to reconcile with his earlier words, both about Kennedy himself, whom he previously called 'one of the greatest evangelists Scotland has ever raised', and about Moody's gospel preaching as 'in its general tendency [...] bound to weaken both the orthodoxy and the evangelism known to Scotland since the Reformation'; these differences would suggest a change of view.[118] Judging historically, there is little doubt that the earlier Murray was correct: Moody's ministry in Scotland functioned not as a slight corrective to five-point Calvinists in the direction of evangelistic warmth, but as a door opened to universal atonement. As MacLeod concluded: 'Moody's communication of the good news arguably reflected McLeod Campbell's emphasis on universal salvation rather than John Calvin's particular redemption', and it promoted the same 'transformation' in the Scottish Church.[119]

Mark Toone described Moody's own doctrinal standpoint on the basis of extensive doctoral research:

> Moody's theology was a modified form of Arminianism. Universal atonement [was] the very heart of his evangelistic method [...] Despite protests to the contrary, supporters of the Moody mission continued to push Westminster dogmatism into the background.[120]

Toone added that, in Scotland, Moody 'contributed to the continuing decline of the rigid orthodoxy found in the Westminster Confession', noting that the key movers behind the declaratory acts that modified subscription, John Cairns and Robert Rainy, were key supporters of Moody's campaigns. Moody 'cannot take credit for single-handedly reshaping the nature of evangelicalism in Scotland', but did 'aid in the operation' by his preaching and leadership.[121] Drummond and Bulloch discern the same change: 'The campaign revealed that the reign of Calvinism in the Free

Church was ending and a less doctrinal and more emotional evangelicalism taking its place.'[122] Alec Cheyne also sees the reception of Moody and Sankey as significant for the development of the Scottish Church, and underline that this significance was exactly as Kennedy warned: they 'laid much emphasis on the convert's decision – which, as John Kennedy of Dingwall realised, was to undermine the traditional Calvinist approach'.[123]

Another aspect of Kennedy's critique was his concern at the instant and easy assurance taught by Moody and his assistants to their converts, which he thought very suspect. Kennedy demanded the traditional 'attestation of faith by works', and was troubled at the lack of concern to promote self-examination in this direction.[124] Ross has rightly observed that this part of the debate reflected the divergence between Highland and Lowland evangelicalism in the late nineteenth century,[125] but on this point it was Kennedy who reflected the historic confessional Calvinism of the Scottish Church, as evident in classic Scottish works on assurance like William Guthrie's *The Christian's Great Interest*. Furthermore, William Enright has observed that Kennedy's rejection of instantaneous conversion as the norm to be expected, in his dispute with Bonar, was simply the recursion of a debate from the 1844 Free Church General Assembly. Older Lowland evangelicals like William Cunningham and John Duncan had then insisted that the three elements of effectual calling identified in the *Westminster Shorter Catechism* as 'conviction of sin', 'enlightening in the knowledge of Christ' and 'renewing of the will' be remembered, anticipated in preaching, and normally expected as sequential in Christian experience.[126] Enright considered Bonar part of a 'pietist school' distinct from the older and more doctrinal evangelicalism of Chalmers and other Disruption leaders.[127]

Considering the debate as a whole, Ross saw a portent of coming separation: 'What was becoming apparent in the controversy between Kennedy and Bonar over the Moody mission was that the two streams of evangelicalism, Lowland and Highland, which had come together in the formation of the Free Church in 1843 were separating again.' The division between the two men was, he argued, between the two sections of the Free Church; it was fundamental and unbridgeable, and thus 'proved to be a marker in the parting of the ways'.[128] In this regard, Ross registered the disagreement in part as reflecting the differing contexts of the two men's ministries: Bonar in a Lowland city surrounded by multitudes unreached by the churches, whereas 'in Dingwall it was different. The Church largely retained its hold on the communal life of the people and there did not appear to be any need at all for a new missionary approach.'[129] This may not be strictly fair, as Kennedy's opposition was against specific features of the Moody campaign, and certainly not against urban evangelism in general. What is clear is that Kennedy was suspicious of those who seemed to desire novel additions to the worship of the local church for their own sake: 'Many there were who merely craved a change, – something to relieve them of the tedium of a routine, in which they found no enjoyment, because they were estranged from God.'[130] A Lowland evangelicalism that embraced the innovations of Moody with enthusiasm, and a Highland Calvinism that rejected them decisively, looked increasingly set to diverge entirely.

Kennedy's assessment of Moody's mission was harsh – and maybe too much so. As a result of false information, he may well have been unreasonably biased against the American evangelist in the early stages of his campaign. Even in his discussion of Moody's doctrine, as Sell remarks, his criticisms may not have been of 'the fairest kind': there were by all accounts real and lasting evangelical conversions from the Moody campaign, and Kennedy had undeniably been more charitable in describing the unusual phenomena of times of revival in the Highland Church. But Kennedy's concern was directed against divergence from his own standpoint, which was traditional Scottish Calvinism: 'He struck a balance, but it was a balance grounded in the Bible and guarded by the Confession.'[131] He rightly discerned in the Moody mission what most contemporary evangelicals seemed to miss: a challenge to confessional doctrine, a rejection of Presbyterian worship, and an easier, lighter gospel that minimised the need for self-examination. Ross's critique of Kennedy hits the mark: 'The problem with Kennedy's refusal to accept Bonar's [demand for a] sense of proportion was that every element in the familiar tradition appeared to him to be equally important.'[132] Kennedy's evangelicalism, which in this context was simply the confessional Calvinistic doctrine and practice of Scottish Presbyterianism hitherto, was a complete package. To abandon the part was to undermine the whole.

With Kennedy's reply published, the specific controversy was allowed to rest; but Kennedy remained deeply concerned at the changed approach to evangelism that the Moody campaign had promoted so successfully in Scotland. In 1879, he wrote in a series of newspaper articles of his concerns at worldliness in the Church, and even though he acknowledged the great activity in foreign mission work in his day, some of which was genuinely fruitful, he warned that this activity did not necessarily indicate the home 'church being in a healthy spiritual condition'. In particular, he warned against evangelistic work undertaken by unqualified individuals: 'Their trail, in all parts of the country, is marked by a growing aversion to the pure gospel and to genuine godliness, and by the spread of Plymouthism, the slimiest of all the isms.'[133] Kennedy saw the easy and superficial gospel of such evangelists as producing the direst results in terms of individuals taking comfort in shallow professions, without evidence of grace and without appetite for deeper teaching. While he did not explicitly blame Moody for the activities of such evangelists, the connection between this critique and the concerns he expressed in *Hyper-evangelism* was evident. In the series of sermons he published in 1883, Kennedy continued to express similar concerns at 'the coming of Revivalists' to a locality with the ostentatious parade of advertisements, choirs and musical instruments. He particularly objected to the way '"cases" are hurriedly and rudely handled, amidst the excitement of an inquiry room . . . and a proclamation is made of results throughout the land'.[134] These practices he contrasted critically with the words of Jesus that 'The Kingdom of God cometh not with observation.'[135]

In 1879, Kennedy opened a new front in his war against the new methods of mass evangelism, assaulting the temperance movement, which he saw as diverging from the gospel. The temperance movement was then acquiring mass popular support, appealing as it did both to the moralising instincts of Victorian society and to its social concern. Alcohol abuse was readily stigmatised as the principal cause, rather than a symptom, of both poverty and crime, and total abstinence was widely urged as the only solution. It was a message that appealed to the moral earnestness of the times, and the movement grew rapidly. The Band of Hope had seven branches in 1871 but 570 by 1887.[136]

The 1870s were the early growth years of this mass movement, which by the 1920s was sufficiently powerful to have, in Edwin Scrymgeour, its own MP. The urging of temperance was not itself controversial: the Victorian middle classes were far less prolific in their drinking than previous generations, and sought to encourage the same change of conduct in the lower reaches of society. The Free Church had a Temperance Committee from 1847, and was instrumental in securing the passing of the Forbes Mackenzie Act of 1853, limiting the opening hours of public houses. However, a minority wanted more extreme action, such as a faction in the United Presbyterian Church demanding that those employed in the liquor trade be prevented from taking office as elders.[137] It was this more doctrinaire faction that formed the core of what became the abstinence movement. Bebbington points out that it had a particular appeal to evangelicals:

> A high proportion of evangelicals mounted a powerful onslaught on strong drink, advocating total abstinence and trying to restrict the availability of alcohol. From their efforts to combat particular problems sprang the broader social gospel movement, dedicated to engaging with the needs of the body as well as those of the soul.[138]

The Highland Church had not historically practised teetotalism: the funeral expenditure in 1849 for John Macdonald, 'the Apostle of the North', included the substantial sum of £9 spent on whisky for the mourners; and Roderick Macleod of Snizort, an outlier in many respects, was considered unusual in urging abstinence from alcohol, and also from tobacco.[139] Evangelical ministers of the Disruption generation, Highland and Lowland alike, were generally wary of such demands, which they considered legalism; ministers like Macdonald and Finlay Cook preached only the need for moderation.[140] But a younger generation of ministers saw the social problems caused by alcohol abuse, and became convinced that only complete abstinence in the Church, in both her teaching and her example, would suffice. It was a rare issue that divided Kennedy from his friend James Begg, but the latter supported the temperance movement vigorously, and was a founder member of the Free Church Abstinence Society.[141]

The abstinence movement was boosted by the support of Moody and Sankey; for example, Moody was asked, 'What can be done to promote temperance in Scotland?' His reply was typical of the dogmatism of the movement: 'Get the ministers to put the infernal stuff away.'[142] Furthermore, temperance became an increasingly important aspect of the ministries of some of Kennedy's colleagues: the biographies of William Ross and Donald John Martin both include lengthy chapters on their activities in promotion of temperance, as though this was intrinsic to their ministerial labours.[143] In addition to dogmatism, the movement was characterised by a certain arrogance. Norman Macfarlane, for example, wrote of Kennedy: 'He wrote pamphlets on Teetotalism in which he was no Reformer. He loitered far behind the advanced guard.'[144] The assumption that 'teetotalism' was the certain destination of evangelicalism was implicit. Yet as Bebbington notes, Kennedy was not alone in his concerns: 'Many [evangelicals] feared it was another gospel, offering a path to self improvement independent of personal faith.' Furthermore, it prepared the way for the broader social gospel movement that focused on the transformation of society more than on individual conversions, thus leading away from traditional evangelistic concerns.[145]

Kennedy's view of wine as legitimate was evident in a sermon he preached in 1866 on the words, 'Let him kiss me with the kisses of his mouth: for thy love is better than wine.' He said that wine is 'greatly accounted of', 'revives the fainting heart', 'cheers as well as revives' and 'moves the giant to use all his strength', in each case urging Christ Himself as 'infinitely more precious'.[146] But when Kennedy published his 1879 pamphlet *Total Abstinence Schemes Examined*, he challenged the abstinence movement directly. In the Introduction, he explained that his involvement in the debate commenced with some remarks he made on the abstinence movement at the Synod, which brought him public condemnation: 'my views were represented as tending to encourage the drunkard in his sin'.[147] In fact, he explained that his purpose in writing was the exact opposite:

> [He realised that] if the teetotal movement, in its various forms, is a misguided effort – that it is neither scripturally based nor scripturally guided – it cannot possibly be successful, and that the sooner it is displaced by what is unobjectionable, the more effectually will the cause of Christian temperance be promoted.[148]

Kennedy stated of himself that he had 'not habitually taken so much as was medically prescribed' to him, and even in unconverted days had never known 'excess of wine'. Drunkenness he condemned as a grievous sin, but that sin required God's forgiveness, not merely to be abandoned: 'If the guilt be not forgiven, and the lust remain unmortified, the man once a drunkard, though now abstinent, is a drunkard still, according to the judgement of God, and as such shall be excluded from His kingdom.' In particular, he denounced any tendency to self-righteousness as a result of a personal choice to abstain from alcohol: 'With the example of Christ before us, it is surely allowable temperately to use it on festive occasions.'[149]

Kennedy declared his opposition to the abstinence movement for its lack of fidelity to Scripture in condemning drink rather than drunkenness, and for its requirement of a vow of abstinence. On the first point, Kennedy noted that the basic Biblical teaching on alcohol was uncontroversial until very recently, when works such as the 'Temperance Bible Commentary' began to insist that the consumption of any alcohol was a sin: 'In all recorded instances of torturing Scripture nothing more revolting appears than the attempts made to explain away all that, under the seal of inspiration, militates against this misrepresentation.' On the second point, Kennedy pointed out the inconsistency of arguing for a vow of abstinence from expediency, that one would not lead others into sin, when such a vow would bind in all situations and circumstances: such a vow could not stand as an absolute moral obligation.[150] Kennedy went on to denounce the movement of 'Good Templarism', which was effectively an order of freemasonry adapted for the temperance movement, for its 'pompous titles', regalia, secrecy, temples for worship, obligations sworn by all members and especially for its liturgy.[151] He quoted at length from the portentous speeches of this organisation, pointing out how the Scriptural quotations given against the use of alcohol had been carefully selected and edited to avoid words condoning the use of wine in moderation. He also objected to the singing of the 'ode to water', and to the 'Christless, graceless' funeral liturgy prescribed by the order.[152] Kennedy also criticised the 'Bands of Hope', which attempted to convey the temperance message to the young, considering their teaching, that all consumption of alcohol was wrong, 'a lie', an intrusion 'upon the province of the family' and dangerous:

> An unscriptural conception of sin is sure to be formed in the minds of the children who composed them. The habit of hearing of one sin, and that, too, the sin of which they are not conscious, and against which they are marshalled, tends to cause an ignoring of all sins besides, and to an education in self conceit, which must vitiate the character of the young, and make them, in later years, intolerable nuisance to all modest minds.[153]

In conclusion, Kennedy urged that the answer to the sin of drunkenness was the gospel of Christ, and its saving effects. By treating drink as the problem, the temperance movement was 'excusing' rather than 'exposing the sin'; drunkenness would be better treated as a crime.[154]

The abstinence movement could not permit such an assault as Kennedy's to go unanswered, and a substantial response appeared later in 1879 from two prominent temperance campaigners, the journalist Frederic Lees and the Congregational minister John Fordyce. As an answer to the charge of pomposity, the pamphlet is not very serviceable; Lees declared self-pityingly, 'there is no rest for the true intellectual warrior, whose sword must be kept always bright and sharp, ready to encounter the foe day by day'. Of the eminent theologians cited by Kennedy, Lees declared: 'Of Hodge I know nothing ... but Edgar and Watts I *do* know. Forty years ago I refuted the former, and three years ago the latter.' He denied that Scripture anywhere sanctioned strong drink: 'The wine sanctioned by the Redeemer is distinctly said to be "excellent" or *good* – and could not, therefore, essentially resemble the prohibited wine.'[155] Fordyce attempted to answer Kennedy more directly, insisting that the desire for alcohol came solely from exposure to it, that the abstinence pledge was a help to men in resisting drink, and especially urging that the Scriptural evidence cited by Kennedy had been misinterpreted to condone the drinking of alcoholic wine.[156] Bands of Hope, Fordyce argued, benefited their young members and taught them only what was moral and right, and abstinence would, if only put into practice, prove more effective in staunching drunkenness than any other proposed solution: he urged it therefore, on the basis of both science and religion.[157]

Typically, Kennedy returned to the fray with a further pamphlet, *A Reply to Some Recent Defences of Total Abstinence Schemes*, addressed particularly to Rev. John Kay, 'the Grand Worthy Chief Templar of Scotland', Lees and Fordyce. He repeated and amplified his criticisms of Good Templarism, noting that Kay's attempts to defend it by analogy from Presbyterian practices were invalid, as the practices of the Church of God were warranted in Scripture, and were in any case less grandiose.[158] Of Lees's attempts to exegete Scripture in support of the abstainers, he wrote: 'They assume certain positions as scientific, and then they proceed to produce harmony by wresting the plain meaning of Scripture.'[159] Kennedy then summarised his objections to abstinence schemes, as 'injudicious ... because they are extreme', and as unscriptural because they had, in his view, no basis in any Biblical instruction: the Hebrew word *yayin* was etymologically derived from the root verb 'to ferment', plainly meant intoxicating wine in the account of Noah's drunkenness, and could not legitimately be applied to any other substance in the account of Abraham's offering to Melchisedec. Christ was called 'a winebibber' because, differing from John the Baptist, he drank wine. Furthermore, the wine he produced in the miracle at Cana was termed 'good' by the ruler of the feast, even though he would not have expected 'good' wine at that later stage, when men's senses were dulled to the distinction, indicating that it was of the same character as the evidently alcoholic wine already served. Above all, wine was appointed to a spiritual purpose at the Last Supper: 'Can anything more thoroughly indicate the unscripturalness of the extreme Abstainer's position, than its generating an impression of this being unsuitable?' Fundamentally, Kennedy thought that abstinence schemes caused 'prejudice against the gospel', 'antagonism to the Church and her mission', and 'an increased disrespect for Scripture': the Church should rather seek help from God in her mission.[160]

In this as in so many areas, Kennedy's influence was potent in the Highland evangelical tradition, and most ministers of subsequent generations seem to have held to his line on alcohol. For example, the Free Presbyterian Church of Scotland engaged in an exceedingly intemperate controversy in the early 1920s, when the Temperance (Scotland) Act came into force, on the question of whether to support the 'no licence' position in the local plebiscites, which then began to be held under that legislation. However, it is significant that the majority, despite favouring 'no licence', firmly rejected 'the notion that it is a disgrace for a man to partake of strong drink, as a beverage, i.e. in sobriety'. Pointedly echoing Kennedy's concerns, they also added condemnation of 'the most dangerous and soul-destroying false doctrine that if a man who had been drinking to excess cease entirely to do so, he is thereby saved'.[161] Similarly, the Scottish theologian John Murray took a lead on the faculty at Westminster Seminary, Philadelphia, in the 1930s, in arguing strongly against the Fundamentalist demand that they teach abstinence as a demand of the Christian life: 'He was vehement in his assertion that for the church to demand abstinence, in the name of Christian holiness, was to set up a standard other than the Word of God.'[162] Alcoholic wine continued to be used for communion in the Free and Free Presbyterian Churches, and abstinence was never a requirement of membership, though some individual ministers, presumably influenced by the temperance movement, did urge the practice from the pulpit.[163]

Kennedy's point in the abstinence controversy was not, of course, to defend drink but to defend the gospel, which he saw being adjusted, and to defend Scripture, which he saw being wrested. These were the same concerns that motivated all his engagement in controversies regarding evangelism. As a young minister, he opposed a lady preacher because he saw the contradiction in a woman purporting to preach the gospel in contravention of the same Scriptures in which that gospel message was conveyed. Later on, he challenged Moody and Sankey for their Arminian tendencies in evangelism, and the Free Church ministers who had allowed themselves to be influenced and shaped by the American evangelists, in contradiction to their Biblical and Confessional commitments. Later still, he dared to oppose the formidable Victorian temperance movement, which he saw twisting the plain meaning of Scripture and promoting a false gospel. Douglas Ansdell makes an interesting comment on the Highland view of the gospel: '[Evangelical religion] was regarded as a new and transforming experience that shaped Highland Society. it must, therefore, be sustained and secured in order to protect its many benefits; social, cultural, moral and institutional.'[164] This precisely identified Kennedy's concern in the various controversies in which he engaged on the subject of evangelism: for him, the many battles were at root one, the defence of the Biblical and confessional Evangel.

Kennedy and Biblical Criticism

As a minister, Kennedy was constantly engaged in the study of the Scriptures, producing at least three separate sermons each week expounding passages of the Bible and applying them to his hearers. In strict parlance, he was therefore a Biblical critic, since the term refers to intelligent engagement with the text rather than any necessarily pejorative description. Kennedy's view of Scripture was that of the *Westminster Confession*, and that shared, at least in public, by all the Presbyterian churches in the wake of the Disruption: the Bible in the original languages was God's Word, given by direct Divine inspiration, and was therefore consistent, correct and authoritative in every detail.[165] The Free Church had inherited what Durkacz called a 'book religion' from their Puritan forebears, shaped in both doctrine and piety by Biblical content and language.[166] As the Victorian era advanced, however, a changing intellectual climate began to influence the general view of Scripture. Darwin's *On the Origin of the Species*, which was published to great acclaim in 1859, undermined confidence in the Biblical cosmology, as did the growing acceptance of Charles Lyell's geological theories regarding the age of the earth. Furthermore, in 1860, *Essays and Reviews*, a composite work by English authors, presented a new and much more radical approach to Biblical scholarship to the public. In the early 1860s, this was further drawn to public attention by major controversies that raged over the Anglican scholar J. W. Colenso's rejection of the Mosaic authorship of most of the Pentateuch, and of the historical accuracy of aspects of its narrative, and over the advanced New Testament criticism of Samuel Davidson of Lancashire Independent College.[167]

The 1860s were, as Cheyne has observed, the crucial decade in the changing theology of Presbyterian Scotland.[168] During that decade, debates over higher criticism entered the mainstream of thought, even in the Scottish Highlands. The Free Church minister William Taylor wrote in March 1866: 'In these days [. . .] the very air around us is filled with scepticism,' with reference in context both to Darwinism and to Biblical criticism.[169] Kennedy was well aware of these currents of thought, and in 1865 delivered a public lecture in Inverness Music Hall on 'The Renaissance of Scepticism'. Barron characterised this lecture as 'condemning the passion for freedom or licence of thought in dealing with the problems of Scripture', adding that Kennedy saw such an approach as the 'revolt of proud intellect against authority'.[170] In 1869, his discussion of creation in *Man's Relations to God* not only excluded Darwinism, but explicitly affirmed that 'from his position in the light of Scripture, in front of the glory of Jehovah in action', the believer must 'be neither drawn nor driven'.[171] In his preaching, lecturing and writing, Kennedy treated the Bible always as the consistent, authoritative Word of God, and in this was undoubtedly typical of the majority of the Free Church ministry up until the 1860s.

But even in the Free Church, times were changing. In 1858, A. B. Davidson was appointed to join the Old Testament department at New College, the first tutor drawn from a younger generation of Free Church ministers who had studied in Germany and been deeply influenced by German Biblical scholarship. Davidson remained at New College for more than four decades, as full Professor of Hebrew from 1863, and greatly influenced the Free Church ministry in favour of higher criticism, though he was cautious about what he put in print.[172] Higher criticism may be reasonably defined as Biblical criticism that is open to questioning the veracity and consistency of the assertions of Scripture.[173] The acceptance of this criticism in Scottish Presbyterianism was the 'Biblical revolution' identified by Cheyne, and he has stressed that 'it was the Free Church that played the leading part', particularly through Davidson and his ablest student, William Robertson Smith.[174] Smith was appointed to the vacant Hebrew chair at the Free Church College, Aberdeen, in 1870, at the remarkably young age of twenty-three, and became an immensely influential academic, called 'one of Britain's finest ever scholars'.[175] However, Smith's public advocacy of higher criticism resulted in a prolonged case before the courts of the Free Church, which eventually resulted in him being deprived of his chair in 1881. Thereafter, he had a very distinguished academic career at Cambridge University, latterly as Professor of Arabic, until his early death.[176]

Some historians have attempted to deny that the advent of higher criticism, and the Robertson Smith case in particular, concerned the inspiration and authority of the Scriptures.[177] However, this is simply disingenuous. The Scottish Victorian higher critics were indeed fervent Christians, but they viewed revelation as gradual and historical, not as a finished product. They believed in God, but dissociated him from the exact words of Scripture. Davidson found 'sporadic flashes of the Divine' in the Old Testament, not a text identifiable in every detail with the 'God that cannot lie'.[178] It is no insult to the higher critics to point out that their view of inspiration radically diverged from that of the older generation of Free Church scholars like Patrick Fairbairn (1805–74), whose *Typology of Scripture* identified detailed prophetic foreshadowing of Christ and the Christian gospel in the fine detail of the Old Testament.[179] Robertson Smith, as Richard Riesen has observed, distinguishes carefully between the Word of God and the Scripture in which it was later recorded; the former he saw as infallible, but not the latter.[180] This was a radical shift – a revolution, indeed – from the reverential view of Scripture advocated by the Disruption generation of Free Church scholars.[181] This distinction, defended by Marcus Dods in a controversial sermon of 1877, itself became the focus of a discipline case against the future Professor. Dods, however, was acquitted of heresy by a decisive vote of the 1878 General Assembly, possibly, Kidd and Wallace have suggested, because the Assembly was preoccupied with the more wide-ranging Robertson Smith case, and possibly because of his less objectionable personality.[182]

But even beyond the exact formulation of the doctrine of inspiration, the new form of criticism had unavoidable theological implications: as the contemporary theologian John Tulloch observed, it 'touched the very root of dogmatic Protestantism'.[183] A critic who considered himself able to discern and explain the alleged inconsistencies of the text of Biblical books could hardly feel bound to every fine detail of doctrine derived from exegesis of these same books. Nigel Cameron agreed, noting that 'what began as literary analysis inevitably spilled over into theological revision'; Drummond and Bulloch concluded that 'the new Biblical Criticism must mean the end of the old Calvinism'.[184] However, the waters were muddied, both by the professional necessity that Free Church ministers continue to declare their entire allegiance to the text of the *Westminster Confession*, and by the genuine evangelistic zeal that some of the higher critics displayed: Robertson Smith himself was reportedly a fine and orthodox preacher.[185]

In December 1875, Smith's views entered the public domain with the publication of the essay 'Bible', in the eighth edition of the *Encyclopaedia Britannica*, which denied the Mosaic authorship of the Pentateuch, with none of the caution or restraint with which Davidson habitually guarded his conclusions. The Established Church minister A. H. Charteris, Professor of Biblical Criticism at Edinburgh University, commenced the assault in an article in April 1876, denouncing Smith's views as heterodox. Within the Free Church, 'the prevailing note was one of indignant protest', as Stewart and Cameron noted, with few prepared at that stage to voice outright support for Smith's conclusions.[186] The College Committee took up consideration of Smith's writings, criticised the article 'Bible' as 'of a dangerous and unsettling tendency' but found no ground for a charge of heresy. However, both shocked conservatives in the Free Church like James Begg, and Smith himself, demanded that the case be tried by a formal libel. Smith was therefore suspended from teaching in 1877, and the cumbersome trial proceeded over three years, following strict and unwieldy Presbyterian process, culminating before the General Assembly in 1880, by which stage the charge had been reduced to a single count, that Smith denied the Mosaic authorship of Deuteronomy.[187]

This apparently trivial issue was, in fact, key to the whole debate over higher criticism: Deuteronomy represented itself as the collected final addresses of Moses to Israel before their entry to the Promised Land, in his capacity as a prophet of God. If, in fact, Deuteronomy was a later book by a later author, even if its claims to Mosaic origin were considered as a literary convention rather than as deliberate forgery, its testimony regarding itself ceased to be strictly true or trustworthy. A direct identification of God with these claims, and, more to the point, the injunctions contained in the text itself, became problematic at best. Furthermore, were such an approach to be applied to New Testament books, higher criticism had the potential to undermine the normative authority of passages of foundational importance to Christian doctrine.[188] The Mosaic authorship of Deuteronomy was not, therefore, peripheral, but rather a vital test case for higher criticism. Whether or not the reverent phrases of the *Confession of Faith* on the inspiration and authority of Scripture could be parsed as permitting this teaching, no one seriously imagined that the Westminster divines shared, or would have sympathised with, such a view. Drummond and Bulloch used a very telling construction in discussing this point: 'The Westminster Confession, as the first exponents of Biblical Criticism in Victorian Scotland were glad to discover, had not been so explicit on the inspiration of the Bible as had been the [older generation of] New College Professors.'[189] The implication of the critics' unfamiliarity with the text was no calumny: for the ministries of many younger men in the Free Church, the *Confession* itself had become increasingly peripheral, and even irrelevant.

Smith's view was both a new interpretation of what inspiration entailed and a whole new perspective on the finished product, the Biblical literature itself. It was no exaggeration for Cameron to call the publication of Smith's arguments in the late 1870s an 'intellectual earthquake' in Scotland, with a seismic impact on the Free Church in particular: indeed, Drummond and Bulloch consider the controversy 'a turning point for the mind of Victorian Scotland'.[190] If Smith's views were to be accepted, the Free Church would have to change beyond all recognition, in its teaching, preaching and, ultimately, its confessional subscription.

But the relevant question before the courts of the Free Church as the libel against Robertson Smith slowly progressed between 1877 and 1880 was strictly whether the *Confession* itself should be read as accommodating such higher criticism as Robertson Smith had published with regard to Deuteronomy.[191] While Kennedy had no immediate involvement in the case, as he was a member neither of Smith's Presbytery nor of his Synod, he certainly held strong views on the inspiration of Scripture, and in 1878 published a pamphlet on the *Confession*'s treatment of the subject. Conscious that the case was on-going in church courts, Kennedy referred only to 'recent discussions' on the *Confession*'s formulation of the doctrine of inspiration. He acknowledged that the *Confession* did not offer a 'definition, in express terms, of the kind or measure of inspiration ascribed to Scripture', but emphasised what it did teach.[192] The *Confession* asserted that God was author of Scripture, that Scripture is 'the Word of God' and that its authority is derived from 'God [who is truth itself]'; therefore, Kennedy argued that to assert errors in the content of Scripture was to blaspheme against 'Him whose words they were'. Furthermore, according to the *Confession*, inspiration extended to the languages in which the Scriptures were written, and therefore referred to specific words: 'The doctrine of the Confession then, is, that the inspiration of Scripture is *plenary* – is *verbal*.' This inspiration was specifically attributed to all the books of the Bible, and must therefore, with regard to them all, be maintained and defended by subscribers to the *Confession*.[193]

Kennedy's opinion of the place of higher critics in the Free Church was evident: 'if they [subscribers] hold and teach views inconsistent with such a doctrine they must either abandon the position secured by their subscription, or retract the opinions which the Confession condemns'. Kennedy acknowledged that those holding divergent views may still benefit from Scripture, but he was concerned about the effect of their teaching on others:

> if they accept their representation of the Bible, as an imperfect record, may not this have the effect of inducing in their minds an utter contempt of all that it contains? I know of no more effective aid to unbelief than that which such teaching must yield.

Kennedy emphasised the importance of an authoritative Word for answering spiritual need: no truly repentant sinner, 'who, for his immortal and sinful soul, desiderates a warrant of hope, that shall be availing and secure, can be content with aught that is not stamped with "thus saith the Lord"'. In dealing with cases where this confidence was being undermined, he urged, 'there should be no faltering in the action of the Church'.[194]

It should be stressed that Kennedy was known to be a gentle and pastoral counsellor to those in real intellectual difficulties. One student who sat under his ministry wrote:

> None knew better the depths of doubt and unbelief into which men's minds are prone to fall, and none was more skilful and successful in dealing with such cases. He did not object to, but rather encouraged, the frankest and fullest confession of intellectual difficulties. These he met with all the resources of his large experience, and with the light which the unerring Word of God brought to bear upon them. [...]
>
> At the same time, he had no sympathy with, and gave no support to, those who merely made difficulties and doubts the apology and lever for overthrowing or unsettling faith in the fundamental truths of the Word of God. Such he did not regard as honest inquirers after truth or humble learners of the wisdom which is from above. As there was no one who could speak more tenderly and kindly, so there were few who could more effectively dispose of error or more scathingly expose the insincere. He held that the highest flights of reason ought to be submitted in the last resort to the light of revelation.[195]

It was evident that Kennedy definitely considered Robertson Smith to fall into the latter category, and such a judgment helps to explain the heated tone of his critique of the Professor. In 1879, for example, Kennedy addressed the Smith case directly in his series of articles in the *Perthshire Courier*, in a tone of considerable frustration:

> We are not to be deterred from referring to the notorious case of Professor Smith, by being reminded that it is still *sub judice*, for we

hold that it should, long ere now, have been finally disposed of. In the first days of the Free Church, its course would have been a very short one; and if dealt with by ecclesiastics who combined a fervent love of the Bible with firmness and wisdom, it would, at any time, and in any place, have been very easily disposed of. Were a man to say, in the face of the Established Church of 1838, or of the Free Church of 1848, that Moses was not the inspired author of Deuteronomy, though the book itself says he was, and the Messiah declared that Moses had written it, he would either have at once to retract his averment, or be allowed no opportunity of repeating it within the church.[196]

He went on to complain of the excessive slowness of the handling of the case and of the evident desire of many of his colleagues to protect Smith from discipline. His words regarding some of these fellow-ministers were sharp in the extreme: 'In the preaching of some of the later additions to the roll of ministers, the repudiation of Confessional theology is as marked as the lack of any traces of a broken heart's experience of the power of the cross.'[197] Kennedy saw the rejection of Westminster theology going hand in hand with a lack of real spirituality.

In May 1880, the case finally came directly before the General Assembly, with Smith's future as Professor of Hebrew in the Aberdeen College in the balance. Kennedy was a commissioner, and was uncharacteristically active on the floor of the Assembly, in debates that indicated his concern at the advance of higher criticism. He seconded the successful motion of Sir Henry Moncrieff that Thomas Smith, an experienced former missionary and staunch constitutionalist, later the biographer of James Begg, be appointed to the vacant chair of Evangelistic Theology at New College. In his speech, he remarked 'they had had more than enough of appointing men who had had no opportunity of acquiring experience in the ministry of the Church', an obvious dig at Davidson and Robertson Smith, neither of whom had ever served in pastoral ministry; the remark was reportedly greeted with hisses and shouts demanding a withdrawal. Kennedy also warned pointedly that a failure to appoint Smith to the chair would be attributed to party feeling.[198] Thomas Smith was certainly conservative, but the chair was a peripheral one and the victory in this vote consequently unimportant.[199] More controversially, Kennedy also seconded a motion that the Edinburgh Presbytery investigate the teaching of an article by A. B. Davidson; this was heavily defeated.[200]

The actual debate on Robertson Smith proved catastrophic for the conservative wing of the Church. Four motions were tabled: Begg moved to proceed to a full heresy trial of Smith; Sir Henry Moncrieff moved, with the support of Robert Rainy, that Smith be dismissed but higher criticism not be condemned; John Laidlaw moved for acquittal but with a statement that Smith's views were not those of the Free Church; and Alexander Beith moved for acquittal, with a warning to Smith to be cautious. Moncrieff's motion, which was evidently the preferred course of the established leadership of the Free Church, reflected the anxiety stirred by Smith's unguarded writings and, in Cheyne's view, also irritation at Smith's personality, but not, crucially, any outright rejection of higher critical scholarship as contrary to the *Confession*.[201] The four motions necessitated a progressive series of votes: Beith's motion defeated Begg's, and then defeated Laidlaw's. The crucial vote was therefore between Beith's motion for acquittal and Moncrieff's for dismissal. Begg and Kennedy, who sat together in the Assembly Hall, had no wish to support Moncrieff's motion that left room in the Free Church for higher criticism. However, they would not let Smith win. As Drummond and Bulloch wrote:

> He and Kennedy of Dingwall, the leader of the Gaelic North, kept their seats until it appeared that Sir Henry would lose. At this point, Begg, according to some accounts, went onto the platform or, according to others, stood on one of the benches. He motioned to his supporters in different parts of the hall to join the queue for Sir Henry's motion until at last all Dr Beith's voters had vanished through the doorway while quite a number still waited to vote for Smith's dismissal. At this point, tired, but satisfied that all was well, Begg ceased to summon his cohorts to the battle and sat down contented.[202]

But Begg had miscalculated: Beith's motion carried by 299 votes to 292. By their abstention, he and Kennedy had permitted Robertson Smith's acquittal and restoration to his chair. Their chagrin may be imagined, though their humiliation was nothing to that of Rainy, whose ruthless policy of sacrificing Smith to preserve liberty for higher criticism had proven such a failure.[203] Throughout the Church, there was consternation at the result: indeed, Kennedy and a number of conservative colleagues, including Begg and Alexander Moody Stuart, in their Sabbath sermons following the conclusion of the Smith case, felt the need to assure their congregations that there was no ground for a separation.[204]

Kennedy called a meeting in his own congregation after his return, to address them more fully on the outcome of the General Assembly, with reference to several issues, but above all, that of the Smith case. As *The Scotsman* reported, 'The Assembly of 1880, he said, was remarkable because for the first time the New Scotland party in the Free Church rose to the power of a majority.'[205] This was an interesting phrase, and the criticism of the 'younger men' that followed made it clear that 'New' in this context referred to the generational shift evident in the Free Church, and indeed in wider society. Kennedy defended his own conduct by insisting that Begg's motion was the only constitutional one and Moncrieff's was 'unconstitutional, because it proposed to condemn before probation'. He would not grant such a precedent to the General Assembly, nor did he merely desire the exclusion of the man, but of his views: 'He repelled with indignation the attempt to fasten on those who refrained from voting then the responsibility of the final result.' The validity of this defence of Kennedy's course of action would, however, later be undermined by his supporting a near-identical motion at the 1881 General Assembly, to relieve Smith of his chair, without condemnation of higher criticism itself.

The extent of Kennedy's disgust at the celebrations of Smith's supporters after the 1880 vote was indicated by his comparison of their conduct with the riot in Ephesus in defence of the cult of Diana, described in Acts 19, with Smith himself called 'their idol'. However, the most significant section of his address followed:

> He had become aware of the existence of a rumour to the effect of ascribing to him an intention of resigning his charge in consequence of the Assembly's decision in the Smith case. In reference to this he would only say that the constitution of the Free Church yet remained unaltered. The faults against which he was disposed to protest were faults in administration. The place to protest against these was within the Church, not outside of its pale. Even the recent decision left the constitution of the Church unchanged, though it indicated a sad decline from faithful testifying on the part of her office-bearers.[206]

That such a rumour would circulate indicated the extent of Kennedy's anger at the handling of the Smith case; his rebuttal of it was, however, both decisive and thoroughly Presbyterian.[207]

But the Robertson Smith case was not over. Just ten days after the Assembly, another volume of the *Encyclopaedia Britannica* was published, with a further article by Smith, on 'Hebrew Language and Literature', written the previous year, repeating and endorsing even more decidedly the theories of German critics like Julius Wellhausen.[208] An Edinburgh minister, George Macaulay, immediately raised a disciplinary complaint before his Presbytery, which was remitted to the Commission of Assembly, which met that August, with Kennedy and many other Highland commissioners in attendance.[209] The Commission appointed a committee to investigate Smith's new writings. Stewart and Cameron probably went too far in stating, 'On this occasion, however, even the professor's friends could not defend his conduct,' for Smith certainly still had his defenders, but their words reflected the general frustration and irritation throughout the Free Church at Smith's unguarded expression of his views.[210] The composition of the Committee was strongly weighted towards Smith's opponents, indicating that the tide of sympathy for the Professor had turned after his latest publications.[211] Even the sympathetic *Glasgow Herald* correspondent noted the difficulty his fresh publication had given his defenders:

> [It] is only explainable on the supposition that he had in October last despaired of pulling through, and concluded that he might as well be hung for a sheep as a lamb. At present efforts of his supporters are devoted to showing that there is not so much difference after all

between a sheep and a lamb. The sheep is after all the same animal, and very little woolier than that which escaped the knife in May last; and, whatever its age, it must be distinguished from heretical goats.[212]

The new article may have challenged Smith's defenders, but for conservatives like Kennedy, it was a fresh provocation. In July 1880, he criticised Smith in a conversation at the close of the Dingwall Presbytery meeting, and some remarks that he made were overheard and published in the newspapers, alleging that Smith had withdrawn some further articles from publication in the *Encyclopaedia Britannica*, which the Editor had described as of an 'extremely pronounced character'.[213] The *Encyclopaedia* Editor, Thomas Baynes, however, in correspondence with Kennedy after the publication of this report, emphatically denied the truth of this allegation, though Kennedy continued to assert that his information was true. At Baynes's instigation, the whole correspondence was published.[214] Though the matter was of no great significance, as an unpublished article could not be a ground for discipline, it bore more than a trace of Kennedy's erroneous conduct with regard to Moody: Baynes's decisive public denial of the allegation would have been very unlikely, were there any truth to Kennedy's assertion.

On 27 October 1880, the committee reported back to the Commission, and Robertson Smith was again suspended from the duties of his chair, pending the outcome of the new case.[215] On 11 November, Kennedy delivered another public lecture in Dingwall, this time directly addressing the Smith case, with very strong language in criticism of Smith and his allies, whom he termed 'Rationalists', adding that 'unsanctified cleverness is a thing which Highlanders have not learned to admire, because they regard it as likely to be rather dangerous than useful to the Church'. Most controversially, he added a demand for summary action: 'Even if it were necessary to depart from strict form in our procedure, it is high time that in dealing with a matter of such cardinal importance we should cease to have our hands tied with red tape.'[216] This latter demand was itself unconstitutional, and neither a constructive nor a temperate contribution to the debate.

His lecture earned Kennedy the severest public criticism of his long and often controversial ministry, with exceedingly sharp words of critique published in the leading Scottish newspapers. 'Vox', for example, desired Kennedy's retirement 'from his assumed leadership of the Highlands', considering it a pity that he had not lived a hundred years earlier, when his gifts 'would have been more appreciated'; and 'A Free Church Highlander' criticised his demand for action against Smith regardless of precedent, which he saw as reminiscent of the extremism of some Covenanters.[217] The *Dundee Courier* went further, calling him 'a petty sort of Ross-shire Pope', and his address 'coarsely unjust'.[218] *The Glasgow Herald*, in similar vein, declared that Kennedy 'may be called the apostle of that Highland Host who came down like enraged shepherds from the northern folds' to the Commission, and termed his address a 'violent outburst', showing less 'regard for justice' than 'pleasure in a heresy hunt'.[219] Kennedy's name was greeted with 'great hissing' at a public meeting held in support of Smith in Aberdeen, and the speaker accused him of pouring out 'virulent invective' against Robertson Smith.[220] Even Kennedy's close friend and fellow-constitutionalist Hugh Martin was evidently uncomfortable with his tone, and sent him a long, somewhat eccentric letter which he also copied to the *Montrose Standard*. Martin disliked his 'pitting of the Highlands and Lowlands against each other', and said of Robertson Smith, who was a personal friend, that he would 'not judge [him] as guilty of worse than thoughtlessness'. However, his on-going affection for Kennedy was evident, and he wished that he were able to undertake a preaching tour alongside him around Highlands and Lowlands alike, in the latter stages of the letter launching into the kind of preaching he believed was called for.[221]

The stress of the extensive controversy over the Smith case may well have been a factor in Kennedy's need to take an extended break on the Continent in the early months of 1881.[222] However, he was a commissioner to the Assembly, and this time, the Free Church leaders were taking no chances: in the run-up to the General Assembly of 1881, Rainy and his colleagues summoned all the principal ministers of the conservative side of the Free Church, Kennedy included, to a council to agree a united strategy for handling the Smith case. Begg demanded a libel on the substance of the issue, but the majority demurred, willing to sacrifice Smith, but not higher criticism in general.[223] On this occasion, the conservative forces would not be divided, and Kennedy followed the lead given, voting to suspend Robertson Smith, though there was no implicit condemnation of the higher criticism.[224] It is evident that this course was not entirely consistent with his declaration the previous year that such a motion was unconstitutional, but truthfully he had no alternative: a motion for a heresy trial would certainly have failed, and if Smith were not suspended, he would return to his teaching post at Aberdeen. With sympathy for Robertson Smith greatly undermined by the Professor's own conduct, the vote fell heavily in favour of his suspension, and the case was at last at a close.

The conservatives knew full well, however, that they had won a hollow victory: a younger generation of Free Church ministers had rallied heavily to Smith's defence, as had (albeit without yet the capacity to register votes) the students' gallery. As James MacLeod observed, the trial was 'almost a caricature' in pitting one generation against another.[225] It was therefore evident that this suspension was merely a temporary expedient; it would not purge the Free Church of higher criticism. The supporters of Smith met the day after his removal from his chair, to issue a declaration and protest against the decision, and in particular an assertion that it left future scholars free to pursue the same questions. The younger professors involved in that meeting, such as T. M. Lindsay and J. S. Candlish, continued freely to teach higher critical approaches to Scripture and church history to Free

Church students.[226] Both by their age and by their uniquely influential positions, these men knew that they controlled the future of the Free Church.

It was in the wake of this Assembly that Kennedy wrote his most unusual publication, *A Purteekler Acoont o' the Last Assembly by Wan o' the Hielan' Host*, a pamphlet on the Robertson Smith case in Scots dialect. Strictly speaking, the work was anonymous, beyond the eponymous attribution to 'wan o' the Hielan' Host', but the attribution to Kennedy was widely attested and the content wholly consistent with his other works.[227] The pamphlet is a rare surviving example of Kennedy's humour. The choice of dialect was, of course, a matter of presentation, not communication: as noted elsewhere, Kennedy had published two of his pamphlets on disestablishment in formal Gaelic prose for monolingual readers, but this pamphlet was an attempt at a down-to-earth appeal to the common sense of his readership with regard to higher criticism. The narrator was proud to 'belave what oor fathers belaved', while the 'Kreetics' were 'brats o' crayturs [who] buld up a skaffal' o' graceless learnin', an' then stan on their toes on the top o' it that they may sput doon on the graves o' their faithers'.[228] Interestingly, the narrator distinguished between lower, or textual critics – 'they micht be doin' a goot wurk' – and the higher criticism – 'thus kind o' work is in great dainger o' no thinkin' o' the Spirit o' God at all, an' o' dalin wi the Bible as uf no han' but man's wus aboot it'. The narrator and his friend Alister had gone as commissioners to the 1881 Assembly, 'to vote against that little black craytur Smuth from Aberdane', who had busied himself for years 'sendin' sparks from his kreetikal anvil unto the een o' a' daysent bodies that kam near hum'. He especially objected to Smith's denial of Mosaic authorship, denial of the Christ-centredness of the Song of Solomon and denial of the historicity of Jonah. These points he defended from the words of Christ about the Pentateuch, attributing the books to Moses, from Christ's citation of the 'sign of Jonah', treating the book as factual history, and from the place of the Song in the canon of Scripture.[229]

Kennedy also used the pamphlet to critique the Assembly decision itself, even though he had reluctantly supported it, pointing out the inconsistency of suspending Smith from his chair while leaving him a minister in good standing: 'what wud be pison to studens cood na be mate for ither people'. The narrator defended his acknowledged vote for the final resolution nonetheless, comparing it to the removal of a leprous stone from a house wall, a reference to the hygienic legislation of Leviticus 14: 33–57, but with obvious disappointment that the Assembly had not gone further, and evident identification of the culprit Kennedy held responsible: 'Och! But there us alwees sum darkness on a Rainy day.'[230] Kennedy's discussion of the principal speakers was amusing: 'Sir Hairy', Henry Moncrieff, who was too much a lawyer, 'an wud hould hus feet on prunceple more staidy'; Rainy, like a tightrope walker, slow and cautious; John Adam, who 'cood screech oot argements that ut wusna aisy to anser'; and 'our ould freend Dr Begg', who, clear and loud, stood 'straicht on prunceple', quoting

Scripture and telling stories in his speeches with ease. His assessments of the speakers on the other side of the debate were a good deal less favourable. But Kennedy reserved his sharpest words for the '*Gobha beag*', Gaelic for 'little Smith', whom he plainly saw as arrogant and outspoken, but 'all hus goots kam un paipar parsals from Shermany'. His talents were 'cluverness an' memary', but not reverence or common sense, and the Devil himself had no lack of the former gifts. Kennedy saw Smith's approach as essentially wrong-headed, taking 'sum luttle duffeekulty, that a luttle panes wud remove', and building critical theories on that weak foundation. The narrator's prediction was solemn: 'Unless he wull repent, he wull grow unto an oot-an-oot enemy o' all revaled truth.'[231] The whole pamphlet demonstrated Kennedy's intense opposition to the higher critical movement.

The Smith case was significant in how it divided the Free Church. The supporters of the Moody campaign, for example, split sharply. Charteris, who had first condemned in print the Professor's writings, and the Bonars, who led calls within the Free Church for decisive disciplinary action, had been key supporters of Moody's work. On the other hand, many of the younger generation of Moody's fellow-labourers, like Alexander Whyte, George Adam Smith and Henry Drummond, backed Robertson Smith without reservation.[232] Ministers were often concerned, but many prominent laymen of the Free Church, like the businessman Charles Cowan, defended Smith.[233] Most Highland ministers regarded Smith's views with horror, but even some of their younger colleagues in the North, like Donald John Martin, read his writings, and those of Marcus Dods, with enthusiasm.[234] As Toone observes of the Smith case, 'the Evangelical party in the Scottish Church was in the midst of transition', but the generational transition was plainly leading away from the traditionally high view of Biblical authority.[235] Cheyne concurs, pointing out that after the Smith case, 'with every year that passed, indeed, the balance of theological opinion seemed to tip a little further to the liberal side'.[236]

Smith's was not the last case fought over higher criticism: further libels were brought in the decades that followed against Marcus Dods, A. B. Bruce and George Adam Smith, all without success, but it was noteworthy that as the years progressed, the concern over higher criticism steadily diminished. Even at its height, the Robertson Smith controversy was never fought with the intensity of the disestablishment campaign, as Kidd and Wallace have pointed out, and they are certainly correct that Rainy viewed the higher criticism cases as 'little more than irritant distractions' from his greater schemes for church union.[237] By the final decade of the nineteenth century, active opposition to the critics was largely evident only amongst the commissioners from the Highlands, the so-called 'Highland Host': indeed, it was left to Kennedy's successor in Dingwall, Murdoch Macaskill, to lead the unsuccessful prosecution of Dods and Bruce.[238] Yet again, the Highland–Lowland divide in the Free Church was evident in the differing responses to the Biblical revolution of the Victorian Church.

Nationally, the tide had turned firmly in favour of higher criticism; in the Free Church, Robertson Smith was both the first and the last casualty of the conflict. In many ways, far from his defeat in 1881 being a decisive blow struck against the higher criticism, the case cemented support for the liberty of the higher critical scholars amongst the majority of a younger generation of Free Churchmen. Cameron noted that the Smith case helped to promote the view that higher criticism was compatible with evangelical theology.[239] David Bebbington agrees on the significance of Robertson Smith's case, noting that his suspension must be seen in the wider context whereby, 'in a solidly Evangelical denomination, Biblical criticism had become accepted' by the early years of the twentieth century. This growing acceptance was, he argued, typical of much of British evangelicalism in the same period.[240] Furthermore, within the Free Church, the acceptance of higher criticism was just one aspect of the wider acceptance of what Kenneth Ross called the 'New Evangelism', an evangelical theology that accommodated itself to the main conclusions of nineteenth-century thought, which 'became a steadily more potent force as the eighties advanced'.[241] Enright, similarly, characterised the Smith case as the 'final conflict' between the older conservative evangelicalism of the Disruption generation and the emerging liberal evangelicalism of the late Victorian era: 'Ironically, Robertson's [*sic*] defeat was the *coup de grace* of older evangelicalism.'[242] Crucially, however, as Ross observed, 'a party of opposition to the New Evangelism was being consolidated', and though small in terms of the national Free Church, it was absolute in its determination to oppose higher criticism. It was from this party, chiefly influenced by Begg and Kennedy, though continuing after their deaths, that the resolution came to continue the Free Church witness, in separate institutional form, if that would prove necessary.[243]

Was Kennedy wrong to use the strong language that he did against Smith? Certainly, the controversy did not always find him at his best. His attempt to justify his abstention in 1880 was undermined by his support for the same course of action against Smith the following year. His refusal to back down from his assertion that Smith had withdrawn further articles from the *Encyclopaedia Britannica* was almost certainly wrong. His demand, later that year, for the Church to discipline Smith without regard for due process was unconstitutional and unhelpful. But from the advantageous perspective of more than a century later, it is hard to disagree with Kennedy's assessment of the devastating significance of the Robertson Smith case for the orthodox Calvinism that he held dear. Smith's teaching and writings, and those of his allies and successors, would prove utterly corrosive to the high view of Scripture and strict adherence to the *Confession* that had marked Kennedy's ministry. John Rogerson was perceptive to note the 'clash of two cultures', the near-total absence of common ground, as Smith and Begg confronted one another on the floor of the Assembly;[244] the contrast would only be greater still if the latter were substituted for his friend Kennedy.

Of course, Robertson Smith was not deliberately seeking to weaken Scottish Calvinist theology. Indeed, in the wider context, he was struggling to preserve evangelical theology, while addressing the scientific discoveries and critical conclusions that appeared to threaten it. Rogerson pointed out that Smith turned to German thought 'to sustain his evangelical beliefs in the light of new knowledge', and thus to resist the secularising trends of late Victorian academia.[245] His conclusions reflected his faith; for example, he asserted that the superiority of the Israelite religion to that of other Semitic peoples proved its Divine origin.[246] But this exposes the weakness at the heart of so-called 'believing criticism': these assertions are themselves then open to invalidation on the basis of further study in comparative religion. Robert Carroll, a modern higher critic, has freely critiqued Smith's Christian presuppositions, his study of Scripture to bolster faith in 'the dogmas of conciliar Christianity', his reconstructed narrative of the prophets as religious reformers, his idealism, his 'anti-Jewish polemic', his 'Orientalism' and so on. Yet in this critique, Carroll uses the tools and approaches that Smith himself helped to legitimise in Scottish scholarship: Robertson Smith, he concedes, 'belongs to that great shaping period of our discipline as biblical scholars', though 'we [. . .] have moved far beyond him now'.[247] In the same volume, Alastair Hunter makes the point even more directly:

> The assumption that the good will of the critic and his (or her) evangelical credentials would defuse the time-bomb of critical biblical scholarship was virtually unquestioned; and the real threat posed by critical scholarship to the most fundamental doctrines of traditional Church teaching was, apparently, not perceived at all by George Adam Smith or by his orthodox supporters.[248]

At root, the higher critics were naïve in believing that critical investigation into the Biblical literature, unfettered by a presupposition of veracity, would yield orthodox conclusions, and thus, Hunter thought, they had done 'deep disservice' to the Church. Hunter could write (in 1995!): 'The Church has yet to face honestly the radical and radically damaging effects of "the higher criticism".' He highlights contemporary critical challenges to the canon, to the doctrine of Christ and even to the Trinity, concluding: 'Higher criticism and traditional doctrine are not in ready harmony.'[249] Yet as a modern liberal scholar has observed, such criticism 'sometimes leads nowhere'. He even added, of such conclusions as were obtained:

> The speculative character of most such results is easily overlooked [. . .] The procedure is a dispiriting one, dull to read, difficult to follow, and largely illusory given the paucity of the results and the conjectural historical realities dotted here and there over the vast span of time. Its most depressing aspect is the no doubt unintentional demeaning of the intelligence of the lawgiver who is responsible for the presentation of the material available to us.[250]

The reality of uncertain criticism being treated as a definitive source of truth, and thereby undermining faith in the truth of the message of Scripture itself, is one of the most troubling aspects of the legacy of the nineteenth-century critics. Ross concluded:

> It was the very strength and conviction of their evangelical faith which persuaded Dods and others that their Christianity was impregnable. It blinded them to the fact that the concessions they made, broke down the orthodox line of defence so that the essence of the faith was exposed to serious danger. They never appreciated the magnitude of what was done in the 1889–92 period.[251]

While one cannot maintain that a choice is necessary between higher criticism and a form of Christian faith, one equally cannot deny that the acceptance of higher critical reasoning necessarily implied a change in the nature of faith – indeed, a revolution. The faith of the higher critics had to look beyond the words and, indeed, beyond the content of the Biblical literature. They claimed to discern 'sporadic flashes of the Divine', to use Davidson's phrase, but such discernment lacked the solidity of any objective foundation.

Alexander Whyte famously claimed to have found reading Robertson Smith reassuring to faith,[252] but the evidence suggests that the higher critics themselves struggled more and more with the logical conclusions of their methodology. Of A. B. Bruce it was reportedly said by one of his closest friends, 'Sandy Bruce died without a single Christian conviction,' while Marcus Dods himself wrote sadly to a friend during his own declining years: 'The Churches won't know themselves fifty years hence. It is to be hoped some little rag of faith may be left when all's done. For my own part I am some-times entirely under water, and see no sky at all.'[253] John Keddie wrote of the destructive nature of higher criticism, asking rhetorically, 'Who would take the Christian faith seriously, if teachers of it did not take the Bible seriously?'[254] It is difficult not to see the labours of the higher critics, believers though they were, as presaging the rise of secularism in twentieth-century Scotland, as the conclusions of the critics were accepted but divorced from any form of Christian faith. A Bible and, more to the point, a Christian faith, presented as the evolved end product of historical and sociological factors, was not one that necessarily commended itself to a new generation.

But had Kennedy and his allies any alternative to higher criticism? It was and is perfectly possible to continue to engage in scholarly study of the Scriptures on the basis of firm conviction of their truth and consistency, as Kennedy recognised when he acknowledged a place for textual criticism 'in the fear o' the Lord', and when he spoke of the critics' identifying and building theories upon 'sum luttle duffeekulty, that a luttle panes wud remove', clearly implying that to follow the latter course would be a more worthy task for believing scholarship.[255] The kind of Biblical criticism practised by New College professor George Smeaton, by professors at conservative institutions like Princeton Theological Seminary, and after 1900 by the faculty of the Free Church College arguably represented the scholarship that Kennedy desired.

When William Robertson Smith died in 1894, he was laid to rest in the graveyard at Keig, Aberdeenshire, where his father had been the Free Church minister. On his stone was inscribed an unusual choice of text, presumably his own: 'The secret of the LORD *is* with them that fear him; and he will shew them his covenant.'[256] Given Kennedy's love of these words, and reliance upon them to support the accounts of mystical experiences in *Days of the Fathers in Ross-shire*, it is hard not to read the choice as a deliberate, albeit posthumous, rejoinder: Smith the higher critic claimed the appellation 'secret of the LORD' for his higher critical scholarship rather than for the Reformed piety of Kennedy and those he admired. The conflict between two views of the Scriptures continued even in death.

Today, it appears evident that the Robertson Smith case was one of the most momentous and significant developments in the history of the Scottish Church, with implications continuing right to the present day. It is a measure of how different is the perspective of history that at the time, it appeared more like a sideshow, even a distraction, from the mass campaign to achieve disestablishment in Scotland. But the Biblical revolution pioneered by Smith would have a far more lasting influence on the Scottish Church, for better or for worse. In engaging in the battle with great vigour and determination, Kennedy rightly discerned its significance for the future of the Scottish Church. For him, it was nothing less than a battle for the truth of Scripture against those asserting its falsehood, and this may explain the faults that excess of zeal engendered. More to the point, by drawing the line so clearly on this issue, Kennedy, alongside Begg and others, helped to prepare for a more decisive stance by their successors in the conservative wing of the Free Church, especially in the Highlands, and particularly that this stance would be taken in absolute rejection of the premises and methodology of Biblical higher criticism.

Conclusion

Kennedy entered controversy with one purpose alone, to defend the Calvinist evangelicalism in which he was reared. He considered the various changes evident in the Victorian Free Church to be progressive steps of departure from the foundations of Reformed theology. He therefore engaged in controversy when he considered that a defence of that heritage was needed, argued for it on the basis of Scripture and the *Confession of Faith*, and positively urged a return to that older evangelicalism which he saw, not without reason, as the legacy inherited by the Disruption Free Church. As a result, the controversies of Kennedy's later ministry, though superficially diverse, really meld one into another: the defence of strict

Sabbath observance, of historic Presbyterian worship, of particular atonement, of Biblical inspiration, and indeed of the Establishment Principle, were all arguably aspects of the same basic conflict over whether or not to maintain the confessional theological heritage of Scottish Presbyterianism. Ross pointed out that the minority of early opponents of union in the 1867 Assembly was strikingly similar to the minority at the same Assembly demanding disciplinary action against W. C. Smith for his looser views on Sabbath observance;[257] similar parallels persisted in the voting patterns of the conservative wing of the Free Church for the rest of the century.

Furthermore, their opponents showed similar consistency, both on the Assembly floor and in wider society. Kennedy wryly commented, in the narrative voice of his Scots pamphlet, on the readiness of *The Scotsman* to do what he considered the work of the Devil: 'Be ut the gospel, or the Sawbath, or the Bible, that the evil wan seeks to oppose, he hes only tull wink at the craytur, for hus pen us alwees reddy for that kind o' wurk.'[258] Kennedy himself frequently made the point that it was a whole movement for change that he contended against, a stream of which one controversy was merely a 'side current', a 'rending wedge' entering the Free Church bringing radical change in fundamental convictions.[259] The fact that historians have come increasingly to concur with Kennedy's own assessment that the scale of change in the nineteenth-century Scottish Church was revolutionary, underlines his far-sightedness in his own day. Equally, the consistent opposition of Free Church leaders like Begg and Kennedy to that liberalising movement helped to engender, especially in the Highlands, a resolute core committed to the older evangelicalism of the Disruption Free Church, prepared, if need be, to maintain that heritage in separate institutional form.

Notes

1. *Westminster Confession of Faith* (1–48), in *The Subordinate Standards and Other Authoritative Documents of the Free Church of Scotland* (Edinburgh, 1955).
2. Ansdell, *The People of the Great Faith*, 113–17.
3. Kennedy, *Sermon Notes*, 39–40.
4. Kennedy, *Sermon Notes*, 160.
5. Hamilton, *Erosion of Calvinist Orthodoxy*, 170–1.
6. Drummond and Bulloch, *Church in Victorian Scotland*, 306–11; Cheyne, *Studies in Scottish Church History*, 26. Smith was 'admonished' by the Free Church General Assembly in 1867, but a motion by Begg that would have begun a formal heresy trial was heavily defeated. Fleming, *History of the Church in Scotland, 1843–1874*, 218–20.
7. Kennedy, 39–40.
8. Letter, *Scotsman*, 29 April 1878.
9. Osgood Mackenzie, *A Hundred Years in the Highlands* [first pub. 1921] (London, 1949), 159–60.
10. E.g., Report, *Scotsman*, 18 September 1888; Noble, *Religious Life in Ross*, xxxvi–xlii.

11. Editorial, *Scotsman*, 3 February 1881.
12. Drummond and Bulloch, *Church in Late Victorian Scotland*, 151-2; Norman Campbell, 'The Sabbath Protest at Strome Ferry in 1883' (299–310), *Scottish Reformation Society Historical Journal*, iii (2013).
13. Interestingly, one of the men, Roderick Finlayson, who acted as their spokesman, was encouraged to study for the ministry, and later, as minister of Daviot Free Church, stood outside the union of 1900; Hugh M. Ferrier, *Echoes from Scotland's Heritage of Grace* (Tain, 2006), 206–7.
14. Report, *Scotsman*, 16 June 1883; Auld, *John Kennedy*, 212.
15. Quoted in Auld, *John Kennedy*, 212–18.
16. Editorial, *Scotsman*, 20 September 1883.
17. Quoted in Campbell, 'The Sabbath Protest', 309.
18. Kennedy, *Sermons*, 528–39.
19. Kennedy, *Sermons*, 534.
20. Kennedy, *Sermons*, 534–9.
21. Kennedy, *Sermon Notes, 1859–1865*, 366–7.
22. *The Directory for Public Worship* (133–68), in *Subordinate Standards of the Free Church*.
23. The first Scottish hymn book was published by a Relief minister in 1786; John Young, 'Scottish Hymn Books Antecedent to the Church Hymnary', *Bulletin of the Hymn Society*, lxi (October 1952), available at: <https://hymnsocietygbi.org.uk/wp-content/uploads/2017/01/T16-Scottish-Hymn-Books.pdf> (last accessed 14 November 2017).
24. Letter, *Scotsman*, 29 April 1878.
25. Cheyne, *Studies*, 18ff.
26. Cheyne, *Studies*, 176.
27. Fleming, *History of the Church in Scotland, 1843–1874*, 116–23.
28. Bebbington, *Dominance of Evangelicalism*, 90.
29. Cheyne, *Studies*, 176.
30. George Smith, *A Modern Apostle: Alexander N. Somerville* (London, 1890), 340–1.
31. Bebbington, *Dominance of Evangelicalism*, 89–90.
32. Ross, *Church and Creed*, 225.
33. *Proceedings and Debates of the General Assembly of the Free Church of Scotland*, 1869, x, 172.
34. *PDGAFCS*, 1872, 321–3.
35. MS Notebook of John Kennedy, from the collection of Dingwall Free Church, and used by permission, 64–8.
36. Ferrier, *Echoes of Grace*, 155.
37. *PDGAFCS*, 1872, 322.
38. *PDGAFCS*, 1872, 323.
39. *PDGAFCS*, 1872, 327.
40. *PDGAFCS*, 1872, 327.
41. Kennedy, *Unionism and its Last Phase*, 18–19.
42. John Kennedy, 'Hyper-evangelism, "Another Gospel", though a Mighty Power' (12–36), in Kennedy and Bonar, *Evangelism: A Reformed Debate*, 30.
43. Kennedy, 'Hyper-evangelism', 31.
44. Kennedy, 'Hyper-evangelism', 31–3.
45. Bonar, 'The Old Gospel' (38–104), in Kennedy and Bonar, *Evangelism*, 78.
46. John Coffey, 'Democracy and Popular Religion: Moody and Sankey's Mission

to Britain, 1873–1875' (93–119), in Eugenio F. Biagini, ed, *Citizenship and Community: Liberals, Radicals and Collective Identities in the British Isles, 1865–1931* (Cambridge, 1996), 93.
47. *PDGAFCS*, 1878, 317ff.
48. Ross, *Church and Creed*, 226–9.
49. John Kennedy, *The Introduction of Instrumental Music into the Worship of the Free Church Unscriptural, Unconstitutional, and Inexpedient: A Speech Delivered in the Free Presbytery of Dingwall* (Edinburgh, 1883).
50. Kennedy, *Introduction of Instrumental Music*, 3–10.
51. Kennedy, *Introduction of Instrumental Music*, 10–14.
52. Kennedy, *Introduction of Instrumental Music*, 18.
53. Sell, *Defending and Declaring the Faith*, 29–30.
54. Kennedy (with M. Mackay), *Divine Religion distinct from all human systems*, 3–5.
55. Kennedy, *Sermons*, 116.
56. Kennedy, *Sermons*, 116, 329, 391, etc.
57. Sell, *Defending and Declaring the Faith*, 29.
58. *PDGAFCS*, 1883, 93–140.
59. Ross, *Church and Creed*, 227.
60. Keddie, *George Smeaton*, 167–8.
61. *The Signal*, iii (1884), 124–8.
62. Munro, 'Lament on the Death of Dr John Kennedy'.
63. Maurice Grant, 'The Heirs of the Disruption in Crisis and Recovery, 1893–1920' (1–36), in Clement Graham, ed., *Crown Him Lord of All: Essays on the Life and Witness of the Free Church of Scotland* (Edinburgh, 1993), 26–31.
64. William Simpson, *A Famous Lady Preacher: A Forgotten Episode in Highland Church History* (Inverness, 1926).
65. Quoted in Campbell, *One of Heaven's Jewels*, 169.
66. Letter, *Scotsman*, 11 October 1862.
67. Campbell, *One of Heaven's Jewels*, 169.
68. Jenny West, 'Gladstone and Laura Thistlethwayte, 1865–75', *Historical Research*, lxxx 368–92 (2007), available at: <http://onlinelibrary.wiley.com/doi/10.1111/j.1468-2281.2006.00397.x/full> (last accessed 4 January 2018).
69. Kennedy, *Sermon Notes, 1859–1865*, 13, 192; see below for more detail on Kennedy's experience in Ireland.
70. John Kennedy, *Sermon Notes, 1866–1874*, 140–2.
71. For a full account, see Brown, *Providence and Empire*, 278–84.
72. MacRae, *Revivals in the Highlands and Islands in the Nineteenth Century*, 171–2.
73. John V. Farwell, *Early Recollections of Dwight L. Moody* (Chicago, 1907), 89–99; cf. John Pollock, *Moody* (Fearn, 1997), 120–2.
74. The full text is reproduced in Farwell, *Early Recollections*, 90–3.
75. Full text in Farwell, *Early Recollections*, 94.
76. Full text of letters in Farwell, *Early Recollections*, 95–8.
77. According to one popular biographer of Moody, its effects were seen 'During early spring'; Pollock, *Moody*, 120. Pollock seems to indicate that Kennedy saw Mackay's letter only *after* publishing *Hyper-evangelism*, which would exonerate the work completely from the charge of bias on this point: however, as the work has no references, it is not clear that this assertion can be substantiated.
78. Drummond and Bulloch, *Church in Victorian Scotland*, 33.
79. Simpson, *Principal Rainy*, 2 vols (London, 1909), i, 408.

80. Bebbington, *Dominance of Evangelicalism*, 43–4.
81. Kennedy, 'Hyper-evangelism', 13.
82. Kennedy, 'Hyper-evangelism', 13–28.
83. Coffey, 'Democracy and Popular Religion', 104.
84. Kenneth R. Ross, 'Calvinists in Controversy: John Kennedy, Horatius Bonar and the Moody Mission of 1873–74' (51–63), *Scottish Bulletin of Evangelical Theology*, ix 1 (1991), 53–4.
85. Kennedy, 'Hyper-evangelism', 29–35.
86. Kennedy, 'Hyper-evangelism', 35–6.
87. MacRae, *Revivals in the Highlands and Islands*, 13–14; cf. Macfarlane, *Rev Donald John Martin*, 90–2.
88. Donald E. Meek, 'The Gaelic Bible, Revival and Mission: The Spiritual Rebirth of the Nineteenth-century Highlands' (114–45), in James Kirk, ed., *The Church in the Highlands* (Edinburgh, 1998), 134; John T. Carson, *Frazer of Tain* (Glasgow, 1966), 29; J. S. McPhail, *Memorial Sermons of the Rev. W. S. McDougall, With a Sketch of his Life* (Edinburgh, 1897), 23; MacRae, *Revivals in the Highlands and Islands*, 102–28.
89. Obituary, *Aberdeen Weekly Journal*, 3 May 1884.
90. Report, *Inverness Advertiser*, 15 August 1863.
91. Bonar, 'The Old Gospel'.
92. Bonar, 'The Old Gospel', 44–7.
93. Bonar, 'The Old Gospel', 58.
94. Bonar, 'The Old Gospel', 61–70.
95. Bonar, 'The Old Gospel', 78–80, 86–90, 98–9.
96. Robert Young, *Hyper-Criticism: An Answer to Dr. Kennedy's 'Hyper-evangelism'* (Edinburgh, n.d., c.1874), *passim*.
97. Notes, *Sword and the Trowel* (March 1875), 268–9.
98. John Kennedy, 'A Reply to Dr Bonar's Defence of Hyper-evangelism' (106–40) in Kennedy and Bonar, *Evangelism*.
99. Kennedy, 'Reply to Dr Bonar's Defence', 112–15.
100. Kennedy, 'Reply to Dr Bonar's Defence', 116–23.
101. Kennedy, 'Reply to Dr Bonar's Defence', 124–33.
102. Kennedy, 'Reply to Dr Bonar's Defence', 134–40.
103. James Barron, 'Memoir of Rev John Kennedy, D.D., Dingwall', originally published in instalments in the *Inverness Courier*, 1893; available at: <http://nesherchristianresources.org/JBS/kennedy/Memoir_of_Dr_Kennedy.html> (last accessed 16 January 2018).
104. Macfarlane, *Apostles of the North*, 103.
105. John Kent, *Holding the Fort: Studies in Victorian Revivalism* (London, 1978), 137; see, e.g., his evangelistic sermon carefully reconciling the gospel offer with Divine sovereignty; Kennedy, *Sermons*, 155–66; cf. discussion of the same point in Sell, *Defending and Declaring the Faith*, 33–4, 231–2n.
106. Stewart and Cameron, *Free Church of Scotland*, 52.
107. Cameron, *Ministers and Men of the Free Presbyterian Church*, x.
108. Beaton, *Some Noted Ministers of the Northern Highlands*, 276.
109. Macleod, *Scottish Theology in Relation to Church History since the Reformation*, 328.
110. Kenneth A. MacRae, *The Resurgence of Arminianism* (Inverness, 1954), 12–15; cf. Iain H. Murray, ed., *Diary of Kenneth A. MacRae* (Edinburgh, 1980), 17, 63; G. N. M. Collins, *The Heritage of our Fathers* [Second Edition] (Edinburgh,

1976), 78–9; Hugh Cartwright, 'Introduction' (9–10) in Kennedy, *Evangelism*, 10.
111. William G. McLoughlin, *Modern Revivalism: Charles Grandison Finney to Billy Graham* (New York, 1959), 212–15; strictly speaking, it was subscription to the *Confession* that was modified rather than the text itself.
112. A. Donald MacLeod, *A Kirk Disrupted: Charles Cowan MP and the Free Church of Scotland* (Fearn, 2013), 298–305.
113. Ross, 'Calvinists in Controversy', 62.
114. George Adam Smith, *Life of Henry Drummond* (London, 1902), 129; Moody himself was an opponent of higher criticism, but as key Scottish lieutenants such as Drummond and Smith himself were part of the higher critical movement, this opposition was not a significant feature of his Scottish campaigns, cf. 58ff., 99; Fleming, *History of the Church in Scotland, 1843–1874*, 234–7.
115. Iain H. Murray, *The Forgotten Spurgeon* (London, 1966), 179–82.
116. Murray, *Forgotten Spurgeon*, 180n. Note that Murray, as editor of an influential British Calvinist magazine, reprinted the entire text of *Hyper-evangelism*; *Banner of Truth*, vi (May 1957), 147–68.
117. Iain H. Murray, *A Scottish Christian Heritage* (Edinburgh, 2006), 187–99.
118. Murray, *Forgotten Spurgeon*, 179–80; cf. the briefer discussion of the debate in Iain H. Murray, *Revival and Revivalism* (Edinburgh, 1994), 398–404, which seems to follow the earlier perspective.
119. MacLeod, *A Kirk Disrupted*, 304–5.
120. M. J. Toone, 'Evangelicalism in Transition: A Comparative Analysis of the Work and Theology of D. L. Moody and his Protégés Henry Drummond and R. A. Torrey' (Unpublished Ph.D. thesis, University of St Andrews, 1988), 103.
121. Toone, 'Evangelicalism in Transition', 141–4.
122. Drummond and Bulloch, *Church in Late Victorian Scotland*, 14.
123. Cheyne, *Transforming of the Kirk*, 82.
124. Kennedy, 'Hyper-evangelism', 28.
125. Ross, *Church and Creed*, 238–41; cf. Ansdell, *People of the Great Faith*, 118–19.
126. Enright, 'Preaching and Theology', 258n.
127. Enright, 'Preaching and Theology', 268–82.
128. Ross, 'Calvinists in Controversy', 52, 60.
129. Ross, 'Calvinists in Controversy', 55.
130. Kennedy, *Evangelism*, 29.
131. Sell, *Defending and Declaring the Faith*, 32–6.
132. Ross, 'Calvinists in Controversy', 62.
133. Kennedy, *Signs of the Times*, 17–19, 55. The reference is to the separatist Christian Brethren, long associated with their early stronghold of Plymouth, who rejected trained ministry, and instead took turns to give devotional addresses in meetings.
134. Kennedy, *Sermons*, 292.
135. Luke 17:2 0, Authorised Version.
136. Tom Lennie, *Glory in the Glen: A History of Evangelical Revivals in Scotland, 1880–1946* (Fearn, 2009), 33.
137. Drummond and Bulloch, *Church in Victorian Scotland*, 25–8.
138. Bebbington, *Dominance of Evangelicalism*, 201.

139. Drummond and Bulloch, *Church in Victorian Scotland*, 25; Kenneth Macdonald, *Social and Religious Life in the Highlands* (Edinburgh, 1902), 100, cf. 198–9 on the typical Highland attitude.
140. T. C. Smout, *A Century of the Scottish People 1830–1950* (London, 1987), 141ff.; Roderick MacLeod, *The Progress of Evangelicalism in the Western Isles, 1800–50* (Unpublished Ph.D. thesis, University of Edinburgh, 1970), 91–4.
141. Donald H. Bishop, 'Church and Society: A Study of the Social Work and Thought of James Begg, A. H. Charteris and David Watson' (Unpublished Ph.D. thesis, University of Edinburgh, 1953), 10, 46–50.
142. Quoted in MacRae, *Revivals in the Highlands and Islands*, 125.
143. Ross, *William Ross of Cowcaddens*, 39–62; Macfarlane, *Donald John Martin*, 93–103.
144. Macfarlane, *Apostles of the North*, 103.
145. Bebbington, *Dominance of Evangelicalism*, 227–30.
146. Kennedy, *Sermon Notes, 1866–1874*, 20–2; the fourth head refers to the imagery of Psalm 78:65.
147. John Kennedy, *Total Abstinence Schemes Examined* (Edinburgh, 1879), 3; an example of criticism of his remarks in the Synod is B. Lynch, *Dr Kennedy and the Temperance Parties* (Edinburgh, 1879), a brief and rather abusive pamphlet defending the abstinence movement against Kennedy's strictures on the basis of the harm caused by alcohol abuse.
148. Kennedy, *Total Abstinence*, 5.
149. Kennedy, *Total Abstinence*, 3–7.
150. Kennedy, *Total Abstinence*, 8–13.
151. For a full discussion of Good Templary in Scotland, cf. Norma Davies Logan, 'Drink and Society: Scotland 1870–1914' (Unpublished Ph.D. thesis, University of Glasgow, 1983), 31–46.
152. Kennedy, *Total Abstinence*, 14–27.
153. Kennedy, *Total Abstinence*, 27–8.
154. Kennedy, *Total Abstinence*, 28–32.
155. F.R. Lees and John Fordyce, *Abstinence Defended* (London, 1879), 2–10.
156. Lees and Fordyce, *Abstinence Defended*, 10–20.
157. Lees and Fordyce, *Abstinence Defended*, 23–32.
158. John Kennedy, *Reply to Some Recent Defences*, 3–18; if Kay's remarks were published in a pamphlet, it has not been located.
159. Kennedy, *Reply to Some Recent Defences*, 19.
160. Kennedy, *Reply to Some Recent Defences*, 24–36.
161. McPherson, *History of the Free Presbyterian Church of Scotland*, 131–7; note that where 'no licence' prevailed in the local vote, licences were not granted to public houses or grocers within the district, but people could still purchase alcohol in hotels with meals and from wholesalers for private consumption: it was not prohibition.
162. Iain H. Murray, 'Life of John Murray' (3:1–158), in *Collected Writings of John Murray*, 4 vols (Edinburgh, 1982), 67.
163. E.g. Rev. Kenneth MacRae; Murray, *Diary of Kenneth MacRae*, 373–6.
164. Douglas Ansdell, 'Disruptions and Continuities in the Highland Church' (89–113), in Kirk, *Church in the Highlands*, 112.
165. Cf. Nicholas R. Needham, *The Doctrine of Holy Scripture in the Free Church Fathers* (Edinburgh, 1991), *passim*.

166. Durkacz, *Decline of the Celtic Languages*, 35; cf. Ansdell, *People of the Great Faith*, 109–12.
167. J.R. Fleming, *A History of the Church in Scotland, 1875–1929* (Edinburgh, 1933), 9; for a fuller comparison, cf. Roger Tomes, 'Samuel Davidson and William Robertson Smith: Parallel Cases?' (67–77), in William Johnstone, ed., *William Robertson Smith: Essays in Reassessment* (Sheffield, 1995).
168. Cheyne, *Studies*, 25.
169. Quoted in W. Taylor, *Autobiography of a Highland Minister* (London, 1897), 116. Taylor had been Free Church Minister of Glass and later Pulteneytown, but had to resign in 1856 due to ill health. He remained active as a writer.
170. Barron, 'Memoir of Rev John Kennedy'.
171. Kennedy, *Man's Relations to God*, 1–2.
172. Strahan, *Andrew Bruce Davidson*, esp. Chs vi–vii.
173. It has also been defined, following Davidson himself, as 'when Scripture is studied like any other book', which expresses the same thought; cf. Nigel M. de S. Cameron, *Biblical Higher Criticism and the Defence of Infallibilism in 19th Century Britain* (New York, 1987), 77–8, 208.
174. Cheyne, *Transforming of the Kirk*, Ch. ii.
175. J.W. Rogerson, quoted in Johnstone, *William Robertson Smith*, 16.
176. For a full if not impartial account of the case, see Simpson, *Life of Principal Rainy*, i, 306–403.
177. E.g. Johnstone, *William Robertson Smith*, 19–20; Carol Smith, 'The Burnet Lectures Series Two and Three' (203–9), in Johnstone, *William Robertson Smith*, 203ff.; in doing so they follow Smith's biographers in an uncritical acceptance of his case before the church courts that his published views did not touch upon the question of Biblical inspiration, cf. J. Sutherland Black and George W. Chrystal, *Life of William Robertson Smith* (London, 1912), Chs v–vi.
178. Quoted in Cheyne, *Transforming of the Kirk*, 42; Titus 1: 2, Authorised Version.
179. Patrick Fairbairn, *The Typology of Scripture* [Second Edition] (Edinburgh, 1854).
180. R. A. Riesen, 'Faith and Criticism in Post-Disruption Scotland, with Particular Reference to A. B. Davidson, W. R. Smith and G. A. Smith' (Unpublished Ph.D. thesis, University of Edinburgh, 1981), 158–62.
181. A. C. Cheyne, 'Bible and Confession in Scotland' (24–40) in Johnstone, *William Robertson Smith*, 32–4.
182. Colin Kidd and Valerie Wallace, 'Biblical Criticism and Scots Presbyterian Dissent in the Age of Robertson Smith' (235–55), in Scott Mandelbrote and Michael Ledger-Lomas, eds, *Dissent & the Bible in Britain, c.1650–1950* (Oxford, 2013), 253–5.
183. Quoted in Drummond and Bulloch, *Church in Late Victorian Scotland*, 52.
184. Cameron, *Biblical Higher Criticism*, 89; Drummond and Bulloch, *Church in Late Victorian Scotland*, 76.
185. Cf. Richard A. Riesen, 'Scholarship and Piety: The Sermons of William Robertson Smith' (86–94), in Johnstone, *William Robertson Smith*.
186. Stewart and Cameron, *The Free Church of Scotland, 1843–1910*, 61.
187. Fleming, *A History of the Church in Scotland, 1875–1929*, 8–12.
188. Interestingly, the Victorian Free Church critics were much more cautious regarding the New Testament, and tended to adopt a 'faith-based position' regarding the gospel narratives; cf. Cameron, *Biblical Higher Criticism*, 252–3.

189. Drummond and Bulloch, *Church in Victorian Scotland*, 252–3.
190. Cameron, *Biblical Higher Criticism*, 287; Drummond and Bulloch, *Church in Late Victorian Scotland*, 52.
191. For a full account of the case, see Drummond and Bulloch, *Church in Late Victorian Scotland*, 54–73.
192. John Kennedy, *The Doctrine of Inspiration in the Confession of Faith* (Dingwall, 1878), 5–6. Alone amongst Kennedy's controversial pamphlets, this was published through the local *Ross-shire Journal* office, and is in a very small format, 18mo, rather than the usual 8vo; the result was a very cheap publication indeed, 'Price Twopence'. These choices may reflect the urgency with which Kennedy viewed the question, and his desire to circulate the material as widely as possible.
193. Kennedy, *Doctrine of Inspiration in the Confession*, 6–9.
194. Kennedy, *Doctrine of Inspiration in the Confession*, 10, 16–22.
195. Quoted in Auld, *John Kennedy*, 121; cf. the thoughtful discussion of 'freedom of thought' in an extract from a lecture with that title; Auld, *John Kennedy*, 323–7.
196. Kennedy, *Signs of the Times*, 40.
197. Kennedy, *Signs of the Times*, 41.
198. Report, *Glasgow Herald*, 31 May 1880; cf. *PDGAFCS*, 1880, 274–8.
199. Cf. Duncan Forrester, 'New Wine in Old Bottles' (259–76), in Wright, David F. and Gary D. Badcock, eds., *Disruption to Diversity: Edinburgh Divinity, 1846–1996* (Edinburgh, 1996), 271–3. Smith was the last holder of this chair; it was suppressed on his retirement.
200. Report, *Glasgow Herald*, 31 May 1880; cf. *PDGAFCS*, 1880, 278–82.
201. Cheyne, 'Bible and Confession in Scotland', 39–40.
202. Drummond and Bulloch, *Church in Late Victorian Scotland*, 69.
203. *PDGAFCS*, 1880, 178–245; cf. Drummond and Bulloch, *Church in Late Victorian Scotland*, 67–9.
204. Report, *Evening Telegraph*, 3 June 1880.
205. Report, *Scotsman*, 10 June 1880.
206. Report, *Scotsman*, 10 June 1880.
207. He was, however, criticised on this point by 'A Highlander', a partisan of the Established Church, who argued that the issues at stake were much greater than those of 1843, an indication of the strength of feeling the case had aroused, even outside the Free Church; cf. Letter, *Scotsman*, 14 June 1880.
208. Fleming, *A History of the Church in Scotland, 1875–1929*, 12–13.
209. Report, *Glasgow Herald*, 12 August 1880.
210. Stewart and Cameron, *The Free Church of Scotland, 1843–1910*, 63.
211. Drummond and Bulloch, *Church in Late Victorian Scotland*, 70–1.
212. Report, *Glasgow Herald*, 12 August 1880.
213. Report, *Evening Telegraph*, 23 July 1880.
214. Letters, *Scotsman*, 9 August 1880; cf. Report, *Dundee Courier*, 11 August 1880.
215. Drummond and Bulloch, *Church in Late Victorian Scotland*, 70–1; Report, *Dundee Courier*, 28 October 1880.
216. Report, *Glasgow Herald*, 12 November 1880; Report, *Edinburgh Evening News*, 12 November 1880.
217. Letters, *Scotsman*, 15 and 17 November 1880. Cf. also Letters, *Glasgow Herald*, 23 and 27 November 1880.

218. Editorial, *Dundee Courier*, 16 November 1880.
219. Editorial, *Glasgow Herald*, 16 November 1880.
220. Report, *Glasgow Herald*, 23 November 1880.
221. Report, *Scotsman*, 27 November 1880. It should be noted that Martin, an eminent theologian, suffered from mental illness in later life and (contrary to many accounts, including the *Oxford Dictionary of National Biography*) eventually died in an asylum in Dundee in 1885; the rambling nature of this letter may suggest that it was symptomatic of Martin's deteriorating condition; cf. Douglas Somerset, 'Life of Hugh Martin' (14–25), *The Bulwark* (October 2008–March 2009).
222. Report, *Evening Telegraph*, 18 February 1881.
223. Report, *Scotsman*, 19 May 1881.
224. *PDGAFCS*, 1880, vii–x.
225. MacLeod, *Second Disruption*, 52–7.
226. Cheyne, *Transforming of the Kirk*, 51–2.
227. E.g., Black and Chrystal, *William Robertson Smith*, 400–1.
228. [John Kennedy], *A Purteekler Acoont o' the last Assembly by Wan o' the Hielan' Host* (Edinburgh, 1881), 3; note how this quotation echoes the imagery of Kennedy's public lecture on Robertson Smith, where he 'regard[ed] any eminence that can be reached without grace as but a scaffold for fools'; Report, *Glasgow Herald*, 12 November 1880.
229. [Kennedy], *Purteekler Acoont*, 4–9.
230. [Kennedy], *Purteekler Acoont*, 10–11.
231. [Kennedy], *Purteekler Acoont*, 12–18.
232. Toone, 'Evangelicalism in Transition', 73–4.
233. MacLeod, *A Kirk Disrupted*, 305ff.
234. Macfarlane, *Donald John Martin*, 118–21; for a middle of the road Highland perspective, minimising the significance of Robertson Smith, cf. Macdonald, *Social and Religious Life in the Highlands*, Ch. 19 and esp. 214–15.
235. Toone, 'Evangelicalism in Transition', 74.
236. Cheyne, *Transforming of the Kirk*, 52.
237. Kidd and Wallace, 'Biblical Criticism and Scots Presbyterian Dissent', 235, 253–5.
238. Cheyne, *Transforming of the Kirk*, 52–7; Fleming, *A History of the Church in Scotland, 1875–1929*, 59; Black and Chrystal, *William Robertson Smith*, 130; John Macaskill, 'Biographical Sketch' (i–xxxv), in Murdoch Macaskill, *A Highland Pulpit* (Inverness, 1907), xviii–xix.
239. Cameron, *Biblical Higher Criticism*, 66ff.
240. Bebbington, *Evangelicalism in Modern Britain*, 184–91; cf. Bebbington, *Dominance of Evangelicalism*, 162–6.
241. Ross, *Church and Creed*, 154–74.
242. Enright, 'Preaching and Theology', 320–1.
243. Ross, *Church and Creed*, 174; MacLeod, *Second Disruption*, 54–5.
244. J.W. Rogerson, *The Bible and Criticism in Victorian Britain* (Sheffield, 1995), 65.
245. Rogerson, *Bible and Criticism*, 70.
246. Rogerson, *Bible and Criticism*, 146–7.
247. Robert P. Carroll, 'The Biblical Prophets as Apologists for the Christian Religion' (148–57), in Johnstone, *William Robertson Smith*.

248. Alastair G. Hunter, 'The Indemnity: William Robertson Smith and George Adam Smith' (60–6), in Johnstone, *William Robertson Smith*, 63.
249. Hunter, 'The Indemnity', 64–5.
250. Calum M. Carmichael, quoted in John W. Keddie, *Preserving a Reformed Heritage: The Free Church of Scotland in the Twentieth Century* (Kirkhill, 2017), 46–7.
251. Ross, *Church and Creed*, 222–3.
252. G. F. Barbour, *The Life of Alexander Whyte* (London, 1923), 222–6.
253. Both quoted in Keddie, *Preserving a Reformed Heritage*, 45–6; cf. the rather sad quotations from Dods in John W. Keddie, 'Movements in the Main-Line Presbyterian Churches in Scotland in the Twentieth Century' (273–97), *Scottish Reformation Society Historical Journal*, iii (2013), 283–5.
254. Keddie, 'Movements in the Main-Line Presbyterian Churches', 282.
255. [Kennedy], *Purteekler Acoont*, 4, 17.
256. Psalm 25: 14, Authorised Version, cited in J. W. Rogerson, 'W. R. Smith's *The Old Testament in the Jewish Church*' (132–47), in Johnstone, *William Robertson Smith*, 147.
257. Ross, *Church and Creed*, 172–3.
258. [Kennedy], *Purteekler Accoont*, 21.
259. *PDGAFCS*, 1872, 323; Kennedy, *Introduction of Instrumental Music*, 14; both quoted above more fully.

Conclusion

By 1883, it was clear that Kennedy was far from well. The General Assembly that year granted his request for permission for Dingwall to call a 'colleague and successor', which would have allowed him to retire from the principal burden of his charge.[1] Kennedy himself took an extended convalescent break on the Continent that year. Hoping to return to Dingwall the following spring, he commenced the journey home but reached only as far as Bridge of Allan, where, on 28 April 1884, John Kennedy died. He was buried in the grounds of the Free Church in Dingwall, as later were his widow and his unmarried daughter. To this day, the Kennedy monument stands alone on that ground, a unique mark of respect to the town's most renowned minister. So widespread was the mourning that a whole volume was published of the obituaries, sermons and posthumous tributes to Kennedy's ministry.[2]

But the full extent of Kennedy's influence is seen only in a broader retrospect. By his preaching and pastoral guidance, he helped to guide the trajectory of evangelicalism in the Highlands in a thoroughly conservative direction that emphasised the authority of Scripture, Divine sovereignty and the need for personal self-examination, and that maintained sacramental practices reflecting these priorities. In his historical and biographical writings, Kennedy challenged readers of his own day to uphold the same priorities as the historic Highland Church, and built a new confidence and cohesion around its distinctive practices in opposition to trends in wider evangelicalism. In his leadership of the Highland part of the constitutionalist party, Kennedy was demonstrably significant in forging a resolute core unchangeably committed to the Free Church constitutional position of 1843. In controversy in the public sphere, Kennedy opposed movements for change in worship, evangelism and Biblical criticism, and helped to unite the Highland people of the Free Church in general opposition to the multifarious revolutions of the Victorian Church, which he saw as a single movement at heart.

For Kennedy, the evangelicalism of the Highlands was nothing less or more than the religion commanded in Scripture, enacted in the Reformation, codified in the *Westminster Confession* and conserved in the stand of the Disruption Free Church. The Highland Church was not pursuing an eccentric cultural tradition, but rather maintaining the Calvinistic heritage that the majority of the Lowland evangelicalism seemed increasingly content to abandon. Kennedy's legacy was evident in 1893, when thousands of

Free Church people in the Highlands separated from a church that had modified its subscription to the *Confession* and its theology by means of a Declaratory Act. It was evident to an even greater degree in 1900, when the majority of Free Church people in the Highlands refused to enter the union with the United Presbyterian Church and continued a separate institutional testimony as the Free Church of Scotland. Arguably, Kennedy's legacy was still evident even in the United Free Church: for example, in the Highlander commissioners who brought a heresy libel against the higher critic George Adam Smith in 1902.

This book has addressed the question: *Why did the evangelical Presbyterianism of the Scottish Highlands diverge so dramatically and enduringly, in theology, worship, piety and practice, from that of Lowland Scotland, between the years 1843 and 1900?* There is no one answer to such a broad question, but the contention of this book is that the thought, leadership and influence of John Kennedy was one major factor in this growing divergence.

Notes

1. Report, *Aberdeen Weekly Journal*, 9 June 1883.
2. [Anon.], *In Memoriam, Rev John Kennedy*.

Bibliography

PRIMARY SOURCES

Manuscript Sources

Free Church of Scotland Records
MS Minute Book of Free Presbytery of Chanonry.
MS Minute Book of Free Presbytery of Dingwall.
MS Notebook of John Kennedy, from the collection of Dingwall Free Church, and used by permission.

National Library of Scotland
MS 2634 fo 74, Blackie Correspondence, Kennedy to Blackie, 25 July 1881.
Register of Births, available at: <www.scotlandspeople.gov.uk>.

Newspapers and Periodicals
Aberdeen Journal.
Aberdeen Weekly Journal.
Athenaeum.
Banner of Truth.
Bulwark.
Caledonian Mercury.
Dundee Courier.
Edinburgh Evening News.
Evening Telegraph.
Glasgow Herald.
Good Words.
Inverness Advertiser.
Inverness Courier.
Liverpool Mercury.
London Review.
North-Eastern Daily Gazette.
Presbyterian.
Principal Acts of the General Assembly of the Free Church of Scotland.
Proceedings and Debates of the General Assembly of the Free Church of Scotland.
Scotsman.
Signal.
Stirling Observer.

Sword and the Trowel.
Watchword.

Publications by John Kennedy
The Lord's Controversy with his People (Edinburgh, 1854).
The Days of the Fathers in Ross-shire [first pub. 1861], [New and Enlarged Edition] (Inverness, 1897).
The Apostle of the North [first pub. 1866] (London, 1867).
Man's Relations to God (Edinburgh, 1869).
The Union Question (Edinburgh, n.d., c.1870).
Unionism and the Union (Edinburgh, 1870).
Reply to the Ten (Edinburgh, 1872).
Unionism and its Last Phase (Edinburgh, 1873).
The Distinctive Principles and Present Position and Duty of the Free Church (Edinburgh, 1875).
Letter to the Members of the Free Church in the Highlands (Edinburgh, 1876).
'Preface' (iii–v), in John Owen, *On Communion with God* [subtitled *Air comh-chomunn nan Naomh ri Dia*, Gaelic trans. by A. Macdougall] (Edinburgh, 1876).
The Constitution of the Church of Scotland and Her Relations to Other Presbyterian Churches as Affected by the Anti-Patronage Act (Edinburgh, 1876).
Air comh-shuidheachadh Eaglais na h-Alba, 'agus a daimhibh ri eaglaisibh cleireach eile, ann an coimh-cheangal ris an Achd leis an do chuireach a' phatronachd air chul (Edinburgh, 1876).
'William MacDonald' (300), *Monthly Record of the Free Church of Scotland*, 173 (December 1876).
'Mackintosh Mackay' (79–88) and 'Donald Sage' (45–52), in J. Greig, ed., *Disruption Worthies of the Highlands* (Edinburgh, 1877).
A Plea in Self-defence Addressed to Leaders of the Disestablishment Party in the Free Church (Edinburgh, 1878).
The Doctrine of Inspiration in the Confession of Faith (Dingwall, 1878).
The Establishment Principle and the Disestablishment Movement (Edinburgh, 1878).
A Reply to Some Recent Defences of Total Abstinence Schemes (Edinburgh, 1879).
Total Abstinence Schemes Examined (Edinburgh, 1879).
A Purteekler Acoont o' the last Assembly by Wan o' the Hielan' Host (Edinburgh, 1881).
The Disestablishment Movement in the Free Church: An Address to Free Churchmen in the Highlands (Edinburgh, 1882).
An gluasad air son an Eaglais a dhealachadh o'n Staid: earail do mhuinntir na h'Eaglais Shaoir anns a Ghaidhealtachd (Edinburgh, 1882).
Sermons Preached in Newington Free Church, Edinburgh: On Occasion of the Death of James Begg, D.D. (Edinburgh, 1883).

The Introduction of Instrumental Music into the Worship of the Free Church Unscriptural, Unconstitutional, and Inexpedient: A Speech Delivered in the Free Presbytery of Dingwall (Edinburgh, 1883).
An Address to Volunteers Delivered at the Opening of the New Drill Hall, Bonar Bridge, in April 1880 (Edinburgh, 1886).
Searmon agus Oraid (Edinburgh, n.d., c.1886).
Sermons [first pub. 1885] (Inverness, 1888).
A Visit to Leper Isle [Second Edition] (Glasgow, 1892).
Expository Lectures, J. K. Cameron, ed. (Inverness, 1911).
(with M. Mackay), *Divine Religion Distinct from all Human Systems, 28 Sermons by the Late Rev John Kennedy and 240 by the Rev M. Mackay* (Dingwall, n.d., 1927).
(with Horatius Bonar), *Evangelism: A Reformed Debate* (Gwynedd, 1997).
Signs of the Times (Aberdeen, 2003).
Sermon Notes, 1859–1865, 1866–1874, 2 vols (Lochmaddy, 2007–8).

Contemporary Publications by Others
[Anon.], 'Puritanism in the Highlands' (307–32), *Quarterly Review*, lxxxix 178 (September 1851).
[Anon.], *Dioghlum o Theagasg nan Aithrichean* (Edinburgh, 1868).
[Anon.], 'Kennedy on Man's Relations to God' (796–809), *British and Foreign Evangelical Review*, xviii (1869).
[Anon.], *The Uig Challenge to be Free* (Glasgow, 1876).
[Anon.], *In Memoriam, Rev John Kennedy, D.D.* (Inverness, n.d., 1884).
[Anon.], 'Macdonald, Duncan George Forbes' in *Dictionary of National Biography*, xxxv (1885–1900), available at: <https://en.wikisource.org/wiki/Macdonald,_Duncan_George_Forbes_(DNB00)> (last accessed 4 August 2016.
'A Highlandman', *A Voice from the Pew: Being a Reply to Dr. Kennedy's Letter to the Members of the Free Church in the Highlands* (Edinburgh, 1876).
Auld, Alexander, *Ministers and Men of the Far North* [first pub. 1869] (Inverness, 1956).
Auld, Alexander, *Life of John Kennedy, D.D.* (London, 1887).
Barron, James, 'Memoir of Rev John Kennedy, D.D., Dingwall', originally published in instalments in the *Inverness Courier*, 1893; available at: <http://nesherchristianresources.org/JBS/kennedy/Memoir_of_Dr_Kennedy.html> (last accessed 16 January 2018).
Begg, James, *Memorial with the Opinions of Eminent Counsel in Regard to the Constitution of the Free Church of Scotland, and Remarks on our Present State and Prospects* (Edinburgh, 1874).
Beith, Alexander, *A Highland Tour* (Edinburgh, 1874).
Beith, Alexander, *To the Men of the North, A Letter* (Edinburgh, 1876).
Black, J. Sutherland and George W. Chrystal, *Life of William Robertson Smith* (London, 1912).
Blaikie, William Garden, *After Fifty Years* (London, 1893).

Bonar, Horatius, *Life of the Rev John Milne of Perth* [Fifth Edition] (New York, 1870).
Boston, Thomas, *Human Nature in its Fourfold State* [first pub. 1720] (Glasgow 1830).
Brown, Thomas, *Annals of the Disruption* (Edinburgh, 1884).
Candlish, Robert S., *The Fatherhood of God* (Edinburgh, 1865).
Candlish, Robert S. et al., *Statement and Appeal: Private Letter to a Minister* (Edinburgh, 1872).
Crawford, Thomas J., *The Fatherhood of God* (Edinburgh, 1867).
Cunningham, William, *Historical Theology*, 2 vols (Edinburgh, 1864).
Fairbairn, Patrick, *The Typology of Scripture* [Second Edition] (Edinburgh, 1854).
Farwell, John V., *Early Recollections of Dwight L. Moody* (Chicago, 1907).
Flavel, John, 'Divine Conduct, or The Mystery of Providence' (iv, 336–497), in *The Whole Works of the Rev Mr John Flavel*, 6 vols (London, 1820).
Fraser, John, 'Rev John Kennedy, D.D.', in *Disruption Worthies of the Highlands* (1886), available at: <http://highlandchristianity.blogspot.co.uk/p/john-kennedy.html> (last accessed 17 November 2014).
Greig, J., ed., *Disruption Worthies of the Highlands* (Edinburgh, 1877).
'Highland Minister', *Disestablishment on Free Church Lines* (Oban, n.d., c.1882).
'Highlander', *The Disestablishment Movement in the Free Church* (Edinburgh, n.d., c.1882).
Innes, A. Taylor, 'The Religion of the Highlands' (413–46), *British and Foreign Evangelical Review*, xxi (July 1872).
'Investigator', *The Church and her Accuser in the Far North* (Glasgow, 1850).
'Lay Member', *An Account of the Present State of Religion Throughout the Highlands of Scotland* (Edinburgh, 1827).
Leask, W. K., *Dr Thomas M'Lauchlan* (Edinburgh, 1905).
Lees, F. R. and John Fordyce, *Abstinence Defended* (London, 1879).
Lynch, B., *Dr Kennedy and the Temperance Parties* (Edinburgh, 1879).
Macaskill, Murdoch, *A Highland Pulpit* (Inverness, 1907).
Macdonald, John, *The Christian: An Elegy in 3 Parts* [trans. John Macleod] (Glasgow, 1906).
Macdonald, Kenneth, *Social and Religious Life in the Highlands* (Edinburgh, 1902).
MacEwen, A. R., *Life and Letters of John Cairns, D.D., LL.D.* (London, 1895).
Macgillivray, Angus, *Sketches of Religion & Revivals of Religion in the Highlands in the Last Century* (Edinburgh, 1859).
Macgregor, Duncan, *Campbell of Kiltearn* [Second Edition] (Edinburgh, 1875).
Macgregor, James, *Disestablishment and the Highlands* (Edinburgh, 1875).
Macgregor, James, *Notes on the Disestablishment Question* (Edinburgh, 1875).
Mackay, J., *Memoir of Rev John MacDonald, Minister of the Free Church at Helmsdale* (Edinburgh, 1861).

Mackeggie, David, *Social Progress in the Highlands Since the Forty Five* (Glasgow, 1906).
Mackenzie, Osgood, *A Hundred Years in the Highlands* [first pub. 1921] (London, 1949).
Maclean, Donald, 'Memoir of Rev John Noble' (xvii–lxxv), in John Noble, *Religious Life in Ross* (Inverness, 1909), xxiii.
Macleod, Donald, 'Thomas Chalmers and Pauperism' (63–78), in Stewart J. Brown and Michael Fry, eds, *Scotland in the Age of Disruption* (Edinburgh, 1993).
McPhail, J. S., *Memorial Sermons of the Rev. W. S. McDougall, With a Sketch of His Life* (Edinburgh, 1897).
MacRae, Alexander, *Revivals in the Highlands and Islands in the Nineteenth Century* (Stirling, n.d., c.1906).
MacRae, Alexander, *Life of Gustavus Aird, A.M., D.D.* (Stirling, 1908).
Macrae, Norman, ed., *Highland Second-Sight* (Dingwall, 1909).
MacTavish, John, *An Address to Free Churchmen* (Inverness, 1882).
MacTavish, John, *Remarks on Dr Kennedy's Pamphlet on Disestablishment* (Inverness, 1882).
Miller, Hugh, *The Testimony of the Rocks* (Edinburgh, 1857).
Mitchell, D. Gibb, *Life of Robert Rainy, D.D.* (Glasgow, n.d.).
Moody Stuart, Kenneth, *Alexander Moody Stuart, D.D.* (Edinburgh, 1899).
Munro, Donald, 'Lament on the Death of Dr John Kennedy who was in Dingwall' (8–17), [translated by C. Johnston], in *Marbhrainn air Dr Begg, bha'n Dun-eidin; 's air Dr. Ceanadaidh bha'n Inbhirfeorathain; agus air daoinibh diadhaidh bh'anns an airde-tuath* (n.p., 1886).
Nicoll, William Robertson, 'The Religion of the Scottish Highlands', *British Weekly*, lxxxiii 4 (1 June 1888).
Noble, John, 'Memoir of the Rev John Kennedy, D.D.' (xxix–clxi), in John Kennedy, *The Days of the Fathers in Ross-shire* [first pub. 1861], [New and Enlarged Edition] (Inverness, 1897).
Noble, John, *Religious Life in Ross* (Inverness, 1909).
Orr, John B., *The Scotch Church Crisis: The Full Story of the Modern Phase of the Presbyterian Struggle* (Glasgow, 1905).
Porter, Bertha, 'Kennedy, John (1819–1884)' in *Dictionary of National Biography*, xxx (1885–1900), available at: <http://en.wikisource.org/wiki/Kennedy,_John_(1819–1884)_(DNB00)> (last accessed 16 May 2014).
Ross, J. M. E., *William Ross of Cowcaddens* (London, 1905).
Ross, Neil M., 'Introduction – A Prince Among Preachers' (vii–xxv), in John Kennedy, *Sermon Notes 1859–1865* (Lochmaddy, 2007).
Sage, Donald, *Memorabilia Domestica, or Parish Life in the North of Scotland* [Second Edition] (Edinburgh, 1889).
Sievewright, James, *Memoirs of the Late Rev. Alexander Stewart, D.D.* (Edinburgh, 1822).

Simpson, Patrick Carnegie, *The Life of Principal Rainy*, 2 vols (London, 1909).
Smith, George, *A Modern Apostle: Alexander N. Somerville* (London, 1890).
Smith, George Adam, *Life of Henry Drummond* (London, 1902).
Smith, Thomas, *Memoirs of James Begg*, 2 vols (Edinburgh, 1885, 1888).
Taylor, W., ed., *Memorials of the Life and the Ministry of Charles Calder Mackintosh* (Edinburgh, 1870).
Taylor, W., *Autobiography of a Highland Minister* (London, 1897).
Thorburn, J. H., *The Church of 1843 Versus a New Celtic Church* (Leith, 1908).
Walker, Norman L., *Chapters from the History of the Free Church of Scotland* (Edinburgh, 1895).
Walker, William, *Additional Reminiscences and a Belated Class-book: King's College, 1836–40* (Aberdeen, 1906).
Robert Young, *Hyper-Criticism: an Answer to Dr. Kennedy's 'Hyper-evangelism'* (Edinburgh, n.d., c.1874).

SECONDARY SOURCES

Unpublished Theses

Bishop, Donald H., 'Church and Society: A Study of the Social Work and Thought of James Begg, A. H. Charteris and David Watson' (Unpublished Ph.D. thesis, University of Edinburgh, 1953).
Dietrich, Ulrich, 'Church and State in the Free Church of Scotland Between 1843–73' (Unpublished M.Th. dissertation, University of Glasgow, 1974).
Enright, W. G., 'Preaching and Theology in Scotland in the Nineteenth Century: A Study of the Context and the Content of the Evangelical Sermon' (Unpublished Ph.D. thesis, University of Edinburgh, 1968).
Logan, Norma Davies, 'Drink and Society: Scotland 1870–1914' (Unpublished Ph.D. thesis, University of Glasgow, 1983).
Macleod, Alasdair J., 'James Begg (1808–1883) and the Death of the Godly Commonwealth: Social Vision and Theological Principle in Nineteenth-Century Scotland' (Unpublished M.Litt. dissertation, University of Glasgow, 2009).
MacLeod, Roderick, 'The Progress of Evangelicalism in the Western Isles, 1800–50' (Unpublished Ph.D. thesis, University of Edinburgh, 1970).
MacLeod Hill, Anne '"Pelican in the Wilderness": Symbolism and Allegory in Women's Evangelical Songs of the Gàidhealtachd' (Unpublished Ph.D. thesis, University of Edinburgh, 2016).
Riesen, R. A., 'Faith and Criticism in Post-Disruption Scotland, with Particular Reference to A. B. Davidson, W. R. Smith and G. A. Smith' (Unpublished Ph.D. thesis, University of Edinburgh, 1981).
Stephen, John Rothney, 'Challenges Posed by the Geography of the Scottish Highlands to Ecclesiastical Endeavor over the Centuries' (Unpublished Ph.D. thesis, University of Glasgow, 2004).

Toone, M. J., 'Evangelicalism in Transition: A Comparative Analysis of the Work and Theology of D. L. Moody and his Protégés Henry Drummond and R. A. Torrey' (Unpublished Ph.D. thesis, University of St Andrews, 1988).

Publications Since 1910

[Anon.], 'Introduction' (v–vi), John Kennedy, *Man's Relations to God* [first pub. 1869] (Trowbridge, 1998).

[Anon.], 'The Prince of Highland Preachers: A Sketch of Dr John Kennedy of Dingwall', available at: <http://reformedbooksonline.com/scottish-theology/free-church-of-scotland/kennedy-john-of-dingwall/the-prince-of-highland-preachers/> (last accessed 15 November 2014).

Ansdell, Douglas, 'The Disruptive Union, 1890–1900 in a Hebridean Presbytery' (55–103), *Records of the Scottish Church History Society*, xxvi (1996).

Ansdell, Douglas, 'Disruptions and Continuities in the Highland Church' (89–113), in James Kirk, ed., *The Church in the Highlands* (Edinburgh, 1998).

Ansdell, Douglas, *The People of the Great Faith: The Highland Church, 1690–1900* (Stornoway, 1998).

Auld, Archibald, *Memorials of Caithness Ministers* (Edinburgh, 1911).

Barbour, G. F., *The Life of Alexander Whyte* (London, 1923).

Beaton, Donald, *Memoir and Remains of Rev Donald Macfarlane* (Glasgow, 1929).

Beaton, Donald, *Some Noted Ministers of the Northern Highlands* [first pub. 1929] (Glasgow, 1985).

Beaton, Donald, *Memoir and Remains of Rev Neil Cameron* (Inverness, 1932).

Bebbington, D. W., *Evangelicalism in Modern Britain* (London, 1989).

Bebbington, David W., *The Dominance of Evangelicalism* (Leicester, 2005).

Beidelman, T. O., *W. Robertson Smith and the Sociological Study of Religion* (Chicago, 1974).

Brown, Callum G., *The Social History of Religion in Scotland Since 1730* (London, 1987).

Brown, Stewart J., *Thomas Chalmers and the Godly Commonwealth* (Oxford, 1982).

Brown, Stewart J., 'The Social Vision of Scottish Presbyterianism and the Union of 1929' (77–96), *Records of the Scottish Church History Society*, xxiv (1992).

Brown, Stewart J., 'Thomas Chalmers and the Communal Ideal in Victorian Scotland' (61–80), *Proceedings of the British Academy*, lxxviii (1992).

Brown, Stewart J., 'Martyrdom in Early Victorian Scotland: Disruption Fathers and the Making of the Free Church' (319–32), in Diana Wood, ed., *Martyrs and Martyrologies* (Oxford, 1993).

Brown, Stewart J., 'The Disruption and the Dream: The Making of New

College, 1843–1861' (29–50), in David F. Wright and Gary D. Badcock, eds, *Disruption to Diversity: Edinburgh Divinity, 1846–1996* (Edinburgh, 1996).

Brown, Stewart J., *Providence and Empire: Religion, Politics and Society in the United Kingdom, 1815–1914* (London, 2008).

Bruce, Steve, 'Social Change and Collective Behaviour: The Revival in Eighteenth Century Ross-shire' (554–72), *British Journal of Sociology*, xxxiv 4 (1983).

Cameron, Ewen A., 'Embracing the Past: The Highlands in Nineteenth-century Scotland' (195–219), in Dauvit Broun, R. J. Finlay and Michael Lynch, eds, *Image and Identity: The Making and Re-making of Scotland Through the Ages* (Edinburgh, 1998).

Cameron, John Kennedy, *The Church in Arran* (Edinburgh, 1912).

Cameron, J. K., *The Clerkship of the General Assembly of the Free Church of Scotland* (Inverness, 1938).

Cameron, Neil, *Ministers and Men of the Free Presbyterian Church* (Glasgow, 1993).

Cameron, Nigel M. de S., *Biblical Higher Criticism and the Defence of Infallibilism in 19th Century Britain* (New York, 1987).

Campbell, Andrew J., *Two Centuries of the Church of Scotland, 1707–1929* (Paisley, 1930).

Campbell, David, ed., *The Suburbs of Heaven: The Diary of Murdoch Campbell* (Kilkerran, 2014).

Campbell, Iain D., *Fixing the Indemnity: The Life and Work of Sir George Adam Smith, 1856–1942* (Carlisle, 2004).

Campbell, Murdoch, *Gleanings of Highland Harvest* [first pub. 1958] (Fearn, 1989).

Campbell, Murdoch, *Memories of a Wayfaring Man* (Glasgow, 1974).

Campbell, Norman, *One of Heaven's Jewels: Rev Archibald Cook of Daviot and the (Free) North Church, Inverness* (Stornoway, 2009).

Campbell, Norman, 'The Sabbath Protest at Strome Ferry in 1883' (299–310), *Scottish Reformation Society Historical Journal*, iii (2013).

Carroll, Robert P., 'The Biblical Prophets as Apologists for the Christian Religion' (148–57), in William Johnstone, ed., *William Robertson Smith: Essays in Reassessment* (Sheffield, 1995).

Carson, John T., *Frazer of Tain* (Glasgow, 1966).

Cartwright, Hugh M., 'Dr John Kennedy' (210–12), *Monthly Record of the Free Church of Scotland* (October 1983).

Cheyne, A. C., *The Transforming of the Kirk* (Edinburgh, 1983).

Cheyne, A. C., 'Bible and Confession in Scotland' (24–40) in William Johnstone, ed., *William Robertson Smith: Essays in Reassessment* (Sheffield, 1995).

Cheyne, A. C., *Studies in Scottish Church History* (Edinburgh, 1999).

Coffey, John, 'Democracy and Popular Religion: Moody and Sankey's Mission to Britain, 1873–1875' (93–119) in Eugenio F. Biagini, ed,

Citizenship and Community: Liberals, Radicals and Collective Identities in the British Isles, 1865–1931 (Cambridge, 1996).
Collins, G. N. M., *Donald Maclean, D.D.* (Edinburgh, 1944).
Collins, G. N. M., *John Macleod, D.D.* (Edinburgh, 1951).
Collins, G. N. M., *Big MacRae: Rev John MacRae, Memorials of a Notable Ministry* (Edinburgh, 1976).
Collins, G. N. M., *The Heritage of our Fathers* [Second Edition] (Edinburgh, 1976).
Collins, G. N. M., *Men of the Burning Heart* (Edinburgh, 1983).
Collins, G. N. M., ed., *Annals of the Free Church of Scotland 1900–1986* (Edinburgh, n.d.).
Davis, Deborah, 'Contexts of Ambivalence: The Folkloristic Activities of Nineteenth-century Scottish Highland Ministers' (207–21), *Folklore*, ciii 2 (1992).
Dawson, J. E. A., 'Calvinism and the Gaidhealtachd in Scotland' (231–53) in A. Pettegree, A. Duke and C. Lewis, eds., *Calvinism in Europe: 1540–1620* (Cambridge, 1994).
Dickson, J. N. Ian, *Beyond Religious Discourse: Sermons, Preaching and Evangelical Protestants in Nineteenth-century Irish Society* (Milton Keynes, 2007).
Drummond, Andrew L. and James Bulloch, *The Church in Victorian Scotland 1843–74* (Edinburgh, 1975).
Drummond, Andrew L. and James Bulloch, *The Church in Late Victorian Scotland 1874–1900* (Edinburgh, 1978).
Durkacz, Victor Edward, *The Decline of the Celtic Languages* [first pub. 1983] (Edinburgh, 1996).
Ewing, W., ed., *Annals of the Free Church of Scotland, 1843–1900*, 2 vols (Edinburgh, 1914).
'Facility', in Dictionary.com, available at: <http://www.dictionary.com/browse/facility> (last accessed 4 August 2016).
Fenyő, Krisztina, *Contempt, Sympathy and Romance: Lowland Perceptions of the Highlands and the Clearances During the Famine Years, 1845–1855* (East Linton, 2000).
Ferrier, Hugh M., *Echoes from Scotland's Heritage of Grace* (Tain, 2006).
Finlayson, Sandy, *Unity and Diversity: The Founders of the Free Church of Scotland* (Fearn, 2010).
Fleming, J. R., *A History of the Church in Scotland, 1843–1874* (Edinburgh, 1927).
Fleming, J. R., *A History of the Church in Scotland, 1875–1929* (Edinburgh, 1933).
Forrester, Duncan, 'New Wine in Old Bottles' (259–76), in David F. Wright, and Gary D. Badcock, eds, *Disruption to Diversity: Edinburgh Divinity, 1846–1996* (Edinburgh, 1996).
Francis, K., W. Gibson, J. Morgan-Guy, B. Tennant and R. Ellison, eds, *The Oxford Handbook of the British Sermon, 1689–1901* (Oxford, 2012).
Gordon, Arthur, *The Life of Archibald Hamilton Charteris* (London, 1912).

Grant, Maurice, 'The Heirs of the Disruption in Crisis and Recovery, 1893–1920' (1–36), in Clement Graham, ed., *Crown Him Lord of All: Essays on the Life and Witness of the Free Church of Scotland* (Edinburgh, 1993).
Hamilton, Ian, *The Erosion of Calvinist Orthodoxy* (Fearn, 2010).
Hamilton, Nigel, *Biography: A Brief History* (Cambridge, MA, 2007).
Hunter, Alastair G., 'The Indemnity: William Robertson Smith and George Adam Smith' (60–6), in William Johnstone, ed., *William Robertson Smith: Essays in Reassessment* (Sheffield, 1995).
Hunter, James, *The Making of the Crofting Community* [New Edition] (Edinburgh, 2000).
Jalland, Pat, *Death in the Victorian Family* (Oxford, 1996).
James Begg Society, available at: <http://easyweb.easynet.co.uk/~jbeggsoc/jbshome.html> (last accessed 15 October 2015).
Johnstone, William, ed., *William Robertson Smith: Essays in Reassessment* (Sheffield, 1995).
Keddie, John W., *George Smeaton* (Darlington, 2007).
Keddie, John W., 'Movements in the Main-line Presbyterian Churches in Scotland in the Twentieth Century' (273–97), *Scottish Reformation Society Historical Journal*, iii (2013).
Keddie, John W., *James MacGregor* (n.p., 2016).
Keddie, John W., *Preserving a Reformed Heritage: The Free Church of Scotland in the Twentieth Century* (Kirkhill, 2017).
Kent, John, *Holding the Fort: Studies in Victorian Revivalism* (London, 1978).
Kidd, Colin and Valerie Wallace, 'Biblical Criticism and Scots Presbyterian Dissent in the Age of Robertson Smith' (235–55), in Scott Mandelbrote and Michael Ledger-Lomas, eds, *Dissent & the Bible in Britain, c.1650–1950* (Oxford, 2013).
Kirk, James, ed., *The Church in the Highlands* (Edinburgh, 1998).
Lee, Hermione, *Biography: A Very Short Introduction* (Oxford, 2009).
Lennie, Tom, *Glory in the Glen: A History of Evangelical Revivals in Scotland, 1880–1946* (Fearn, 2009).
MacColl, Allan W., *Land, Faith and the Crofting Community* (Edinburgh, 2006).
Macdonald, George, *Men of Sutherland* [first pub. 1937] (Dornoch, 2014).
MacDonald, Ian R., *Aberdeen and the Highland Church, 1785–1900* (Edinburgh, 2000).
Macfarlane, Donald, *Memoir and Remains of Rev Donald Macdonald* (Glasgow, 1903).
Macfarlane, Norman C., *Rev Donald John Martin* (Edinburgh, 1914).
Macfarlane, Norman C., 'John Kennedy' (100-05), in *Apostles of the North* (Stornoway, 1931), available at: <http://highlandchristianity.blogspot.co.uk/p/john-kennedy-by-norman-c-macfarlane.html> (last accessed 22 May 2014).
Macfarlane, Norman C., *Apostles of the North* [first pub. 1931] (Stornoway, n.d.).

Machin, G. I. T., *Politics and the Churches in Great Britain, 1869 to 1921* (Oxford, 1987).
Machin, Ian, 'Voluntaryism and Reunion, 1874–1929' (221–38), in Norman MacDougall, ed., *Church, Politics and Society: Scotland, 1408–1929* (Edinburgh, 1983).
Macinnes, Allan I., 'Evangelical Protestantism in the Nineteenth-century Highlands' (43–65), in G. Walker and T. Gallagher, eds, *Sermons and Battle-hymns: Protestant Popular Culture in Modern Scotland* (Edinburgh, 1990).
Macinnes, Dr John, 'Religion in Gaelic Society' (222–42), *Transactions of the Gaelic Society of Inverness*, lii (1980–2).
Macinnes, Rev. John, *The Evangelical Movement in the Highlands of Scotland, 1688–1800* (Aberdeen, 1951).
McIntosh, Alistair, *Island Spirituality* (Kershader, 2013).
MacKillop, Allan Macdonald, *A Goodly Heritage*, Sine Martin, ed. (Inverness, 1988).
Mackillop, Andrew, *'More Fruitful than the Soil': Army, Empire and the Scottish Highlands, 1715–1815* (East Linton, 2000).
Maclean, Malcolm, *The Lord's Supper* (Fearn, 2009).
Maclean, Norman, *Life of James Cameron Lees* (Glasgow, 1922).
MacLeod, A. Donald, *A Kirk Disrupted: Charles Cowan MP and the Free Church of Scotland* (Fearn, 2013).
Macleod, Donald, 'The Highland Churches Today' (146–76), in James Kirk, ed., *The Church in the Highlands* (Edinburgh, 1998).
MacLeod, James Lachlan, *The Second Disruption* (East Linton, 2000).
Macleod, John, *Scottish Theology in Relation to Church History Since the Reformation* (Edinburgh, 1943).
Macleod, John, 'An Argyllshire Worthy' (231–85), in G. N. M. Collins, *John Macleod, D.D.* (Edinburgh, 1951).
Macleod, John, *By-paths of Highland Church History* (Edinburgh, 1965).
MacLeod, John, *Banner in the West: A Spiritual History of Lewis and Harris* (Edinburgh, 2008).
McLoughlin, William G., *Modern Revivalism: Charles Grandison Finney to Billy Graham* (New York, 1959).
Macnaughton, Colin, *Church Life in Ross and Sutherland* (Inverness, 1915).
McPherson, Alexander, ed., *History of the Free Presbyterian Church of Scotland, 1893–1970* (Inverness, 1973).
MacRae, Innes, *Dingwall Free Church: The Story of 100 Years and more* (Dingwall, 1970).
MacRae, Kenneth A., *The Resurgence of Arminianism* (Inverness, 1954).
Matheson, Ann, 'Preaching in the Churches of Scotland' (152–66), in Francis, K., W. Gibson, J. Morgan-Guy, B. Tennant and R. Ellison, eds, *The Oxford Handbook of the British Sermon, 1689–1901* (Oxford, 2012), 165.
Meek, Donald E., 'Saints and Scarecrows: The Churches and Gaelic Culture

in the Highlands since 1560' (3–22), *Scottish Bulletin of Evangelical Theology,* xiv (1996).

Meek, Donald E., *The Scottish Highlands, the Churches and Gaelic Culture* (Geneva, 1996).

Meek, Donald E., 'The Gaelic Bible, Revival and Mission: The Spiritual Rebirth of the Nineteenth-century Highlands' (114–45), in James Kirk, ed., *The Church in the Highlands* (Edinburgh, 1998), 134.

Meek, Donald E., *The Quest for Celtic Christianity* (Boat of Garten, 2000).

Middleton, Roy, 'Jonathan Ranken Anderson and the Free Church of Scotland – Part I' (135–274), *Scottish Reformation Society Historical Journal,* iv (2014).

Middleton, Roy, 'Jonathan Ranken Anderson and the Free Church of Scotland – Part II' (211–318), *Scottish Reformation Society Historical Journal,* v (2015).

Middleton, Roy, 'Jonathan Ranken Anderson's Critique of the Free Church of Scotland in the 1850s' (321–51), *Scottish Reformation Society Historical Journal,* v (2015).

Millar, Gordon F., 'Innes, Alexander Taylor (1833–1912)', *Oxford Dictionary of National Biography* (Oxford, 2005), available at: <http://www.oxforddnb.com/view/article/41289> (last accessed 5 July 2016).

Mowat, I. R. M., *Easter Ross, 1750–1850* (Edinburgh, 1981).

Munro, Rev. Donald, *Records of Grace in Sutherland* (Edinburgh, 1953).

Murray, Iain H., *The Forgotten Spurgeon* (London, 1966).

Murray, Iain H., ed., *Diary of Kenneth A. MacRae* (Edinburgh, 1980).

Murray, Iain H., 'Life of John Murray' (3: 1–158), in *Collected Writings of John Murray,* 4 vols (Edinburgh, 1982).

Murray, Iain H., *Revival and Revivalism* (Edinburgh, 1994).

Murray, Iain H., *The Old Evangelicalism* (Edinburgh, 2005).

Murray, Iain H., *A Scottish Christian Heritage* (Edinburgh, 2006).

Murray, Iain H., *The Undercover Revolution* (Edinburgh, 2009).

Needham, Nicholas R., *The Doctrine of Holy Scripture in the Free Church Fathers* (Edinburgh, 1991).

Paton, David, *The Clergy and the Clearances* (Edinburgh, 2006).

Pollock, John, *Moody* (Fearn, 1997).

Riesen, Richard A., 'Scholarship and Piety: The Sermons of William Robertson Smith' (86–94), in William Johnstone, ed., *William Robertson Smith: Essays in Reassessment* (Sheffield, 1995).

Roberts, Maurice J., 'John Kennedy of Dingwall' (4–31), *The Banner of Truth* (August–September 1984).

Rogerson, J. W., *The Bible and Criticism in Victorian Britain* (Sheffield, 1995).

Rogerson, J. W., 'W. R. Smith's *The Old Testament in the Jewish Church*' (132–47), in William Johnstone, ed., *William Robertson Smith: Essays in Reassessment* (Sheffield, 1995).

Ross, Kenneth R., *Church and Creed in Scotland: The Free Church Case 1900–1904 and its Origins* (Edinburgh, 1988).

Ross, Kenneth R., 'Calvinists in Controversy: John Kennedy, Horatius Bonar and the Moody Mission of 1873–74' (51–63), *Scottish Bulletin of Evangelical Theology*, ix 1 (1991).

Ross, Neil M., 'Introduction – A Prince Among Preachers' (vii–xxv), in John Kennedy, *Sermon Notes 1859–1865* (Lochmaddy, 2007).

Schmidt, Leigh Eric, *Holy Fairs: Scotland and the Making of American Revivalism* (Grand Rapids, 2001).

Scott, Hew, *Fasti Ecclesiae Scoticanae*, 6 vols [New Edition] (Edinburgh, 1917).

Sell, Alan P. F., *Defending and Declaring the Faith: Some Scottish Examples, 1860–1920* (Exeter, 1987).

Sell, Alan P. F., 'Kennedy, John (1819–1884)', *Oxford Dictionary of National Biography* (Oxford, 2004), available at: <http://www.oxforddnb.com/view/article/15386> (last accessed 28 March 2022).

Simpson, William, *A Famous Lady Preacher: A Forgotten Episode in Highland Church History* (Inverness, 1926).

Sinclair, James S., ed., *Rich Gleanings After the Vintage from 'Rabbi' Duncan* (London, 1925).

Smith, Carol, 'The Burnet Lectures Series Two and Three' (203–9), in William Johnstone, ed., *William Robertson Smith: Essays in Reassessment* (Sheffield, 1995).

Smith, John A., 'Free Church Constitutionalists and the Establishment Principle' (99–119), *Northern Scotland*, xxii (2002).

Smout, T. C., *A Century of the Scottish People 1830–1950* (London, 1987).

Stevenson, John, *Fulfilling a Vision: The Contribution of the Church of Scotland to School Education, 1772–1872* (Eugene, OR, 2012).

Stewart, Alexander and J. Kennedy Cameron, *The Free Church of Scotland, 1843–1910* (Edinburgh, 1910).

Strahan, James, *Andrew Bruce Davidson, D.D., LL.D., D.Litt.* (London, 1917).

Strong, Rowan, *Episcopalianism in Nineteenth-Century Scotland* (Oxford, 2002).

The Subordinate Standards and Other Authoritative Documents of the Free Church of Scotland (Edinburgh, 1955).

Taylor, David, *The Wild Black Region, Badenoch 1750–1800* (Edinburgh, 2016).

Tomes, Roger, 'Samuel Davidson and William Robertson Smith: Parallel Cases?' (67–77), in William Johnstone, ed., *William Robertson Smith: Essays in Reassessment* (Sheffield, 1995).

West, Jenny, 'Gladstone and Laura Thistlethwayte, 1865–75', *Historical Research*, lxxx 368–392 (2007), available at: <http://onlinelibrary.wiley.com/doi/10.1111/j.1468-2281.2006.00397.x/full> (last accessed 4 January 2018).

Withers, C. W. J., *Gaelic Scotland: The Transformation of a Culture Region* (London, 1988).

Withers, C. W. J., 'The Historical Creation of the Scottish Highlands'

(143–56), in I. Donnachie and C. Whatley, eds, *The Manufacture of Scottish History* (Edinburgh, 1992).

Wolffe, John, 'Begg, James (1808–1883)', *Oxford Dictionary of National Biography* (Oxford, 2004), available at: <http://www.oxforddnb.com/view/article/1959> (last accessed 7 January 2017).

Wright, David F. and Gary D. Badcock, eds, *Disruption to Diversity: Edinburgh Divinity, 1846–1996* (Edinburgh, 1996).

Young, John, 'Scottish Hymn Books Antecedent to the Church Hymnary', *Bulletin of the Hymn Society*, lxi (October 1952), available at: <https://hymnsocietygbi.org.uk/wp-content/uploads/2017/01/T16-Scottish-Hymn-Books.pdf> (last accessed 14 November 2017).

Index

Aberdeen, 19, 29, 30, 54, 56, 87, 189, 202, 206, 210
Aberdeen, University of, 18, 19, 21, 99
Abraham (Biblical character), 199
Adam (Biblical character), 122–4, 128
Adam, John, 150, 168n, 211
Aird, Gustavus, 30, 58, 64n, 82, 146–7
Amyraldianism *or* Amyraldism, 20, 120, 141, 142, 145, 162n
Amyraut, Moses, 162n
Anderson, Jonathan Ranken, 73–4, 110n
Anglican *see* Church of England
Annals of the Disruption (book), 24
Annals of the Free Church of Scotland (book), 50, 64n
Ansdell, Douglas, 5, 6, 24, 49, 84–5, 108, 147, 160, 200
Antinomianism, 53, 173, 187
Anti-Patronage Act *see* Patronage
Applecross, 55, 84, 121, 134
Arabic (language), 202
Argyll, Free Church Synod of, 65n, 136
Argyllshire, 3, 88, 136
Arminianism, 120, 127, 162n, 192–3
Arminius, Jacobus, 162n
Arnot, William, 144
Arran, Isle of, 168n
Athenaeum, The (periodical), 81
Atonement (doctrine), 5, 117–20, 124–7, 130–4, 140–7, 160, 162n, 186, 191–3
Auld, Alexander, 5, 6, 20, 31, 35, 36, 38–9, 43–4, 62n, 66n, 82, 83, 128–9, 139
Australia, 9, 28

Balmacara, 19
Balmer, Robert, 119
Bands of Hope, 196, 198–9
Baptist (denomination), 33, 44, 95, 107, 142, 176
Baptism (sacrament), 55–8, 79, 173
Barron, James, 33, 39, 190, 201
Baynes, Thomas, 209

Beaton, Donald, 121, 191
Bebbington, David W., 130, 147, 176–7, 186–7, 196–7, 213
Begg, James, 29, 96, 112n, 131, 161n, 165n, 173, 196–7
  leader of the Free Church constitutionalists, 59, 117, 132–40, 143, 146–9, 154, 158, 160, 166n, 177, 180, 183, 203, 206–7, 210–13, 216–17
  reviewer of books, 130, 139, 166n
Beith, Alexander, 9, 61n, 103, 153, 206–7
Bethune, Hector, 25
Biblical criticism, 1, 10, 155, 157, 181, 183, 192, 201–16, 221n, 223n, 227
Blackie, John Stuart, 51–2
Bonar, Andrew, 185, 212
Bonar, Horatius, 94–5, 100–1, 179, 185–6, 188–95, 212
Boston, Thomas, 87, 122
Boyd, Annie, 69n
Bridge of Allan, 227
British and Foreign Evangelical Review, The (periodical), 129, 163–4n
Brown, Callum, 8
Brown, John, 119–20, 142
Brown, Stewart J., 18–19, 22, 24, 148–9
Bruce, A. B., 129–30, 212, 215
Bruce, Steve, 108
Buccleuch (Edinburgh), 183
Budge, David, 37
Bulloch, James *see* Drummond, Andrew L., and Bulloch, James
Bunyan, John, 86, 107, 115n
Burghead, 29
Burns, William Chalmers, 54, 188–9

Cairns, John, 133, 150, 173, 193
Caithness, 3, 10, 22, 28, 37, 82, 136, 139
Calvin, John, 6, 19, 193
Calvinism, 20, 42, 47, 60, 74, 149, 151, 203, 213–14

Calvinism (*cont.*)
  as characteristic of Highland Evangelicalism, 1–3, 17, 52–3, 133, 139, 159–60, 171, 216, 227–8
  as opposed to campaign evangelism, 184–96
  as opposed to theories of universal atonement, 118–32
Cambridge, 87, 202
Cambuslang, 66n
Cameron, John Kennedy, 47, 190–1, 203, 208
Cameron, Neil, 66n, 191
Cameron, Nigel M. de S., 203–4, 213
Campbell, Andrew J., 55, 140
Campbell, David, 92
Campbell, Murdoch, 5–6, 12n, 107, 116n
Campbell, Norman, 50, 107
Candlish, James S., 65n, 210–11
Candlish, Robert S., 87, 120–1, 123, 128, 132, 140, 143, 145, 146
Carroll, Robert P., 214
Cartwright, Hugh M., 191
Chalmers, Thomas, 1, 18, 22, 87, 118, 145, 148, 154, 194
Chanonry, Free Church Presbytery of, 1, 23, 58, 63n
Charteris, Archibald H., 148, 157, 161, 203, 212
Cheyne, A. C. (Alec), 4, 74, 118–19, 176, 194, 201–2, 207, 212
Chicago, 185–6
Christ, 1–2, 20–3, 25, 35–7, 41–3, 45–6, 52–6, 74, 102–3, 118–22, 125–8, 131, 133, 140–2, 158, 162n, 172, 175, 178, 185, 190, 194, 197–9, 202, 211, 214
Christian Brethren (Plymouth), 221n
Church of England, 87, 176, 121, 130, 201
Church of Ireland, 142
Church of Scotland (Established Church), 1, 3, 8–11, 16–18, 20–2, 25–6, 30, 40, 57, 59, 63n, 69n, 87, 117–18, 121, 140, 148–61, 168n, 169n, 172, 176–7, 181, 203, 206–7, 224
Claim of Right (1842), 73, 154–5
Coffey, John, 187
Colenso, J. W., 201
Collins, George N. M., 191
Communion (sacrament), 20, 24, 28–31, 35, 37, 48, 52, 55–60, 64n, 67n, 69n, 75, 78, 105, 138, 139, 157, 158, 172, 182, 184, 200
Confessional subscription, 1, 4, 13n, 18, 104, 106, 108, 118, 120, 127, 130–1, 139, 145, 149, 151, 155–61, 178–81, 184, 187, 191, 194–5, 200, 203–7, 217, 221n, 227–8
Conon Bridge, 50
Conservative (political party)/Tory, 5, 22, 159
Cook, Archibald, 83
Cook, Finlay, 52, 196
Cowal, 34
Cowan, Charles, 191–2, 212
Craig, George, 191
Cramond, 72
Crawford, Archibald, 34, 35–6, 105, 131
Crawford, Duncan, 37
Crawford, Thomas, 121, 128, 132
Creich, 28, 29, 35, 55, 58, 82, 100, 105
Cunningham, William, 4, 87, 120, 140, 194
Cunningham Lectures, 121

Daily Review, The (periodical), 32
Darwin, Charles, 15, 201
David (Biblical character), 78, 139, 175
Davidson, A. B., 202–3, 206, 215, 223n
Davidson, Samuel, 201
Declaratory Act (Free Church), 183–4, 193, 228
Declaratory Act (United Presbyterian), 119–20, 155, 193
Dickson, J. N. Ian, 41
Dietrich, Ulrich, 135–6
Dingwall, 25, 29, 35, 38, 69, 147, 174, 184, 209, 227
  Established Church congregation of, 25–6, 87, 157
  Free Church building, 5, 26, 27, 64n, 227
  Free Church congregation of, 1, 4, 9, 24–7, 49, 58, 64n, 65n, 67n, 162n, 171–2, 176, 212, 227
  Free Church presbytery of, 26, 59, 135, 173, 209
Dingwall Museum, 64n
Disruption *see* Free Church of Scotland
Dods, Marcus, 64n, 202, 212, 215, 226n
Dornoch, 49

Duff, Alexander, 135
Duff, Donald, 49–50
Duncan, John, 194
Dundee, 29, 37, 66n, 225n
Dundee Courier, The (periodical), 209
Dunoon, 28, 65n
Durkacz, Victor, 9, 201
Drummond, Andrew L. and Bulloch, James, 8, 73, 132–3, 136, 138, 147–8, 151, 186, 193–4, 203–4, 207, 222n
Drummond, Henry, 212, 221n

Eadie, John, 172
Edgar, John, 199
Edinburgh, 29, 73, 80, 83, 84, 93, 139, 143, 150, 153, 173, 183, 185, 188, 189, 206, 208
Edinburgh, University of, 15, 121, 157, 203
Education question, 149, 165n, 167–8n
Edwards, Jonathan, 86
Elder, Robert, 149
Elijah (Biblical character), 64n, 189
Elisha (Biblical character), 64n
Encyclopaedia Britannica (book), 203, 208–9, 213
England, 87, 88, 184
Enright, William G., 4, 121, 194, 213
Episcopalianism and Scottish Episcopal Church, 8, 17, 25, 61n, 156
Erskine, Ebenezer, 53–4, 179
Erskine, Thomas, 121
Established Church *see* Church of Scotland
Establishment principle, 1, 117, 140–61, 217
Evangelical Alliance, 142
Evangelical Union, 191
Evangelicalism, 26, 30, 34, 40–1, 47–52, 55, 66n, 91–6, 99, 118–21, 129–30, 147, 152, 154, 164n
  divergence of Highland from Lowland, 1–11, 74–89, 100–10, 117, 121, 139, 158–61, 173, 180–217, 227–8
  history in the Highlands, 75–80, 172
  Kennedy as Highland Evangelical, 15–25, 60, 71–2
Evangelistic campaigns, 2, 53–4, 100–1, 148–9, 178–80, 185–96, 212, 221n
Evans, Christmas, 107
Evolution, theory of, 15, 122

Fairbairn, Andrew, 121
Fairbairn, Patrick, 202
Farwell, John V., 186
Fatherhood of God (doctrine), 4, 118–32
Fenyő, Krisztina, 6
Ferintosh, 89; *see also* Urquhart
Finlay, Robert Bannatyne, 159
Finlayson, Roderick, 218n
Finlayson, Sandy, 5, 140, 146
Flavel, John, 106
Fleming, J. R., 138, 192
Fodderty, 28, 34
Forbes Mackenzie Act, 196
Fordyce, John, 198–9
France, 184
Francis, Keith W., 31, 40
Fraser, John, 23, 31, 38–9, 46, 62n
Free Church College, Aberdeen, 202, 206
Free Church College, Edinburgh (post-1900), 216
Free Church College, Glasgow, 65n, 73–4
Free Church Defence Association, 133
'Free Church Minister' (pseudonym), 130
Free Church of Scotland
  Constitutionalist party, 1–2, 11, 59, 117, 136, 138, 144, 146, 148–52, 157, 159, 169n, 183, 206, 210
  continuance after 1900, 1, 5, 7, 9–11, 31, 51, 80, 86, 161, 168n, 183–4, 200, 216, 218n, 228
  Disestablishment controversy, 5, 95, 148–61, 168n, 171, 175, 183, 211–12, 216
  Disruption, 1, 3, 5, 10, 21–6, 30, 32, 38, 49, 60, 63n, 73, 87, 148, 152, 154–6, 161, 172, 176, 194, 196, 201–2, 213, 216–17, 227
  General Assembly, 2, 5, 9, 10, 23, 27, 30, 55, 57–9, 88, 92, 117–21, 132–46, 149–51, 154, 159, 161, 164–6n, 168n, 176–7, 180–5, 194, 202–3, 206–11, 213, 217, 227
  in the Highlands *see* Highlands
  Presbyteries *see under individual names*
  Progressive party, 11, 206–11
  Synods *see under individual names*
  Union controversy, 2–4, 6–7, 9, 29, 117, 120, 122, 127, 129–30, 132–48, 151, 154–5, 156–7, 160–1, 164–6n, 171, 177, 181, 185, 188, 217, 228

Free Presbyterian Church of Scotland, 1, 3, 5, 24, 50, 57, 63n, 80, 86, 168n, 191, 200

Gaelic, 1, 3, 15–16, 18–19, 23, 25, 66n, 85, 88, 94, 133, 138, 139, 176, 188, 207
  as historical factor, 8–10
  elegies for Kennedy, 37–8, 47, 51, 174, 183
  use by Kennedy in ministry, 26–9, 31–2, 67n, 165
  use by Kennedy in publications, 82, 169n, 211–12
Gaelic Chapel, Edinburgh, 93
Gairloch, 29, 173
Garve, 184
geography as historical factor, 7–9, 135
Gibson, James, 73–4, 111n, 177
Gillies, Neil, 58–9
Gladstone, William E., 149–50, 155, 184
Glasgow, 19, 26, 28, 29, 65n, 73–4, 87, 107, 118, 120, 165n, 172
Glasgow Herald, The (periodical), 32, 80–1, 95, 129, 131, 159, 208–10
Glenelg, Free Church Synod of, 22, 136, 138
Good Templarism, 198–9
Grange (Edinburgh), 183, 188
Grant, George, 33, 105
Greek (language), 39, 44
Greenock, 26, 28, 29, 37, 65n
Guthrie, Thomas, 73, 87
Guthrie, William, 194
Guyon, Madame, 107

Hamilton, Ian, 120, 141, 143, 166n
Hamilton, Robert, 105
Hebrew (language), 199, 202, 206, 208
Hebrides, 3
Henderson, Alexander (of Caskieben), 18
Highlands
  divergence in evangelicalism *see* Evangelicalism
  geographical region, 1–11, 15–20, 22–5, 28–32, 35, 48–52, 54–5, 58–60, 61n, 66–67n, 72–9, 82, 84–8, 94–5, 121, 134–9, 146–7, 152–61, 172–4, 177, 180, 182, 185, 188–90, 201, 210, 216–17, 227–8
Highland Land Law Reform Association, 10, 14n

'Highland Minister' (pseudonym), 156–7
'Highlander' (pseudonym), 224n
Hodge, Charles, 199
Hog, Thomas, 76, 83, 107
House of Commons *see* Parliament
hymns, 132–3, 140, 166n, 176–84, 187, 189, 218n
Howe, John, 107
Hunter, Alastair, 214
Hunter, James, 10–11, 13n, 108

Innes, Alexander Taylor, 6, 83, 89
Inverness, 3, 9, 15, 29, 30, 141, 159, 165n, 173, 182, 185, 188
Inverness Courier, The (periodical), 81, 95, 96–7
Inverness Music Hall, 135, 201
'Investigator' (pseudonym for Kenneth Phin), 10, 13n, 16
Ireland, 54, 94, 142, 184, 189, 219n
Israel, 44–5, 72, 78, 110n, 153, 203, 214

Jack, Hector, 50
Jalland, Pat, 91
James Begg Society, 131
John the Baptist (Biblical character), 199
Jonathan (Biblical character), 139

Kay, John, 199, 222n
Keddie, John W., 215
Keig, 216
Kelman, John, 185–6
Kennedy, Donald (brother of John), 22, 58, 63n, 134
Kennedy, John (of Caticol), 28
KENNEDY, JOHN (of Dingwall), 4, 62–5n, 112n, 117, 171, 227–8
  Address to Volunteers . . . (pamphlet), 156, 169n
  Annotationes Quotidianae [Daily Jottings], 21, 62n
  as a biographer, 89–99, 109–10, 114n, 169n
  as a Highland evangelical, 1, 4–6, 11, 15–25, 60–1, 227–8
  as a historian, 71–89, 109–10
  birth and early life, 15–18, 167n
  Constitution of the Church of Scotland . . ., The (pamphlet), 153–4

Disestablishment Movement in the Free Church, The (pamphlet), 73, 155–6, 169n
Disruption, experience of, 21–3
Distinctive Principles . . . of the Free Church, The (pamphlet), 151–3
Divine Religion . . . (book), 40
Doctrine of Inspiration . . ., The (pamphlet), 204–5, 224n
Establishment Principle . . ., The (pamphlet), 22–3, 154
Evangelical conversion, 18–21
Expository Lectures (book), 42–4
Hyper-evangelism (pamphlet), 53, 101, 179, 185–8, 191–5, 219n
in the atonement controversy, 117–32, 160–1
in the Biblical criticism controversy, 201–17, 224–5n
in the Establishment controversy, 147–61
in the evangelism controversies, 184–200, 219n
in the temperance controversy, 196–200, 222n
in the Union controversy, 132–47, 160–1, 164–5n
in the worship controversies, 171–84, 216–17
Introduction of Instrumental Music . . ., The (pamphlet), 180–2
Letter to . . . the Free Church in the Highlands (pamphlet), 152–3
licensing, 1, 23, 62–3n
Lord's Controversy . . ., The (pamphlet), 71, 73, 184
Man's Relations to God (book), 71, 121–32, 135, 160–1, 162n, 201
ministry in Dingwall, 25–7
Pastoral ministry, 48–61
Plea in Self-defence . . ., A (pamphlet), 154–5
preaching ministry, 27–47, 60–1, 66–8n, 220n
Purteekler Acoont o' the last Assembly . . . (pamphlet), 211–12, 225n
Reply to Dr Bonar's Defence . . . (pamphlet), 54, 101, 189–90, 195
Reply to Some Recent Defences . . . (pamphlet), 199
Reply to the Ten (pamphlet), 143–4

Sermon Notes (books), 4, 39–42, 67n, 172, 175, 182, 184, 197, 222n
Sermons (book), 28, 39, 43–6, 82, 158, 174–5, 182, 195–6, 220n
Sermons Preached in Newington Free Church . . . (pamphlet), 29, 139, 166n
Signs of the Times (pamphlet), 56, 111n, 155, 195, 205–6
The Apostle of the North (book), 27, 71, 89, 92–9, 139, 169n
The Days of the Fathers in Ross-shire (book), 6, 17, 18, 28, 48, 56, 71–90, 96, 99, 100–10, 136, 216
Total Abstinence Schemes Examined (pamphlet), 196–8
Union Question, The (pamphlet), 135, 141–2, 165n, 171
Unionism and its Last Phase (pamphlet), 145–6
Unionism and the Union (pamphlet), 142–3, 165n
unpublished writings, 4–5, 6, 97, 114n, 162n
View of supernatural experiences, 100–10
Visit to Leper Isle (pamphlet), 115n
Kennedy, John (of Greenock), 65n
Kennedy, John (of Killearnan), 15, 17, 20, 63n, 76, 89–91, 102
Kennedy, (Mrs) Mary, 28, 80, 158
Kent, John, 190
Kidd, Colin, and Wallace, Valerie, 202, 212
Killearnan, 15, 17–18, 20, 23, 24, 58–9, 63n, 90–1, 102, 134
Kilmallie, 24, 33
Kinglassie, 184
Kingussie, 9

Laidlaw, John, 206–7
Lairg, 35, 36, 37, 173
Lancashire Independent College, 201
Land disputes, 10–11, 13n, 15, 24
'Lay Member' (pseudonym), 87–8
Leask, W. Keith, 84, 138
Leckie, J. H., 119
Lee, Hermione, 89–90
Lees, Frederic R., 198–9
Lees, James Cameron, 118
Leith, 173, 184, 185–6
Lewis, Isle of, 28, 30, 138, 152

Liberal (political party), 5, 149, 155, 159, 175
Lillingston, Isaac, 19, 103
Lochaber, 33, 66n
Lochalsh, 103
Lochbroom, 30, 90
Lochcarron, 76, 121, 174
Lochcarron, Free Church Presbytery of, 138
Loch Shin, 173
London, 29, 33, 44, 94, 96, 174
London Review, The (periodical), 81
Lord Advocate, 157-8, 169n
Love, John, 68n, 87, 107, 189-90
Lowlands
  divergence in evangelicalism *see* Evangelicalism
  geographical region, 1-11, 15-16, 18, 22, 29-30, 50, 55-61, 72, 75, 79-88, 110, 131, 136, 159, 173, 176-7, 184, 188-9, 194, 210, 228
Lyell, Charles, 201

MacAskill, Murdoch, 11, 14n, 65n, 212
Macaulay, Aeneas, 121
Macaulay, George, 208
MacColl, Alexander, 173
MacColl, Allan W., 2, 7, 9-10, 11, 85
McCrie, Thomas, 164n
Macdonald, Donald, 24, 63n
Macdonald, Duncan G. F., 96-9, 114n, 115n, 169n
Macdonald, John (of Ferintosh), 27-8, 54, 71, 76, 83, 89, 92-9, 196
Macdonald, John (of Helmsdale), 54, 86
Macdonald, Kenneth, 6, 55, 84, 86-7, 134, 137-8, 158, 225n
Macdonald, William, 91
MacEwan, Alexander, 133
Macfarlane, Donald, 34-5
Macfarlane, Norman C., 27, 32, 33, 51, 137, 158, 190, 197
Macgillivray, Angus, 86, 88
Macgregor, Duncan, 82
Macgregor, James, 140-1, 143, 153
Macgregor, Malcolm, 50, 135, 158
Machin, G. I. T. (Ian), 149, 150
Macinnes, Allan I., 3
Macinnes, (Dr) John, 9
Macinnes, (Rev.) John, 2, 5, 48, 107-8, 121

Maciver, Angus, 152, 168n
Mackay, George, 173
Mackay, John (College friend of Kennedy), 19-21
Mackay, John (of Chicago), 185-6
Mackay, John (of Lybster), 86-7
Mackay, Murdoch, 40, 67n
Mackay, Mackintosh, 28, 92
Mackenzie, Forbes, 28
Mackenzie, Lachlan, 43, 76, 107
Mackenzie, Mary *see* Kennedy, Mary
Mackenzie, Osgood, 173
M'Killigan, John, 76
MacKillop, Allan Macdonald, 9, 24, 27
Mackintosh, Charles, 65n
Maclaren, John, 80
M'Lauchlan, Thomas, 84, 130
MacLean, John, 50
Maclean, Malcolm, 53, 57
Maclean, Norman, 7
MacLeod, A. Donald, 191-3
Macleod, Donald, 24, 57
MacLeod, James Lachlan, 5, 7, 13n, 85-6, 138, 210
Macleod, John, 24, 31, 34, 44, 47, 50, 83, 105, 120, 131, 191
MacLeod, John, 5, 57, 99
Macleod, Marion, 105
Macleod, Norman (of Campbeltown), 88
Macleod, Norman (of Glasgow), 148, 172
Macleod, Norman (of New Zealand), 82-3
Macleod, Roderick, 55, 196
McLeod Campbell, John, 20, 118-19, 121, 193
MacLeod Hill, Anne, 66n
McLoughlin, William, 191
MacNab, Duncan, 64n
MacNeilage, Archibald, 34
MacPherson, Mary, 174
MacRae, Alexander, 138
MacRae, Duncan, 35
MacRae, Innes, 64n
MacRae, John, 64-5n
MacRae, Kenneth, 191
Macrae, Mary, 103
MacTavish, John, 156
Martin, Donald John, 118, 197, 212
Martin, Hugh, 146, 149, 177, 210, 225n
Mastricht, Petrus van, 56
Matheson, Ann, 40

Matheson, James, 105
Maurice, F. D., 121
Meek, Donald, 3, 6, 85, 89, 91, 188
Men (Highland evangelical leaders), 3, 10, 33, 48–51, 60, 76–8, 80–7, 105
Methodism, 21, 25
Miller, Hugh, 122, 145, 154
Mitchell, D. Gibb, 72, 74
Moncrieff, Sir Henry W., 58–9, 143, 149–50, 168n, 183, 206–7, 211
Moody, D. L., 53–4, 100–1, 149, 179, 185–95, 197, 200, 209, 212, 221n
Moody Stuart, Alexander, 68n, 207
Moray, Free Church Synod of, 136
Morison, James, 119–20
Munro, Donald, 37–8, 47, 51, 183
Murray, Iain H., 192–3, 221n
Murray, John, 200
Murray, William, 48–9
musical instruments, 115n, 176–84, 187, 189, 195

Nathan, Timothy, 50
Nairnshire Telegraph, The (periodical), 32
New College, Edinburgh, 73–4, 120, 140–1, 153, 183, 202, 204, 206, 216
Newington (Edinburgh), 29, 139
Nicholson, Catherine, 27
Nicoll, William Robertson, 31, 32, 46, 103
Nixon, William, 143, 146, 150
Noah (Biblical character), 199
Noble, John, 35, 133, 139–40
Northern Chronicle, The (periodical), 32

Oban, 37
Obsdale, 139
Olrig, 28, 67n, 82
Orr, John Boyd, 7

Parliament, 5, 15, 149–50, 159, 161
Paton, David, 3, 49, 84
Patronage, and Anti-Patronage Act, 21–2, 140, 148, 150–3, 156, 158
Peel, Robert, 22
Perthshire, 3, 25
Perthshire Courier, The (periodical), 155, 205
Pollock, John, 219n
Poolewe, 59
Porter, Bertha, 63n
potato famine, 6, 24

Presbyterian, The (periodical), 129
'Presbyterian' (pseudonym), 55, 100, 173, 176
Presbyterianism, 1, 3, 5, 8, 10, 17–19, 25–6, 47, 48, 53, 56, 60–1, 72, 74, 76, 81, 83–4, 86, 89, 90, 106, 108, 110, 117–19, 139, 148–61, 162n, 171–2, 176, 178–9, 186–95, 199, 201–17, 227–8
Princeton Theological Seminary, 216

Quarterly Review, The (periodical), 77

race as historical factor, 6–7, 16, 89
Rainy, Robert, 11, 14n, 16, 30, 58–9, 74, 95–6, 129, 132, 133, 136, 137, 148–50, 159, 183, 193, 206–7, 210–12
Reformed Presbyterian Church of Scotland, 164n
Revival and revivalism, 3, 9, 19, 25, 54, 75, 83, 86, 91, 94, 99, 142, 145, 184–5, 188–91, 195
Riesen, Richard A., 202
Rogerson, John W., 213–14
Roman Catholicism, 8, 11, 17, 156
Rose, William, 59
Ross, Alexander, 74
Ross, Free Church Synod of, 22, 50, 58, 65n, 134–6, 143
Ross, Georgina, 93
Ross, Kenneth, 2, 57, 74, 141, 177, 180, 187–8, 192, 194–5, 213, 215, 217
Ross, William, 138, 197
Rosskeen, 30
Ross-shire, 3, 16–18, 24–6, 28, 75–91, 103, 109–10, 173, 188, 209
Ross-shire Farmers Club, 59
Ryle, J. C., 130

Sabbath observance, 3, 52, 78, 145, 155, 171–5, 183–4, 216–17
Sage, Aeneas, 121
Sage, Donald, 87, 92
Sankey, Ira D., 179–80, 186, 191, 194, 197, 200
Schmidt, Leigh Eric, 56
Scotsman, The (periodical), 55, 95, 100, 135, 173, 174–5, 184, 207, 217
Scott, William, 120
Scottish Episcopal Church *see* Episcopalianism

'Secret of the Lord' (theological concept), 2, 5, 100–10, 216
Sell, Alan P. F., 5, 129–30, 182, 195
Shakespeare, William, 62n
Shepherd, Henry, 66n
Shieldaig, 24, 63n
Signal, The (periodical), 183
Simpson, Patrick Carnegie, 16, 95–6, 133, 136–7, 143, 186
Smeaton, George, 74, 183, 216
Smith, Sir George Adam, 4, 11n, 192, 212, 214, 221n, 228
Smith, John A., 5, 158
Smith, Thomas, 59, 149, 168n, 206, 224n
Smith, Walter Chalmers, 172
Smith, William Robertson, 4, 51, 74, 181, 202–17, 223n, 225n
sociology as historical factor, 6, 10–11, 13n, 108–9, 215
Spurgeon, Charles H., 32, 33, 44, 95, 142, 173, 176, 185, 189, 192
Stephen, John Rothney, 8–9
Stevenson, John, 149
Stewart, Alexander (of Cromarty), 39
Stewart, Alexander (of Free St Columba's, Edinburgh), 120, 190–1, 203, 208
Stewart, Alexander (of Moulin and Dingwall), 25–6, 87
Stirling Observer, The (periodical), 81
Stornoway, 28, 37, 105, 118, 158
Stratherrick, 50
Strathpeffer, 30, 157, 188
Strome Ferry, 173–5
Sutherland, 3, 29, 35, 57, 105
Sutherland and Caithness, Free Church Synod of, 22, 136
Sword and the Trowel, The (periodical), 189

Tain, 26, 28, 83, 188
Tain, Free Church Presbytery of, 60
Taylor, William, 201, 223n
Temperance movement, 196–200, 222n
Thistlethwayte, Laura, 184, 200
Thomson, Andrew, 4
Thurso, 15, 30, 185
Toone, Mark J., 193, 212

Tory *see* Conservative
Tulloch, John, 203

Uig (Isle of Lewis), 152, 158, 168n
United Free Church of Scotland, 1, 3–5, 9, 32, 137
United Presbyterian Church of Scotland, 2–4, 117, 119–20, 122, 127, 129–30, 132–51, 153, 155, 161, 164n, 166n, 172–3, 179, 188, 196, 228
United Secession Church, 119–20
Urray, 30
Urquhart, 50, 93–4, 135, 158; *see also* Ferintosh

Victoria, Queen, 15
'Vox' (pseudonym), 209

Walker, William, 23, 32
Wallace, Valerie *see* Kidd, Colin, and Wallace, Valerie
Watchword, The (periodical), 130, 133, 135, 138, 139
Watson, John ('Ian Maclaren'), 16
Watts, Robert, 199
Wellhausen, Julius, 208
Wesley, John and Charles, 21
Westminster Confession of Faith, 20, 53, 57, 106, 118–21, 154–5, 171, 178, 191, 193, 201, 203–4, 227
Westminster Directory for Public Worship, 176, 184
Westminster Shorter Catechism, 10, 55, 194
Westminster Standards, 118–21, 131, 135, 139, 141, 148–9, 151, 160, 176, 183–4, 206
Westminster Theological Seminary, 200
Whitefield, George, 21
Whyte, Alexander, 212, 215
Wick, 29
Wilberforce, William, 19
Withers, Charles, 9
Wood, Julius, 132, 140
worship controversy, 2, 4, 10, 132, 140–7, 152, 154–5, 161, 171–84, 186, 188, 190, 192, 194–5, 217, 227–8

Young, Robert, 189